143 Mallard Street, Suite E
Saint Rose, Louisiana 70087
www.kaplanfinancial.com

At press time, this edition contains the most complete and accurate information currently available. Owing to the nature of certification examinations, however, information may have been added recently to the actual test that does not appear in this edition. Please contact the publisher to verify that you have the most current edition.

This publication is designed to provide accurate and authoritative information in regard to the subject matter covered. It is sold with the understanding that the publisher is not engaged in rendering legal, accounting, or other professional services. If legal advice or other expert assistance is required, the services of a competent professional should be sought.

To submit comments or suggestions, please send an email to errata@kaplan.com.

KAPLAN REVIEW FOR THE CFP® CERTIFICATION EXAMINATION,
VOLUME IV: INCOME TAX PLANNING, 10th Edition
©2006 DF Institute, Inc. All rights reserved.

Published by DF Institute, Inc.

Printed in the United States of America.

ISBN: 1-4195-8556-8

PPN: 4302-4501

06	07	10	9	8	7	6	5	4	3	2	1
J	F	M	A	M	J	J	A	S	O	N	D

If found, please notify the following:

Name of CFP® Candidate:_____

Address:_____

City, State, Zip:_____

Phone:_____

E-mail: _____

Additional information on review materials and live
instructional review courses near you is available at:

www.kaplanfinancial.com

Please visit our Web site regularly
for updates to this and other products!

For answers to your technical questions on the contents of this text, please contact us at:

fpstudent@kaplan.com

PRODUCTS AND SERVICES FOR THE CFP® CERTIFICATION EXAMINATION

KAPLAN FINANCIAL REVIEW COURSES FOR THE CFP® CERTIFICATION EXAMINATION

Kaplan Financial offers several options to meet the diverse needs of candidates--the Live Review Course, which offers both traditional and virtual classrooms, and the Online Review Course.

THE LIVE REVIEW COURSE

Traditional Classroom Program

Kaplan Financial offers the Traditional Classroom Program in over 30 classes in more than 19 states across the country. The Five-Day Review is an intensive program consisting of 38 hours of instruction conducted Wednesdays through Sundays. The Six-Day Review consists of 48 hours of instruction conducted over two (nonconsecutive) weekends, Friday through Sunday. Instruction consists mainly of teaching substantive material and mastering both knowledge and application. The course includes working problems to assure that the substantive materials taught can be applied to the exam-like questions, as well as actual exam-management techniques.

The Virtual Classroom Program

Kaplan Financial's Virtual Review is an instructor-led, Web-based program that provides all the benefits of a classroom review from the convenience of the learner's home or office. This program format is a great option for those who have access to the Web and prefer not to incur the expense of travel. This course is an intensive program consisting of 48 hours of instruction conducted over 17 three-hour sessions held on Mondays, Wednesdays, and Thursdays. Learners receive real-time interaction with the instructor and students and access to a recorded playback option. Playbacks remain active until the first day of the CFP® Certification Examination.

THE ONLINE REVIEW COURSE

For students who have completed the Kaplan University Certificate in Financial Planning, this course provides an extensive review of the concepts covered in our six-course program. The Online Review proceeds through the topics listed by CFP Board, beginning with a detailed outline of each topic to highlight key aspects of the material and concluding with review questions that will help you assess your mastery of each topic. The course also includes a 300-item simulation that can be used by prospective CFP® certificants to prepare for the exam.

VOLUMES I – VI

Volumes I – VI contain complete reference outlines that give detailed coverage of the six tested areas of the CFP® Certification Examination. Each volume contains examples, illustrations, and an index. Combined, the six volumes offer over 1,500 multiple-choice problems to prepare you for the exam. The answers and explanations for each multiple-choice problem are also provided. The answers to the multiple-choice problems are identified by topical categories to assist you in focusing your study efforts. The Introduction to each volume presents helpful tips on what to expect when taking the exam, tips for studying, sample study plans, and tips for solving both straight and combination-type multiple-choice problems. The Introduction also forecasts the number of questions expected in each area of the exam. Each volume has been updated to reflect law and inflation adjustments through January 2006.

VOLUME VII – CASE BOOK

Volume VII – Case Book provides the exam candidate with 16 comprehensive cases, 40 item sets (mini cases) and Cognitive Connection questions. The answers and explanations for each multiple-choice question are provided and the text has been updated to reflect law and inflation adjustments through January 2006. This text prepares you for the three comprehensive cases given on the exam. Your preparation in this area is extremely important since case-type questions are weighted more heavily than the general multiple-choice questions. Our students who have used the *Case Book* have said that this book is a <u>must</u> if you want to be prepared for the exam!

VOLUME VIII – MOCK EXAM AND SOLUTIONS

Volume VIII – Mock Exam and Solutions simulates the 10-hour comprehensive CFP® exam. The text is broken up into three mock exams, each containing multiple-choice questions, item sets, and a comprehensive case. This text can serve as a diagnostic tool useful in identifying the areas of strength and weakness in a study plan and can be used to create a unique study program to meet your individual needs. This text is also updated to reflect law and inflation adjustments through January 2006.

UNDERSTANDING YOUR FINANCIAL CALCULATOR

Understanding Your Financial Calculator is designed to assist you in gaining proficiency in using and understanding your financial calculator. In addition to helping master the keystrokes for the financial calculator, it is also designed to assist students with the underlying financial theory-type problems given on the exam. Being familiar with the financial calculations is critical, since mastering these problems is an important step to passing the exam.

All calculations are worked out **step-by-step** showing keystrokes and displays for five of the most popular financial calculators. These include: HP-17B II, HP-12C, HP-10BII, TI-BAII Plus, and Sharp EL-733A.

Understanding Your Financial Calculator covers the basic operations of the calculators, basic time value of money calculations, fundamental problems (such as mortgages, education needs analysis, and retirement needs analysis), investment planning concepts, calculations (such as IRR, YTM, YTC, Sharpe, Treynor, Jensen, and standard deviation), and more. This text also includes a student workbook with over 200 basic, intermediate, and advanced practice problems and calculations. This text is a great reference for the exam and for practitioners.

FINANCIAL PLANNING FLASHCARDS

Kaplan Financial's Financial Planning Flashcards were created as a study supplement to *Volumes I – VI* study materials. The Flashcards include over 1,000 cards covering topics in each of the areas on the exam and can help you learn basic concepts and definitions. Flashcards provide an excellent way to learn the material by prompting you to recall facts and information quickly. Their portability makes them a valuable study tool for those on the go!

TEST BANK SOFTWARE

Our computerized Test Bank is an interactive software product including over 1,700 questions taken from *Volumes I-VI, Released Cases and Questions,* and additional practice questions written by our authors. The software will allow you to keep score, track your time and progress, and break down your score by sections.

From the Publisher

This text is intended as the basis for preparation for the CFP® Certification Examination (the exam), either as self-study or as part of a review course. The material is organized according to the six functional areas tested on the exam and is presented in an outline format that includes examples with questions and illustrations to help candidates quickly comprehend the material.

We have structured the material into *six* manageable study units:

Volume I: Fundamentals

Volume II: Insurance Planning

Volume III: Investments

Volume IV: Income Tax Planning

Volume V: Retirement Planning

Volume VI: Estate Planning

The multiple-choice problems and item sets within each volume have been grouped into primary categories that correspond to the major topic headings in the outlines. In addition, the answers also identify more specific topical categories within each study unit.

We are indebted to Certified Financial Planner Board of Standards, Inc. for permission to reproduce and adapt their publications and other materials.

We welcome any comments concerning materials contained in or omitted from this text. Please send your written comments to Kaplan Financial, 143 Mallard Street, Suite E, St. Rose, Louisiana 70087, or fax your comments to us at (504) 461-9860.

Wishing you success on the exam.

Kaplan Financial

ACKNOWLEDGMENTS AND SPECIAL THANKS

We are most appreciative of the tremendous support and encouragement we have received from everyone throughout this project. We are extremely grateful to the users of out texts who were gracious enough to provide us with valuable comments.

We very much appreciate the continued support of the many registered programs who have adopted our Review Materials. We understand that our success is a direct result of that support.

We greatly appreciate the assistance of the following individuals who reviewed the outlines and problems and solutions for technical accuracy:

- Tim Bellows, JD, CFP®
- Rey Belyeu, MBA, CFP®
- Ed Clark, CASL, CFP®
- Randy Martinez, MS, CPA, CFP®
- Scott Wasserman, CPA/PFS, ChFC, RFC, CFP®

We have received so much help from so many people, it is possible that we inadvertently overlooked thanking someone. If so, it is our shortcoming, and we apologize in advance. Please let us know if you are that someone, and we will correct it in our next printing.

We deeply appreciate the cooperation of CFP Board for granting us permission to reproduce and adapt their publications and other materials. CFP Board's Standards of Professional Conduct, copyrighted by CFP Board, is reprinted (or adapted) with permission.

Thanks to John J. Dardis for granting us permission to use material from "Estate & Benefit Planning Symposium" in *Volume VI – Estate Planning*.

INTRODUCTION

Introduction

Volumes I – VI serve as the basis for preparation for the CFP® Certification Examination (the exam) either as self-study materials or as part of a review course. These volumes are organized by the six topic areas tested on the exam. Each volume presents its core content in outline format using examples, questions, and exhibits to help candidates quickly comprehend the material. The core content is followed by multiple-choice questions with answers and rationales provided to test candidates' mastery of the material.

Volumes I-VI **cover the following topics:**

Volume I – Fundamentals

Volume II – Insurance Planning

Volume III – Investments

Volume VI – Income Tax Planning

Volume V – Retirement Planning

Volume VI – Estate Planning

ABOUT THE CFP® CERTIFICATION EXAMINATION (THE EXAM)

EXAMINATION PROCEDURES

Read carefully the procedures outlined in the *Guide to CFP® Certification*. The section entitled "CFP® Certification Examination" covers:

- Dates of examinations
- Alternate test dates and test facilities
- Fees for the examination
- Scheduling confirmations
- Withdrawal from the exam
- Medical emergencies
- Items to bring to the examination

- Examination misconduct
- Examination scoring
- Score reports
- Pass score
- Reexamination procedures
- Review and appeals

A copy of the *Guide to CFP® Certification* may be obtained from:

Certified Financial Planner Board of Standards, Inc.
1670 Broadway, Suite 600
Denver, CO 80202-4809
Telephone: (800) 487-1497
           (303) 830-7500
Fax: (303) 860-7388
Website: www.cfp.net
E-mail: mail@CFPBoard.org

DATE GIVEN

The exam is generally given on the third Friday and Saturday of March, July, and November each year.

Friday (1 session – afternoon)	4 hours
Saturday (2 sessions)	6 hours
Total	**10 hours**

Exam Dates	Application Deadline
March 17-18, 2006	February 1, 2006
July 21-22, 2006	June 7, 2006
November 17-18, 2006	October 10, 2006

For future exam dates, contact CFP Board at www.CFP-Board.org or call (303) 830-7500.

QUESTION TYPES

The examination consists of approximately 285 multiple-choice questions. The majority of these are stand-alone questions that contain all relevant information within the body of a problem. Also included are item set questions where one fact pattern will be used to answer several questions. A portion of the exam is in the form of case analysis. Each session of the exam contains one case with 15-20 questions. The information needed to answer these questions is generally found within the body of the case. These cases can be several pages long, making it difficult to efficiently organize the information to answer the questions.

The stand-alone questions, item sets, and case questions may test only one particular area of financial planning, such as investments. Many of the questions, however, are integrated questions, meaning that more than one topic is covered in the question. For example, a question might integrate investments and taxation. These integrated questions are designed to test your ability to analyze fact situations involving many planning considerations.

DISTRIBUTION OF TOPICS

The topics on the exam are targeted as follows:

Topic Covered	Percent of the Exam
Fundamentals	13%
Insurance	10%
Investments	19%
Income Tax	17%
Employee Benefits*	8%
Retirement	18%
Estates	15%
Total	**100%**

* The majority of topics within the employee benefits section are discussed in the retirement section. The remaining topics in employee benefits are discussed in the tax and insurance sections. For an in-depth breakdown of all topics, please refer to the updated topic lists found later in this Introduction.

Cognitive Levels Tested (Target)	Percent of the Exam
Knowledge Level	5%
Comprehension/Application	35%
Analysis/Synthesis/Evaluation	60%
Total	**100%**

Scoring Method	Point Value per Question	Approximate Number	Points	Percent
Stand-alone questions and item sets	2 points	235	470	76%
Case questions	3 points	50	150	24%
Total		**285**	**620**	**100%**

The examination division of CFP Board assigns the value weights to questions according to type, cognitive level, and level of difficulty.

TIME AND TIME ANALYSIS

There are 10 hours of examination time.

1. Friday (4 hours) – 1 case, item sets, and multiple choice.

2. Saturday (morning session – 3 hours) – 1 case, item sets, and multiple choice.

3. Saturday (afternoon session – 3 hours) – 1 case, item sets, and multiple choice.

4. Approximately 285 questions overall.

5. Case questions 15-20 per case.

	Time (minutes)	Approximate Number of Multiple-Choice Questions	Average Time
Average indicated time per stand-alone and item set question	400	235	1.5 – 1.7 minutes each (Friday and Saturday)
Average indicated time per case question	200	50	4.0 minutes each (Friday and Saturday)
Average indicated time per question	600	285	2.1 minutes each (Overall)

You should strive to average 1.5 minutes per question throughout your study of *Volumes I – VI*. The cases and case analyses presented in *Volume VII: Case Book* should provide you with a realistic approximation of exam conditions regarding cases. The case multiple-choice questions should take about 75-90 minutes per set, including reading the case.

PASS RATES

The pass rates have ranged from 42% to 66% on recent exams. This exam is a pass/fail professional exam with no partial credit. Therefore, it is vitally important that you be thoroughly prepared for all the topics covered on this examination.

KAPLAN FINANCIAL'S PASS RATES

The Kaplan Financial Live Instructional Reviews have consistently averaged a 70% to 80% first-time pass rate, which is 20% higher than the national average.

TOPIC LISTS FOR THE CFP® CERTIFICATION EXAMINATION

Applies to July 2006 CFP® Certification Examination (page 1 of 7)

The following topics, based on the 1999 Job Analysis Study, are the basis for the CFP® Certification Examinations. Each exam question will be linked to one of the following topics, in the approximate percentages indicated following the general headings. Questions may be at the evaluation level, which is the highest cognitive level in Bloom's taxonomy, or at any lower level. Questions often will be asked in the context of the financial planning process.

In addition to being used for the CFP® Certification Examination, this list indicates topic coverage requirements to fulfill the pre-certification educational requirement, and the topics that will be granted continuing education credit by CFP Board.

(References to sections (§) in this list refer to sections of the Internal Revenue Code.)

GENERAL PRINCIPLES OF FINANCIAL PLANNING (13%)

1. Financial planning process
   A. Purpose, benefits and components
   B. Steps
      1) Establishing client-planner relationships
      2) Gathering client data and determining goals and expectations
      3) Determining the client's financial status by analyzing and evaluating general financial status, special needs, insurance and risk management, investments, taxation, employee benefits, retirement, and/or estate planning
      4) Developing and presenting the financial plan
      5) Implementing the financial plan
      6) Monitoring the financial plan
   C. Responsibilities
      1) Financial planner
      2) Client
      3) Other advisors

2. CFP Board's *Code of Ethics and Professional Responsibility* and *Disciplinary Rules and Procedures*
   A. *Code of Ethics and Professional Responsibility*
      1) Preamble and applicability
      2) Composition and scope
      3) Compliance
      4) Terminology
      5) Principles
         a) Principle 1 – Integrity
         b) Principle 2 – Objectivity
         c) Principle 3 – Competence
         d) Principle 4 – Fairness
         e) Principle 5 – Confidentiality
         f) Principle 6 – Professionalism
         g) Principle 7 – Diligence
      6) Rules
   B. *Disciplinary Rules and Procedures*

3. CFP Board's *Financial Planning Practice Standards*
   A. Purpose and applicability
   B. Content of each series (use most current *Practice Standards*, as posted on CFP Board's Web site at www.CFP.net)
   C. Enforcing through *Disciplinary Rules and Procedures*

4. Personal financial statements
   A. Balance sheet (statement of financial position)
   B. Cash flow statement
   C. Pro Forma statements

5. Budgeting
   A. Discretionary vs. non-discretionary
   B. Financing strategies
   C. Saving strategies

6. Emergency fund planning
   A. Adequacy of reserves
   B. Liquidity vs. marketability
   C. Liquidity substitutes

7. Credit and debt management
   A. Ratios
   B. Consumer debt
   C. Home equity loan and home equity line of credit
   D. Secured vs. unsecured debt
   E. Bankruptcy
   F. Consumer protection laws

8. Buying vs. leasing
   A. Calculation
   B. Adjustable and fixed-rate loans
   C. Effect on financial statements

9. Function, purpose and regulation of financial institutions
   A. Banks
   B. Credit unions
   C. Brokerage companies
   D. Insurance companies
   E. Mutual fund companies
   F. Other

10. Client attitudes and behavioral characteristics
    A. Cultural
    B. Family
    C. Emotional
    D. Life cycle and age
    E. Level of knowledge, experience and expertise
    F. Risk tolerance

11. Educational funding
    A. Needs analysis
    B. Tax credits and deductions
    C. Qualified state tuition plans (§529 plans)
    D. Education IRAs
    E. Savings bonds or CDs
    F. Government grants and loans
    G. Other sources
    H. Ownership of assets
    I. Tax ramifications

12. Financial planning for special circumstances
    A. Divorce
    B. Disabilities
    C. Terminal illness
    D. Non-traditional families
    E. Job change and job loss, including severance packages
    F. Dependents with special needs

13. Economic concepts
    A. Supply and demand
    B. Fiscal policy
    C. Monetary policy
    D. Economic indicators
    E. Business cycles
    F. Inflation, deflation and disinflation
    G. Yield curve

14. Time value of money concepts and calculations
    A. Present value
    B. Future value
    C. Ordinary annuity and annuity due

Applies to July 2006 CFP® Certification Examination (page 2 of 7)

D. Net Present Value (NPV)
E. Internal Rate of Return (IRR)
F. Irregular cash flows
G. Inflation adjusted earning rates
H. Serial payments

15. Characteristics and consequences of types of entities
    A. Sole proprietorship
    B. Partnership
       1) General
       2) Limited
       3) Limited Liability Partnership (LLP)
       4) Family Limited Partnership (FLP)
    C. Limited Liability Company (LLC)
    D. Corporation
       1) S corporation
       2) C corporation
       3) Professional Corporation (PC)
    E. Association
    F. Trust
    G. Selection of business form
    H. Acquisition and disposition

16. Characteristics and consequences of property titling
    A. Common law vs. community property
    B. Sole ownership
    C. Joint tenancy with right of survivorship (JTWROS)
    D. Tenancy by the entireties
    E. Tenancy in common
    F. Trust ownership
    G. Uniform Transfers to Minors Act (UTMA) and Uniform Gifts to Minors Act (UGMA)

17. Financial services industry regulation requirements
    A. Registration and licensing
    B. Reporting
    C. Compliance
    D. State securities and insurance laws

18. Business Law
    A. Contracts
    B. Torts
    C. Agency
    D. Negotiable instruments
    E. Professional liability
    F. Fiduciary liability
    G. Arbitration and mediation

19. Quantitative analysis
    A. Probability analysis
    B. Modeling and simulation
    C. Sensitivity analysis

20. Monetary settlement planning
    A. Structured settlements
    B. Legal settlements
    C. Lottery winnings and monetary windfalls
    D. Lump sum retirement distributions
    E. Insurance proceeds
    F. Other

INSURANCE PLANNING AND RISK MANAGEMENT (10%)

21. Principles of insurance
    A. Definitions and application
       1) Risk
       2) Peril
       3) Hazard
       4) Law of large numbers
       5) Adverse selection
    B. Response to risk
       1) Retain
       2) Transfer
       3) Control
       4) Reduce
       5) Avoid
    C. Mortality vs. morbidity

22. Analysis and evaluation of risk exposures
    A. Personal
       1) Death
       2) Disability
       3) Poor health
       4) Unemployment
       5) Outliving one's capital
    B. Property
       1) Real
       2) Personal
       3) Auto
    C. Liability
       1) Negligence
       2) Libel
       3) Slander
       4) Malpractice
    D. Business-related risks
    E. Calculation of benefits

23. Legal aspects of insurance
    A. Indemnity
    B. Insurable interest
    C. Contract requirements
    D. Contract characteristics

24. Property and casualty insurance (individual and business)
    A. Real property
    B. Automobile and recreational vehicles
    C. Business
    D. Business activity
    E. Personal property
    F. Umbrella liability

25. General business liability
    A. Professional liability
    B. Errors and omissions
    C. Directors and officers
    D. Product liability

26. Health insurance (individual)
    A. Hospital-surgical
    B. Major medical
    C. Traditional indemnity
    D. Preferred Provider Organization (PPO)

E. Health Maintenance Organization (HMO)
F. Medicare supplemental insurance
G. Other

27. Disability income insurance (individual)
    A. Occupational definitions and application
       1) Total
       2) Partial
       3) Residual
    B. Benefit period
    C. Elimination period
    D. Benefit amount
    E. Riders
    F. Taxation of benefits

28. Long-term care insurance (individual and joint)
    A. Basic provisions
    B. Eligibility
    C. Benefit amount and period
    D. Elimination period
    E. Inflation protection
    F. Nursing home and in-home care
    G. Comparing and selecting policies
    H. Tax implications and qualification
    I. Appropriateness of coverage

29. Life insurance
    A. Fundamentals
    B. Types
    C. Contractual provisions
    D. Dividend options
    E. Non-forfeiture and other options
    F. Settlement options
    G. Policy replacement
    H. Tax issues and strategies
    I. Policy ownership issues and strategies, including split-dollar

30. Viatical settlements
    A. Legal principles
    B. Requirements
    C. Tax implications
    D. Planning
    E. Ethical concepts and planning

31. Insurance needs analysis and rationale
    A. Life insurance amount required
       1) Liquidity and survivor income needs
       2) Human life value
       3) Capital retention
    B. Disability insurance
    C. Long-term care insurance
    D. Health insurance
    E. Property insurance
    F. Liability insurance

32. Taxation of life, disability and long-term care insurance
    A. Income
    B. Gift
    C. Estate

Applies to July 2006 CFP® Certification Examination (page 3 of 7)

D. Generation-Skipping Transfer Tax (GSTT)
E. Ownership issues
F. Beneficiary issues
G. Withdrawals

33. Insurance policy selection
A. Purpose of coverage
B. Length of time required
C. Risk tolerance
D. Cash flow constraints

34. Insurance company selection and due diligence
A. Financials
B. Ratios
C. Ratings
D. Mutual vs. stock
E. Reinsurance
F. Investments
G. Underwriting
H. Federal and state law

EMPLOYEE BENEFITS PLANNING (8%)

35. Employee benefit plans
A. Group life insurance
   1) Types and basic provisions
      a) Group term
      b) Group permanent
      c) Dependent coverage
   2) Income tax implications
   3) Employee benefit analysis and application
B. Group disability insurance
   1) Basic provisions and limitations
      a) Definitions of disability
      b) Own occupation limits
      c) Integration with Social Security, workers' compensation or other income
      d) Income tax implications
   2) Employee benefit analysis and application
C. Group medical insurance
   1) Types and basic provisions
      a) Indemnity
      b) Preferred Provider Organization (PPO)
      c) Health Maintenance Organization (HMO)
      d) Dental and vision plans
   2) Income tax implications
   3) Employee benefit analysis and application
   4) COBRA provisions
D. Cafeteria plans and flexible spending accounts
   1) Basic provisions and eligible benefits
   2) Income tax implications
   3) Employee benefit analysis and application
E. Other employee benefits

   1) Fringe benefits
   2) Voluntary Employees Beneficiary Association (VEBA)
   3) Salary continuation plans
   4) Prepaid legal services
   5) Group long-term care insurance
   6) Other

36. Employee stock options
A. Basic provisions
   1) Company restrictions
   2) Transferability
   3) Retirement
   4) Vesting schedule
   5) Expiration
   6) Availability to non-employees (directors, board members, etc.)
   7) Cashless exercise
B. Incentive Stock Options (ISOs)
   1) Income tax implications (regular, AMT, basis)
      a) Upon grant
      b) Upon exercise
      c) Upon sale
   2) Holding period requirements
   3) Disqualifying dispositions
   4) Planning opportunities and strategies
C. Non-qualified stock options
   1) Income tax implications (regular, AMT, basis)
      a) Upon grant
      b) Upon exercise
      c) Upon sale
   2) Gifting opportunities
      a) Unvested/vested
      b) Exercised/unexercised
      c) Gift tax valuation
      d) Payment of gift tax
   3) Planning opportunities and strategies
   4) Employee benefits analysis and application
D. Planning strategies for employees with both incentive stock options and non-qualified stock options
E. Election to include in gross income in the year of transfer (§83(b) election)

37. Stock plans
A. Employee Stock Purchase Plans (ESPPs)
   1) Basic provisions
   2) Income tax implications
   3) Special tax benefits
   4) Employee benefit analysis and application
B. Phantom stock and other employee stock plans
   1) Basic provisions
   2) Income tax implications
   3) Special tax benefits
   4) Employee benefit analysis and application

38. Non-qualified deferred compensation
A. Basic provisions and differences from qualified plans
B. Types of plans and applications
   1) Supplemental Executive Retirement Plans (SERPs)
   2) Rabbi trusts
   3) Secular trusts
   4) Hybrids
C. Tax implications
   1) Constructive receipt
   2) Substantial risk of forfeiture
D. Funding methods
E. Strategies

39. Employer/employee insurance arrangements
A. Business continuation (buy/sell) plans
B. Business overhead disability plan
C. Executive/owner benefits (§162)
D. Split-dollar
E. Key employee insurance
F. Transfer of ownership and tax issues

INVESTMENT PLANNING (19%)

40. Types and use of investment vehicles
A. Certificates of deposit and cash equivalents
B. U.S. Government and agency securities
   1) Bills, notes and bonds
   2) Inflation-adjusted securities
   3) Treasury strips
C. Municipal bonds
   1) General obligation
   2) Revenue
D. Corporate bonds
   1) Investment grade
   2) High-yield
   3) Convertible
   4) Callable
E. Promissory notes
F. Insurance-based investments
   1) Guaranteed Investment Contracts (GICs)
   2) Annuities
      a) Fixed
      b) Variable
G. Stock
   1) Common
   2) Preferred
   3) Warrants and rights
H. Derivatives
   1) Options
   2) Futures
I. Exchange traded funds
J. Index securities
K. Investment companies
   1) Unit investment trusts
   2) Open-end mutual funds
   3) Closed-end investment companies
L. Real Estate Investment Trust (REIT)

Applies to July 2006 CFP® Certification Examination (page 4 of 7)

M. Real estate (investor-managed)
N. Private placements/venture capital
O. Limited partnerships
P. Asset-backed securities
Q. Natural resources
R. Tangible assets
S. American Depository Receipts (ADR)

41. Types of investment risk
    A. Inflation
    B. Interest rate
    C. Market
    D. Business
    E. Liquidity
    F. Reinvestment
    G. Political (sovereign)
    H. Exchange rate

42. Measures of investment risk
    A. Coefficient of determination (R^2)
    B. Variability of returns
    C. Standard deviation
    D. Beta
    E. Covariance
    F. Semi-variance

43. Measures of investment returns
    A. Annualized return
    B. Real (inflation-adjusted) return
    C. Total return
    D. Risk-adjusted return
    E. After-tax return
    F. Holding period return
    G. Internal Rate of Return (IRR)
    H. Yield-to-maturity
    I. Yield-to-call
    J. After-tax yield
    K. Realized compound yield

44. Time-influenced security valuation concepts
    A. Net present value
    B. Future value
    C. Bond duration and convexity
    D. Internal Rate of Return (IRR)

45. Bond and stock valuation methods
    A. Capitalized earnings
    B. Dividend growth models
    C. Ratio analysis
       1) Price/earnings
       2) Price/free cash flow
       3) Price/sales
       4) Price/Earnings/Growth (PEG)
    D. Intrinsic value
    E. Book value

46. Portfolio management and measurement concepts
    A. Modern portfolio theory
    B. Performance measures
       1) Sharpe ratio
       2) Treynor ratio
       3) Jensen ratio
    C. Investment policy statements

D. Appropriate benchmarks
E. Time- vs. dollar-weighted rate of return
F. Probability analysis, including Monte Carlo

47. Formula investing
    A. Dollar-cost averaging
    B. Dividend reinvestment
    C. Bond ladders and barbells
    D. Other

48. Investment strategies
    A. Market timing
    B. Passive investing (indexing)
    C. Fundamental analysis
    D. Buy and hold
    E. Portfolio immunization
    F. Swaps and collars
    G. Technical analysis
    H. Efficient market anomalies
    I. Other

49. Asset allocation and portfolio diversification
    A. Strategic asset allocation
       1) Application of client lifecycle analysis
       2) Client risk tolerance measurement and application
       3) Asset class definition and correlation
    B. Tactical asset allocation (re-balancing strategies)
    C. Passive vs. active portfolio management
    D. Individual stock selection
    E. Strategies for dealing with concentrated portfolios

50. Efficient Market Theory (EMT)
    A. Strong form
    B. Semi-strong form
    C. Weak form
    D. Anomalies

51. Asset pricing models
    A. Capital Asset Pricing Model (CAPM)
    B. Multi-factor Asset Pricing Model (APM)
    C. Option pricing model (Black-Scholes)
    D. Binomial option pricing
    E. Other

52. Leverage of investment assets
    A. Margin requirement
    B. Margin calls

53. Hedging and option strategies
    A. Options
    B. Puts and calls
    C. Short sales

54. Tax efficient investing
    A. Mutual funds
       1) Turnover

       2) Short-term/long-term/ unrealized capital gains
    B. Stocks
       1) Tax management
       2) Wash sale rule
    C. Bonds
       1) Taxable Equivalent Yield (TEY)
       2) Premium/discount considerations
       3) SEC yield

55. Investment strategies in tax-advantaged accounts
    A. Capital gain vs. ordinary income
    B. Tax advantages
    C. Net Unrealized Appreciation (NUA)
    D. Appropriate assets for tax-advantaged vs. taxable accounts

56. Taxation of investment vehicles
    A. Mutual funds
       1) Basis determination
       2) Taxation
    B. Stocks
       1) Dividends
       2) Basis determination
       3) Capital gains/losses (long vs. short)
       4) Liquidations
       5) Stock splits/dividends
       6) Warrants and rights
       7) Other
    C. Bonds
       1) U.S. Government
       2) Agency
       3) Municipal
       4) Zero-coupon
       5) Treasury Inflation-Protection Securities (TIPS)
    D. U.S. savings bonds
    E. Annuities
    F. Limited partnership
    G. Unit investment trust
    H. Other

INCOME TAX PLANNING (17%)

57. Income tax law fundamentals
    A. Sources of authority
       1) Primary
       2) Secondary
    B. Research sources

58. Tax compliance
    A. Filing requirements
    B. Authority to represent clients before the IRS (Circular 230)
    C. Audits
    D. Penalties

59. Income tax fundamentals and calculations
    A. Filing status
    B. Gross income
    C. Adjusted gross income
    D. Itemized deductions

Applies to July 2006 CFP® Certification Examination (page 5 of 7)

1) Types
2) Limitations
E. Personal and dependency exemptions
F. Taxable income
G. Tax liability
H. Tax credits
I. Payment of tax
J. Estimated payments and withholding requirements
K. Kiddie tax
L. Imputed income

60. Tax accounting methods
A. Cash method
B. Accrual method
C. Hybrid method
D. Long-term contracts
E. Installment sales
F. Accounting periods
G. Method changes (entity)

61. Tax characteristics of entities
A. Taxation at entity level
B. Flow-through of income and losses to shareholders
C. Special taxes at entity level for flow-through entities
1) Built-in gains tax
2) LIFO recapture
3) Excess net passive income tax
4) Personal holding company tax
5) Other
D. Use of losses
E. Taxation at dissolution

62. Income taxation of trusts and estates
A. General issues
1) Filing requirements
2) Deadlines
3) Choice of taxable year
4) Tax treatment of distributions to beneficiaries
5) Rate structure
B. Grantor trusts
C. Simple trusts
D. Complex trusts
E. Trust income
1) Trust accounting income
2) Trust taxable income
3) Distributable Net Income (DNI)
F. Estate income tax

63. Basis
A. Original basis
B. Adjusted basis
C. Original issue discount
D. Carryover basis
E. Step-up in basis
F. Impact of community property and common law on basis

64. Cost-recovery concepts
A. Modified Accelerated Cost Recovery System (MACRS)

1) Cost basis
2) Half-year convention
3) Mid-quarter convention
B. Repairs
C. Special elections (§179)
D. Amortization

65. Tax consequences of like-kind exchanges
A. Reporting requirements
B. Qualifying transactions
C. Multiple properties
D. Liabilities
E. Boot
F. Related party transactions

66. Tax consequences of gain or loss on sale of assets
A. Holding period
B. Sale of residence
1) Reporting
2) Exclusion
C. Capital assets (§1221)
D. Depreciation recapture
1) Personal or real property used in trade or business (§1231)
2) Rules for personal property (§1245)
3) Rules for real property (§1250)
E. Related parties
F. Wash sales
G. Bargain sales
H. §1244 stock (small business stock election)

67. Alternative Minimum Tax (AMT)
A. Individual and corporate AMT
1) Mechanics
2) Preferences and adjustments
3) Exclusion items vs. deferral items
4) Credit (creation, usage and limitations)
B. Small business exemption

68. Tax management techniques
A. Tax credits
B. Alternative Minimum Tax (AMT) planning
1) Incentive Stock Options (ISOs)
2) Charitable gifts
3) Stock redemption agreements
C. Accelerated deductions
D. Deferral of income
E. Estimated taxes and withholdings
F. Net operating losses

69. Passive activity and at-risk rules
A. Definitions
B. Computations
C. Treatment of disallowed losses
D. Disposition of passive activities
E. Real estate exceptions

70. Tax implications of changing circumstances

A. Marriage
1) Filing status
2) Children
3) Common law and community property
B. Divorce
1) Alimony
2) Child support
3) Qualified Domestic Relations Order (QDRO)
C. Death (final income tax return)

71. Charitable contributions and deductions
A. Qualified entities
1) Public charities
2) Private charities
B. Deduction limitations
C. Carryover periods
D. Appreciated property and the AMT
E. Partial interest gifts to charity
F. Non-deductible contributions
G. Appraisals
H. Substantiation requirements
I. Charitable contributions by business entities

RETIREMENT PLANNING (18%)

72. Retirement needs analysis
A. Assumptions for retirement planning
1) Inflation
2) Retirement period and life expectancy
3) Lifestyle
4) Total return
B. Financial needs
1) Living costs
2) Charitable and beneficiary gifting objectives
3) Medical costs, including long-term care needs analysis
4) Other (trust and foundation funding, education funding, etc.)
C. Income sources
1) Total return assumptions
2) Probabilistic analysis assumptions
D. Alternatives to compensate for projected cash-flow shortfalls

73. Social Security [Old Age, Survivor, and Disability Insurance (OASDI)]
A. Eligibility and benefit
1) Retirement
2) Disability
3) Survivor
4) Family limitations
B. How benefits are calculated
C. Working after retirement
D. Taxation of Social Security

74. Medicare
A. Eligibility
B. Coverage provided by Parts A and B

Applies to July 2006 CFP® Certification Examination (page 6 of 7)

1) Benefits covered by Medicare
2) Benefits not covered under Medicare
C. Cost of coverage

75. Types of retirement plans
  A. Characteristics
    1) Qualified plans
    2) Non-qualified plans
    3) Government plans (§457 plans)
  B. Types of qualified plans
    1) Defined contribution
      a) Money purchase
      b) Profit-sharing (age-weighted, 401(k), ESOP, etc.)
      c) Target benefit
    2) Defined benefit
      a) Traditional
      b) Cash balance

76. Qualified plan rules and options
  A. Feasibility of installation of a qualified plan
    1) Client objectives
    2) Constraints
  B. Qualified plan coverage and eligibility requirements
    1) Age and service requirements
    2) Coverage requirements
    3) Minimum participation
    4) Highly compensated
    5) Controlled group
  C. Qualified plan vesting schedule
    1) Types
    2) Top-heavy plans
  D. Integration with Social Security/ disparity limits
    1) Defined benefit plans
    2) Defined contribution plans
  E. Factors affecting qualified plan contributions or benefits
    1) Tax considerations
    2) Nature of defined contribution
    3) Nature of defined benefit
    4) Comparison of defined contribution and defined benefit
    5) Definition of compensation
    6) Multiple plans
    7) Special rules for self-employed (non-corporations)
  F. Top-heavy plans
    1) Definitions
    2) Vesting
    3) Effects on contributions or benefits
  G. Loans from qualified plans

77. Other tax-advantaged retirement plans
  A. Types
    1) Traditional IRA
    2) Roth IRA, including conversion analysis
    3) SEP
    4) SIMPLE

5) §403(b) plans
6) §457 plans
  B. Basic provisions
    1) Eligibility
    2) Contribution limits
    3) Deductibility
    4) Distribution options

78. Regulatory considerations
  A. Employee Retirement Income Security Act (ERISA)
  B. Department of Labor (DOL) regulations
  C. Fiduciary obligations
  D. Prohibited transactions
  E. Reporting requirements

79. Plan selection for businesses (key factors affecting selection)
  A. Owner's personal objectives
    1) Tax considerations
    2) Capital needs at retirement
    3) Capital needs at death
  B. Business' objectives
    1) Tax considerations
    2) Cash flow situation and outlook
    3) Employee demographics
    4) Comparison of defined contribution and defined benefit plan alternatives

80. Investment considerations for retirement plans
  A. Suitability
  B. Time horizon
  C. Fiduciary considerations
  D. Prohibited transactions
  E. Unrelated Business Taxable Income (UBTI)
  F. Life insurance

81. Distribution rules, alternatives and taxation
  A. Premature distributions
    1) Penalties
    2) Substantially equal payments (§72(t))
  B. Election of distribution options
    1) Lump sum distributions
    2) Annuity options
    3) Rollover
    4) Direct transfer
  C. Required minimum distributions
    1) Rules
    2) Calculations
    3) Penalties
  D. Beneficiary considerations
  E. Qualified Domestic Relations Order (QDRO)
  F. Taxation of distributions
    1) Waiver
    2) Cost basis recovery

ESTATE PLANNING (15%)

82. Methods of property transfer at death
  A. The probate process
    1) Testate succession
    2) Intestate succession
    3) Advantages and disadvantages of probate
    4) Assets subject to probate
    5) Techniques of avoiding probate
    6) Ancillary probate
  B. Operation of law (title)
  C. Transfers through trusts
  D. Transfers by contract

83. Estate planning documents
  A. Wills
    1) Legal requirements
    2) Types of wills
    3) Avoiding will contests
  B. Powers of attorney
    1) For health care
    2) For property
    3) Durable feature
    4) Special or limited powers
    5) General powers
  C. Advance medical directives (e.g., living wills)
  D. Trusts
  E. Marital agreements
  F. Business agreements
  G. Other

84. Gifting strategies
  A. Suitability of gifting as a planning strategy
  B. Techniques for gift-giving
  C. Appropriate gift property
  D. Strategies for closely-held business owners
  E. Gifts of present and future interests
  F. Tax implications
    1) Income
    2) Gift
    3) Estate
    4) Generation-Skipping Transfer Tax (GSTT)

85. Gift taxation and compliance
  A. Filing requirements
  B. Calculation
    1) Annual exclusion and applicable credit
    2) Split gifts
    3) Prior taxable gifts
    4) Education and medical exclusions
    5) Marital and charitable deductions
    6) Tax liability

86. Incapacity planning
  A. Definition of incapacity/ disability

Applies to July 2006 CFP® Certification Examination (page 7 of 7)

B. Care of client's dependents
C. Care of person and property
D. Disability insurance
E. Long-term care insurance
F. Medicaid planning
G. Viatical settlements
H. Business disability coverage
I. Social Security disability benefits

87. Estate tax calculation and compliance
    A. The gross estate
       1) Inclusions
       2) Exclusions
    B. Deductions
    C. Adjusted Gross Estate (AGE)
    D. Deductions from the adjusted gross estate
    E. Taxable estate
    F. Adjusted taxable gifts rule
    G. Tentative tax base
    H. Tentative tax calculation
    I. Credits
       1) Gift tax payable
       2) Unified credit
       3) Prior transfer credit
       4) State death tax

88. Satisfying liquidity needs
    A. Sale of assets
    B. Life insurance
    C. Other

89. Powers of appointment
    A. Use and purpose
    B. General and special (limited) powers
       1) 5+5 power
       2) Crummey provisions
       3) Distributions for health, education, maintenance and support
       4) Other
    C. Tax implications

90. Types, features and taxation of trusts
    A. Classification
       1) Simple and complex
       2) Revocable and irrevocable
    B. Rule against perpetuities
    C. Selected provisions
       1) Spendthrift clauses
       2) Perpetuity clauses
       3) Other
    D. Taxation of trusts and estates (income, gift and estate)

91. Qualified interest trusts
    A. Grantor Retained Annuity Trusts (GRATs)
    B. Grantor Retained Unitrusts (GRUTs)
    C. Qualified Personal Residence Trusts (QPRTs or House-GRITs)
    D. Tangible personal property trusts
    E. Limitations on the valuation of remainder interests of qualified interest trusts (§2702)

92. Charitable giving
    A. Considerations for contributions and transfers
    B. Requirements for a gift to qualify for a charitable deduction
    C. Charitable remainder trusts
       1) Unitrusts (CRUT)
       2) Annuity trusts (CRAT)
    D. Charitable lead trusts
       1) Unitrusts (CLUT)
       2) Annuity trusts (CLAT)
    E. Pooled income funds
    F. Private foundations
    G. Other types of charitable gifts
    H. Income tax charitable deduction limitations

93. Use of life insurance in estate planning
    A. Advantages and disadvantages
    B. Ownership, beneficiary designation and settlement options
    C. Life insurance trusts
    D. Gift and estate taxation
    E. Income taxation

94. Valuation issues
    A. Estate freezes
       1) Corporate and partnership recapitalizations (§2701)
       2) Transfers in trust
    B. Valuation issues with family partnerships and LLCs
       1) Minority discounts
       2) Marketability discounts
       3) Blockage discounts
       4) Key person discounts
    C. Valuation techniques and the federal gross estate

95. Marital deduction
    A. Characteristics
    B. Terminable interest rule and exceptions
    C. QTIP planning and the prior transfer credit
    D. Special planning for non-citizen spouses
    E. Marital deduction and by-pass planning

96. Deferral and minimization of estate taxes
    A. Deductions and credits
    B. Lifetime planning techniques
    C. Postmortem planning techniques
       1) Qualified disclaimers
       2) Alternative valuation date
       3) Relief provisions for business owners' and farmers'/ranchers' estates
          a) Deferral of estate tax (§6166)
          b) Corporate stock redemptions (§303)
          c) Special use valuation (§2032A)

          d) Qualified family-owned business exclusion (§2057)
    D. Optimal QTIP planning

97. Intra-family and other business transfer techniques
    A. Characteristics
    B. Techniques
       1) Buy-sell agreements
       2) Installment notes
       3) Self-canceling installment notes
       4) Private annuities
       5) Transfers in trust
    C. Federal income, gift, estate and Generation-Skipping Transfer Tax (GSTT) implications

98. Disposition of estate
    A. Tax and non-tax consequences of various estate plans (outright distributions, transfers in trust, etc.)
    B. Estate planning for non-traditional relationships
       1) Children of another relationship
       2) Cohabitation
       3) Adoptions
       4) Same-sex relationships
       5) Communal relationships

99. Generation-Skipping Transfer Tax (GSTT)
    A. Identify transfers subject to the GSTT
       1) Direct skips
       2) Taxable distributions
       3) Taxable terminations
    B. Impact of the GSTT on lifetime transfers
       1) Outright transfers of cash or property
       2) Transfers in trust
    C. Exemptions and exclusions for the GSTT
       1) Outright gifts qualifying for the gift tax annual exclusion
       2) The GSTT exemption
       3) Qualified transfer payments (educational and medical)

100. Fiduciary responsibilities
    A. Duties of fiduciaries
    B. Selection of fiduciaries

101. Income in Respect of a Decedent (IRD)
    A. IRD assets
    B. IRD income tax deduction

TOPIC LISTS FOR THE CFP® CERTIFICATION EXAMINATION (CONTINUED)

Applies to November 2006 and March 2007 CFP® Certification Examination (page 1 of 8)

The following topics, based on the 2004 Job Analysis Study, are the basis for the CFP® Certification Examinations. Each exam question will be linked to one of the following topics, in the approximate percentages indicated following the general headings. Questions will pertain to all levels in Bloom's taxonomy with an emphasis on the higher cognitive levels. Questions often will be asked in the context of the financial planning process and presented in an integrative format.

In addition to being used for the CFP® Certification Examination, this list indicates topic coverage requirements to fulfill the pre-certification educational requirement. Continuing education (CE) programs and materials that address these topics will be eligible for CFP Board CE credit.

(References to sections (§) in this list refer to sections of the Internal Revenue Code)

First Test Date: November 2006

GENERAL PRINCIPLES OF FINANCIAL PLANNING (11%)

1. Financial planning process
   A. Purpose, benefits, and components
   B. Steps
      1) Establishing client-planner relationships
      2) Gathering client data and determining goals and expectations
      3) Determining the client's financial status by analyzing and evaluating general financial status, special needs, insurance and risk management, investments, taxation, employee benefits, retirement, and/or estate planning
      4) Developing and presenting the financial plan
      5) Implementing the financial plan
      6) Monitoring the financial plan
   C. Responsibilities
      1) Financial planner
      2) Client
      3) Other advisors

2. CFP Board's *Code of Ethics and Professional Responsibility* and *Disciplinary Rules and Procedures*
   A. *Code of Ethics and Professional Responsibility*
      1) Preamble and applicability
      2) Composition and scope
      3) Compliance
      4) Terminology
      5) Principles
         a) Principle 1 – Integrity
         b) Principle 2 – Objectivity
         c) Principle 3 – Competence
         d) Principle 4 – Fairness
         e) Principle 5 – Confidentiality
         f) Principle 6 – Professionalism
         g) Principle 7 – Diligence
      6) Rules
   B) *Disciplinary Rules and Procedures*

3. CFP Board's *Financial Planning Practice Standards*
   A) Purpose and applicability
   B) Content of each series (use most current *Practice Standards*, as posted on CFP Board's Web site at www.CFP.net)
   C. Enforcement through *Disciplinary Rules and Procedures*

4. Financial statements
   A. Personal
      1) Statement of financial position
      2) Statement of cash flow
   B. Business
      1) Balance sheet
      2) Income statement
      3) Statement of cash flows
      4) *Pro forma* statements

5. Cash flow management
   A. Budgeting
   B. Emergency fund planning
   C. Debt management ratios
      1) Consumer debt
      2) Housing costs
      3) Total debt
   D. Savings strategies

6. Financing strategies
   A. Long-term vs. short-term debt
   B. Secured vs. unsecured debt
   C. Buy vs. lease/rent
   D. Mortgage financing
      1) Conventional vs. adjustable-rate mortgage (ARM)
      2) Home equity loan and line of credit
      3) Refinancing cost-benefit analysis
      4) Reverse mortgage

7. Function, purpose, and regulation of financial institutions
   A. Banks
   B. Credit unions
   C. Brokerage companies
   D. Insurance companies
   E. Mutual fund companies
   F. Trust companies

8. Education planning
   A. Funding
      1) Needs analysis
      2) Tax credits/adjustments/ deductions
      3) Funding strategies
      4) Ownership of assets
      5) Vehicles
         a) Qualified tuition programs (§529 plans)
         b) Coverdell Education Savings Accounts
         c) Uniform Transfers to Minors Act (UTMA) and Uniform Gifts to Minors Act (UGMA) accounts
         d) Savings bonds
   B. Financial aid

 CERTIFIED FINANCIAL PLANNER™ | CFP®

Applies to November 2006 and March 2007 CFP® Certification Examination (page 2 of 8)

9. Financial planning for special circumstances
   A. Divorce
   B. Disability
   C. Terminal illness
   D. Non-traditional families
   E. Job change and job loss
   F. Dependents with special needs
   G. Monetary windfalls

10. Economic concepts
    A. Supply and demand
    B. Fiscal policy
    C. Monetary policy
    D. Economic indicators
    E. Business cycles
    F. Inflation, deflation, and stagflation
    G. Yield curve

11. Time value of money concepts and calculations
    A. Present value
    B. Future value
    C. Ordinary annuity and annuity due
    D. Net present value (NPV)
    E. Internal rate of return (IRR)
    F. Uneven cash flows
    G. Serial payments

12. Financial services regulations and requirements
    A. Registration and licensing
    B. Reporting
    C. Compliance
    D. State securities and insurance laws

13. Business law
    A. Contracts
    B. Agency
    C. Fiduciary liability

14. Consumer protection laws
    A. Bankruptcy
    B. Fair credit reporting laws
    C. Privacy policies
    D. Identity theft protection

INSURANCE PLANNING AND RISK MANAGEMENT (14%)

15. Principles of risk and insurance
    A. Definitions
    B. Concepts
       1) Peril
       2) Hazard
       3) Law of large numbers
       4) Adverse selection
       5) Insurable risks
       6) Self-insurance
    C. Risk management process

D. Response to risk
   1) Risk control
      a) Risk avoidance
      b) Risk diversification
      c) Risk reduction
   2) Risk financing
      a) Risk retention
      b) Risk transfer
E. Legal aspects of insurance
   1) Principle of indemnity
   2) Insurable interest
   3) Contract requirements
   4) Contract characteristics
   5) Policy ownership
   6) Designation of beneficiary

16. Analysis and evaluation of risk exposures
    A. Personal
       1) Death
       2) Disability
       3) Poor health
       4) Unemployment
       5) Superannuation
    B. Property
       1) Real
       2) Personal
       3) Auto
    C. Liability
       1) Negligence
       2) Intentional torts
       3) Strict liability
    D. Business-related

17. Property, casualty and liability insurance
    A. Individual
       1) Homeowners insurance
       2) Auto insurance
       3) Umbrella liability insurance
    B. Business
       1) Commercial property insurance
       2) Commercial liability insurance
          a) Auto liability
          b) Umbrella liability
          c) Professional liability
          d) Directors and officers liability
          e) Workers' compensation and employers liability

18. Health insurance and health care cost management (individual)
    A. Hospital, surgical, and physicians' expense insurance
    B. Major medical insurance and calculation of benefits
    C. Continuance and portability
    D. Medicare
    E. Taxation of premiums and benefits

19. Disability income insurance (individual)
    A. Definitions of disability
    B. Benefit period

C. Elimination period
D. Benefit amount
E. Provisions
F. Taxation of premiums and benefits

20. Long-term care insurance (individual)
    A. Eligibility
    B. Services covered
    C. Medicare limitations
    D. Benefit period
    E. Elimination period
    F. Benefit amount
    G. Provisions
    H. Taxation of premiums and benefits

21. Life insurance (individual)
    A. Concepts and personal uses
    B. Policy types
    C. Contractual provisions
    D. Dividend options
    E. Nonforfeiture options
    F. Settlement options
    G. Illustrations
    H. Policy replacement
    I. Viatical and life settlements

22. Income taxation of life insurance
    A. Dividends
    B. Withdrawals and loans
    C. Death benefits
    D. Modified endowment contracts (MECs)
    E. Transfer-for-value
    F. §1035 exchanges

23. Business uses of insurance
    A. Buy-sell agreements
    B. Key employee life insurance
    C. Split-dollar life insurance
    D. Business overhead expense insurance

24. Insurance needs analysis
    A. Life insurance
    B. Disability income insurance
    C. Long-term care insurance
    D. Health insurance
    E. Property insurance
    F. Liability insurance

25. Insurance policy and company selection
    A. Purpose of coverage
    B. Duration of coverage
    C. Participating or non-participating
    D. Cost-benefit analysis
    E. Company selection
       1) Industry ratings
       2) Underwriting

2

Applies to November 2006 and March 2007 CFP® Certification Examination (page 3 of 8)

26. Annuities
   A. Types
   B. Uses
   C. Taxation

EMPLOYEE BENEFITS PLANNING (8%)

27. Group life insurance
   A. Types and basic provisions
      1) Group term
      2) Group permanent
      3) Dependent coverage
   B. Income tax implications
   C. Employee benefit analysis and application
   D. Conversion analysis
   E. Carve-out plans

28. Group disability insurance
   A. Types and basic provisions
      1) Short-term coverage
      2) Long-term coverage
   B. Definitions of disability
   C. Income tax implications
   D. Employee benefit analysis and application
   E. Integration with other income

29. Group medical insurance
   A. Types and basic provisions
      1) Traditional indemnity
      2) Managed care plans
         a) Preferred provider organization (PPO)
         b) Health maintenance organization (HMO)
         c) Point-of-service (POS)
   B. Income tax implications
   C. Employee benefit analysis and application
   D. COBRA/HIPAA provisions
   E. Continuation
   F. Savings accounts
      1) Health savings account (HSA)
      2) Archer medical savings account (MSA)
      3) Health reimbursement arrangement (HRA)

30. Other employee benefits
   A. §125 cafeteria plans and flexible spending accounts (FSAs)
   B. Fringe benefits
   C. Voluntary employees' beneficiary association (VEBA)
   D. Prepaid legal services
   E. Group long-term care insurance
   F. Dental insurance
   G. Vision insurance

31) Employee stock options
   A. Basic provisions
      1) Company restrictions
      2) Transferability
      3) Exercise price
      4) Vesting
      5) Expiration
      6) Cashless exercise
   B. Incentive stock options (ISOs)
      1) Income tax implications (regular, AMT, basis)
         a) Upon grant
         b) Upon exercise
         c) Upon sale
      2) Holding period requirements
      3) Disqualifying dispositions
      4) Planning opportunities and strategies
   C. Non-qualified stock options (NSOs)
      1) Income tax implications (regular, AMT, basis)
         a) Upon grant
         b) Upon exercise
         c) Upon sale
      2) Gifting opportunities
         a) Unvested/vested
         b) Exercised/unexercised
         c) Gift tax valuation
         d) Payment of gift tax
      3) Planning opportunities and strategies
      4) Employee benefits analysis and application
   D. Planning strategies for employees with both incentive stock options and non-qualified stock options
   E. Election to include in gross income in the year of transfer (§83(b) election)

32. Stock plans
   A. Types and basic provisions
      1) Restricted stock
      2) Phantom stock
      3) Stock appreciation rights (SARs)
      4) Employee stock purchase plan (ESPP)
   B. Income tax implications
   C. Employee benefit analysis and application
   D. Election to include in gross income in the year of transfer (§83(b) election)

33. Non-qualified deferred compensation
   A. Basic provisions and differences from qualified plans
   B. Types of plans and applications
      1) Salary reduction plans
      2) Salary continuation plans
      3) Rabbi trusts
      4) Secular trusts
   C. Income tax implications
      1) Constructive receipt
      2) Substantial risk of forfeiture
      3) Economic benefit doctrine
   D. Funding methods
   E. Strategies

INVESTMENT PLANNING (19%)

34. Characteristics, uses and taxation of investment vehicles
   A. Cash and equivalents
      1) Certificates of deposit
      2) Money market funds
      3) Treasury bills
      4) Commercial paper
      5) Banker's acceptances
      6) Eurodollars
   B. Individual bonds
      1) U.S. Government bonds and agency securities
         a) Treasury notes and bonds
         b) Treasury STRIPS
         c) Treasury inflation-protection securities (TIPS)
         d) Series EE, HH, and I bonds
         e) Mortgage-backed securities
      2) Zero-coupon bonds
      3) Municipal bonds
         a) General obligation
         b) Revenue
      4) Corporate bonds
         a) Mortgage bond
         b) Debenture
         c) Investment grade
         d) High-yield
         e) Convertible
         f) Callable
      5) Foreign bonds
   C. Promissory notes
   D. Individual stocks
      1) Common
      2) Preferred
      3) American depositary receipts (ADRs)
   E. Pooled and managed investments
      1) Exchange-traded funds (ETFs)
      2) Unit investment trusts
      3) Mutual funds
      4) Closed-end investment companies

Applies to November 2006 and March 2007 CFP® Certification Examination (page 4 of 8)

5) Index securities
6) Hedge funds
7) Limited partnerships
8) Privately managed accounts
9) Separately managed accounts
F. Guaranteed investment contracts (GICs)
G. Real Estate
  1) Investor-managed
  2) Real estate investment trusts (REITs)
  3) Real estate limited partnerships (RELPs)
  4) Real estate mortgage investment conduits (REMICs)
H. Alternative investments
  1) Derivatives
    a) Puts
    b) Calls
    c) Long-term Equity AnticiPation Securities (LEAPS®)
    d) Futures
    e) Warrants and rights
  2) Tangible assets
    a) Collectibles
    b) Natural resources
    c) Precious metals

35. Types of investment risk
A. Systematic/market/nondiversifiable
B. Purchasing power
C. Interest rate
D. Unsystematic/nonmarket/diversifiable
E. Business
F. Financial
G. Liquidity and marketability
H. Reinvestment
I. Political (sovereign)
J. Exchange rate
K. Tax
L. Investment manager

36. Quantitative investment concepts
A. Distribution of returns
  1) Normal distribution
  2) Lognormal distribution
  3) Skewness
  4) Kurtosis
B. Correlation coefficient
C. Coefficient of determination (R^2)
D. Coefficient of variation
E. Standard deviation
F. Beta
G. Covariance
H. Semivariance

37. Measures of investment returns
A. Simple vs. compound return

B. Geometric average vs. arithmetic average return
C. Time-weighted vs. dollar-weighted return
D. Real (inflation-adjusted) vs. nominal return
E. Total return
F. Risk-adjusted return
G. Holding period return
H. Internal rate of return (IRR)
I. Yield-to-maturity
J. Yield-to-call
K. Current yield
L. Taxable equivalent yield (TEY)

38. Bond and stock valuation concepts
A. Bond duration and convexity
B. Capitalized earnings
C. Dividend growth models
D. Ratio analysis
  1) Price/earnings
  2) Price/free cash flow
  3) Price/sales
  4) Price/earnings ÷ growth (PEG)
E. Book value

39. Investment theory
A. Modern portfolio theory (MPT)
  1) Capital market line (CML)
    a) Mean-variance optimization
    b) Efficient frontier
  2) Security market line (SML)
B. Efficient market hypothesis (EMH)
  1) Strong form
  2) Semi-strong form
  3) Weak form
  4) Anomalies
C. Behavioral finance

40. Portfolio development and analysis
A. Fundamental analysis
  1) Top-down analysis
  2) Bottom-up analysis
  3) Ratio analysis
    a) Liquidity ratios
    b) Activity ratios
    c) Profitability ratios
    d) Debt ratios
B. Technical analysis
  1) Charting
  2) Sentiment indicators
  3) Flow of funds indicators
  4) Market structure indicators
C. Investment policy statements
D. Appropriate benchmarks
E. Probability analysis, including Monte Carlo
F. Tax efficiency
  1) Turnover
  2) Timing of capital gains and losses

3) Wash sale rule
4) Qualified dividends
5) Tax-free income
G. Performance measures
  1) Sharpe ratio
  2) Treynor ratio
  3) Jensen ratio
  4) Information ratio

41. Investment strategies
A. Market timing
B. Passive investing (indexing)
C. Buy and hold
D. Portfolio immunization
E. Swaps and collars
F. Formula investing
  1) Dollar cost averaging
  2) Dividend reinvestment plans (DRIPs)
  3) Bond ladders, bullets, and barbells
G. Use of leverage (margin)
H. Short selling
I. Hedging and option strategies

42. Asset allocation and portfolio diversification
A. Strategic asset allocation
  1) Application of client lifecycle analysis
  2) Client risk tolerance measurement and application
  3) Asset class definition and correlation
B. Rebalancing
C. Tactical asset allocation
D. Control of volatility
E. Strategies for dealing with concentrated portfolios

43. Asset pricing models
A. Capital asset pricing model (CAPM)
B. Arbitrage pricing theory (APT)
C. Black-Scholes option valuation model
D. Binomial option pricing

INCOME TAX PLANNING (14%)

44. Income tax law fundamentals
A. Types of authority
  1) Primary
  2) Secondary
B. Research sources

4

Applies to November 2006 and March 2007 CFP® Certification Examination (page 5 of 8)

45. Tax compliance
   A. Filing requirements
   B. Audits
   C. Penalties

46. Income tax fundamentals and calculations
   A. Filing status
   B. Gross income
      1) Inclusions
      2) Exclusions
      3) Imputed income
   C. Adjustments
   D. Standard/Itemized deductions
      1) Types
      2) Limitations
   E. Personal and dependency exemptions
   F. Taxable income
   G. Tax liability
      1) Rate schedule
      2) Kiddie tax
      3) Self-employment tax
   H. Tax credits
   I. Payment of tax
      1) Withholding
      2) Estimated payments

47. Tax accounting
   A. Accounting periods
   B Accounting methods
      1) Cash receipts and disbursements
      2) Accrual method
      3) Hybrid method
      4) Change in accounting method
   C. Long-term contracts
   D. Installment sales
   E. Inventory valuation and flow methods
   F. Net operating losses

48. Characteristics and income taxation of business entities
   A. Entity types
      1) Sole proprietorship
      2) Partnerships
      3) Limited liability company (LLC)
      4) Corporations
      5) Trust
      6) Association
   B. Taxation at entity and owner level
      1) Formation
      2) Flow through of income and losses
      3) Special taxes
      4) Distributions
      5) Dissolution
      6) Disposition

49. Income taxation of trusts and estates
   A. General issues
      1) Filing requirements
      2) Deadlines
      3) Choice of taxable year
      4) Tax treatment of distributions to beneficiaries
      5) Rate structure
   B. Grantor/Nongrantor trusts
   C. Simple/Complex trusts
   D. Revocable/Irrevocable trusts
   E. Trust income
      1) Trust accounting income
      2) Trust taxable income
      3) Distributable net income (DNI)
   F. Estate income tax

50. Basis
   A. Original basis
   B. Adjusted basis
   C. Amortization and accretion
   D. Basis of property received by gift and in nontaxable transactions
   E. Basis of inherited property (community and non-community property)

51. Depreciation/cost-recovery concepts
   A. Modified Accelerated Cost Recovery System (MACRS)
   B. Expensing policy
   C. §179 deduction
   D. Amortization
   E. Depletion

52. Tax consequences of like-kind exchanges
   A. Reporting requirements
   B. Qualifying transactions
   C. Liabilities
   D. Boot
   E. Related party transactions

53. Tax consequences of the disposition of property
   A. Capital assets (§1221)
   B. Holding period
   C. Sale of residence
   D. Depreciation recapture
   E. Related parties
   F. Wash sales
   G. Bargain sales
   H. Section 1244 stock (small business stock election)
   I. Installment sales
   J. Involuntary conversions

54. Alternative minimum tax (AMT)
   A. Mechanics
   B. Preferences and adjustments
   C. Exclusion items vs. deferral items

   D. Credit: creation, usage, and limitations
   E. Application to businesses and trusts
   F. Planning strategies

55. Tax reduction/management techniques
   A. Tax credits
   B. Accelerated deductions
   C. Deferral of income
   D. Intra-family transfers

56. Passive activity and at-risk rules
   A. Definitions
   B. Computations
   C. Treatment of disallowed losses
   D. Disposition of passive activities
   E. Real estate exceptions

57. Tax implications of special circumstances
   A. Married/widowed
      1) Filing status
      2) Children
      3) Community and non-community property
   B. Divorce
      1) Alimony
      2) Child support
      3) Property division

58. Charitable contributions and deductions
   A. Qualified entities
      1) Public charities
      2) Private charities
   B. Deduction limitations
   C. Carryover periods
   D. Appreciated property
   E. Non-deductible contributions
   F. Appraisals
   G. Substantiation requirements
   H. Charitable contributions by business entities

RETIREMENT PLANNING
(19%)

59. Retirement needs analysis
   A. Assumptions for retirement planning
      1) Inflation
      2) Retirement period and life expectancy
      3) Lifestyle
      4) Total return
   B. Income sources
   C. Financial needs
      1) Living costs

5

CERTIFIED FINANCIAL PLANNER™ | CFP®

Applies to November 2006 and March 2007 CFP® Certification Examination (page 6 of 8)

2) Charitable and beneficiary gifting objectives
3) Medical costs, including long-term care needs analysis
4) Other (trust and foundation funding, education funding, etc.)
D. Straight-line returns vs. probability analysis
E. Pure annuity vs. capital preservation
F. Alternatives to compensate for projected cash-flow shortfalls

60. Social Security (Old Age, Survivor, and Disability Insurance, OASDI)
A. Paying into the system
B. Eligibility and benefit
1) Retirement
2) Disability
3) Survivor
4) Family limitations
C. How benefits are calculated
D. Working after retirement
E. Taxation of benefits

61. Types of retirement plans
A. Characteristics
1) Qualified plans
2) Non-qualified plans
B. Types and basic provisions of qualified plans
1) Defined contribution
a) Money purchase
b) Target benefit
c) Profit sharing
1) 401(k) plan
2) Safe harbor 401(k) plan
3) Age-based plan
4) Stock bonus plan
5) Employee stock ownership plan (ESOP)
6) New comparability plan
7) Thrift plan
2) Defined benefit
a) Traditional
b) Cash balance
c) 412(i) plan

62. Qualified plan rules and options
A. Nondiscrimination and eligibility requirements
1) Age and service requirements
2) Coverage requirements
3) Minimum participation
4) Highly compensated employee (HCE)
5) Permitted vesting schedules
6) ADP/ACP testing
7) Controlled group

B. Integration with Social Security/disparity limits
1) Defined benefit plans
2) Defined contribution plans
C. Factors affecting contributions or benefits
1) Deduction limit (§404(c))
2) Defined contribution limits
3) Defined benefit limit
4) Annual compensation limit
5) Definition of compensation
6) Multiple plans
7) Special rules for self-employed (non-corporations)
D. Top-heavy plans
1) Definition
2) Key employee
3) Vesting
4) Effects on contributions or benefits
E. Loans from qualified plans

63. Other tax-advantaged retirement plans
A. Types and basic provisions
1) Traditional IRA
2) Roth IRA, including conversion analysis
3) SEP
4) SIMPLE
5) §403(b) plans
6) §457 plans
7) Keogh (HR-10) plans

64. Regulatory considerations
A. Employee Retirement Income Security Act (ERISA)
B. Department of Labor (DOL) regulations
C. Fiduciary liability issues
D. Prohibited transactions
E. Reporting requirements

65. Key factors affecting plan selection for businesses
A. Owner's personal objectives
1) Tax considerations
2) Capital needs at retirement
3) Capital needs at death
B. Business' objectives
1) Tax considerations
2) Administrative cost
3) Cash flow situation and outlook
4) Employee demographics
5) Comparison of defined contribution and defined benefit plan alternatives

66. Investment considerations for retirement plans
A. Suitability

B. Time horizon
C. Diversification
D. Fiduciary considerations
E. Unrelated business taxable income (UBTI)
F. Life insurance
G. Appropriate assets for tax-advantaged vs. taxable accounts

67. Distribution rules, alternatives, and taxation
A. Premature distributions
1) Penalties
2) Exceptions to penalties
3) Substantially equal payments (§72(t))
B. Election of distribution options
1) Lump sum distributions
2) Annuity options
3) Rollover
4) Direct transfer
C. Required minimum distributions
1) Rules
2) Calculations
3) Penalties
D. Beneficiary considerations/ Stretch IRAs
E. Qualified domestic relations order (QDRO)
F. Taxation of distributions
1) Tax management techniques
2) Net unrealized appreciation (NUA)

ESTATE PLANNING (15%)

68. Characteristics and consequences of property titling
A. Community property vs. non-community property
B. Sole ownership
C. Joint tenancy with right of survivorship (JTWROS)
D. Tenancy by the entirety
E. Tenancy in common
F. Trust ownership

69. Methods of property transfer at death
A. Transfers through the probate process
1) Testamentary distribution
2) Intestate succession
3) Advantages and disadvantages of probate
4) Assets subject to probate estate
5) Probate avoidance strategies

6

Applies to November 2006 and March 2007 CFP® Certification Examination (page 7 of 8)

6) Ancillary probate administration
B. Transfers by operation of law
C. Transfers through trusts
D. Transfers by contract

70. Estate planning documents
   A. Wills
      1) Legal requirements
      2) Types of wills
      3) Modifying or revoking a will
      4) Avoiding will contests
   B. Powers of Attorney
   C. Trusts
   D. Marital property agreements
   E. Buy-sell agreements

71. Gifting strategies
   A. Inter-vivos gifting

   B. Gift-giving techniques and strategies
   C. Appropriate gift property
   D. Strategies for closely-held business owners
   E. Gifts of present and future interests
   F. Gifts to non-citizen spouses
   G. Tax implications
      1) Income
      2) Gift
      3) Estate
      4) Generation-skipping transfer tax (GSTT)

72. Gift tax compliance and tax calculation
   A. Gift tax filing requirements
   B. Calculation
      1) Annual exclusion
      2) Applicable credit amount
      3) Gift splitting
      4) Prior taxable gifts
      5) Education and medical exclusions
      6) Marital and charitable deductions
      7) Tax liability

73. Incapacity planning
   A. Definition of incapacity
   B. Powers of attorney
      1) For health care decisions
      2) For asset management
      3) Durable feature
      4) Springing power
      5) General or limited powers
   C. Advance medical directives (e.g. living wills)
   D. Guardianship and conservatorship
   E. Revocable living trust
   F. Medicaid planning

G. Special needs trust

74. Estate tax compliance and tax calculation
   A. Estate tax filing requirements
   B. The gross estate
      1) Inclusions
      2) Exclusions
   C. Deductions
   D. Adjusted gross estate
   E. Deductions from the adjusted gross estate
   F. Taxable estate
   G. Adjusted taxable gifts
   H. Tentative tax base
   I. Tentative tax calculation
   J. Credits
      1) Gift tax payable
      2) Applicable credit amount
      3) Prior transfer credit

75. Sources for estate liquidity
   A. Sale of assets
   B. Life insurance
   C. Loan

76. Powers of appointment
   A. Use and purpose
   B. General and special (limited) powers
      1) 5-and-5 power
      2) Crummey powers
      3) Distributions for an ascertainable standard
      4) Lapse of power
   C. Tax implications

77. Types, features, and taxation of trusts
   A. Classification
      1) Simple and complex
      2) Revocable and irrevocable
      3) Inter-vivos and testamentary
   B. Types and basic provisions
      1) Totten trust
      2) Spendthrift trust
      3) Bypass trust
      4) Marital trust
      5) Qualified terminable interest property (QTIP) trust
      6) Pour-over trust
      7) §2503(b) trust
      8) §2503(c) trust
      9) Sprinkling provision
   C. Trust beneficiaries: Income and remainder
   D. Rule against perpetuities
   E. Estate and gift taxation

78. Qualified interest trusts
   A. Grantor retained annuity trusts (GRATs)

B. Grantor retained unitrusts (GRUTs)
C. Qualified personal residence trusts (QPRTs or House-GRITs)
D. Valuation of qualified interests

79. Charitable transfers
   A. Outright gifts
   B. Charitable remainder trusts
      1) Unitrusts (CRUTs)
      2) Annuity trusts (CRATs)
   C. Charitable lead trusts
      1) Unitrusts (CLUTs)
      2) Annuity trusts (CLATs)
   D. Charitable gift annuities
   E. Pooled income funds
   F. Private foundations
   G. Donor advised funds
   H. Estate and gift taxation

80. Use of life insurance in estate planning
   A. Incidents of ownership
   B. Ownership and beneficiary considerations
   C. Irrevocable life insurance trust (ILIT)
   D. Estate and gift taxation

81. Valuation issues
   A. Estate freezes
      1) Corporate and partnership recapitalizations (§2701)
      2) Transfers in trust
   B. Valuation discounts for business interests
      1) Minority discounts
      2) Marketability discounts
      3) Blockage discounts
      4) Key person discounts
   C. Valuation techniques and the federal gross estate

82. Marital deduction
   A. Requirements
   B. Qualifying transfers
   C. Terminable interest rule and exceptions
   D. Qualified domestic trust (QDOT)

83. Deferral and minimization of estate taxes
   A. Exclusion of property from the gross estate
   B. Lifetime gifting strategies
   C. Marital deduction and bypass trust planning
   D. Inter-vivos and testamentary charitable gifts

7

Copyright © 2005 by Certified Financial Planner Board of Standards Inc. All rights reserved.

CERTIFIED FINANCIAL PLANNER™ | **CFP**®

Applies to November 2006 and March 2007 CFP® Certification Examination (page 8 of 8)

84. Intra-family and other business transfer techniques
   A. Characteristics
   B. Techniques
      1) Buy-sell agreement
      2) Installment note
      3) Self-canceling installment note (SCIN)
      4) Private annuity
      5) Transfers in trust
      6) Intra-family loan
      7) Bargain sale
      8) Gift or sale leaseback
      9) Intentionally defective grantor trust
      10) Family limited partnership (FLP) or limited liability company (LLC)
   C. Federal income, gift, estate, and generation-skipping transfer tax implications

85) Generation-skipping transfer tax (GSTT)
   A. Identify transfers subject to the GSTT
      1) Direct skips
      2) Taxable distributions
      3) Taxable terminations
   B. Exemptions and exclusions from the GSTT
      1) The GSTT exemption
      2) Qualifying annual exclusion gifts and direct transfers

86. Fiduciaries
   A. Types of fiduciaries
      1) Executor/Personal representative
      2) Trustee
      3) Guardian
   B. Duties of fiduciaries
   C. Breach of fiduciary duties

87. Income in respect of a decedent (IRD)
   A. Assets qualifying as IRD
   B. Calculation for IRD deduction
   C. Income tax treatment

88. Postmortem estate planning techniques
   A. Alternate valuation date
   B. Qualified disclaimer
   C. Deferral of estate tax (§6166)
   D. Corporate stock redemption (§303)
   E. Special use valuation (§2032A)

89. Estate planning for non-traditional relationships
   A. Children of another relationship
   B. Cohabitation
   C. Adoption
   D. Same-sex relationships

ADDENDUM

The following topics are an addendum to the *Topic List for CFP® Certification Examination*. Although individuals taking the CFP® Certification Examination will not be tested directly over these topics, CFP Board registered programs are strongly encouraged to teach them in their curricula) Continuing education (CE) programs and materials that address these topics will be eligible for CFP Board CE credit.

1. Client and planner attitudes, values, biases and behavioral characteristics and the impact on financial planning
   A. Cultural
   B. Family (e.g. biological; non-traditional)
   C. Emotional
   D. Life cycle and age
   E. Client's level of knowledge, experience, and expertise
   F. Risk tolerance
   G. Values-driven planning

2. Principles of communication and counseling
   A. Types of structured communication
      1) Interviewing
      2) Counseling
      3) Advising
   B. Essentials in financial counseling
      1) Establishing structure
      2) Creating rapport
      3) Recognizing resistance
   C. Characteristics of effective counselors
      1) Unconditional positive regard
      2) Accurate empathy
      3) Genuineness and self-awareness
   D. Nonverbal behaviors
      1) Body positions, movements, and gestures
      2) Facial expressions and eye contact
      3) Voice tone and pitch
      4) Interpreting the meaning of nonverbal behaviors
   E. Attending and listening skills
      1) Physical attending
      2) Active listening
      3) Responding during active listening; leading responses
   F. Effective use of questions
      1) Appropriate types of questions
      2) Ineffective and counterproductive questioning techniques

8

CERTIFIED FINANCIAL PLANNER™ | **CFP**®

PLAN YOUR STUDY TIME

BE PREPARED TO SPEND THE TIME

- The CFP® Certification Examination (the exam) will demand a great deal of your time and effort. Make passing a priority in your life. If it is not in your top three or four priorities at this time, perhaps you should wait until it is.

- A comprehensive review will take you approximately 300 hours including any time spent in or out of class. This time will vary depending on your level of knowledge in the base material and your experience in the practice or simulated practice of financial planning. Whether or not you attend a live review will also impact the amount of study time necessary to pass. The Kaplan Financial Live Review will focus you on what you need to know to pass the exam and will streamline your study efforts.

- Do not fool yourself! This exam is comparable to other professional exams, such as the CPA exam, CFA exams, or Bar exam, and is extremely rigorous.

KNOW YOUR FINANCIAL CALCULATOR

- You need a very thorough knowledge of your financial calculator. It is imperative that you are familiar with the time-value-of-money calculations, as well as the underlying financial theory. If you are deficient in this area, you should take the time (approximately 6-8 hours) to learn the calculator before beginning your study program.

- Work problems 76-124 in *Volume I – Fundamentals of Financial Planning* as practice. Also, work thoroughly through *Understanding Your Financial Calculator* book.

- It is especially helpful to learn the keystrokes. Pay close attention to where the cash flows occur in time. Mastering these problems is an important step in passing the exam.

- We recommend the HP-12C, HP-10B, HP-10BII, or an equivalent.

DEVELOP A STUDY PLAN

- The exam is comprehensive and encompasses an enormous amount of material and information. Studying on a regular basis will be a great asset in accomplishing your goal of passing the exam. With work, family, eating, and sleeping, much of the day is already gone. For this reason, it is important to develop a study plan and keep study materials with you at all times.

- Get organized. Make a preliminary study plan keeping all specifics (such as date, number of problems attempted, number correct, total time (hours), etc.). Your study plan should be divided into the six subject areas for more manageable use of your study time. You may want to use the sample study plan at the end of this section to track your progress.

- You will need self-discipline to adhere to your plan.

SAMPLE YOUR KNOWLEDGE

- It is crucial to begin your study program by first evaluating your current knowledge. Once you have an idea of what you currently know, you must then determine the areas in which you are deficient. Basically, you must determine where your strengths and weaknesses lie.

- We recommend that you sample your knowledge by taking a random sample of 20 multiple-choice questions in each of the six major areas from Volumes I- IV*. Be sure to mark the time that you start and the time that you finish. Put a (G) by any questions where you had to guess the answer.

- If you score above 70% in any area, take another sample and continue with this method as long as your percentage correct stays above 70%. Continue until you have answered all the questions. Anytime you score less than 70%, you should carefully read the entire outline in the front of the book that relates to the material you have been testing, then, take another sample.

- Note the questions you answer incorrectly and the topics they cover. Go over those questions and allow time to devote more study time to the areas to which they pertain.

- Most candidates will need practice in some topical areas in each of the above. Don't be discouraged.

- We recommend that you write down your progress in your study plan. Try to get each topic to 65%-70% correct with one or more above 80%. You are almost certain to pass.

- Evaluation:

    - 80% or more correct and 1.7 minutes or less per question = extremely well prepared.

    - 70% or more correct and 1.7 minutes or less per question = well prepared.

    - 50-60% or more correct and 2.0 minutes or less per question = marginally prepared (risk).

    - Less than 50% and/or over 2.0 minutes per question = need serious review (serious risk).

* Students may also use the Test Bank software (sold separately), that contains over 1700 questions. For more information regarding this product please contact a Kaplan Financial Customer Service Representative at 1-888-694-3568.

TIME MANAGEMENT

- After you determine your areas of strength and weakness, you should be able to estimate the number of hours you will need to study in order to pass the exam. At this point, you should take out your calendar, and count the number of weeks you have remaining to study prior to the exam. Divide the number of hours you need to study by the number of weeks until the exam. This will allow you to determine the number of hours you must study per week. This figure can then be further refined into hours to study per weekday and per weekend, etc.

- For example, Paul is taking the exam in November. It is now the middle of July, and he has just received his Kaplan Financial materials. He purchased *Volumes I – VIII, Understanding Your Financial Calculator,* the *Financial Planning Flashcards,* and the *Test Bank.* He has registered for and plans to attend a Kaplan Financial Live Instructional Review. He has 17 weeks until the exam and has decided that he needs to study a full 350 hours to pass. Based on this information, he will need to study 20 hours per week. To accomplish this goal, Paul decided to study 2 hours each weekday and 10 hours on the weekend (except for the weeks he attends the Live Review). He will always carry at least one section of the flashcards with him so that he can make the best use of any "downtime" he encounters. Using this information (along with Paul's knowledge of his own areas of strength and weakness), Paul decided the following schedule would be appropriate:

Week	Topics to Cover	Hours
1	*Understanding Your Financial Calculator*	20
2	*Vol. I – Fundamentals* – text (all) and questions (half)	20
3	*Vol. I – Fundamentals* – questions (half) and *Vol. II – Insurance Planning* text (all)	20
4	*Vol. II – Insurance Planning* questions (all) and *Vol. III – Investments Planning* text (half)	20
5	*Vol. III – Investments* text (half) and questions (all)	20
6	*Vol. VI – Estate Planning* text (all) and questions (half)	20
7	*Vol. VI – Estate Planning* questions (half) and *Vol. V – Retirement & Employee Benefit Planning* text (all)	20
8	*Vol. V – Retirement Planning.* questions (all) and *Vol. IV – Income Tax Planning* text (half)	20
9	*Vol. IV – Income Tax Planning* text (half) and questions (all)	20
10	*Volume VII – Case Book* – Item Sets, Cognitive Connections and catch-up	20
11	*Test Bank* and attend Live Review	34
12	*Test Bank* and attend Live Review	34
13	*Vol. VII – Case Book* (half)	20
14	*Vol. VII – Case Book* (half)	20
15	*Vol. VIII – Mock Exam and Solutions* and review	12
16	Review weak topics and catch-up	20
17	Review weak topics	10

MONTHLY CALENDAR

- You might find it beneficial to invest in a large monthly calendar and hang it where you will see it every day. Be sure to mark all of your upcoming commitments with regard to work, family, outside activities, etc., on your calendar. This will help you plan and anticipate any time constraints that may lead to obstacles in your study program. For example, during Week 3 of Paul's schedule, he knows that he must attend an out-of-town wedding and will only have time to study the two hours he is on the airplane. Even though he will make good use of his flashcards during that time, he still must adjust his schedule to spend more time studying during Weekend 2 and on the weekdays during Weeks 2 and 3 in order to compensate for the fluctuation in his study program. You may find that you will need to cancel commitments or turn down new commitments you would otherwise accept in order to maintain your focus. Remember, your study time for the CFP® Certification Examination is limited and must be one of your top priorities!

- You will also want to indicate on your calendar the subject areas on which you plan to focus your study time each week. This will help you plan which commitments you will and will not be able to accept as weeks go by. For example, in Week 8 Paul's brother calls and wants to schedule dinner for Week 9. Paul knows that he will be studying Income Tax Planning (his hardest subject) and that this area might require more study time than other areas. Thus, Paul decides that he should not schedule any additional events for Week 9, and declines.

- Make the most of your travel time to and from the Live Review. For example, because Paul will be traveling to and from the Live Review by train, he can study the remaining sections of his flashcards.

WEEKLY CALENDAR

- Before you begin your first week of study, list all of the activities in which you participate. Determine how long each activity takes to complete and whether or not this activity is performed at a specific time each day, week, month, etc.

- Make sure to include your work hours, drive time, family time, meals, sleep, and any other miscellaneous activities you might do that take up your time. You may want to use the sample schedule at the end of this section to track your activities.

- Once you have logged your activities in your weekly and monthly calendars, review your schedule, and decide which time slots are full and which are open. Using this information, you should be able to develop a realistic study plan for each day. If you find that your current activities do not leave you enough free time to study, you will need to eliminate enough activities so that you will have adequate study time to prepare for the exam. If you discover that you do not have the appropriate amount of time for exam preparation, it would be to your benefit to postpone taking the exam until it is a higher priority or until you have fewer commitments. Before each week begins, review your weekly schedule and update it for any new commitments. Although you will need to be flexible with your scheduled study time, it is important to stick with your scheduled study time as much as possible. Try to anticipate missed study time and be sure to reschedule the missed time for another day.

MAKE A DAILY TO-DO LIST

- Before you begin each study session, make a tentative list of what you want to accomplish during your study time. You may also want to keep a spiral notebook or binder so you will be able to continuously evaluate and reevaluate your progress. Write down the number of pages that you plan to read and/or the number of problems that you plan to work during your study session. Be realistic when you write this list and work very hard to stick to your study plan.

PREPARE TO STUDY

There are many ways you can maximize the benefits of your study time. The following are some of our suggestions to most efficiently and effectively study:

CREATE A SUITABLE STUDY ENVIRONMENT

The most important thing you can do to help facilitate your studying is to create a suitable study environment. Your study area should be:

1. Quiet. You want to find a place that is free from all extraneous noise (including the television and disruptive people).

2. Away from distractions. Stay away from areas where there are a lot of distractions. For example, try not to study close to a telephone, since you might be tempted to answer it and talk. You might also want to try to avoid studying at work or at home if coworkers or family members will interrupt you.

3. Study in a well lit location. You will want to study in an area where you will be able to see the information as well as stay awake and alert.

4. Be comfortable, but not too comfortable. You want to be relaxed so that you see studying as a beneficial activity and not a punishment. You should not, however, let yourself get so comfortable that you will be tempted to fall asleep.

5. Have all of your materials readily available. Gather everything you will need during your study session beforehand. This includes pencils, pens, books, highlighters, a calculator, and paper. Try to sit at a desk or table so that you have a firm writing surface and room for all of your materials.

USE THE MULTIPLE-CHOICE QUESTIONS TO DIRECT YOUR STUDY

- Keep in mind that you should not spend the majority of your study time on material you've already learned. There is a natural tendency to do so, as it is a lot more fun and certainly more comforting, but unfortunately, counter-productive. The subject in which you scored the lowest should be studied the most. The multiple-choice questions can be used as a monitoring tool if you keep thorough records. We recommend that you study the multiple-choice questions and the outlines as needed.

BECOME THOROUGHLY KNOWLEDGEABLE WITH THE MATERIAL

- The exam is professionally rigorous and tests across Bloom's Taxonomy of Cognitive Learning. You can expect a small percentage of problems to test at the knowledge level and a much larger percentage to test at the application, synthesis, and evaluation levels.

- The difference in passing and failing is the difference between being thoroughly prepared and proactive, versus being casually acquainted and reactive. For example, when you think of IRAs, your mind should create a picture of the following topics that relate to IRAs:

  - Eligibility
  - Deductible/nondeductible
  - Allocation between spouses
  - Transferability
  - Rollover
  - Assignment/pledging
  - Investments
  - Penalties

  - Distribution prior to 70½
  - Minimum distributions
  - Roth IRAs and Coverdell Education Savings Accounts
  - Death
  - Inclusion in Gross Estate
  - QDRO
  - Active participation in a pension plan
  - Joint life distribution

- You should be immediately prepared and ready to answer any question about any subtopic in IRAs. If the mentioning of IRAs does not bring anything to mind, or if only a few of the listed topics come to mind, you are not thoroughly knowledgeable.

- The problem with being only casually acquainted with the material is twofold: (1) you take too much time thinking of an answer, and (2) you let the exam lead you to incorrect answers. You must discipline yourself to aggressively answer the questions and you must monitor the time it takes you to answer the average multiple-choice question. Remember, when you are thoroughly knowledgeable, the questions are fairly easy. When you are only casually acquainted, the questions are much harder and take longer to answer.

TEXTBOOK PREVIEWING

As you are reviewing all of the texts, there are two things you should do:

- Be sure to study the title of each section. Not only will this preview what you are about to read, it will also help you to narrow your scope of study.

- Look for relationships. This is extremely important. By looking for relationships between current information and subjects you have read about previously, you can learn to group concepts together and increase memory retention. Most of the questions on the CFP® Exam tie many topics and subjects together into one question, so it is important to look for relationships.

THINGS TO MARK

- Definitions. Often knowing a word's definition can help you to distinguish terms that might otherwise prove confusing. On the exam, knowing the definition of key words and concepts can often help you eliminate possible answers on multiple-choice questions.

- Signal words. Words such as, "and," "or," "except," "not," and "also," indicate the relationships between concepts.

- Key words and phrases. Key words are words or phrases that should instantly bring to mind a number of questions, issues, or ideas relating to the topics identified by the key words or phrases. For example, the phrase "substantial and reoccurring" is a key phrase that relates to the funding of profit-sharing plans. Keywords and phrases are the foundation on which you should build your basis of knowledge.

NOTE-TAKING METHODS

- Flashcards or note cards. Notes taken on note cards can also be used as valuable tools for review. You can use them as flashcards, which are much more portable than textbooks or notebooks, and force memory recall, which is a requirement of the exam. You can create your own flashcards or use Kaplan Financial's Financial Planning Flashcards which number over 1,000, to enhance your studying when you're on the go.

- Study notes. Traditional study notes allow you to trigger key concepts that you have read about. This is crucial for review purposes. Study notes should be rewritten within 48 hours of taking them to clarify any areas that seem ambiguous.

STUDY METHODS

SQ3R Study System

- Survey. Glance through material and get a general idea about the key information within the text.

- Question. Think about questions that could be asked about the material. If the section title is "Key Concepts of Estate Planning," a possible question might be, "*What are the key concepts of estate planning?*"

- Read. Read through the material carefully, marking the text and taking notes as you go.

- Recite. After each section, pretend that you are lecturing to a friend or colleague on the material. Are you able to retain the information?

- Review. Be sure to go over each section and review information about which you might be confused.

SOAR Study Formula

- Survey the book. Skim over the outline topics. Review the table of contents to see the major categories of information. Review the index for important topics and keywords. Also look at each individual section and review the topics, major points, and information contained within each section.

- Organize. Organize the information that you have read and taken notes on. Some ways to facilitate this are to:

    - Underline books.
    - Make notes for books (charts, note cards, etc.)

- Anticipate. Anticipate the information that you think will be tested. Formulate possible test questions, and evaluate your ability to answer these questions correctly in a testing environment.

- Recite and Review. Just as with the SQ3R method, the SOAR method places final emphasis on being able to recite information as if lecturing on its key points and reviewing any areas where you have deficiencies.

MNEMONICS

- Mnemonics literally translates to, "to help the memory." These are techniques that can be incorporated into your study plan in order to increase your retention of information. The most common use of mnemonics is to create an acronym or a sentence with the first letter of each keyword. For instance, "PRIME" is an acronym used to help students remember systematic risks. P-R-I-M-E stands for Purchasing Power Risk, Reinvestment Rate Risk, Interest Rate Risk, Market Risk, and Exchange Rate Risk.

KAPLAN'S FINAL TIPS

- Avoid whining. Avoid whining about your having to know or learn some area of financial planning that is technical and that most planners have to look up. One purpose of the exam is to serve as gatekeeper to the profession; another is to help you develop a healthy sense of professional humility about what you know. Also, clients will expect you to know everything.

- Study what you don't know. Your lowest-scoring subject should be the subject you study the most.

- Think positively. It will help you pass.

- Find a way to make it fun. Don't fight the problem.

STUDY PLAN

Date	# Attempted	# Correct	% Correct	Average Time per Question	Study Outline	Total Time	Notes

WEEKLY ACTIVITIES/COMMITMENTS

Time	Monday	Tuesday	Wednesday	Thursday	Friday	Saturday	Sunday
12 am							
1							
2							
3							
4							
5							
6							
7							
8							
9							
10							
11							
12 pm							
1							
2							
3							
4							
5							
6							
7							
8							
9							
10							
11							

SOLVING MULTIPLE-CHOICE QUESTIONS

Read the last line (the requirement) first.

- The last line will generally be the question part of the problem and will identify the types of important information that will be needed to answer the question.

- From Example 1 on the following page, "How many personal and dependency exemptions can Mike and Pam claim on their 2006 income tax return?"

- This last sentence identifies the type of information needed from the body of the problem. You can now look for key information while reading through the body of the problem.

Read the question carefully.

- Underline the concepts, words, and data, and make important notes of data or relevant rules to help formulate your answer.

Formulate your answer.

- Do not look at the answer choices presented on the exam until you have formulated your answer. Looking at the answer choices may have a tendency to distract you or change your thinking.

Select your answer if it is presented.

- Write your answer or circle it directly on the examination.

- Watch the clock and enter answers on the answer sheet as you go, or all at once at the end. If at the end, be sure you have enough time. Be consistent.

Review other answer choices for the following:

- Was your answer sufficiently precise?

- Was your answer complete?

If your answer is not presented:

- You know you are incorrect. Alternatives:
    - Reread question and requirements.
    - Evaluate answers presented.
    - Guess.
    - Skip the question and come back to it later.
    - Note: You are not penalized for guessing, so, if time is running out, be sure to fill in all of the open questions.

SOLVING A-TYPE QUESTIONS

STRAIGHT MULTIPLE-CHOICE QUESTIONS

1. **Example.**

   Mike and Pam, ages 67 and 65, respectively, filed a joint tax return for 2006. They provided all of the support for their 19-year-old son, who had $2,200 of gross income. Their 23-year-old daughter, a full-time student until her graduation on June 25, 2006, earned $2,700, which was 40% of her total support during the year. Her parents provided the remaining support. Mike and Pam also provided total support for Pam's father, who is a citizen and life-long resident of Columbia. How many personal and dependency exemptions can Mike and Pam claim on their 2004 income tax return?

   Question 1 Analysis

Step 1	Read last line and identify the topic: Personal and dependency exemptions.
Step 2	Read question and make notes:

   - Mike and Pam   ⇒ 2 personal exemptions.

   - 19-year-old son   ⇒ 1 dependency exemption (because gross income test is met).

   - 23-year-old daughter   ⇒ 1 dependency exemption (because full-time student for five months).

   - Pam's father   ⇒ None (because he is not a citizen). Note: He could qualify if a citizen of Mexico or Canada.

Step 3	Count exemptions (four) and select answer (c).

   a. 2.

   b. 3.

   c. 4.

   d. 5.

   e. None of the above.

   Answer: (c)

   Exemptions are allowed for Mike, Pam, their son, and their daughter. They are not entitled to an exemption for Pam's father because he was not a citizen or resident of the U.S. or other qualifying country. Their son qualifies as a dependent because his gross income was less than the exemption amount ($3,300 in 2006). The gross income test is waived for their daughter, who was a full-time student for at least five months during the year.

2. **Example.**

George, whose wife died in November 2005, filed a joint tax return for 2005. He did not remarry and has continued to maintain his home for his two dependent children. In the preparation of his tax return for 2006, what is George's filing status?

Question 2 Analysis

Step 1	Read last line and identify the topic: Filing status for George for 2006.
Step 2	Read question and make notes:
	• Wife died 11/05.
	• Joint return filed for 2005.
	• Unmarried with two dependents.
Step 3	With these facts and notes, you should immediately recall that the surviving spouse's filing status can be used for the two years following the year of death of the first spouse if there is a dependent child.
Step 4	Delete the clearly wrong answers by striking through them (e.g., delete answer (d) – he is not married). This will help you to focus on the viable alternatives.
Step 5	Select answer (b).

  a. Single.

  b. Qualified widow/widower.

  c. Head of household.

  d. Married filing separately.

  e. None of the above.

Answer: (b)

George correctly filed a joint return in 2005. He will file as a qualified widower for 2006.

3. **Example.**

Brian, an employee of Duff Corporation, died December 25, 2006. During December, Duff Corporation made employee death payments of $10,000 to his widow and $10,000 to his 17-year-old son. What amounts can be excluded from gross income by the widow and son in their respective tax returns for 2006?

Question 3 Analysis

Step 1	Read last line and identify the topic: Amounts excluded from gross income for 2006.
Step 2	Read question and make notes:
	• Brian died during 2006.
	• Employee death payments of $10,000 to widow and $10,000 to son.
Step 3	With these facts and notes, you should recall that the law allowing an exclusion for death benefits was repealed.
Step 4	Analysis:
	• Total amount excludable = $0.
	• Total death benefits = $20,000.
Step 5	Select answer (a).

	Widow	Son
a.	$0.	$0.
b.	$2,500.	$2,500.
c.	$5,000.	$5,000.
d.	$7,500.	$7,500.
e.	$10,000.	$10,000.

Answer: (a)

No death proceeds are excludable.

4. Example.

Clark Roberts wants to retire in nine years. He needs an additional $300,000 (today's dollars) in nine years to have sufficient funds to finance this objective. He assumes inflation will average 5.0% over the long run, and he can earn a 4.0% compound annual after-tax return on investments. What will be Clark's payment at the end of the second year?

Question 4 Analysis

Step 1	Read last line and identify the topic: TVM serial payment second year-end.
Step 2	Read question and make notes:

- Needs $300,000 in today's dollars in nine years.

- Inflation rate = 5%, earnings rate = 4%.

Step 3   Analysis:

FV	=	$300,000	
i	=	-0.95238	$[((1.04 \div 1.05) - 1) \times 100]$
N	=	9	
PV	=	0	
PMT	=	$34,623.42	Payment at the beginning of the year 1.
		x 1.05 = $36,354.60	Payment at the end of year 1.
		x 1.05 = $38,172.33	Payment at the end of year 2.

Step 4   Select answer (b).

a. $38,244.62.

b. $38,172.33.

c. $36,354.60.

d. $34,623.42.

e. None of the above.

Answer: (b)

$36,354.60 × 1.05 = $38,172.33. This is an example of a serial payment. A serial payment is not an annuity due or ordinary annuity level payment. A serial payment increases annually at the rate of inflation.

5. **Example.**

   Taxpayer gives her son property with a basis to donor of $35,000 and a fair market value of $30,000. No gift tax is paid. Son subsequently sells the property for $33,000. What is his recognized gain (or loss)?

   Question 5 Analysis

Step 1	Read last line and identify the topic: Gain or loss on sale of donated property. Note: This topic should bring to mind the important points for this area, such as basis and sales price.
Step 2	Read question and make notes:

   - FMV < Basis.

   - FMV < Sales Price < Basis.

   - If an asset is sold between the gain basis and the loss basis, there will be no gain or loss.

Step 3	Select answer (a).

   a. No gain or loss.

   b. Loss.

   c. Gain.

   d. None of the above.

   Answer: (a)

   The son's basis is $35,000 for gains. His loss basis is $30,000. Since his selling price of $33,000 is between the gain and the loss basis, there is no recognized gain or loss.

CALCULATION-TYPE QUESTIONS

6. **Example.**

   Helen, a single taxpayer, purchases an airplane for $130,000. In order to obtain financing for the purchase, Helen issues a lien on her personal residence in the amount of $130,000. At the time, the residence had a fair market value of $400,000 and a first mortgage of $320,000. For the plane loan, Helen may claim as qualified residence interest the interest on what amount?

   Question 6 Analysis

Step 1	Read last line and identify the topic: Qualified residence interest/home equity limit.
Step 2	Read question and make notes:

   - QRI limit to $1,000,000 debt or fair market value, whichever is less.
   - Home equity line is limited to the lesser of equity, or $100,000.

   Step 3   Analysis:

FMV	$400,000	
First Mortgage	- 320,000	
	$80,000	Equity limit

   Step 4   Answer $80,000. Select answer (b).

   a. $30,000.

   b. $80,000.

   c. $100,000.

   d. $130,000.

   e. None of the above.

Answer: (b)

Home equity loans are limited to the lesser of:

- The fair market value of the residence, reduced by acquisition indebtedness, or
- $100,000.

Thus, $400,000 (fair market value) − $320,000 (first mortgage) provides a limit of $80,000. Interest on the remaining $50,000 of the loan will be treated under the consumer interest rules (i.e., not deductible).

7. **Example.**

Connie wants to withdraw $1,200 at the beginning of each month for the next 5 years. She expects to earn 10% compounded monthly on her investments. What lump sum should Connie deposit today?

Question 7 Analysis

Step 1	Read last line and identify the topic: Analysis of PMT (AD).
Step 2	Read question and make notes: PV problem.
Step 3	Analysis:

- PV
- N
- i
- PMT
- N

Step 3	Fill out information and identify objective.

PV	=	?
N	=	60
i	=	10% ÷ 12
PMT	=	$1,200 (annuity due)
FV	=	Not applicable (put 0 in cell to eliminate any numbers)

Step 4 Calculate PV_{AD} = $56,949.10. Answer (b).

If your result was $56,478.44, you calculated an ordinary annuity (payments at the end of the period) instead of an annuity due.

Make sure that your calculator is in "begin" mode.

a. $56,478.44.

b. $56,949.10.

c. $58,630.51.

d. $59,119.10.

e. None of the above.

Answer: (b)

PMT_B	=	$1,200
i	=	0.8333 (10 ÷ 12)
N	=	60 (5 × 12)
PVAD	=	$56,949.10

8. **Example.**

Gary has received an inheritance of $200,000. He wants to withdraw equal periodic payments at the beginning of each month for the next 5 years. He expects to earn 12% compounded monthly on his investments. How much can he receive each month?

Question 8 Analysis

Step 1	Read last line and identify the topic: Analysis of PMT (AD).
Step 2	Analysis:

- PV
- N
- i
- PMT
- N

Step 3	Fill out information and identify objective.

PV	=	$200,000
N	=	60
i	=	$12 \div 12$
Objective $\Rightarrow \mathrm{PMT_{AD}}$	=	$4,404.84 – therefore answer (a)
FV	=	Not applicable

Note closeness of answer (b); make sure you have the annuity due, ordinary annuity issue correct. Does answer (c) or (d) make any sense? No, 60 payments at those levels would be 2-3 million.

Step 4	Select answer (a).

    a. $4,404.84.

    b. $4,448.89.

    c. $49,537.45.

    d. $55,481.95.

    e. None of the above.

Answer: (a)

PV	=	$200,000
i	=	1.00 (12 ÷ 12)
N	=	60 (5 × 12)
$\mathrm{PMT_{AD}}$	=	$4,404.84

EVALUATE ANSWERS

9. **Example.**

On January 1, Father (Mike) loaned Daughter (Allison) $90,000 to purchase a new personal residence. There were no other loans outstanding between Mike and Allison. Allison's only income was $30,000 salary and $4,000 interest income. Mike had investment income of $200,000. Mike did not charge Allison interest. The relevant federal rate was 9%. Which of the following statements is correct regarding the transaction?

   a. Allison must recognize $8,100 (0.09 × $90,000) imputed interest income on the loan.

   b. Mike must recognize imputed interest income of $4,000.

   c. Mike must recognize imputed interest income of $8,100.

   d. Allison is allowed a deduction for imputed interest of $8,100.

   e. None of the above.

Question 9 Analysis

In order to answer this type of question, you must evaluate each presented option.

Step 1	Read each option and identify the topic(s): Lender's imputed interest.
Step 2	Read question and make notes:
	• No interest on loans < $10,000.
	• No interest on loans < $100,000 if no income.
Step 3	Analysis of answer choices:
	a. No, it is not Allison that would impute interest information.
	b. Looks correct, Mike's inputed interest is equal to lesser of Allison's interest income or federal rate.
	c. Is federal rate; therefore, wrong.
	d. Allison is wrong person.
	e. (b) and (c) are both possible.
Step 4	Select answer (b).

Answer: (b)

The $100,000 exemption applies, and thus Mike's imputed interest income is limited to Allison's net investment income.

10. **Example.**

Judy estimates her opportunity cost on investments at 12%, compounded annually. Which one of the following is the best investment alternative?

    a.   To receive $50,000 today.

    b.   To receive $250,000 at the end of fourteen years.

    c.   To receive $40,000 at the end of four years and $120,000 eight years later.

    d.   To receive $5,000 at the beginning of each six-month period for nine years, compounded semiannually.

    e.   To receive $60,000 at the end of three years.

Question 10 Analysis

Step 1   Read each option and identify the topic(s): Present value.

Step 2   Read question.

Step 3   Analysis of answer choices:

	(a)	**(b)**	**(c)**	**(d)**	**(e)**
FV		$250,000.00	$120,000.00		$60,000.00
N		14	12	18	3
i		12	12	6	12
PMT				$5,000 AD	
Objective $\Rightarrow$ PV	$50,000.00	$51,154.95	$30,801.01	$57,386.30	$42,706.81
FV			$40,000.00		
N			4		
i			12		
PV			$25,420.72		
Total			$56,221.73		

Step 4   Select answer (d).

Answer: (d)

PMT	=	$5,000
i	=	6 (12 ÷ 2)
N	=	18 (9 × 2)
PV$_{AD}$	=	$57,386.30

SOLVING K-TYPE QUESTIONS

EVALUATE EACH K-TYPE STATEMENT

11. Example.

Which, if any, of the following transactions is/are permissible regarding an IRA?

1. A nonspouse IRA beneficiary must distribute the balance of an IRA, where distribution had begun, over a period not exceeding five years.

2. A nonspouse IRA beneficiary may distribute the balance of an IRA, where distribution had not begun, over the life expectancy of the beneficiary.

3. A beneficiary spouse of a deceased owner of an IRA can delay any distribution of such IRA until April 1 following the year in which such heir or beneficiary is 70½.

4. A spouse beneficiary of a deceased owner IRA can roll such IRA balance into her own IRA, even if distributions had begun to the owner prior to death.

Question 11 Analysis

Step 1	Read last line and identify the topic. Note: positive/are or negative/are not. IRA/Distributions.
Step 2	Read question.
Step 3	Analysis of statements:
	1. False.
	2. True.
	3. True.
	4. True.
Step 3	Read answers.
Step 4	Select answer (d).

   a.   1 and 2.

   b.   2 and 3.

   c.   1, 2, and 3.

   d.   2, 3, and 4.

   e.   1, 2, 3, and 4.

Answer: (d)

Statement 1 is incorrect. The option is to pay at least as fast as the original payment schedule. For K-type questions, anchor yourself in certainty. Include the answers that are certainly correct and exclude any answer with a statement that is certainly incorrect.

---

12. **Example.**

Which of the following is/are deductible for adjusted gross income?

1. Alimony paid to the taxpayer's former spouse.

2. Capital losses.

3. Ordinary and necessary expenses incurred in a business.

4. A deductible individual retirement account (IRA) contribution.

Question 12 Analysis

Step 1	Read last line and identify the topic: Note: is/are verses are not/AGI.
Step 2	Read question.
Step 3	Analysis of statements:
	1. True.
	2. Let's suppose I don't know.
	3. Let's suppose I don't know.
	4. True.
Step 4	Evaluate answers.
	a. 1 only *(definitely incorrect)*
	b. 4 only *(definitely incorrect)*
	c. 1 and 4 *(possible answer)*
	d. 1, 3, and 4 *(possible answer)*
	e. 1, 2, 3, and 4 *(possible answer)*
Step 5	Evaluate answers 2 and 3 above.
Step 4	Select answer (e).

a. 1 only.

b. 4 only.

c. 1 and 4.

d. 1, 3, and 4.

e. 1, 2, 3, and 4.

Answer: (e)

All are deductible for adjusted gross income.

13. Example.

Which of the following would best describe the action of a fiscal policy economist?

1. Increase in government spending.

2. Decrease in the money supply.

3. Decrease in income taxes.

4. Increase in the inflation rate.

Question 14 Analysis

Step 1	Read last line and identify the topic: Fiscal policy.
Step 2	Read question and make notes:
	• Fiscal is taxation and spending; monetary is interest rates.
Step 3	Analysis of statements:
	1. Yes, fiscal.
	2. Do not know.
	3. Yes, fiscal.
	4. Do not know.
Step 4	Evaluate answers.
	a. Possible answer.
	b. Possible answer.
	c. No.
	d. No.
	e. No.
Step 5	Reevaluate statements: Statement 4 is incorrect, therefore (a) is incorrect.
Step 4	Select answer (b).

a. 1, 2, 3, and 4.

b. 1 and 3.

c. 2 only.

d. 2 and 4.

e. 1 only.

Answer: (b)

Fiscal policy economists believe that the economy can be controlled through the use of government spending and income tax adjustments. Answer (c) is the answer to describe economists who believe that economic activity is controlled through the use of the money supply. Answer (a) is incorrect since that answer describes all the choices that include both fiscal policy as well as monetary policy economists. Answer (d) is incorrect because inflation is determined by market factors. Answer (e) partially describes the actions of a fiscal policy economist.

YOUR COMMENTS FOR VOLUMES I – VI

Our goal is to provide a high-quality product to you and other CFP® candidates. With this goal in mind, we hope to significantly improve our texts with each new edition. We welcome your written suggestions, corrections, and other general comments. Please be as detailed as possible and send your written comments to:

Kaplan Financial
143 Mallard Street, Suite E
St. Rose, Louisiana 70087
(504) 461-9860 Fax

	Volume	Page	Question	Comments (please be as specific as possible)
1.				
2.				
3.				
4.				
5.				
6.				
7.				
8.				
9.				
10.				
11.				
12.				
13.				
14.				
15.				

Name

Address

Phone _____ (Work) _____ (Home) _____ (Fax)

E-mail_____   Do you require a response? _____YES   _____NO

TABLE OF CONTENTS

SOLUTIONS

TABLE OF EXHIBITS

TABLE OF APPENDICES

INCOME TAX PLANNING

Outlines and Study Guides

Income Tax

I. TAX LAW – LEGISLATIVE, ADMINISTRATIVE, AND JUDICIAL

A. LEGISLATIVE SOURCES OF THE TAX LAW.

1. The Internal Revenue Code (IRC).

   a. The Internal Revenue Code is the highest source of authority.

   b. In 1939, Congress codified (separated and organized) the federal tax laws. The IRC was recodified in 1954. The Tax Reform Act of 1986 (TRA) renamed the 1954 code the Internal Revenue Code of 1986.

   c. The IRC is located in Title 26, with income taxes located in Subtitle A. IRC is normally quoted by code sections, which are typically broken down in sub-parts. For example, Section 150(e)(1)(A) cites Section 150, subsection (e), paragraph (1), and subparagraph (A).

2. Objective of treaties – The U.S. is a partner to over 40 income tax treaties with other countries. The primary purpose of these treaties is to establish primary taxing authority. When treaties conflict with the IRC, the Technical and Miscellaneous Revenue Act of 1988 provides that the most recent prevails. Anytime a taxpayer takes a position where treaty overrides law, the taxpayer must disclose the conflict on the appropriate tax return or a penalty may apply.

B. EXECUTIVE SOURCES OF THE TAX LAW.

1. Treasury Department Regulations (Regs) – The U.S. Treasury Department interprets the Code and issues Regulations – the highest source of authority next to the Code. Regulations have the full force and effect of the law. Income tax regulations are cited by the number 1, followed by the applicable code section. For example, a regulation dealing with Code Section 72 would be cited as Reg 1.72.

2. Revenue Rulings – Revenue Rulings provide interpretations of the tax law with regard to taxable income, deductions, and credits. They are issued by the National Office of the IRS to deal with problems more specific than Regulations. Rulings do **not** have the full force of law and do not carry the force and effect of Regulations but can be cited as precedent. They are published by the government to give guidance to IRS personnel and taxpayers.

   a. Rulings are identified by the year released and the ruling number for the year. For example, Rev. Rul. 99-28 was the 28th ruling released in 1999.

   b. Before relying on a Revenue Ruling as support, care should be taken that the ruling has not been affected by subsequent law changes, administrative rulings, or judicial decisions.

3. Revenue Procedures – Revenue Procedures explain the internal management practices and procedures of the IRS.

   a. Often, the IRS uses Revenue Procedures to distribute information to the general public. For example, tax tables and inflation-indexed amounts (standard deductions, exemptions, etc.) are released to the public in the form of a Revenue Procedure.

   b. Like Revenue Rulings, Revenue Procedures are identified by year issued and the number of issue (e.g., Rev. Proc. 2000-01 which discusses user fees for private letter rulings).

4. Letter Rulings – three types.

a. Private Letter Ruling (PLR) – At the request of a taxpayer, the National Office of the IRS will describe its position on a specific tax issue (typically a proposed transaction).

   1) Although a PLR applies only to the taxpayer who requested it, PLRs are considered substantial authority for the purpose of avoiding accuracy-related penalties.

   2) The IRS does not officially publish PLRs. They do purge the PLRs of taxpayer identifying information and make them available to commercial sources who, in turn, make them available to the general public.

   3) A PLR cannot be cited as precedent by anyone other than the taxpayer who requested the ruling, but can provide guidance to the IRS's position on specific topics.

b. Determination Letters – Issued by the area District Director in response to a taxpayer request about a completed transaction.

   1) A determination letter provides guidance on the application of the tax law only to the party making the request.

   2) Determination Letters are not published or made available to the public.

c. Technical Advice Memorandum (TAMs) – A ruling from the IRS National Office usually prompted by a request from an agent performing an audit who needs clarification that cannot be provided by the local office. The ruling concerns a completed transaction and only applies to the taxpayer whose audit prompted the ruling.

EXHIBIT 1: ADMINISTRATIVE SOURCES OF TAX LAW

Type	Issued By	Description
Regulation	U. S. Treasury	Has the full force and effect of law.
Revenue Ruling	National Office of the IRS	Addresses questions of income, deductions, and credits in the context of a specific set of facts.
Revenue Procedure	National Office of the IRS	Explains IRS practices and procedures. Used to distribute information to taxpayers.
Private Letter Ruling (PLR)	National Office of the IRS	Issued in response and applies only to a taxpayer request about a proposed transaction.
Determination Letter	District Director	Issued in response to a taxpayer request about a completed transaction.
Technical Advice Memorandum	National Office of the IRS	Requested by agent to clarify issue encountered in an audit in progress.

Note: All of the administrative sources of law listed above are considered to be sources of substantial authority for the purposes of the requirements of IRC Section 6662. This code section imposes a penalty on the substantial underpayment of tax except where the taxpayer has substantial authority for the position taken on the return.

C. JUDICIAL SOURCES OF TAX LAW.

1. The judicial process.

   a. Any tax-related dispute that cannot be resolved by the taxpayer and the IRS or by using the administrative review process may be taken to the Federal Courts. If not resolved by a court of original jurisdiction (trial court), an appeal may be made and the dispute can be taken to the appropriate appellate court.

2. The federal judicial system has three trial courts:

   a. The U.S. District Court.

      i. Hears cases on legal matters involving tax and nontax issues, has one judge per court (typically a generalist), and is located in the taxpayer's jurisdiction. A jury trial is available in this court.

      ii. Because of the existence of a jury, the taxpayer must first pay any deficiency assessed and then sue for a refund. The taxpayer is the plaintiff in such a civil matter.

      iii. This is usually where a taxpayer would take an emotional or nontax-specific (valuation) issue rather than a technical tax issue (interpretation of IRC).

      iv. Decisions can vary significantly among the different districts.

b. The U.S. Court of Federal Claims.

    i. Decides monetary claims against the United States, has 16 judges, and has a nationwide jurisdiction. A jury trial is not available in this court.

    ii. The taxpayer must first pay any deficiency assessed and then sue for a refund. The taxpayer is the plaintiff in such a civil matter.

    iii. Must follow only appeals decisions rendered by the Federal District of the Court of Appeals, not the Circuit Court of Appeals.

c. The U.S. Tax Court.

    i. Decides tax cases only, has 19 judges, and has nationwide jurisdiction. A jury trial is not available in this court.

    ii. The taxpayer does not have to pay the deficiency prior to trial. Payment will only become due if there is an adverse judgment.

    iii. The Small Cases Division of the U.S. Tax Court decides cases where the amount in dispute does not exceed $50,000. There is no appeal from the Small Cases Division of the U.S. Tax Court, and the decisions of the Small Cases Division have no precedential value.

3. Appellate courts.

a. There are 11 geographical circuit courts of appeals (usually referred to by circuit number and hearing cases originating in specified states), the Washington, D.C. Court of Appeals, and the Court of Appeals for the Federal Circuit.

b. The location of an appeal will depend on where the litigation originated.

c. District Courts, the Tax Court and the Court of Federal Claims must follow the precedents set by the Court of Appeals of their jurisdiction. In other words, the Tax Court and the U.S. District Court follow the precedents set in the appeals court in the taxpayer's home circuit. The Court of Federal Claims must follow decisions of the Court of Appeals for the Federal Circuit.

d. A Court of Appeals in one jurisdiction is not required to follow the decisions of a Court of Appeals in another jurisdiction.

e. All courts must follow the decisions of the U.S. Supreme Court. The U.S. Supreme Court infrequently hears tax cases, as most major cases are settled in the appellate or lower courts.

EXHIBIT 2: THE JUDICIAL PROCESS

	U.S. District Court	U.S. Court of Federal Claims	U.S. Tax Court	U.S. Tax Court, Small Claims Division
Number of Courts	95	1	1	1
Number of Judges	1 (per court)	16	19	19
Jurisdiction	District	National	National	National
Subject Matter	Criminal and Civil	Claims against Government	Tax only	Tax only
When to Use?	Emotional issue	District court has ruled unfavorably on the issue	Technical tax issue	Deficiency is less than $50,000
Pay Deficiency First?	Yes	Yes	No	No
Jury Available?	Yes	No	No	No
Appeal	U.S. Court of Appeals	U.S. Court of Appeals – Federal Circuit	U.S. Court of Appeals	None

Example

If John lost his tax case in the U.S. District Court he would appeal to the U.S. Court of Appeals. Appeals from the U.S. District Court go to the taxpayer's home circuit of the U.S. Court of Appeals.

D. RESEARCH SOURCES OF TAX LAW.

1. Tax services – There are several comprehensive multi-volume services that provide tax research assistance.

   a. Research Institute of America (RIA).

      i. RIA publishes the Federal Tax Coordinator, which is a multi-volume set with periodic updates.

      ii. Includes lengthy explanatory text for the Internal Revenue Code and regulations.

      iii. Organized by topic, with volumes arranged alphabetically.

      iv. Also offers a Practice Aids volume, which contains tax planning strategies and ideas.

   b. Commerce Clearing House (CCH).

      i. CCH publishes the Standard Federal Tax Reporter, which is a multi-volume set with periodic updates.

      ii. Includes lengthy explanatory text for the Internal Revenue Code and regulations, as well as explanation of court decisions.

        iii. Organized by Internal Revenue Code section, in sequence.

        iv. Also offers a Citator volume, which contains cross referencing of court decisions.

   c. The Bureau of National Affairs, Inc. (BNA).

        i. BNA publishes Income Tax Portfolios, which is a multi-volume set with periodic updates.

        ii. Includes lengthy explanatory text for the Internal Revenue Code and regulations.

        iii. Organized by topic, with a separate portfolio for each topic.

2. Periodicals – in addition to the comprehensive tax services available for research, there are various periodicals, such as newsletters, magazines, and internet services.

   a. Tax newsletters and magazines include:

        i. Taxes – The Tax Magazine.

        ii. Tax Notes.

        iii. Journal of Taxation.

        iv. BNA Daily Tax Report.

        v. BNA Financial Planning Journal.

   b. Tax internet services include:

        i. CCH Tax Research Network.

        ii. Leimberg Information Services.

        iii. Lawthreads.

        iv. www.IRS.gov.

        v. RIA Checkpoint.

II. TAX RATES AND BRACKETS

A. RATES AND BRACKETS.

1. The following exhibit represents the 2006 tax rates and brackets.

EXHIBIT 3: 2006 TAX RATES AND BRACKETS

Single – Schedule X

If taxable income is: Over --	But not over --	The tax is:	Of the amount over --
$0	$7,550	-------------- 10%	$0
7,550	30,650	$755.00 + 15%	7,550
30,650	74,200	4,220.00 + 25%	30,650
74,200	154,800	15,107.50 + 28%	74,200
154,800	336,550	37,675.50 + 33%	154,800
336,550	------------	97,653.50 + 35%	336,550

Head of Household – Schedule Z

If taxable income is: Over --	But not over --	The tax is:	Of the amount over --
$0	$10,750	-------------- 10%	$0
10,750	41,050	$1,075.00 + 15%	10,750
41,050	106,000	5,620.00 + 25%	41,050
106,000	171,650	21,857.50 + 28%	106,000
171,650	336,550	40,239.50 + 33%	171,650
336,500	------------	94,656.50 + 35%	336,550

Married Filing Jointly or Qualifying Widow(er) – Schedule Y-1

If taxable income is: Over --	But not over --	The tax is:	Of the amount over --
$0	$15,100	-------------- 10%	$0
15,100	61,300	$1,510.00 + 15%	15,100
61,300	123,700	8,440.00 + 25%	61,300
123,700	188,450	24,040.00 + 28%	123,700
188,.450	336,550	42,170.00 + 33%	188,450
336,550	------------	91,043.00 + 35%	336,550

Married Filing Separately – Schedule Y-2

If taxable income is: Over --	But not over --	The tax is:	Of the amount over --
$0	$7,550	--------------- 10%	$0
7,550	30,650	$755.00 + 15%	7,550
30,650	61,850	4,220.00 + 25%	30,650
61,850	94,225	12,020.00 + 28%	61,850
94,225	168,275	21,085.00 + 33%	94,225
168,275	------------	45,521.50 + 35%	168,275

III. BASIC TAX FORMULA AND INFLATION-ADJUSTED AMOUNTS

A. THE TAX FORMULA.

Income (broadly conceived)	$xx,xxx	
Less: Exclusions from Gross Income	(x,xxx)	*Section VI. Gross Income – Exclusions – Topics 8, 21, 27 & 34*
Gross Income	$xx,xxx	*Section V. Gross Income – Inclusions – Topics 27, 34, 46, 47, 57 & 60*
Less: Deductions for Adjusted Gross Income	(x,xxx)	*Section VII. Deductions for Adjusted Gross Income – Topics 8, 46 & 47*
Adjusted Gross Income (AGI)	$xx,xxx	
Less: The Greater of--		
Total itemized deductions or standard deduction	(x,xxx)	*Section VIII. Basic Standard Deduction and Additional Standard Deductions – topic 46*
Less: Personal and Dependency Exemptions	(x,xxx)	*Section IX. Personal and Dependency Exemptions – Topic 46*
Taxable Income	$xx,xxx	

B. REQUIRED TAX PAYMENTS.

1. Employer must withhold income taxes and FICA (Social Security and Medicare) taxes from an employee's paycheck.

2. Taxpayers who receive income that is not subject to withholding must make quarterly estimated tax payments.

   a. For calendar-year taxpayers, estimated payment due dates are 4/15, 6/15, 9/15 and 1/15 of the following year. If the 15th falls on a Saturday or Sunday, the due date will be the following Monday.

   b. To avoid an underpayment penalty, taxpayers must make estimated payments that are the lesser of:

      • 90% of the tax liability shown on the current year return.

      • 100% of tax liability shown on prior year return if AGI is $150,000 or less.

      • If AGI is > $150,000, then required payment based on prior year return is based on 110% of the prior year's tax liability.

3. No penalty is imposed if the taxpayer did not have a tax liability for the previous year.

EXHIBIT 4: EXEMPTIONS

Item	2006	Text Reference
Personal and Dependency Exemptions	$3,300	VIII.A.
Exemption Phaseout begins at – Married/Joint	$225,750	VIII.D.
Exemption Phaseout begins at – Single	$150,500	VIII.D.
Exemption Phaseout begins at – Head of Household	$188,150	VIII.D.
Exemption Phaseout begins at – Married/Separate	$112,875	VIII.D.

EXHIBIT 5: STANDARD DEDUCTIONS/OVER 65 OR BLIND GET AN ADDITIONAL STANDARD DEDUCTION*

Item	2006 Basic Standard Deduction	2006 Additional Standard Deduction*	Text Reference
Married/Joint	$10,300	$1,000	VII.
Single	$5,150	$1,250	VII.
Head of Household	$7,550	$1,250	VII.
Married/Separate	$5,150	$1,000	VII.
Standard Deduction for an Individual Claimed as a Dependent	$850	$1,250	IX.B.

*Example: If you are 65, blind, and single you receive double the additional standard deduction: $1,250 for age 65 or over and $1,250 for being blind.

EXHIBIT 6: OTHER INFLATION-ADJUSTED AMOUNTS

Item	2006	Text Reference
Itemized Deduction Phaseout AGI threshold – Married/Joint, Single, and Head of Household	$150,500	XV.H.
Itemized Deduction Phaseout AGI threshold – Married/Separate	$75,250	XV.H.

IV. GROSS INCOME – INCLUSIONS

A. DEFINITION.

1. Gross income is broadly defined as "all income from whatever source derived" (Internal Revenue Code Section 61(a)). The following is a partial list of gross income:

EXHIBIT 7: ITEMS INCLUDED IN GROSS INCOME

• Alimony Received	• Cost of group term life insurance for coverage over $50,000
• Annuities (partial)	• Hobby income
• Awards	• Interest
• Back pay	• Jury duty fees
• Bargain purchase by employee	• Living quarters, meals
• Bonuses	• Mileage allowance
• Breach of contract damages	• Military pay
• Business income	• Notary fees
• Certain compensatory damages	• Partnership income
• Clergy fees	• Pensions
• Commissions	• Prizes
• Compensation for services	• Professional fees
• Death benefits from employer	• Punitive damages
• Debts forgiven	• Rent
• Director fees	• Rewards
• Dividends	• Royalties
• Embezzled funds	• Salaries
• Employee awards	• Severance pay
• Employee benefits – limited	• Strike and lockout benefits
• Estate and trust income	• Supplemental unemployment
• Farm income	• Tips and gratuities
• Fees	• Travel allowance
• Gains from illegal activities	• Unemployment compensation
• Gains from sale of property	• Wages
• Gambling winnings	

2. Gross income is not limited to cash received. It may be realized in any form, whether in money, property, or services.

3. When a taxable sale or exchange occurs, the seller is permitted to recover his or her investment (or other adjusted basis) in the property before gain or loss is recognized.

B. ACCOUNTING PERIODS.

1. In General:

    a. Taxable income is generally computed based on an annual accounting period, known as a taxable year.

    b. A taxable year is the annual period over which income is measured for income tax purposes.

    c. A calendar year is a 12-month period ending on December 31. Most individuals and many businesses use a calendar year.

    d. A fiscal year is a 12-month period ending on the last day of any month other than December. Many businesses use a fiscal year based on the natural business year (i.e., A school may have a fiscal year that begins in August).

2. Requirements.

    a. All taxpayers may use a calendar year. A fiscal year may be adopted only by taxpayers who maintain adequate records.

    b. The accounting period is initially established when an individual or business files its initial income tax return. Once the accounting period has been established, the taxpayer cannot change it without IRS consent.

3. Tax year for business entities.

    a. Partnerships – must generally use the same tax year as the tax year of the partners, unless the partnership can establish a business purpose for having a different tax year.

    b. S corporations – must generally use the calendar year, unless the S corporation can establish a business purpose for having a different tax year.

    c. If a partner or S corporation shareholder has a different tax year than the partnership or S corporation, the partner or shareholder must report their share of the entity's income in their taxable year within which the entity's tax year ends.

Example

Orentlich Partners is a partnership with a fiscal year ending on September 30. Bethany, a 20% partner in the partnership, is a calendar year individual taxpayer. For the taxable year ending September 30, 2006, Orentlich had operating income of $100,000. Orentlich also had operating income of $30,000 for the period of October 1, 2006, through December 31, 2006. Bethany must report $20,000 (20% partnership interest × $100,000 partnership income) on her year 2006 income tax return. Any income earned by the partnership from October 2006 through December 2006 will be reported on Bethany's 2007 tax return.

C. ACCOUNTING METHODS.

1. Cash method.

    a. Taxpayer generally reports income when cash is collected (or taxpayer has constructive receipt) and reports expenses when cash payments are made.

    b. For fixed assets, (i.e., equipment) the cash-basis taxpayer claims a deduction through depreciation in the same manner as an accrual-basis taxpayer.

c. Prepaid expenses must be capitalized and amortized if the life of the asset extends "substantially beyond" the end of the tax year.

d. The cash method can be used by:

   i. Individuals.

   ii. Partnerships that do not have C corporations as partners.

   iii. Corporations or partnerships, if annual gross receipts for all prior years do not exceed $5 million.

   iv. Certain farming businesses.

   v. Qualified personal service corporations in the fields of accounting, law, engineering, health, consulting, architecture, actuarial science, or performing arts.

e. Exceptions for Cash-Basis Taxpayers.

   i. Constructive receipt – If income is available, it is subject to income tax even though it is not physically in the taxpayer's possession. An example of this is accrued interest on a savings account. Under the constructive receipt of income concept, the interest is taxed to the depositor in the year it is available rather than the year actually withdrawn.

   ii. Series E and Series EE bonds – The income on these savings bonds can be tax deferred. A cash-basis taxpayer has the choice to either (1) defer income recognition until maturity or redemption, or (2) elect to include in gross income the annual increment in redemption value.

      A) When a taxpayer elects to report the income from the bonds on an annual basis, the election applies to all such bonds the taxpayer owns at the time of the election.

      B) Before September 2004, if a cash-basis taxpayer had not made the election to report interest currently on Series E or EE bonds held, he or she could have exchanged these bonds for HH bonds and defer interest recognition until the HH bonds matured.

   iii. Original issue discount – Under the general rules, the cash-basis taxpayer would not report the original issue discount (the difference between the original loan and the amount due at maturity) as interest income until the year the amount is collected, although an accrual-basis taxpayer would claim the interest as it is earned. However, the Code treats cash-basis and accrual-basis taxpayers the same by requiring that the original issue discount be reported when it is earned regardless of the accounting method.

   iv. Amounts received under an obligation to repay – No income is realized in receipt of borrowed funds. Receipt of funds is not necessarily a taxable event. For example, a deposit on equipment rental is not taxable until forfeited.

Example

Peggy, a cash-basis taxpayer, has the following items of income for 2006:

- Salary $40,000.

- $5,000 bonus check issued and available at payroll office (but not picked up until 1/5/07).

- Borrowed $10,000 on a home equity line.

- Original Issue Discount corporate bond, accrual amount of $2,000.

- A U.S. savings bond that increased in redemption value by $200. Last year she elected to include the annual increment in redemption value in income.

Her gross income for the year is:

Salary	$40,000	
Bonus	5,000	(included because of constructive receipt rule)
OID	2,000	(although not received in cash, this is an exception for cash-basis taxpayer)
Savings bond	200	(she must be consistent in her election on this bond)
Total gross income	$47,200	

The proceeds on the home equity line are not included in gross income because Peggy is obligated to repay.

---

2. Accrual Method.

   a. This method reports expenses when incurred and income when earned for any single tax year.

   b. Expenses do not have to be paid to be deductible, nor does income have to be received to be taxable. The controlling factor for the accrual method is when the income was earned or the expenses incurred.

   c. Exceptions for Accrual-Basis Taxpayers.

      i. Prepaid income – For tax purposes, prepaid income is taxed in the year of receipt. Prepaid rents and prepaid interest may not be deferred by the accrual-basis taxpayer.

      ii. Deferral of advance payments for goods – A taxpayer can elect to defer recognition of income for advance payments for goods if the method of accounting for the sale is the same for tax and financial reporting.

      iii. Deferral of advance payments for services – Taxpayers can defer recognition of income for advance payments for services to be performed by the end of the tax year following the year of receipt. No deferral is allowed if the taxpayer might be required to perform any services after the tax year following the year of receipt of the advance payment.

Examples

- Julia, an accrual-basis taxpayer, owns an office building. On December 1, 2006, she rented the unit to a tenant that had a rather shaky credit history. As a result, she asked him for a year's rent in advance that amounted to $18,000. Julia must claim the entire $18,000 rent in 2006.

---

3. Long-Term Contracts.

   a. In General.

      i. A long-term contract is any contract for the manufacture, building, installation, or construction of property.

      ii. To be considered a long-term contract, the contract must not be completed within the same year it was entered into.

      iii. If the contract is a manufacturing contract, it will only be considered a long-term contract if it involves the manufacture of a unique item not normally carried in inventory (such as machinery) and normally requires more than 12 months to manufacture.

      iv. Generally, long-term contracts must be accounted for using the percentage-of-completion method. However, home construction contracts and contracts of small businesses can be accounted for using the completed contract method.

   b. Percentage-of-Completion Method.

      i. Requires the taxpayer to recognize a portion of the gross profit on the contract based on the estimated percentage of the contract completed.

      ii. The portion of the contract price reportable in a given year is based on the following ratio:

$$\text{Total contract price} \times \frac{\text{Costs incurred during the current period}}{\text{Total estimated costs for the contract}}$$

Example

In September 2006, Johnson Corporation entered into a contract to build a hotel that will be completed by December 2007. The contract price was $2,000,000, and the estimated costs of construction were $1,000,000. During 2006 actual costs incurred were $600,000. In 2007, the hotel was completed at a total cost of $1,100,000. Johnson Corporation will report the following income in 2006 and 2007:

	2006	2007
Revenue reported on tax return	$1,200,000 *	$800,000
(Costs)	(600,000)	(500,000)
Net income	$600,000	$300,000

*($600,000 ÷ $1,000,000) = 60% × $2,000,000 = $1,200,000

---

iii. If less than 10% of the total estimated contract costs have been incurred, the taxpayer may choose to defer reporting of the revenue until the year in which the 10% threshold has been reached.

iv. If the percentage-of-completion method is used for a contract, special "look-back" provisions apply in the tax year the contract is completed.

    A) Annual income must be recomputed based on actual final costs rather than estimated costs.

    B) Interest will be owed by or payable to the taxpayer if there was an underpayment or overpayment for any tax year.

Example

Assuming the same facts as in the previous example, Johnson Corporation's income should have been $490,000 in 2006, as calculated below. Johnson overstated income by $110,000 ($600,000 reported – $490,000). As a result, the IRS is required to pay Johnson interest on the overpayment of the related tax.

	2006
Revenue based on actual costs	$1,090,000*
(Costs)	(600,000)
Net income	$490,000

*($600,000 ÷ $1,100,000) = 54.5% × $2,000,000 = $1,090,000

2007 income would also be adjusted for the difference.

	2007
	$810,000 *
	(500,000)
	$310,000

* This is without considering any interest income from the IRS which is not part of the calculation.

---

c. Completed Contract Method.

   i. The completed contract method allows the taxpayer to defer revenue recognition until the contract is completed.

   ii. The completed contract method can only be used in two situations:

     A) Home construction contracts – at least 80% of the costs are related to buildings containing no more than four dwelling units.

     B) Small contractors – contracts completed within two years by contractors with average annual gross receipts (for the last three years) of $10,000,000 or less.

d. Alternative Minimum Tax (AMT) Consequences.

   i. The percentage-of-completion method must be used for AMT purposes, except for home construction contracts, which can use the completed contract method.

   ii. If a small contractor uses the completed contract method for regular tax purposes, there will be an AMT adjustment required each year of the contract.

   iii. There is no AMT adjustment required for home construction contracts, since they can be accounted for using the completed contract method for both regular tax and AMT purposes.

4. Installment Sales.

a. See Section XVIII. Property Transactions – Topic L – "Installment Sales." on page 137 for details on the installment method of accounting.

5. Hybrid method.

a. A combination of the accrual and the cash method of accounting.

b. The taxpayer may account for some items of income using the accrual method (e.g., sales) and other items using the cash method (e.g., interest income).

6. Accounting method changes.

a. Once an accounting method has been adopted, it cannot be changed without approval from the IRS.

b. Changes in accounting methods may include:

   i. A change from the cash to accrual basis.

   ii. A change in inventory valuation (FIFO to LIFO, etc.).

   iii. A change from the completed contract method to the percentage-of-completion method for long-term contracts.

c. Taxpayers who change their method of accounting must make certain adjustments to income in the year of the change (or over a longer period, if certain conditions are met). The adjustments are necessary to prevent the omission or duplication of income and deductions.

Example

Kalfoglou Enterprises is a corporation that switched from the cash method of accounting to the accrual method of accounting this year. At the end of last year, the company's outstanding receivables were $40,000. If Kalfoglou Enterprises were allowed to switch to the accrual method of accounting without any income adjustment, $40,000 would completely escape taxation. Therefore, the company must report $40,000 in income in this year as a result of the change in accounting method.

    d. A change in accounting method is different from a correction of an error on a tax return. An error, such as a mathematical mistake, can be corrected on an amended return without IRS approval. If the correction changes the amount of tax due, interest and penalties may apply, or a refund for the taxpayer may be due.

D. INCOME SOURCES.

  1. Personal services.

    a. When an employee renders services to his employer's customer, the employer is taxed on the income received from the customer. The employer then pays deductible compensation to the employee who has taxable compensation.

    b. Assignment of income.

      i. Under the assignment of income concept, a taxpayer cannot avoid income tax by assigning income earned to some other person or entity.

Example

Jill, who is in the highest income tax bracket, directs her employer to pay $18,000 of her salary to her son, who is a college student in the lowest income tax bracket. Jill cannot assign the income to her son because Jill earned it. If her employer pays the money to her son, her W-2 will include the $18,000 and she will have been deemed to have made a gift to her son. This will require her to file a gift tax return.

  2. Income from property – Income from property (such as stocks, bonds, and rental property) must be included in the gross income of the owner of the property. This discourages, for example, owners giving away coupons from bearer bonds prior to the payment date.

    a. Interest is accrued daily.

    b. Dividends are paid at the discretion of the corporation and, unlike interest, do not accrue daily. They accrue after declaration and date of record.

    c. Dividends are taxed to the person who is entitled to receive them. If a taxpayer sells stock after a dividend has been declared but before the record date, the dividend will be taxed to the purchaser, instead of the seller (date of record is controlling).

    d. The income-producing property must also be assigned for the income to be taxed to the assignee.

Examples

- Joe, a taxpayer in the highest income tax bracket, owns rental property that generates $2,000 of rental income per month. Joe instructs the tenant of his rental property to pay the rent to Joe's daughter, Mary, who is in the 15% income tax bracket.

  Since Joe owns the rental property, the payment of rent to his daughter will be an assignment of income. Joe will be taxed on the rental income, even though his daughter received the actual payments.

- Cornelius owns 20 shares of Qualco stock. Qualco declares a dividend on September 1, for shareholders of record September 15, payable October 15. If Cornelius sells his shares on September 16, he will still have dividend income, even though he did not own the stock at the dividend payment date, because he held it on the date of record.

3. Income from partnerships, S corporations, trusts and estates.

    a. Partnerships and S corporations are pass-through entities.

    b. Income from partnerships is taxed to the partners at their own individual rates. The partnership must file an informational return (Form 1065). Each partner receives a K-1 indicating his or her share of the partnership income.

    c. The shareholders, rather than the corporation, pay the tax on an S corporation's income. An S corporation files Form 1120S. Each shareholder receives a K-1 indicating his or her share of the S corporation income.

    d. The beneficiaries of estates and trusts generally are taxed on income that is distributed from the trust. Any income not distributed is taxed to the estate or trust, according to the trust tax schedule.

Example

Carla is a calendar-year taxpayer. She receives a K-1 on March 1, 2006, from a partnership that has a January 31 year end. The income will be included on her 2006 tax return, since she must report her partnership distributive share for the partnership tax year ending in her tax year.

4. Income in community property states.

    a. In a community property state, one-half of the earnings of each spouse is considered owned by the other spouse (a one-half undivided individual interest).

    b. Community property spouses living apart – A spouse (or former spouse) will be taxed only on actual earnings from personal services if all of the following conditions are met:

        i. The spouses live apart for the entire year.

        ii. They do not file a joint return.

        iii. No portion of the earned income was transferred between the spouses.

E. ALIMONY AND SEPARATE MAINTENANCE PAYMENTS.

1. Alimony and separate maintenance payments are deductible by the payor and are includible in the gross income of the payee.

2. Post-1984 divorce agreements and decrees.

    a. To avoid confusing alimony (a taxable event) and property settlements (a nontaxable event), Congress developed rules to classify the payments. Payments are classified as alimony only if all of the following conditions are satisfied:

        i.   The payments are made in cash.

        ii. The agreement or decree does not specify that the payments are not alimony for federal income tax purposes.

        iii. The payee and payor are not members of the same household at the time the payments are made.

        iv. There is no liability to make the payments for any period after the death of the payee.

        v.   Payments are made directly to payee spouse or to third party for direct benefit of payee spouse (e.g., making the mortgage payment).

3. Front-loading (also referred to as alimony recapture).

    a. A measure to discourage disguising property settlements as alimony.

    b. If there is more than a $15,000 decrease in alimony payments between any of the first 3 years, there may be alimony recapture.

    c. The formula to calculate alimony recapture is as follows (this formula is the same as the one in the Code but uses different variable names).

    $$R_3 = R_1 + R_2$$

    $$R_2 = P_2 - (P_3 + 15,000)$$

    $$R_1 = P_1 - \left[\frac{(P_2 - R_2 + P_3)}{2} + \$15,000 \right]$$

R_1 = Recapture Year 1	P_1 = Payments Year 1
R_2 = Recapture Year 2	P_2 = Payments Year 2
R_3 = Recapture Year 3	P_3 = Payments Year 3

    Note: R_2 cannot be less than zero. If you get a negative number, then you set R_2 equal to zero.

    d. Alimony recapture affects the third year of alimony payments only. R_3 will be claimed as income by the original payor and claimed as a deduction from income by the payee. In other words, the effect of the original transaction is reversed. (No cash changes hands; this is merely a tax transaction.)

Example

Ann and Mark divorce in 2005. Mark will make the following alimony payments:

2005	$60,000
2006	$40,000
2007	$20,000
2008	$40,000

Recapture is calculated as follows:

$$R_2 = \$40,000 - (\$20,000 + \$15,000) = \$5,000$$

$$R_1 = \$60,000 - \left[\frac{(\$40,000 - \$5,000 + \$20,000)}{2} + \$15,000\right] = \$17,500$$

$$R_3 = \$5,000 + \$17,500 = \$22,500$$

In 2007, Mark will include $22,500 in gross income, and Ann will have a $22,500 deduction for AGI.

Shortcut Method (the easy way):*

$$R_3 = P_1 + P_2 - 2P_3 - \$37,500$$

$$R_3 = \$60,000 + \$40,000 - (2 \times \$20,000) - \$37,500$$

$$R_3 = \$22,500$$

*The shortcut method will not always work, but may be used to help estimate recapture when there are three payments. For example, if there is not at least a $15,000 decrease each year, then the formula will not work.

---

    e.   Divorcing taxpayers may, as a tax-planning strategy, purposely create alimony recapture where the payor's income tax bracket in the third year is expected to be less than the bracket in the first year, and where the payee's bracket in the third year is expected to be greater than in the first year.

Example

Dave and Sue's divorce became final on January 2nd of the current year. Dave is an executive for a Fortune 500 company, and Sue is starting her own business this year. In the current year (Year 1 of the divorce agreement), Dave expects his marginal income tax rate to be 35%, while Sue's marginal income tax rate will be 25%, due to some initial expenses of her new business. Two years from now (Year 3 of the divorce agreement), Dave will retire, and will be in the 15% tax bracket, while Sue's business, a sole proprietorship, will cause her to be in the 35% tax bracket. Dave intentionally front-loaded his alimony payments to Sue ($60,000 in Year 1, $40,000 in Year 2, and $20,000 in Year 3), resulting in alimony recapture for Dave of $22,500 (see previous example for calculation of recapture amount) in Year 3.

In Year 1, Dave will get a deduction of $60,000, when his tax rate is 35%. Sue will include the alimony received in her gross income, when her tax rate is only 25%.

In Year 3, Dave must report (in his gross income) the alimony recapture of $22,500, when his tax rate will be only 15%. Sue would get a deduction of $22,500, when her tax rate is 35%.

F. CHILD SUPPORT.

1. Money received for child support is not includible as taxable income by the payee and is not deductible by the payor.

2. Distinguishing alimony from child support is sometimes difficult. If payments are reduced when the child reaches a certain age, marries, or dies, the amount of the reduction is presumed to be child support, and the remainder is considered alimony if it meets the alimony criteria.

Example

As part of their divorce agreement, David must pay Michelle $4,000 per month. In five years, when their daughter attains age 18, the payments are reduced to $2,800 per month.

The reduction of $1,200 ($4,000 – $2,800) will be considered child support and will never be deductible by David.

G. INTEREST ON BELOW-MARKET LOANS.

1. Generally income is not recognized unless it is realized. However, in instances where a lender has issued a below-market-rate loan, the lender may be required to recognize (impute) interest income or the borrower may receive an interest expense deduction when, in fact, no interest has been received or paid.

    a. Imputed interest is calculated using the federal government's borrowing rate, compounded semiannually and adjusted monthly.

    b. If the interest charged on the loan is less than the federal rate, the imputed interest is the difference in interest determined using the federal rate and that determined using the actual rate.

2. The imputed interest rules apply to the following types of below-market-rate loans:

a. Gift loans – The lender has interest income and the borrower has interest expense to the extent of imputed interest. In addition, a gift has been made to the borrower in the amount of imputed interest.

b. Compensation-related loans – Employer loans to employees. The corporation has interest income and compensation expense for the amount of the imputed interest. The borrower will have compensation income and interest expense (may or may not be deductible) for the same amount.

c. Corporation-shareholder loans – A loan to a nonemployee shareholder by the corporation. The corporation will have interest income and a dividend distribution for the amount of the imputed interest. The shareholder/borrower will have dividend income and interest expense (may or may not be deductible) for the same amount.

d. Tax avoidance loans – Loans that significantly affect the borrower or lender's federal tax liability.

3. Exceptions and limitations to the imputed interest rules.

a. No interest is imputed on total outstanding gift loans in the aggregate of $10,000 or less between individuals, unless the proceeds are used to purchase income-producing property. There is also an exception for compensation-related or corporation – shareholder loans that are less than or equal to $10,000.

b. On loans between individuals greater than $10,000 and less than or equal to $100,000, the imputed interest cannot exceed the borrower's net investment income (from all sources) for the year. A further exception is carved out by law stating that if the borrower's net investment income for the year does not exceed $1,000, no interest is imputed on loans of $100,000 or less.

c. If the principal purpose of the loan is tax avoidance, none of the exceptions apply.

Example

On January 1, Richie loaned his daughter, Lori Beth, $90,000 to purchase a new personal residence. There were no other loans outstanding between Richie and Lori Beth. Lori Beth's only income was $30,000 salary and $4,000 interest income. Richie had investment income of $200,000. Richie did not charge Lori Beth interest. The relevant federal rate was 9%.

Richie must recognize imputed interest income of $4,000. The $100,000 exemption applies and, thus, Richie's imputed interest income (and Lori Beth's imputed interest expense) is limited to Lori Beth's net investment income. In addition, Richie is deemed to have made a gift to Lori Beth of $4,000. The gift is eligible for the annual exclusion.

H. PRIZES AND AWARDS.

1. Cash and the fair market value of prizes and awards are included in gross income. If you win a dream vacation on a game show, the fair market value of your prize is income to you.

2. When the winner has an option of taking a lump sum or an annuity, if the annuity is chosen, current inclusion of the full value of the prize is not required.

3. If the winner receives the award for religious, charitable, scientific, educational, artistic, literary, or civic achievement <u>and</u> turns the proceeds over to a governmental unit or qualifying charity, the award may be excluded from income.

I. INCOME FROM ANNUITIES.

1. As the value of the annuity increases, the annuitant does not report any income because it has not been constructively received.

2. Tax treatment of withdrawals before the scheduled annuity starting date.

   a. Withdrawals (including loans) on contracts issued <u>after August 13, 1982,</u> are included in gross income up to the total interest earned (LIFO basis recovery).

      i. Amounts received in excess of post-August 13, 1982 increases in cash value are treated as a recovery of capital until the taxpayer's cost has been entirely recovered.

      ii. The taxpayer may also be subject to a 10% penalty for early withdrawals unless he or she is over 59 1/2 years of age, deceased or disabled. This penalty would apply only to the taxable portion of the withdrawal.

   b. Collections before the annuity start date on contracts issued on August 13, 1982 or earlier, are subject to FIFO tax treatment, so that adjusted tax basis is received first and is not taxable.

3. Tax treatment of annuity payments received on and after the annuity starting date.

   a. The annuitant can exclude (as a recovery of capital) the proportion of each payment that the investment (cost) in the contract bears to the expected return under the contract. The exclusion amount is calculated as follows:

   $$\frac{\text{Investment}}{\text{Expected Return}} \times \text{Annuity Payment} = \text{Exclusion Amount}$$

   b. To determine the amount taxable, subtract the exclusion amount from the total annuity payment received. For retirement plan distributions, the IRS provides a simplified method for calculating exclusions.

   c. For contracts issued on December 31, 1986 or earlier, the exclusion ratio is used for all payments, even if payments are made past the expected life expectancy. This allows the taxpayer to exclude more than his basis if he lives past his life expectancy.

   d. For contracts issued after December 31, 1986, the exclusion ratio is only used to the extent of recovered basis. Thus, the taxpayer will not use the exclusion ratio for payments made after life expectancy.

Example

Wendy, a 55-year-old woman, has begun receiving an annuity over her life expectancy of 25.5 years. She receives $1,500 per month. Her contributions to the annuity were after tax and amounted to $91,800. Payments began April 1st of this year. Wendy can exclude $2,700 of the annuity payments received this year.

Exclusion ratio is $91,800 ÷ ($1,500 × 12 × 25.5) = 20%.

20% × $1,500 × 9 months = $2,700.

J. GROUP TERM LIFE INSURANCE.

1. An employee can exclude premiums paid by the employee's employer on the first $50,000 of group term life insurance.

2. Only employees are eligible for this benefit (partners, proprietors and greater than 2% S corporation owners are not employees).

3. If the group term life insurance amount exceeds $50,000, the taxable amount of the benefit is computed by applying the premium from the Uniform Premium Table to the excess coverage (see Exhibit 8: "Cost per $1,000 of Protection for One Month (Section 79)").

4. If the plan is discriminatory, key employees lose the $50,000 exclusion. They must include in income the greater of the actual cost of the insurance or the premium calculated using the Uniform Premium Table.

EXHIBIT 8: COST PER $1,000 OF PROTECTION FOR ONE MONTH (SECTION 79)

Age	Cost
Under 25	$0.05
25 through 29	$0.06
30 through 34	$0.08
35 through 39	$0.09
40 through 44	$0.10
45 through 49	$0.15
50 through 54	$0.23
55 through 59	$0.43
60 through 64	$0.66
65 through 69	$1.27
70 or older	$2.06

See Reg. 1.79-3(d)(2)

Example

Taxpayer is 51 years old and works for Employer A. Taxpayer's coverage with Employer A is $80,000. Taxpayer pays premiums of $50 a year under the Employer A group plan.

Calculate the amount to include in the taxpayer's income as follows:

Employer A coverage (in thousands)	$80
Less: Exclusion (in thousands)	($50)
Excess amount (in thousands)	$30
Multiply by cost per $1,000 per month, age 51 (from table)	$0.23
Cost of excess insurance for 1 month (0.23 × 30)	$6.90
Multiply by number of full months coverage at this cost	12
Cost of excess insurance for tax year	$82.80
Less: Premiums paid	($50.00)
Cost to include in income as wages (W-2)	**$32.80**

K. UNEMPLOYMENT COMPENSATION.

1. Unemployment compensation benefits are included in gross income (in lieu of wages).

L. SOCIAL SECURITY BENEFITS.

1. As much as 85% of Social Security benefits can be included in gross income.

2. The amount subject to tax is based upon the taxpayer's modified adjusted gross income.

3. The taxable amounts can be determined by one of two formulas using the modified adjusted gross income (MAGI).

4. MAGI is AGI from all sources (less Social Security) plus the foreign income exclusion and any tax-exempt interest income.

5. Calculation of the taxable amount.

    a. Two base amounts are established:

        i. First base amount.

            A) $32,000 for married filing joint.

            B) $0 for married taxpayers who do not live apart for the entire year but file a separate return.

            C) $25,000 for all other taxpayers.

        ii. Second base amount.

            A) $44,000 for married individuals filing joint.

            B) $0 for married taxpayers who do not live apart for the entire year but file a separate return.

            C) $34,000 for all other taxpayers.

b. If MAGI plus one-half of Social Security exceeds the first set of base amounts, but not the second set, the taxable amount of Social Security is the lesser of the following:

   i. 0.50 (Social Security Benefits), or

   ii. 0.50 (MAGI + 0.50 (Social Security) – base amount).

c. If MAGI plus one-half of Social Security exceeds the second set of base amounts, the taxable amount of Social Security is the lesser of the following:

   i. 0.85 (Social Security Benefits), or

   ii. Sum of 0.85 (MAGI + 0.50 (Social Security) – second base amount), plus lesser of:

   • Amount included through application of the first formula, or

   • $4,500 ($6,000 for married filing jointly).

M. FICA TAX.

1. FICA tax consists of the Social Security tax (OASDI) and the Medicare tax (HI).

2. For OASDI, a rate of 6.2% is applied to wages, with a base cap of $94,200 in 2006 (indexed to changes in average wages). Employers must match this rate for employees. Self employed pay a total OASDI rate of 12.4% on net income.

3. The Medicare tax has no ceiling for earnings subject to the hospital insurance portion (HI) of the Social Security tax. The HI tax is 1.45% for both the employee and the employer. Self-employed taxpayers pay 2.9% on net income.

4. When calculating self-employment tax, the taxpayer reduces net earnings from self-employment by 50% of the self-employment rate. In addition, the self-employed taxpayer may deduct one-half of the self-employment tax paid as a deduction for AGI.

PLANNING TIPS

1. Since S corporation earnings (other than salaries) are not considered self-employment income, they are not subject to FICA tax. It may be possible, in some cases, to decrease salaries to avoid a portion of the HI tax. However, the salaries paid must be reasonable.

2. Structure payments to reflect rental or interest income that is not subject to FICA. Note, however, that rental of personal property may be subject to FICA.

3. A shareholder in a personal service S corporation may want to accumulate funds in the S corporation, instead of personally, to avoid the increased FICA tax.

V. GROSS INCOME – EXCLUSIONS

A. INTRODUCTION.

Only those items that are specifically excluded by statute are excludable from income. Generally, items excluded are those that are donative in nature, a return of capital, socially desirable, a matter of legislative grace, usually resulting from the lobbying efforts of a special interest group, or that make you whole again. Exhibit 9: "Exclusions from Gross Income" lists the exclusions from gross income.

EXHIBIT 9: EXCLUSIONS FROM GROSS INCOME

Items Characterized by Love, Affection, or Assistance
Gifts, bequests, and inheritances (Section 102) Scholarships (Section 117) Life insurance proceeds paid by reason of death (Section 101) Accelerated Death Benefits, including sale of policy to a viatical settlement provider (Section 101)
Personal and Welfare Items
Injury or sickness payments (Section 104) Amounts received under insurance contracts for certain living expenses (Section 123) Reimbursement for the costs of caring for a foster child (Section 131)
Employer-Provided Benefits
a. Fringe Benefits

Accident and health benefits (Sections 105 and 106)
    Medical/Health Savings Accounts reimbursements (Section 106)
    Long-term care insurance benefits (Section 7702)
    Lodging and meals furnished for the convenience of the employer (Section 119)
    Employee achievement awards (Section 74(c))
    Employer contributions to employee group term life insurance (Section 79)
    Benefits received through cafeteria plans (Section 125)
    Educational assistance payments (Section 127)
    Child or dependent care (Section 129)
    Services provided to employees at no additional cost to the employer (Section 132)
    Employee discounts (Section 132)
    Working condition and de minimis fringes (Section 132)
    Athletic facilities provided to employees (Section 132)
    Qualified transportation fringe benefit (Section 132)
    Tuition reductions granted to employees of educational institutions (Section 117)
    Adoption assistance (Section 137)

b. Military Benefits
Combat pay (Section 112)   Housing, uniforms, and other benefits (Section 134)
c. Foreign Earned Income   Choice between foreign earned income exclusion and foreign income credit (Section 911)
Investments
Interest on state and local government obligations (Section 103) Gain exclusion (50%) for Small Business Stock (Section 1202)
Benefits for the Elderly
Social Security benefits (partial, see Section IV.- "Social Security Benefits." .) (Section 86)
Other Benefits
Income from discharge of indebtedness under bankruptcy or insolvency (Section 108) Recovery of a prior year's deduction that yielded no tax benefit (Section 111) Educational savings bonds (Section 135) Gain from sale of personal residence-$250,000 single exclusion; $500,000 for married filing joint (Sec. 121)

B. GIFTS, BEQUESTS, AND INHERITANCES.

1. A gift is defined by the courts as a voluntary transfer of property by one to another without adequate (valuable) consideration.

2. The recipient (donee) of a gift or inheritance is allowed to exclude the value of the property from gross income. However, the recipient of a gift of income-producing property is subject to tax on any income subsequently earned from the property.

C. SCHOLARSHIPS.

1. Scholarship recipients (must be a candidate for a degree) may exclude from gross income amounts used for tuition and related expenses (books, fees, but not room and board), provided the conditions of the grant do not require that the funds be used for other purposes.

2. If the scholarship is received in one year and spent in the subsequent year, the student does not have to include in income the amount in excess of qualified expenses until all expenditures have been made. The amount would be taken into income in the year resolution occurs.

3. Employees of nonprofit educational institutions are allowed to exclude a tuition waiver from gross income, if the waiver is pursuant to a qualified tuition reduction plan.

4. Payments by a donor made directly to an educational institution are qualified payments, are not includible in the student's income and are not subject to gift tax.

Example

*   On June 1, 2006, Mark was awarded a full tuition scholarship for his freshman year at Dalton University. He began his freshman year in August 2006 and completed it in May 2007. One half of the tuition is due 8/1/2006 and one-half is due 1/1/2007 Since the scholarship was for tuition only, nothing will be included in Mark's gross income in 2006 or 2007.

*   On January 1, 2006, David was awarded a post-graduate fellowship grant of $6,000 by a tax-exempt educational organization. David is not a candidate for a degree and was awarded the grant to continue his research. The grant was awarded for the period August 1, 2006, through July 31, 2007. On August 1, 2006, David elected to receive the full amount of the grant.

    Since David is not a candidate for a degree, he must include all of the grant received on his 2006 tax return. The issue of proration between years is not relevant in this case.

D. LIFE INSURANCE PROCEEDS (PRESUMED GIFT).

1. In General.

    a. Proceeds paid to a beneficiary because of death of the insured are generally exempt from income tax.

    b. If the proceeds are received in installment payments, any interest income will be taxable.

Example

Susan, a widow, elected to receive the proceeds of a $200,000 face value insurance policy on the life of her deceased husband in ten annual installments of $22,000 each (beginning last year). In the current year, she received $22,000, which included $2,000 interest. Susan must include the $2,000 interest in her gross income.

---

2. Cashing in the policy before insured's death.

   a. If the owner cancels the policy and receives the cash surrender value, the owner must recognize ordinary income gain to the extent the amount received exceeds the cost basis of the policy.

   b. Losses are not deductible.

   c. Withdrawals or loans are received as FIFO.

3. Transfer for valuable consideration.

   a. If an existing policy is transferred for valuable consideration, the insurance proceeds are includible in the gross income of the transferee to the extent the proceeds exceed their basis (amount paid for policy plus any subsequent premiums paid).

   b. There are five instances when the transfer of a policy will not result in loss of exclusion treatment. These include transfers to:

      i. The insured.

      ii. A partner of the insured.

      iii. A partnership in which the insured is a partner.

      iv. A corporation in which the insured is an officer or shareholder.

      v. A transferee (such as a child) whose basis in the policy is determined by reference to the transferor's basis (tax-free exchange or gift).

4. Viatical agreements.

   a. Amounts received under the sale of a life insurance contract on the life of a terminally ill or chronically ill individual are excluded from gross income. The exclusion also applies to the sale/assignment of a contract to a qualified "viatical" settlement provider.

   b. A terminally ill individual is an individual that has been certified by a physician as having an illness or condition that can reasonably be expected to result in death within 24 months of the date of certification.

   c. A chronically ill individual is generally a person who is unable to perform at least two activities of daily living (e.g., eating, bathing) for a period of at least 90 days. If the individual is chronically ill, the benefits will only be excluded from income to the extent they are used for long-term care services.

   d. Under the tranfer for value rule, the purchaser of the life insurance policy will be taxed on any benefits received in excess of the purchaser's basis.

Example

Erwin Scott was recently diagnosed with a rare liver disorder and has been certified by his physician, on July 15 of the current year, as terminally ill. Erwin immediately resigned from his sales position with ABC Company and sold his life insurance policy with a face value of $500,000 to a viatical settlement provider (VSP) for $340,000. Erwin paid $30,000 in premiums over the last few years.

Since Erwin was certified as terminally ill, none of the proceeds he received from the VSP will be taxable to him. If instead he was certified as chronically ill, the proceeds would be excluded from his gross income only if the proceeds were used for long-term care services.

5. Modified endowment contract (MEC).

    a. An MEC is a life insurance policy issued after June 21, 1988, that fails the seven-pay test.

        i. Seven-pay test – contract is an MEC if the premiums paid during the first 7 years of the contract exceed the total of the net level premiums that would have been paid if the policy provided for paid-up benefits after the 7th year.

    b. In the case of withdrawals or loans from the MEC, basis is recovered last (LIFO). As a result, withdrawals (including loans) to the extent of earnings are currently taxed. This is different from a traditional life insurance policy, which features FIFO basis recovery.

    c. If the policyholder has no plans to borrow money against the MEC, it may be an effective estate planning tool because the classification as a MEC does not affect the taxation of the death benefit, as the death benefit is received by the beneficiary tax-free, provided there has been a transfer for value.

E. COMPENSATION FOR INJURIES AND ILLNESS.

1. Taxability of damages received.

    a. Compensatory damages.

        i. If the damages are awarded for physical injury or sickness, the damages are excludable from gross income (special damages).

        ii. Personal, nonphysical, damages (e.g., emotional distress, business reputation damages, breach of contract, age discrimination, sexual harassment, slander and libel, pain and suffering) must be included in gross income (general damages).

    b. Punitive damages are generally included in gross income.

2. Workers compensation amounts received are excluded by statute from gross income.

3. Taxation of accident and health insurance benefits (for accidents and illness) depends on whether the premiums were paid by the employer or the employee. Benefits collected under an accident and health insurance policy purchased by the taxpayer are excludable. For example, a taxpayer collects payments under a disability policy. If the taxpayer purchased the policy, the payments are not included in income. If the taxpayer's employer purchased the policy, the payments are included in income.

F. EMPLOYER-PROVIDED BENEFITS

1. Accident and health plans.

   a. Premiums – Premiums paid by the employer for accident, health, and disability insurance policies are deductible for the employer and excludable from the employee's income.

   b. Benefits paid under employer-sponsored health and accident plans.

      i. If the payments are received for the medical care of the employee, spouse, or dependents, the payments are not included in the taxpayer's income.

      ii. Payments for permanent loss or the loss of the use of a member or function of the body or permanent disfigurement of the employee, spouse, or dependent are not included in the taxpayer's income.

      iii. Other insurance benefits collected are included in gross income.

      iv. If a taxpayer pays the cost of a disability policy with after-tax dollars, any subsequent benefits are not taxable. If the employer pays the premiums, the benefits are taxable. If the employer and taxpayer each pay a portion of the premium, there will be a fractional allocation to the nontaxed benefits based on contributions to the plan.

   c. Employees are not taxed on the value of coverage under a long-term care plan provided by their employer. This exclusion does not apply if coverage is reimbursed under a tax-free flexible spending plan or provided through a cafeteria plan.

   d. Contributions made by an employer to a medical savings plan or health savings account are not included in the employee's income.

2. Meals and lodging.

   a. Excludable by employee if furnished by the employer on the business premises for the employer's convenience.

   b. If free lodging is an employee benefit, the employee must be required to accept it as a condition of employment in order to exclude it from his income.

Example

Tom is the manager of a hotel. To be available in emergency situations, Tom's employer requires that he live in one of the hotel rooms without charge. The value of the room is $1,500 per month if occupied each night. The hotel is ordinarily 70% occupied. If Tom did not live there, he would live in an apartment that would rent for $900 per month. The room is furnished for the convenience of the employer on the employer's premises and is a requirement of Tom's employment. Therefore, Tom will not be required to report the benefit as income.

---

3. Group term life insurance – See "Group Term Life Insurance." on page 27.

4. Child and dependent care services – Employees can exclude up to $5,000 in child care expenses paid by their employer to enable the employee to work. If the taxpayer is married, the exclusion is limited to the income of the lesser-paid spouse. In addition, child care provided under a cafeteria plan is not eligible for the dependent care credit.

5. Athletic facility provided to employees – The value of a health facility or gymnasium provided by the employer on the premises solely for the use of employees and the employee's dependents is excluded from the employee's gross income. If the employer pays the health club dues (public health club) of an employee, the dues are taxable to the employee.

6. Educational assistance.

   a. Qualified employer-provided educational assistance is excluded from gross income.

   b. The exclusion is subject to an annual ceiling of $5,250.

   c. The exclusion applies to both undergraduate and graduate education.

   d. Cannot discriminate in favor of highly compensated employees.

7. Cafeteria plans.

   a. Under a cafeteria plan, an employer offers his employee the choice between cash or selected nontaxable benefits. If the employee chooses the benefit, it remains nontaxable. If the employee chooses cash equal to the cost of the benefit, the cash is included in income. A cafeteria plan can also provide employees an opportunity to buy certain benefits with after-tax contributions.

8. No additional cost services – Excluded from income under the following conditions:

   a. The employee receives services, not property.

   b. The employer does not incur substantial additional cost, including forgone revenue, in providing the services to the employee.

   c. The services are offered to customers in the ordinary course of the business in which the employee works (e.g., travel privileges for employees of an airline).

   d. Nondiscrimination provision – If the plan is discriminatory in favor of highly compensated employees, then the highly compensated are denied exclusion treatment.

9. Qualified employee discounts – When an employer offers goods or services to an employee at a discount, the discount can be excluded from income if:

   a. In the case of property, it is not real property or investment-type personal property.

   b. The property or services are offered in the same line of business in which the employee works.

   c. In the case of property, the exclusion is limited to the gross profit component of the price to customers.

   d. In the case of services, the exclusion is limited to 20% of the customer price.

   e. Nondiscrimination provision – If the plan is discriminatory in favor of highly compensated employees, then the highly compensated are denied exclusion treatment.

10. Working condition fringes – When an employer provides property or services to an employee that an employee could have deducted had she paid for them herself, the value of the property or services is a nontaxable fringe. Discrimination does not affect the exclusion status.

Example

Frances is a member of her state CPA society. Her employer pays the annual dues. This is a nontaxable fringe since Frances could have deducted it as an employee business expense had she paid them herself.

---

11. De minimis fringes – The benefits are so small that accounting for them is impractical. They are, therefore, excludable. For example, the personal use of a company-owned computer or copy machine is considered a nontaxable de minimis fringe benefit. Discrimination does not affect the exclusion status.

12. Qualified transportation fringes – To encourage mass transit for commuting to and from work, this fringe benefit is nontaxable and includes:

    a. Transportation in a commuter highway vehicle between the employee's residence and the place of work.

    b. A transit pass within limits ($105/month for 2006).

    c. Qualified parking within limits ($205/month for 2006).

    d. The dollar limits are adjusted annually for inflation.

13. Employer-Provided Adoption Assistance.

    a. Employer-provided adoption assistance can be excluded from an employee's income. The maximum exclusion is $10,960 for 2006 per eligible child, including special needs children.

    b. Phaseout of adoption assistance. The adoption assistance exclusion is phased out beginning at modified AGI of $164,410 with complete phaseout at $204,410 (2006).

14. Employer-provided auto – Personal use of an employer-provided car is usually a taxable fringe benefit. The taxable amount is determined by the employer and included on the employee's W-2.

15. See Exhibit 10: "Summary of Fringe Benefits" for a summary of fringe benefit exclusions, along with the effect of discriminatory application.

EXHIBIT 10: SUMMARY OF FRINGE BENEFITS

Fringe Benefit	Exclusion	Effect of Discrimination in Favor of Highly Compensated
Premiums on employer-provided health insurance	Employee excludes from gross income	Highly compensated must include excess benefits in income
Employer-paid premiums on Group Term Life	Premiums paid on coverage up to $50,000 excluded	Key employees must include greater of actual cost or table cost in income $50,000 exclusion not available
No additional cost services	Excluded as long as in line of business and no additional cost incurred	No exclusion for highly compensated employees if plan is discriminatory
Qualified employee discounts for goods	Excluded to extent discount does not exceed gross profit	No exclusion for highly compensated employees if plan is discriminatory
Qualified employee discounts for services	Exclusion limited to 20% of customer price	No exclusion for highly compensated employees if plan is discriminatory
Meals and lodging	Excluded if furnished by the employer on the business premises for employer's convenience Lodging must be a condition of employment	N/A
Employer-provided child and dependent care services	Exclude up to $5,000, limited to the income of the lesser-paid spouse	No exclusion for highly compensated employees if plan is discriminatory
Athletic facility provided to employees	Excluded if provided on employer's premises solely for use of employees	N/A
Educational assistance	Undergraduate and graduate, excluded up to $5,250/year	No exclusion for highly compensated employees if plan is discriminatory
Working condition fringes	Excluded if the expenses would have been deductible by the employee	No effect
De minimis fringes	Excluded if immaterial	No effect
Qualified transportation	Excluded with limit for transit passes, commuter van, and parking	No effect
Adoption assistance	Limit of $10,960 (2006) per child with AGI phaseout $164,410 – $204,410	No exclusion for highly compensated employees if plan is discriminatory

G. INVESTMENT RELATED.

1. Interest on certain state and local government obligations – The interest on state and local government obligations is exempt from federal income taxation. However, the exemption does not apply to gains on the sale of tax-exempt securities.

2. Educational savings bonds.

    a. A taxpayer may elect to exclude interest on Series EE U.S. government savings bonds from gross income if the bond proceeds are used to pay qualified higher education expenses.

    b. The following requirements must be met:

        i.   The savings bonds are issued after December 31, 1989.

        ii. The savings bonds are issued to an individual who is at least 24 years old before the time of issuance.

        iii. The savings bonds are issued at a discount.

    c. It should also be noted that the exclusion does not apply to married couples filing separate returns.

    d. The exclusion is limited by a Modified AGI (MAGI) threshold. For 2006, the threshold begins at $94,700 on a joint return ($63,100 on others) and is completely phased out at $124,700 ($78,100 others).

3. Life insurance – The annual increase in the cash surrender value of the policy is not taxable. By borrowing on the policy cash surrender value, the owner can actually receive the policy increase in value in cash, without recognizing income (FIFO basis recovery).

4. Noncorporate investors can exclude up to 50% of the gain they realize on qualified small business stock (Section 1202). Any remaining gain is taxed at the 28% capital gains rate.

    a. The stock must be issued after 8/10/93.

    b. The stock must be held more than five years.

    c. Exclusion limited to greater of $10 million or ten times the taxpayer's basis in the stock.

    d. 7% of excluded amount of gain (3.5% of total gain) is a tax preference item for Alternative Minimum Tax (AMT) purposes for stock disposed of on or after March 6, 2003 and before tax year beginning in 2008.

H. OTHER BENEFITS.

1. Tax benefit rule.

    a. A rule that limits the recognition of income from the recovery of an expense or loss properly deducted in a prior year to the amount of the deduction that generated the tax benefit. For example, a taxpayer who claims the standard deduction in 2006 receives a $500 state income tax refund in 2007. The refund is not taxable because the taxpayer did not deduct the state income taxes paid. If the taxpayer had claimed $12,000 of itemized deductions in 2006, the $500 refund would have been taxable in 2007.

    b. In other words, if a taxpayer obtains a deduction for an item in one year and in a later year recovers all or a portion of the prior deduction, the recovery is included in gross income in the year received (such as a state tax refund on taxes deducted in the prior year).

2. Income from discharge of indebtedness.

   a. Generally, if a lender forgives a borrower's debt, the borrower must report the forgiven debt as income.

   b. Bankrupt and insolvent taxpayers may exclude the income.

   c. If a taxpayer transfers appreciated property to satisfy a debt, income is realized. The transaction is treated as a sale of the appreciated property followed by payment of a debt.

   d. When a creditor forecloses on a piece of property, it is treated as a sale or exchange.

   e. In some special instances, the taxpayer is allowed to reduce the basis of the asset by the realized gain from discharge of debt. Included are discharge of qualified real property business indebtedness, a seller's cancellation of the buyer's indebtedness and forgiveness of student loans.

   f. Students who are granted loans which are forgiven in return for working in the state after graduation, do not have to include the debt forgiveness in their income.

3. Foreign earned income.

   a. The U.S. taxes all income of its citizens regardless of where it is earned. Without special provisions, U.S. taxpayers could be in danger of having non-U.S. income taxed twice, once by the U.S. and again by the foreign country.

   b. The following options are available to mitigate double taxation:

      i. Include the foreign income in taxable income and then claim a credit for foreign taxes paid, or

      ii. Exclude up to $80,000 (for years 2002 – 2007) if the foreign earnings from U.S. gross income.

   c. Foreign earned income is the earnings from the taxpayer's personal services in a foreign country.

   d. To qualify for the exclusion, the taxpayer must be either:

      i. A bona fide resident of the foreign country.

      ii. Present in a foreign country for at least 330 days during any 12 consecutive months.

   e. The exclusion is limited to an indexed amount per year. A taxpayer who is present in the country for less than the entire year must prorate the exclusion using the following formula:

$$\text{Maximum Exclusion} \times \frac{\text{Number of days present in foreign country}}{\text{Number of days in entire year}}$$

   f. Taxpayers who live and work abroad may elect to exclude amounts for employer-provided foreign housing costs.

I. EDUCATIONAL INCENTIVES.

1. Coverdell Education Savings Accounts (formerly Education IRA).

    a. Contributions.

        i. Up to $2,000 per beneficiary (under 18) may be contributed to a Coverdell Education Savings Account.

        ii. The contribution is phased out at certain Modified Adjusted Gross Income (MAGI) levels. MAGI is defined as AGI increased by any amounts excluded due to foreign earned income.

            A) The $2,000 contribution is phased out at the following MAGI levels:

Taxpayer Filing Status	MAGI Phaseout
Single	$95,000 – 110,000
Married Filing Jointly	$190,000 – 220,000

    b. Distributions and Rollovers.

        i. Distributions from such accounts used to pay qualified education expenses of an eligible student are excluded from income.

        ii. The amounts must be distributed to the beneficiary by age 30 if unused. Then, distributions are taxable and subject to 10% penalty.

        iii. A Coverdell Education Savings Account may be rolled over to the account of a new beneficiary who is a member of the same family free of taxation and the penalty.

        iv. A taxpayer may claim the HOPE Scholarship Credit or Lifetime Learning Credit for a taxable year and also exclude from gross income amounts distributed from a Coverdell Education Savings Account on behalf of the same student, provided the distribution is not used for the same educational expenses for which a credit is claimed.

    c. Qualified Education Expenses.

        i. Qualified education expenses include tuition, fees, books, supplies, and equipment required for the enrollment or attendance of the designated beneficiary at an eligible education institution. Qualified education expenses may include room and board, provided the student is enrolled at an eligible institution on at least a half-time basis.

        ii. Eligible education institutions generally include accredited post-secondary educational institutions offering credit toward a bachelor's degree, an associate's degree, a graduate-level or professional degree, or another recognized post-secondary credential. Qualified elementary and secondary school expenses (kindergarten through grade 12) are also eligible.

2. Qualified Tuition Plans (529 Plans).

   a. Earnings on qualified tuition plans accumulate free from income tax.

   b. Distributions from qualified tuition programs are excluded from gross income to the extent that the distribution is used to pay for qualified higher education expenses.

   c. A taxpayer can claim a HOPE Scholarship Credit or Lifetime Learning Credit for a taxable year and also exclude from gross income amounts distributed from a qualified tuition program on behalf of the same student (provided the distribution is not used for the same expenses for which a credit is claimed).

   d. A transfer from one qualified tuition program for the benefit of a designated beneficiary to another qualified tuition program for the benefit of the same beneficiary (rollover) is not considered a distribution.

3. See Retirement Planning outline for a discussion of tax incentives available through regular IRAs and Roth IRAs.

4. See "Interest on Educational Loans." on page 46.

5. See "Cafeteria plans." on page 36.

VI. DEDUCTIONS FOR ADJUSTED GROSS INCOME

These deductions are subtracted from a taxpayer's gross income to arrive at adjusted gross income. Deductions for adjusted gross income (AGI) include:

A. ORDINARY AND NECESSARY EXPENSES INCURRED IN A TRADE OR BUSINESS.

1. Expenses related to a taxpayer's trade or business are deductions for AGI.

2. These expenses, along with the revenue from the business, are reported on Schedule C of an individual's Form 1040 if the individual is a sole proprietor.

3. Unreimbursed business expenses of an employee are deductible as miscellaneous itemized deductions, subject to the 2% of AGI floor (a deduction from AGI).

B. ONE-HALF OF SELF-EMPLOYMENT TAX PAID.

1. To help mitigate the burden of paying both halves of FICA, self-employed individuals are allowed a deduction for AGI of one-half of self-employment tax paid.

2. For self-employed individuals, the self-employment tax is based on net income.

C. ALIMONY PAID TO TAXPAYER'S EX-SPOUSE.

1. Alimony paid to an ex-spouse is a deduction for AGI.

2. A spouse who receives alimony must include the alimony as taxable income.

D. PAYMENTS TO KEOGH AND SELF-EMPLOYED SEPs AND SIMPLE PLANS.

1. See the Retirement Planning Section for details of contribution limits, deductions, and distribution rules.

2. Keoghs must be established by year-end and funded by the extension due date. The maximum contribution is dependent on the type of plan.

3. SEPs must be established and funded by the extended due date of the employer. SEP contribution limits are covered in the Retirement Planning Section.

E. IRA CONTRIBUTIONS.

1. For 2006, taxpayers can contribute a maximum of $4,000 for themselves and $4,000 for their spouse (working or nonworking). If the contribution is made to a Traditional IRA, the contribution may be deductible. See the Retirement Planning Section for rules regarding the deductibility and limitations of contributions to a Traditional IRA.

2. Roth IRA contributions are never deductible.

F. MOVING EXPENSES.

1. General.

    a. Allowed with commencement of work at a new place.

    b. The distance between the new job and the old residence must be at least 50 miles greater than the distance between the old job and the old residence.

        i. The location of the new residence is irrelevant.

Example

Davin moved to a new home less than 50 miles from his former home because he changed job locations. His old job was 3 miles from his former home. Davin's new job is 60 miles from the former home. Because Davin's new job is 57 miles farther from his former home than the distance from his former home to his old job, he meets the 50-mile distance test.

---

     c.   Must be employed full-time at the new job for 39 weeks during the next 52 weeks.

     d.   If self-employed, the requirement is 78 weeks of full-time work in the next 104 weeks.

2.   Moving expenses include:

     a.   Moving of household goods and personal effects.

     b.   Travel to the new location (including lodging) and out-of-pocket travel of 18 cents per mile (for 2006).

         i.   No meal deduction is allowed.

         ii.   No house-hunting expenses are deductible.

         iii.   No temporary living expenses are deductible.

     c.   Tax treatment.

         i.   Qualified expenditures reimbursed/paid by the employer are not reported on the employee's Form W-2 (and employer payment is not included in income).

         ii.   Qualified, unreimbursed expenditures are deductible by the taxpayer for AGI.

         iii.   Unqualified expenditures paid by or reimbursed by the employer are included in the employee's gross income and deducted by the employer as compensation.

Example

Karen is transferred by her employer from New Orleans to Houston. Her expenses are not reimbursed and are as follows:

Cost of moving household furnishings	$1,600
Transportation costs	300
Meals en route	400
Lodging en route	250
	$2,550

Her qualified moving expenses are $2,150.

($1,600 + $300 + $250) = $2,150. Meals are not deductible while moving.

G. FORFEITED INTEREST PENALTY FOR PREMATURE WITHDRAWAL OF TIME DEPOSITS.

1. Any forfeited interest on withdrawals from Certificate of Deposits (CDs) is deductible for AGI.

Example

Dan has immediate need for a large amount of cash and his most liquid asset is a 3-year CD that does not mature for 18 more months. When he redeems the CD early, the bank charges him 3 months interest as a penalty. The 3 months' interest is reportable as income, but it is also a deduction for AGI.

H. CAPITAL LOSSES.

1. Capital losses can offset capital gains without limit.

2. Capital losses can offset ordinary income up to a maximum of $3,000 per year.

3. Unused capital losses are carried forward indefinitely. Capital losses cannot be carried back.

I. SELF-EMPLOYED HEALTH INSURANCE PREMIUMS.

1. Self-employed taxpayers and wage earners who are more-than-2% shareholders of an S corporation can take a 100% deduction (not to exceed net earnings from self-employment) for amounts paid for health insurance for taxpayers, spouses, and dependents.

J. CONTRIBUTIONS TO ARCHER MEDICAL SAVINGS ACCOUNT (ARCHER MSAS).

1. Employees of small employers and self-employed individuals with high deductible health insurance plans can make tax-deductible contributions to an Archer MSA and use the funds accumulated in the Archer MSA to pay medical expenses. If the employer makes the contributions, they are excluded from the employee's income.

2. Earnings generated by the plan are not taxable, and distributions from an Archer MSA used to pay medical expenses are not taxable.

3. Distributions not used for medical expenses are taxable and subject to a 15% penalty tax. The 15% penalty does not apply to distributions made after age 65 or upon death or disability.

K. CONTRIBUTIONS TO HEALTH SAVINGS ACCOUNTS (HSAS).

1. HSAs have characteristics similar to the MSAs. It is possible to have both an MSA and HSA, but contributions to the MSA will reduce contribution limits to the HSA plan. You may also rollover your preexisting MSA into an HSA plan.

2. The HSA plans allow qualifying individuals with high-deductible health insurance plans to make tax-deductible cash contributions (above-the-line deductions). HSA funds can be used to reimburse the individual tax free for qualifying medical expenses.

3. If an individual makes withdrawals for expenses other than qualifying medical expenses, the amount will be subject to income tax and a 10% penalty. The 10% penalty does not apply to withdrawals after age 65.

4. Earnings generated by the plan are not taxable, and distributions from an HSA used to pay medical expenses are excludable from taxable income.

5. If the employer makes the contributions, they are excluded from the employee's income.

L. Interest on Educational Loans.

1. In General.

   a. Interest paid on qualified educational loans is deductible in arriving at adjusted gross income (above-the-line deduction).

   b. Loan proceeds must have been used for higher education tuition, fees, room, board, and other necessary expenses (e.g., transportation).

   c. The taxpayer may not be claimed as a dependent of another and deduct interest on education loans.

2. Limitations:

   a. The maximum allowable annual deduction is $2,500. The deduction is phased out at certain modified adjusted gross income (MAGI) levels.

   b. MAGI phaseout levels by filing status:

Filing Status	MAGI Phaseout
Single	$50,000 – $65,000
Married Filing Jointly	$105,000 – $135,000

M. Adjusted Gross Income (AGI).

1. This subtotal serves as the basis (amount) for computing percentage limitations on certain itemized deductions such as charitable (≤50% of AGI), medical (> 7.5% of AGI), casualty losses (> 10% of AGI) and miscellaneous itemized deductions (> 2% of AGI). AGI also serves as a benchmark for limiting total itemized deductions, personal and dependency exemptions, and passive rental real estate losses. Many states start their calculation of taxable income with federal AGI.

VII. BASIC STANDARD DEDUCTION AND ADDITIONAL STANDARD DEDUCTIONS

A. BASIC STANDARD DEDUCTION.

1. Basic standard deduction amounts are based on filing status.

EXHIBIT 11: STANDARD DEDUCTION AMOUNT

Filing Status	2006
Single	5,150
Married filing jointly	10,300
Qualifying widow(er)	10,300
Head of household	7,550
Married filing separately	5,150

B. ADDITIONAL STANDARD DEDUCTION.

1. A taxpayer who is age 65 or blind qualifies for an additional standard deduction depending on the filing status. Two additional standard deductions are allowed for a taxpayer who is age 65 and blind.

EXHIBIT 12: AMOUNT OF EACH ADDITIONAL STANDARD DEDUCTION

Filing Status	2006
Single	1,250
Married, filing jointly	1,000
Qualifying widow(er)	1,000
Head of household	1,250
Married filing separately	1,000

Example

The 2006 standard deduction for a taxpayer who is age 55, single, and blind is $6,400 ($5,150 + $1,250).

The 2006 standard deduction for a married couple where both are 68 years old and both are blind is $14,300 [$10,300 + (4 × 1,000)].

VIII. PERSONAL AND DEPENDENCY EXEMPTIONS

A. PERSONAL EXEMPTIONS

1. An individual may claim a personal exemption for himself/herself.

2. An individual may also claim a personal exemption for his/her spouse if a joint return is filed

3. The personal exemption amount is $3,300 for 2006.

B. DEPENDENCY EXEMPTIONS.

1. A taxpayer can claim an additional exemption for each individual who qualifies as a dependent of the taxpayer.

2. A dependency exemption can be claimed if an individual is either a "qualifying child" or "qualifying relative" of the taxpayer.

    a. Qualifying Child – a taxpayer may claim an individual as a dependent if the individual satisfies all of the following requirements:

        i. The individual must meet one of the following relationships:

            A) Child, step-child, foster child, or adopted child of the taxpayer.

            B) Brother, sister, stepbrother, or stepsister of the taxpayer.

            C) Descendants of any of the individuals listed above.

        ii. The individual must live with the taxpayer for more than half of the taxable year.

        iii. The individual must pass an age test (meet one of the following):

            A) Individual is under age 19 at the close of the tax year.

            B) Individual is a full-time student and under the age of 24 at the close of the tax year.

            C) Individual is totally and permanently disabled at any time during the tax year.

        iv. The individual must not have provided more than half of his or her own support during the tax year.

        v. The individual cannot claim any other individual as a dependent.

        vi. The individual may not file a joint return for the tax year (unless the only reason a return was filed was to obtain a refund of tax withheld).

        vii. The individual generally must also be a U.S. citizen, U.S. national, or a resident of the United States, Canada, or Mexico.

    b. Qualifying Relative – a taxpayer may claim an individual as a dependent if the individual satisfies all of the following requirements:

        i. The individual is not a qualifying child of the taxpayer, as defined above.

        ii. The individual must satisfy one of the following two requirements:

            A) The individual bears a specified relationship to the taxpayer, including parent, in-law, niece, nephew, aunt, or uncle.

            B) The individual is unrelated to the taxpayer, but the individual resided in the taxpayer's principal home during the tax year.

      iii. The individual's gross income for the year must be less than the exemption amount ($3,300 for 2006).

      iv. The taxpayer provides over one-half of the individual's support for the tax year.

      v. The individual cannot claim any other individual as a dependent.

      vi. The individual may not file a joint return for the tax year (unless the only reason a return was filed was to obtain a refund of tax withheld).

      vii. The individual generally must also be a U.S. citizen, U.S. national, or a resident of the U.S., Canada, or Mexico.

3. As long as all the tests are met, a dependency exemption can be taken for a person who dies during the year, without any reduction.

4. Eligible taxpayers are generally free to agree among themselves who will claim a dependency exemption for an individual who can be claimed by more than one taxpayer.

    a. Only one person can claim a dependency exemption for an individual (exemption cannot be pro-rated).

    b. If more than one individual files a return claiming the same individual as a dependent, the "tie-breaker" rules apply.

IF	THEN the child will be treated as the qualifying child of the
only one of the persons is the child's parent parent	parent
both persons are the child's parent,	parent with whom the child lived for the longer period of time. If the child lived with each parent for the same amount of time, then the child will be treated as the qualifying child of the parent with the highest AGI.
none of the persons are the child's parent,	person with the highest AGI.

Example

- Erin and Brian, both age 50, filed a joint return for the current year. They provided all the support for their 19-year-old daughter who had no income. Their 23-year-old son, a full-time student at a university, had $5,000 of income and provided 70% of his own support.

  Three exemptions are allowed: two personal exemptions for Erin and Brian, and one dependency exemption for their daughter. No exemption is allowed for their son. Although the gross income test is waived, they did not meet the support test for him.

- Dennis, age 50, filed a joint return with his wife, Kelly, age 24. Their son, Derek, was born December 16 of the taxable year. Dennis provided 60% of the support for his 73-year-old widowed mother until May 1, when she died. His mother's only income was from Social Security benefits totaling $3,500.

  The couple is entitled to four exemptions – Dennis, Kelly, their son Derek, and Dennis' mother. An exemption is allowed for a dependent who was alive during any part of the taxable year. Dennis' mother's Social Security income is excluded from gross income; thus, it is not considered in applying the gross income test.

- Andre provided more than one-half of the support for his cousin, his niece and his foster parent. None of them were members of Andre's household. None of these relatives had any income, nor did any of them file an individual or joint return. All of the relatives are U.S. citizens. Of the potential dependents listed, only the niece is a qualifying relative.

C. STANDARD DEDUCTION WHEN CLAIMED AS A DEPENDENT.

1. The standard deduction of a person who may be claimed as a dependent of another is limited to the greater of (a) $850 (for 2006), or (b) earned income plus $300. However, in no event can a dependent's standard deduction be greater than the regular standard deduction. No personal exemption is allowed.

Example

Andrea is claimed as a dependent on her parents' return. During 2006, she earned $2,900 as a runner for her Dad's law firm. She also has $2,000 in dividend and interest income. Andrea's standard deduction is $3,200 ($2,900 + 300). She receives no personal exemption since she is claimed as a dependent on someone else's return.

D. PHASEOUT OF EXEMPTIONS.

1. The amount you can claim as a deduction for exemptions is phased out when your adjusted gross income (AGI) exceeds a certain level based on your filing status. These levels are as follows:

EXHIBIT 13: PHASEOUT OF EXEMPTIONS

Filing Status	2006 AGI Phaseout
Married filing separately	$112,875 – 174,125
Single	$150,500 – 273,000
Head of household	$188,150 – 310,650
Married filing jointly	$225,750 – 348,250
Qualifying widow(er)	$225,750 – 348,250

2. Reduce the dollar amount of exemptions by 2% for each $2,500, or part of $2,500 ($1,250 if married filing separately), that AGI exceeds the threshold amount.

Example

Taxpayers (MFJ) have AGI of $275,000 in 2006. These taxpayers have a total of 5 personal and dependency exemptions. Determine their actual deductible personal and dependency exemption.

5 exemptions × $3,300		$16,500
AGI Income	$275,000	
Threshold	(225,750)	
Difference	$49,250	
Divide by 2,500	19.70	
Round up to next integer	20	
Multiply by 2%	40%	
Apply personal & dependency exemption (40% × $16,500 = $6,600)		(6,600) Loss due to threshold
		$9,900 Exemption amt. after phaseout

Note: It is unlikely that the exam will test this type of calculation.

---

3. Beginning in 2006, the phaseout of personal exemptions is reduced. The phaseout is completely eliminated for tax years after 2009.

IX. TAX DETERMINATION

A. COMPUTATION OF NET TAXES PAYABLE/REFUND DUE.

1. Estimated taxes, taxes previously withheld, and tax credits are subtracted from tax liability to reduce the tax due dollar-for-dollar. Tax credits include earned income credit, credit for child and dependent care expenses, credit for the elderly, and foreign tax credit.

2. An underpayment penalty will apply if an insufficient amount has been paid. See Section "Required Payments" on page 11 for ways to avoid the penalty.

3. Prior year's tax that must be paid by high-income (high income is defined as exceeding $150,000 AGI) taxpayers to avoid the estimated tax penalty is 110% of prior year's tax for 2006.

B. KIDDIE TAX.

1. The kiddie tax applies to any unearned income of a minor under age 14. This income is taxed at the parents' highest marginal rate. The net unearned income is the amount taxed at the parents' rate, computed as follows:

   Total Unearned Income

   Less: $850 for 2006.

   Less: The greater of:

   - $850 for 2006, or
   - The amount of the allowable itemized deductions directly connected with the production of the unearned income.

   Equals: Net unearned income.

Example

Ann is 11 years old and earned $5,200 from baby sitting in 2006. She also had interest from her savings account of $2,000. Ann's net unearned income is:

$2,000	Gross unearned income
(1,700)	Kiddie tax threshold
$300	Net unearned income taxed at parents' rate

Ann's taxable income is:

$5,200	Baby sitting
2,000	Savings account interest
$7,200	Gross income
(5,150)	Standard deduction (Earned Income plus $300 but limited to $5,150)
(0)	Personal exemption
$2,050	Taxable income

Of the $2,050 in taxable income, $300 ($2,000 – $1,700) is taxed at her parents' highest rate and $1,750 is taxed at Ann's rate.

X. FILING CONSIDERATIONS

A. FILING STATUS.

1. There are five filing status categories:

   a. Single.

   b. Married Filing Jointly.

   c. Married Filing Separately.

   d. Head of Household.

   e. Qualifying Widow(er) with dependent child (also called surviving spouse).

2. Single.

   a. An unmarried, separated, or divorced individual who does not qualify for another status must file as a Single taxpayer.

   b. There are exceptions. For example, abandoned spouses who live apart may be able to use the more advantageous Head of Household rate schedule.

   c. Marital status is determined as of the last day of the tax year, except when a spouse dies during the year in which case the survivor may file Married Filing Jointly.

3. Married Filing Jointly or Separately.

   a. Married individuals are allowed to file joint returns or separate returns.

   b. When filing separate returns, each spouse reports only his or her own income, exemptions, deductions, and credits. In addition, each spouse must use the tax rate for married persons filing separately.

   c. The tax law places limits on married taxpayers filing separately. For example, they cannot take the credit for child and dependent care expenses, the earned income credit, or any education credits. In addition, if one spouse itemizes, then the other should generally itemize because the standard deduction would be reduced to zero (some exceptions apply.)

   d. It is usually advantageous for married persons to file a joint return since the combined amount of tax is generally lower.

   e. Special situations may exist which result in a lower married filing separate tax liability (e.g., spouse with low income has high medical expenses). It is wise to compute the tax under both assumptions to determine the most advantageous filing status.

4. Head of Household.

   a. Unmarried individuals who maintain a household for a qualifying person are entitled to use the Head of Household rates.

   b. This rate schedule ranks between the Joint and the Single return tax rate schedules.

   c. To qualify for Head of Household rates, a taxpayer must pay more than half the cost of maintaining a household for a qualifying person, and the household must be the qualifying person's principal home.

    d.   Qualifying persons.

        i.   Child, grandchild, stepchild, or adopted child. A single child does not have to be a dependent. A married child must qualify as a dependent unless the child is claimed by the noncustodial parent under a written court agreement.

        ii.   Other relatives that the taxpayer claims as dependents. Qualifying relatives are limited to parents, grandparents, siblings, half-siblings and stepsiblings, stepparents, in-laws, and, if related by blood, uncles, aunts, nephews and nieces.

        iii.   Parents may be claimed as the qualifying person for Head of Household even when not a member of the household. If the taxpayer maintains a separate home for parents and pays more than half the cost of upkeep on that home, or pays more than half the cost of a rest home or home for the elderly, then the taxpayer may claim Head of Household filing status.

EXHIBIT 14: QUALIFYING PERSONS

Qualifying Person	Claimed as a Dependent	Must Live in Taxpayer's Home > Half of the Year
Single Child	No	Yes
Married Child	Yes[1]	Yes
Other Relative	Yes	Yes
Parents	Yes	No[2]

[1] Qualifies as dependent unless noncustodial spouse claims the exemption.
[2] Taxpayer pays more than half of the cost of separate home or elder care home.

    5.   Qualifying Widow(er) with dependent child.

        a.   A taxpayer with a deceased spouse will file Married Filing Jointly with two personal exemptions in the year of the death of the spouse.

        b.   Taxpayer may be eligible to use Qualifying Widow(er) with dependent child as the filing status for two years following the year of death of a spouse. For example, if taxpayer's spouse died in 2006 and taxpayer has not remarried, the taxpayer may be able to use this filing status for 2007 and 2008. The taxpayer would file Married Filing Jointly for 2006.

        c.   This filing status entitles the taxpayer to use joint return tax rates with one personal exemption and the highest standard deduction amounts (if taxpayer does not itemize deductions). This status does not authorize the taxpayer to file a joint return or claim an exemption for the deceased spouse.

        d.   Eligibility rules for filing as a Qualifying Widow(er) with dependent child.

           i.   A taxpayer is eligible to file as a Qualifying Widow(er) with dependent child if taxpayer meets all of the following tests:

              A)   Taxpayer was entitled to file a joint return with spouse for the year spouse died (it does not matter whether the taxpayer actually filed a joint return).

              B)   The taxpayer did not remarry before the end of the tax year in question.

C) The taxpayer has a child, stepchild, adopted child, or foster child who qualifies as a dependent for that year.

D) The taxpayer paid more than half the cost of upkeep of the home that is the main home for the taxpayer and the child for the entire year except for temporary absences.

Example

John Reed's wife died in 2006. John has not remarried. He continued during 2007 and 2008 to maintain a home for himself and his dependent child. For 2006, he was entitled to file a joint return. For 2007 and 2008, he may file as a Qualifying Widower with a dependent child. After 2008, he may file as Head of Household if he qualifies (otherwise Single).

B. FILING REQUIREMENTS.

1. The following individuals are not required to file unless their income is equal to or exceeds their exemption amount plus the applicable standard deductions:

   a. Single Individuals.

   b. Head of Households.

   c. Surviving Spouses.

2. Married Filing Jointly individuals are not required to file unless their combined gross income equals or exceeds the basic standard deduction, plus twice the exemption amount. Married Filing Separately must file if income equals or exceeds the exemption amount.

3. See Exhibit 15: "Filing Levels (Required to File)" for 2006 required filing levels.

4. Filing requirements for dependents – If someone claims the taxpayer as a dependent, filing requirements for the dependent are controlled by the amount and type of income of the dependent. See "C. Standard Deduction When Claimed as a Dependent." on page 50.

Type of Income	Filing Required If Income Equals or Exceeds
Earned income only	Standard deduction amount including additional standard deduction amounts for age and blindness.
Unearned income only	Standard deduction[1] including additional standard deduction amounts for age and blindness.
Earned income and unearned income	Standard deduction[2] including additional standard deduction for age and blindness.

[1] With no earned income, the standard deduction would be $850 (2006) plus any additional amounts.
[2] Greater of $850 (2006) or earned income plus $300 plus any additional amounts.

Example

- In 2006, a single individual, who is claimed by a parent as a dependent, has earned income of only $3,800. No return would be required since the income is less than the standard deduction amount ($5,150).

- In 2006, a single, blind individual, who is claimed by a parent as a dependent, has unearned income only amounting to $1,200. The dependent does not need to file since gross income does not exceed $2,100 ($850 + 1,250 (additional standard deduction for blindness)).

- In 2006, a single individual, claimed as a dependent by a parent, has earned income of $2,000 and unearned income of $1,800 (total income-$3,800). This taxpayer must file since the earned and unearned income total is more than the standard deduction of $2,300 (earned income plus $300).

5. Selecting the proper form – Depending on the level of complexity, an individual taxpayer may file a Form 1040, Form 1040A, or Form 1040EZ.

C. RETURN DUE DATE.

1. Return is due on the 15th day of the fourth month after the end of the tax year. If this date falls on a weekend/holiday, return is due the next business day.

2. A six-month extension of time to file can be requested on Form 4868.

3. If taxpayer overpays taxes and wants a refund, a claim must be filed by the later of three years from the date the return was filed (if filed early, return is counted as filed on the due date) or two years from the date tax was last paid.

D. DECEDENT'S FINAL INCOME TAX RETURN.

1. A final income tax return must be filed for a decedent for the portion of the tax year that ends on the date of the decedent's death.

2. The return is due on the filing date that would have applied if death had not occurred. This would be April 15th for a calendar-year individual. Typically, the final income tax return will be filed by the executor or the administrator of the estate.

3. The surviving spouse may file a joint return with the decedent if the following conditions are met:

   a. An executor or administrator has not been appointed by the time the joint return is prepared.

   b. An executor or administrator has not been appointed before the extended due date of the tax return for the surviving spouse.

   c. The decedent did not previously file a tax return for the tax year.

4. Income inclusion.

   a. Cash-basis taxpayer – only income actually or constructively received up to the date of death is included in the decedent's final income tax return. This could include any uncashed payroll or dividend checks.

   b. Accrual-basis taxpayer – generally, only income accrued up to the date of death is included in the decedent's final income tax return.

5. Deductions.

    a. Cash-basis taxpayer – the expenses the decedent paid before death are deductible on the final income tax return.

    b. Accrual-basis taxpayer – the expenses for which the decedent was liable before death, regardless of whether the expenses were paid, are deductible on the final income tax return.

    c. Even though the return is for a short period, the standard deduction and personal exemption amounts are allowed in full.

EXHIBIT 15: FILING LEVELS (REQUIRED TO FILE)

Filing Status	2006 Gross Income
Single	
Under 65	$8,300
65 or older	$9,550
Married Filing Joint Return	
Both spouses under 65	$16,900
One spouse 65 or older	$17,900
Both spouses 65 or older	$18,900
Married Filing Separate Return	
All – whether or not 65 or older	$3,300
Head of Household	
Under 65	$10,850
65 or older	$12,100
Qualifying Widow(er)	
Under 65	$13,600
65 or older	$14,600

Note: The additional standard deduction for age is taken into account, but the additional standard deduction for blindness is not.

XI. DEDUCTIONS AND LOSSES

A. CLASSIFICATION OF DEDUCTIBLE EXPENSES – FOR VERSUS FROM AGI.

1. Deductions for Adjusted Gross Income (AGI) are identified in Section 62 of the Code. Deductions for AGI, which are often referred to as "above-the-line" deductions, include expenses relating to a trade or business, alimony paid, 50% of self-employment tax paid, capital loss deduction, interest penalty for early withdrawal of savings, deductible IRA contributions, student loan interest, and moving expenses.

2. Itemized deductions are deductions from AGI. Itemized deductions, which are often referred to as "below-the-line" deductions, include charitable contributions, medical expenses, mortgage interest, taxes paid, casualty losses, and unreimbursed employee business expenses.

3. Section 162 allows deductions for expenses incurred in a trade or business while Section 212 allows deductions for expenses incurred in connection with investment activities.

   a. Most expenses incurred in a trade or business are deductions for AGI (above-the-line) while investments expenses are deductions from AGI (with the exception of expenses incurred to produce rents and royalties).

   b. Both Section 162 and Section 212 expenses must have a profit motive.

4. Reporting procedures – Deductions for AGI are reported on the front (page 1) of Form 1040. Deductions from AGI are itemized deductions reported on Schedule A.

B. ORDINARY, NECESSARY, AND REASONABLE REQUIREMENTS.

1. Ordinary and necessary requirement – Expenses are necessary if a prudent person would make the same expenditure in the same situation. Expenses are ordinary if it is normal or customary to make the expenditure (not capital).

2. Reasonableness requirement – In addition to ordinary and necessary, there is a reasonableness requirement typically associated with compensation amounts and particularly with closely held corporations.

   a. C Corporation – if a distribution from a C corporation is classified as a dividend, the distribution will be double-taxed, once to the corporation and once to the recipient-shareholder.

      i. If the IRS determines that compensation paid by a corporation to a shareholder is unreasonably high, the excess compensation will be classified as a dividend (double-taxed).

      ii. The burden of proof is on the company. There is no standard formula to determine reasonableness of compensation.

      iii. In determining reasonableness, the IRS will consider the following factors:

         A) Size of the company.

         B) Duties of the employee receiving the compensation.

         C) Qualifications of the employee.

         D) Salaries for similar executives.

         E) Conflicts of interest.

F) Salary of shareholder compared to gross income of company.

G) Evidence of a consistent compensation plan.

b. S Corporation – a distribution from an S corporation is generally treated as a tax-free return of capital. Therefore, an S corporation shareholder would probably desire a distribution from an S corporation rather than a salary, which is subject to FICA taxes.

    i. If the IRS determines that compensation paid by an S corporation to a shareholder is unreasonably low, the IRS will likely reclassify any excess of the distribution as salary.

    ii. The salary will be subject to FICA taxes.

C. DEDUCTIONS AND LOSSES – TIMING OF EXPENSE RECOGNITION.

1. Taxpayer method of accounting.

   a. The two most common methods of accounting are the cash method and the accrual method.

   b. A cash-basis taxpayer generally gets a deduction when the expense has been paid.

   c. An accrual-basis taxpayer generally gets a deduction when the expense is incurred.

2. Cash basis requirements.

   a. Deduction is allowed only when paid. Income is not recognized until cash is constructively received.

   b. Capital outlays (even if made in cash) are not current deductions except as depreciation, amortization, or depletion.

   c. Prepaid expenses are required to be capitalized and amortized only if the life of the asset extends more than one taxable year after the year of payment.

3. Accrual basis requirements.

   a. Taxpayer takes a deduction/claims income when all the events have occurred to create the taxpayer's liability/right to receive income and the amount of the liability/income can be determined with reasonable accuracy (all events test).

   b. Economic performance test must also be satisfied for deductions.

D. DISALLOWED DEDUCTIONS.

1. The IRC and the courts deny deductions for activities that are contrary to public policy.

   a. Fines and bribes are not deductible.

   b. Bribes, kickbacks, and other illegal payments are disallowed.

   c. Expenses relating to the trafficking of controlled substances (i.e., drugs) are disallowed.

2. Political contributions – Political contributions are not deductible whether paid to Political Action Committees or directly to political candidates.

3. Lobbying activities.

   a. No deduction allowed.

   b. Exceptions allowed for local, monitoring, and de minimis (< $2,000 annual).

4. Disallowance of deductions for capital expenditures – No current deduction is available for buildings, betterments, or permanent improvements made to property. The taxpayer must capitalize and depreciate these expenditures over an appropriate period.

    a. Capital expenditures can be depreciated using ACRS (pre-1987) or MACRS (post 1986) tax depreciation methods. The asset must have an ascertainable life (e.g., land has none and, therefore, is not depreciable).

    b. Intangible assets are amortized over 15 years (including goodwill).

5. Personal expenditures – Deductions of this nature are only deductible if a section of the IRC specifically allows it (Section 262).

6. Expenditures made on behalf of others.

    a. No deduction is allowed for expenditures that benefit another taxpayer, but an exception is allowed for payment of medical expenses. Medical expenditures for a spouse or dependents are deductible by a taxpayer.

Example

Fred paid the following expenses for his dependent son during the current year:

Principle payment on son's automobile loan	$15,000
Payment of interest on above loan	1,500
Payment of son's medical expenses	4,000
Payment of son's property taxes (ad valorem)	1,000

The $4,000 medical expenses are deductible by Fred. The other items are not incurred for the taxpayer's benefit or are a result of the taxpayer's legal obligation and are not tax deductible.

---

7. Tax-exempt income related expenses and interest – If income is tax-exempt, taxpayer cannot deduct any expenses/interest related to that income.

E. LIMITED DEDUCTIONS (COMPENSATION, INVESTIGATION OF A NEW BUSINESS, HOBBY LOSSES, AND VACATION RENTAL HOMES).

1. Executive compensation – Maximum of $1,000,000 on the deductibility of executive compensation of large, publicly held corporations. Excluded from this cap are commissions, performance based bonuses, tax-qualified retirement contributions, and payments excluded from gross income.

2. Investigation expenses related to a new business.

    a. If a taxpayer investigates a business that is similar to the one he is already in, the expenses are deductible whether or not he acquires the business.

b. If a taxpayer investigates a business that is a new line of business and acquires the business, the expenses should be capitalized and amortized over 60 months. If he does not acquire the business, the expenses are nondeductible.

	TP Already in a Similar Business	**TP Not Already in Similar Business**
TP acquires the business	Expenses currently deductible	Capitalize costs and can elect to amortize over 60-month period
TP does _not_ acquire business	Expenses currently deductible	Not deductible

---

Example

Kristin, a calendar-year, cash-basis taxpayer, owns and operates furniture rental outlets in Georgia. She wants to expand to other states. During the current year, she spends $20,000 investigating furniture stores in Alabama and $12,000 investigating stores in Florida. She acquires the Alabama stores, but not the stores in Florida. Since she is already in the business, the expenses in both Alabama and Florida are deductible.

---

3. Losses incurred in hobby activities.

   a. Classification as a hobby or business is important because it affects the deductibility of losses. If an activity is deemed to be a hobby, any losses incurred may not be fully deductible. If an activity is a trade or business, the losses are deductible and can offset other taxpayer income.

   b. Is an activity a hobby or a trade/business? The answer depends on whether there was intent to earn a profit. IRS Regulations and court cases specify the factors to be considered as follows:

      i. Whether the activity is conducted in business-like manner.

      ii. Expertise of the taxpayers or their advisers.

      iii. Time and effort expended.

      iv. Expectation that the assets of the activity will appreciate in value.

      v. Previous success of the taxpayer in the conduct of similar activities.

      vi. History of income or losses from the activity.

      vii. Relationship of profits earned to losses incurred.

      viii. Financial status of the taxpayer (is there other income?)

      ix. Elements of personal pleasure or recreation in the activity.

      x. Conducting business professionally, time spent, regular hours, etc.

   c. If activity generated profits for 3 out of 5 years, the burden of proof is on the IRS, rather than the taxpayer, to prove that the activity is NOT a business.

   d. Hobby income is reduced first by taxes and interest, then by other noncapital-related expenses, then by expenses that affect basis.

e. Gross hobby income is reported on page 1 of Form 1040 (other income), and hobby expenses are reported on Schedule A (itemized deductions) as miscellaneous itemized deductions subject to the 2% of AGI floor.

Example

Sara pursued a hobby of selling antique furniture in her spare time. During the year, she sold furniture for $3,000. She incurred expenses as follows:

Cost of goods sold	$2,000
Supplies	1,200
Interest on loan to get business started	800
Advertising	750

Assuming that the activity is a hobby, and that she cannot itemize this year, she should include $3,000 in income and deduct nothing for AGI since hobby expenses must be itemized, and she cannot itemize.

---

4. Vacation home rentals.

   a. Restrictions are designed to prevent taxpayers from holding personal-use vacation homes and generating deductible rental losses. Tax treatment depends on the relative time rented vs. personal use.

EXHIBIT 16: VACATION HOMES

Type	Description	Treatment
Personal Use	Property rented less than 15 days a year	• Exclude rental income from gross income • Expenses nondeductible except mortgage interest and taxes (Schedule A)
Rental	If the rental property is rented at least 15 days a year and is not used for personal use more than the greater of 14 days per year or 10% of rental days, it is classified as primarily rental use.	• Allocate expenses between business and personal • Can deduct loss up to $25,000 (phased out at AGI between $100,000–$150,000) • Report income and expenses on Schedule E
Mixed Use (vacation status)	Rental property rented at least 15 days a year and used for personal use more than the greater of 14 days per year or 10% of rental days.	• Deduct expenses (in order of interest/taxes, operating, and then depreciation, up to amount of income) • Cannot deduct loss • Report income and expenses on Schedule E (apply hobby rules)

b. Primarily personal use – If property is rented <15 days per year, it is a personal residence.

   i. Rent is excluded from gross income and normal personal residence deductions apply (i.e., mortgage interest and taxes).

   ii. Income is not claimed.

c. Primarily rental use – If the rental property is rented at least 15 days a year and is not used for personal use more than the greater of 14 days per year or 10% of rental days, it is classified as primarily rental use.

   i. A loss can be used to offset other taxpayer income.

   ii. The expenses must be allocated between personal and rental days.

   iii. Passive activity loss rules may apply.

   iv. Reported on Schedule E, with income/loss carried to front of 1040.

d. Both personal and rental use (mixed use).

   i. If the property is rented too much for b (above) and used personally too much for c (above), expenses can be deducted only to extent of income (i.e., there can be no deductible loss. This is the same as the hobby loss rules – deemed to be not-for-profit).

   ii. The order that expenses are deducted is the same as for hobby losses (interest and taxes, operating expenses, expenses that affect basis).

   iii. Income and allowable expenses are reported on Schedule E.

Example

Doug and Cathy own a house at the beach. The house was rented to unrelated parties for 8 full weeks during the current year. Doug and Cathy used the house 16 days for their vacation during the year. After properly dividing the expenses between rental and personal use, it was determined that a loss was incurred as follows:

Gross rental income ($800 per week)		$6,400
Less: allocable mortgage interest and property taxes	$5,000	
Other allocated expenses	3,000	(8,000)
Net rental loss		($1,600)

This is a mixed-use property. The deductible rental expenses are limited to the gross rental income. They cannot take a net loss – similar to the hobby loss rule. The interest and taxes allocated to personal use may be deductible on Schedule A as itemized deductions.

---

5. Related-party losses.

   a. These transactions are restricted to prevent transactions which generate paper losses without any real economic loss suffered by either party.

b.   Losses between related parties are disallowed but may be recovered if at the eventual sale to an unrelated party the property is sold for a gain. In such a case, the seller can offset any gain with the previously disallowed loss. If the deduction is not recovered at a subsequent sale, it is lost forever.

c.   Related parties include the immediate family (brothers, sisters, spouse, ancestors, and lineal descendants), closely held corporations (own > 50%), sister corporations, etc.

Example

On January 10, 2005, Billy sold stock with a cost of $6,000 to his son, Patrick, for $4,000 (its fair market value). On July 31, 2006, Patrick sold the same stock for $5,000 in a bona fide arms length transaction.

Neither Billy nor Patrick has a recognized gain or loss in either 2005 or 2006. Billy has a $2,000 realized loss in 2005 but cannot recognize it. Billy forever loses the ability to take a deduction for the loss. Patrick has a realized gain of $1,000 in 2006. He can reduce his gain by Billy's loss (up to the amount of gain). Patrick has no gain or loss in 2006. The remaining $1,000 loss is no longer available to any taxpayer.

F.   OTHER DEDUCTIONS AND LOSSES.

1.   Legal and Accounting Fees.

   a.   When legal/accounting fees are incurred in connection with trade or business or for the production of rents and royalties, they are deductible FOR AGI. If these fees are incurred in the determination of any tax, they are deductible FROM AGI.

   b.   Legal fees incurred for personal purposes are nondeductible.

   c.   Legal fees related to the acquisition of an asset are added to the basis of the property.

2.   Worthless Securities.

   a.   Securities must be completely worthless to be deducted. Losses are deemed to be capital losses occurring on the last day of the year in which they become worthless, thereby creating increased potential for long-term capital loss treatment (net capital loss deduction remains limited to $3,000 per year).

3.   Small business stock (Section 1244 – applies to losses only).

   a.   Generally any security loss is capital in nature, but Section 1244 allows ordinary loss treatment if the loss is sustained by an individual who acquires the securities directly from the corporation (which must meet certain requirements).

   b.   Section 1244 losses are limited to $50,000 annually ($100,000 for joint filers). Any losses in excess of the limits are capital losses.

   c.   In order to qualify for Section 1244 treatment, the corporation must receive less than $1,000,000 in capital for stock at time of issue.

   d.   Section 1244 applies only to losses on the investment, not to gains.

Examples

- Tom, a single taxpayer, owns Section 1244 stock he purchased three years ago for $80,000. This year, he sold all of the Section 1244 stock for $10,000, incurring a loss of $70,000. He had no other investment transactions for the year.

  Since Tom is single, the first $50,000 of the loss on the Section 1244 stock will be treated as ordinary loss. The remaining $20,000 ($70,000 – $50,000) loss will be treated as a capital loss, of which Tom can currently deduct $3,000. The remaining capital loss of $17,000 can be carried forward.

- On October 15, 2006, Kurt purchased stock in Tech Corporation (the stock is not small business stock) for $2,000. On June 15, 2007, the stock became worthless.

  Kurt will have a $2,000 long-term capital loss. Worthless securities are treated as becoming worthless on the last day of the tax year; therefore, it is a long-term capital loss even though his actual holding period was only eight months. If the stock had been Section 1244 stock, Kurt would have had a $2,000 ordinary loss.

---

4. Bad Debts.

   a. Specific charge-off method.

      i. Specific charge-off method is usually required.

      ii. Deductions are only allowed in year of worthlessness.

      iii. If a previously deducted bad debt is later collected, income is recognized only if a tax benefit was received.

   b. Business bad debts.

      i. Bad debts are sales or revenues (accounts receivable) on credit that later become worthless. A deduction is only allowed if the income from the receivable was previously included in income (i.e., if accrual basis, because income was reported at time of service; not for cash basis because no payment means income was never reported).

      ii. There must be an identifiable relationship between the creation of the debt and the trade/business.

      iii. Deduction is allowed when business debts become partially or wholly worthless.

      iv. Business bad debts are deductible as an ordinary loss in year incurred.

   c. Nonbusiness (personal) bad debts.

      i. Some nonbusiness debts can be written off, but they must be wholly worthless.

      ii. Nonbusiness bad debt is debt not related to the taxpayer's trade or business.

      iii. Nonbusiness bad debts are always considered short-term capital losses.

iv. It does not matter what the borrowed funds are used for (because the deduction relates to the lender not the borrower).

Type of Debt	Deduction
Business – Partial or whole	Ordinary loss in year incurred
Nonbusiness – Wholly worthless	Short-term capital loss in year incurred
Nonbusiness – Partially worthless	None

Examples

- XYZ, Inc. is an accrual-basis taxpayer. XYZ uses the accounts receivable aging approach to calculate their accounting allowance for bad debts. The following information is available for the current year related to bad debts.

Credit sales	$450,000
Collections on credit sales	$375,000
Amount added to the allowance account	$60,000
Beginning balance in the allowance account	$25,000
Bad debts written off in the current year	$32,000

[handwritten note: Accrual entered into income so loss can be claimed]

The tax deduction for bad-debt expense for XYZ, Inc. for the current year is $32,000. Only the specific charge-off method can be used. Allowances for estimated expenses are not allowed for tax purposes.

- Bob Doll, CPA, files his tax return using the cash method. In April 2006, Bob billed a client $4,500 for the following professional services:

Estate planning	$3,000
Personal tax return preparation	$1,000
Compilation of business financial statements	$500

No part of the $4,500 was ever paid. In April 2006, the client declared bankruptcy, and the $4,500 obligation became totally uncollectible. No loss is allowed for Bob because the indebtedness was never taken into income since Bob was a cash-basis taxpayer.

---

5. Loans between related parties.

   a. The question is whether this is a bona fide loan or a gift.

   b. To be a loan, there must be an enforceable obligation to pay a specific amount of money.

   c. Other considerations are collateral, collection efforts, intent, interest paid, etc.

6. Loss of deposits in insolvent financial institutions.

   a. Loss of deposits may be deducted as personal casualty losses instead of nonbusiness bad debts, but they are then subject to 10% AGI limit and $100 floor.

   b. This may be elected only by qualified individuals (i.e., not >1% owners, relatives or officers).

   c. Amount of loss equals basis less amount to be received.

7. Business casualty losses or held-for-production-of-income casualty losses.

   a. The identifiable event must be sudden, unexpected, or unusual.

   b. Losses related to business/trade property are deductible for AGI. They are not subject to the $100 or 10% AGI floors to which individuals are held.

   c. Losses relating to property held for profit are not subject to the $100 and 10% floors and are deductible for AGI only if the property is held for rent or royalty. Other for-profit property losses are deductible from AGI (included in other miscellaneous itemized deductions) and are subject to a 2% AGI floor.

   d. If completely destroyed, the loss is the adjusted basis of the property. If partially destroyed, the loss is the lesser of the adjusted basis or the decline in the FMV of the property (preevent and postevent).

   e. For a discussion of personal casualty losses see Section XV. Itemized Deductions on page 92.

G. NET OPERATING LOSSES (NOL).

1. The purpose of allowing NOLs is to create an equitable situation for cyclical businesses that might otherwise lose substantial money without receiving any tax benefit. The inequality would cause excessive average taxes for a business with irregular income and/or expenses when compared to a business with the same average income but with uniform income and expenses.

2. Carryback and carryover periods.

   a. General rules – Net operating losses can be carried back two years preceding the loss year and forward 20 years following the loss year.

   b. Sequence of use of NOLs – The oldest is completely written off prior to using any of the more recent NOLs. Each loss is computed and maintains its own integrity.

   c. Election to forgo carryback – This election is irrevocable. The election produces a tax advantage if the taxpayer was in a low tax bracket in earlier years and expects to be in a higher bracket in the carryforward years.

XII. DEPRECIATION, COST RECOVERY, AMORTIZATION, AND DEPLETION

A. INTRODUCTION.

1. Taxpayers may recover the cost of certain assets used in trade/business through depreciation, amortization, or depletion. The amount of annual recovery depends on the type of property, when it was acquired, and the elected method of recovery.

2. Property eligible for capital recovery includes personalty, realty, and intangibles. The property must have a determinable useful life and be subject to wear and tear, decay or decline from natural causes, or obsolescence.

3. The basis of an asset must be reduced by the cost recovery taken and by not less than the amount the taxpayer could have taken. In other words, if you don't take the depreciation allowed, you still have to reduce the basis by the allowable depreciation.

B. MODIFIED ACCELERATED COST RECOVERY SYSTEM (MACRS).

1. Under MACRS, tangible personalty is either 3-year, 5-year, 7-year, 10-year, 15-year, or 20-year property. The percentages are based on 200% declining balance for 10-year-and-less property, and 150% declining balance for 15-year and 20-year property.

   a. Both 200% declining balance and 150% declining balance switch over to straight-line depreciation when it results in a larger deduction.

   b. A half-year convention is used (half-year depreciation is allowed during the year placed in service and a half-year depreciation in the year of disposition). However, the mid-quarter convention may apply (see discussion below).

2. Under MACRS, residential real estate has a 27.5-year life; nonresidential has a 39-year life.

   a. Cost recovery percentages are calculated using straight line.

   b. Mid-month convention is used (a half-month depreciation allowed for month placed in service and a half-month for month of disposition).

3. IRS tables provide the statutory percentages.

   a. The statutory percentage is applied against the asset cost (no reduction for salvage value).

   b. The tables incorporate the conventions for the year/month placed in service.

4. Mid-quarter convention.

   a. In order to reduce the benefits of the half-year convention for property placed in service late in the year, the mid-quarter convention was developed. If more than 40% of the personal property is placed in service during the last quarter of the year, the mid-quarter convention applies to all personal property assets placed in service that year.

   b. In the first year of service, first-quarter assets get 10.5 months of depreciation, second-quarter assets get 7.5 months, third-quarter assets get 4.5 months, and fourth-quarter assets get 1.5 months.

   c. The mid-quarter convention does not apply to real property.

C. ELECTION TO EXPENSE ASSETS.

1. Section 179 allows an annual write-off of the cost of tangible personal property used in a trade or business and placed in service during 2006.

    a. The maximum write-off under Section 179 for tangible personal property other than sports utility vehicles and luxury autos is $108,000 for 2006.

        i. The $108,000 limit would apply to purchases of office equipment, business computers, etc.

        ii. The $108,000 limit would also apply to vehicles with a gross vehicle weight in excess of 14,000 pounds.

    b. The maximum write-off under Section 179 for sports utility vehicles is $25,000 for 2006.

        i. A sports utility vehicle is defined as any four wheeled vehicle primarily designed for the carrying of passengers over public streets, that has a gross vehicle weight in excess of 6,000 pounds and not more than 14,000 pounds.

        ii. An auto that weighs 6,000 pounds or less is subject to the luxury auto depreciation rules, discussed under Section E, Business Use of Listed Property.

2. Annual limitations.

    a. If the total amount of property placed in service for a given year is above $430,000, the allowance is reduced dollar-for-dollar for any amount over $430,000. No carryover is allowed.

    b. The amount of the deduction cannot exceed the taxable income from total trade/business of the taxpayer (carryforward is available).

Example

- In 2006, Roth Corporation purchased and placed in service a piece of machinery costing $200,000. Assuming Roth had taxable income of $52,000 (without regard to Section 179 expense), the maximum Section 179 expense that can be taken is $52,000. $108,000 is eligible, but the amount is limited to the taxable income. $56,000 ($108,000 − $52,000) will be carried forward to 2007.

- In 2006, Roth Corporation purchased $20,000 in new equipment and had taxable income (without regard to Section 179 expense) of $200,000. Section 179 expense of $20,000 can be taken in 2006. Neither of the annual limitations apply.

---

3. Effect on adjusted taxable basis.

    a. The adjusted taxable basis of the property is reduced by the amount of the Section 179 deduction taken and is adjusted for the property placed in service limitation. It is not adjusted for the income limitation.

Example

The adjusted taxable basis of the property acquired by Roth is:

Year 2006 = $200,000 − 108,000 = $92,000 for equipment purchased in 2006.

Example

In 2006, Babe Corp. purchased and placed in service a machine to be used in its manufacturing operations. This machine cost $437,000. What portion of the cost may Babe elect to treat as an expense rather than as a capital expenditure assuming net taxable income of $600,000?

Maximum allowable §179 expense for 2006	$108,000
Reduction ($437,000 – $430,000)	(7,000)
Allowed §179 expense	101,000
Cost of property	437,000
§179 expense	(101,000)
Adjusted taxable basis of property	336,000*

*Ignoring any depreciation allowable.

D. REPAIRS VS. CAPITAL EXPENDITURES.

1. The cost of repairing business property is currently deductible as a business expense. A repair could include:

   a. An incidental expense that does not materially add to the value of the property.

   b. An incidental expense that does not appreciably prolong the life of the property.

   c. An expense that maintains the property in its normal operating state.

2. If a cash outlay is considered a capital expenditure, the cash outlay is not currently deductible. Instead, the cost must be capitalized and depreciated over the property's useful life. A capital expenditure could include:

   a. Expenditures that materially add to the value of the property.

   b. Expenditures that substantially prolong the property's useful life.

   c. Expenditures as part of a general plan of renovating, improving, or altering the property.

Example

Tom Hall operates Hall's Limo, a limousine service. Tom occasionally incurs expenses for the upkeep of his limos. These expenses, which include items such as spark plugs, oil changes, and labor, would be considered repair and maintenance expenses since the expenses do not significantly prolong the limo's useful life. However, if Tom replaced the transmission at a cost of $800, the expense would be considered a capital improvement.

E. BUSINESS USE OF LISTED PROPERTY.

Listed property includes passenger automobiles, entertainment assets, computers, and phones. If the business usage of listed assets is > 50%, then the taxpayer may use the statutory percentages for depreciation. If business usage is ≤ 50%, then the taxpayer is limited to straight line.

---

1. Autos and other listed property used predominantly in business.

   a. The percentage of business use must be above 50%. The 50% test is based on business use only and not on production of income. However, if the test is met, then the cost recovery amount is based on both the business and production of income usage.

   b. The amount of cost recovery available is based on the percentage of the total use that is business related.

   c. There is a limit on annual depreciation. This limit is applied prior to the adjustment for business use percentage. The caps are adjusted for inflation each year.

Placed in Service	1st Year Depreciation	2nd Year Depreciation	3rd Year Depreciation	4th Year and Later
2005	$3,260*	$5,200	$3,150	$1,875

2. Autos and other listed property not used predominantly in business.

   a. The depreciation for this property must be based on the straight-line method and the alternative depreciation system (ADS) which require a 5-year period for autos.

   b. The dollar limits previously described are still applicable.

   c. If the property fails the 50% test, it must be depreciated using the straight-line method even if it later could pass the 50% test.

3. Change from predominantly business use – If property initially passes the 50% test but later fails the test, the property is subject to cost recovery recapture. The amount of recapture is the amount of cost recovery claimed less the amount that could have been claimed if the straight-line method had been used from the beginning.

4. Leased automobiles – In order to prevent circumvention of the cost recovery rules by leasing, an annual inclusion amount (figured from IRS tables) is required to be reported as gross income. The amount reported is based on the fair market value, the number of days of use during the year, and the percentage of business vs. personal use. The effect is to reduce the deduction of the lease payments by the inclusion amount.

5. Substantiation requirements – Records must substantiate the taxpayer's claims pertaining to amount of expenditures, business purpose, and percentage use for business purposes.

Example

Catherine purchased an automobile in 2005 for $20,000. During 2006, she uses the car 40% for personal and 60% for business reasons. The MACRS statutory percentage for 5-year property, year 2 is 32%. Catherine's depreciation deduction for 2006 is $3,840. Catherine's depreciation deduction using the MACRS percentage is $6,400 (32% × $20,000). This is limited to $5,200. The business percentage is then applied to $5,200. $5,200 × 60% = $3,840.

F. ALTERNATIVE DEPRECIATION SYSTEM (ADS).

1. ADS must be used for alternative minimum tax adjustments, international asset use, tax-exempt entities, tax-exempt bond financed assets, and assets from certain discriminating countries for earnings and profit purposes.

2. For personal property, taxpayers may use 150% declining balance instead of 200% declining balance and compute the ordinary tax instead of adjusting for the AMT. However, the period must be based on ADS, not the usual asset-class periods.

G. AMORTIZATION.

1. Certain intangible assets are amortizable over 15 years.

2. Section 197 assets include goodwill, trademarks, covenants not to compete, copyrights, and patents if they are used in a trade or business or for the production of income. Self-created intangibles are not considered amortizable assets under Section 197.

Example

Maria acquired a business on July 1 of the current year. The purchase price included a copyright valued at $30,000. Maria can claim $1,000 of amortization in the current year. The annual amortization will be $30,000 ÷ 15 = $2,000. Maria held it only six months during the current year.

H. DEPLETION.

1. Natural resources (except land) are subject to depletion. An owner of the resource is someone who acquires economic interest and receives income from the resource. The owner is entitled to a deduction for AGI to recover his costs. There are four types of expenditures: cost of natural resources, cost of intangible development, tangible asset costs, and operating costs.

2. Intangible drilling and development costs.

    a. There are two options for the taxpayer:

        i.   Expense in year incurred.

        ii. Capitalize and deplete.

    b. After the election is made, all future expenditures of a similar nature are handled the same way. Generally, the expense option is more advantageous.

3. Depletion methods.

    a. There are two depletion methods:

        i.   Cost.

        ii. Percentage.

    b. This is an annual election and usually the method yielding the larger deduction is chosen.

    c. Cost depletion – The asset basis is divided by the estimated total number of recoverable units of the asset and then multiplied by the number of units sold (not produced) to determine the amount of the deduction for the year. If the estimated total number of recoverable units is inaccurate, future calculations are based on a revised estimate.

    d. Percentage depletion – A statutory percentage is applied to the gross income from the property (limited to 50% of the gross income). This method is unrelated to the cost or basis of the asset.

e. Effect of intangible drilling costs on depletion – If the costs are capitalized, the basis of the property is increased and the cost depletion increases. If the costs are expensed, the 50% depletion limits may apply.

Example

Mr. Coleman owns a sulfur mine that had 100,000 total estimated tons when he purchased it for $2,000,000. In the current year, 20,000 tons were extracted and 18,000 tons were sold. The statutory percentage for sulfur is 22%. Gross income for the year was $1,000,000. His depletion deduction for the current year is $360,000.

Cost Method: $\dfrac{\$2,000,000}{100,000} \times 18,000 = \$360,000$

Percentage Method: 22% × 1,000,000 = $220,000.

Mr. Coleman's depletion deduction will be $360,000 (the higher of the two methods).

XIII. PASSIVE ACTIVITY LOSSES

A. TAX SHELTER INVESTMENTS.

1. Primarily, tax shelter investments defer or eliminate taxes for the investor. Before Congress curbed tax shelter abuse, the shelters allowed paper losses in excess of the amount of capital the investor provided due to the high expenses (depreciation, interest, development, etc.) and low revenues in the early years of a project.

2. Two major changes in the IRC have significantly reduced the benefit of tax shelters:

   a. At-risk limits.

   b. Passive activity loss limits.

3. At-risk limits are applied before the passive activity loss limits.

B. AT-RISK LIMITS.

1. The maximum deductible loss for an activity is limited to the amount that the investor has at risk at the end of the current tax year (i.e., the potential economic loss).

2. The amount at risk is the total of the cash and property invested and the debt for which the investor is personally liable (typically referred to as "recourse" debt). The amount is adjusted annually based on the taxpayer's share of profit or loss from the venture.

3. If a loss is disallowed because of at-risk rules, the loss can be carried forward and taken in the first year that the at-risk amount becomes a positive amount (enough to absorb the loss) or when the investment is sold.

Example

In 2006, Bob invested $50,000 for a 20% interest in a partnership in which he was a material participant during the year. The partnership incurred a loss, and Bob's share was $75,000.

Since Bob has only $50,000 of capital at risk, he cannot deduct more than $50,000 against his other income. Bob's nondeductible loss of $25,000 can be carried over and used when the at-risk provisions allow. If Bob has taxable income of $45,000 from the partnership in 2007 and no other transactions that affect his at-risk amount, he can use all of the $25,000 loss carried over from 2006. In this case, he would only recognize $20,000 of taxable income from the partnership.

C. PASSIVE ACTIVITY LOSS LIMITS.

1. Apply to:

   a. Individuals.

   b. Estates.

   c. Trusts.

   d. Closely Held C Corporations.

   e. Personal Service Corporations (PSCs).

2. In general, the passive activity loss rules divide all income into active, passive, and portfolio. The rules then limit the deduction for passive losses to the amount of passive income only (with exceptions for real estate activities).

3. The limits are applied to closely held corporations to prevent an individual or business from incorporating solely to take advantage of passive losses. Closely held corporations may offset passive losses against active income, but not portfolio income.

4. The limits are applied to Personal Service Corporations (PSCs) to prevent professionals from forming a PSC and using it to acquire investments that produce passive losses to deduct against active corporate profits. A PSC is a corporation where the primary economic activity is the performance of personal services by the owners of the corporation.

D. CLASSIFICATION OF INCOME AND LOSSES.

1. Taxpayer must classify income and losses into active, passive, or portfolio. Passive loss limitations prevent the taxpayer from deducting passive losses against active or portfolio income.

2. Active income examples are:

   a. Wages, salaries, and other employee compensation.

   b. Trade/business income when taxpayer is a material participant.

   c. Intangible property income when taxpayer significantly contributed to the creation.

   d. Qualified low-income housing project income.

3. Portfolio income examples are:

   a. Interest, dividends, annuities, and royalties.

   b. Gain/loss from disposition of property that produces portfolio income or is held for investment.

E. PASSIVE ACTIVITIES DEFINED.

1. Either of the following conditions creates a passive activity.

   a. The taxpayer does not materially participate (except oil and gas partnerships).

   b. The activity is a rental activity (even if the taxpayer does materially participate).

2. If the answer is "yes" to any of the following, the taxpayer is a material participant:

   a. Does taxpayer complete more than 500 hours of participation during the year?

   b. Does the individual's participation in the activity constitute substantially all of the participation in the activity of all individuals (including individuals who are not owners) for the year?

   c. Does taxpayer participate for more than 100 hours, and is this amount equal to or more than any other participant in the activity?

   d. Is the activity a significant participation activity (i.e., >100 hours of participation), and does total participation in all such activities exceed 500 hours?

   e. Did the taxpayer materially participate in the activity in at least five of the last ten years?

   f. Is the activity a personal service activity, and did the taxpayer materially participate in the activity in any of the three previous years?

   g. Using the existing facts and circumstances, did the taxpayer participate on a regular, continuous, and substantial basis during the year?

3. An oil or gas activity that involves a working interest in any oil or gas property that a taxpayer owns directly or through an entity that does not limit the taxpayer's liability interest is not a passive activity. Therefore, losses can be applied against active and portfolio income. This exception is applied on a well-by-well basis.

4. Limited partners are not material participants because they are not allowed to participate in the management of the business.

5. Rental Activities.

   a. Unless excepted by the Code, all rental activities are deemed passive. Rental activities occur when payments are received for the use of tangible property. If an activity is excepted by the Code, it must still pass the material participation test to be considered active.

   b. An activity is not rental under any of the following 6 conditions:

      i. The average customer use is 7 days or less.

      ii. The average customer use is 30 days or less, and the owner provides significant personal services.

      iii. The owner also provides extraordinary services (rental period is irrelevant).

      iv. The rental activity is incidental to a nonrental activity of taxpayer (investment or trade/business).

      v. The property is customarily made available during business hours for nonexclusive use by customers (e.g., golf course).

      vi. The property is used in a partnership, S corporation, or joint venture where the owner has an interest.

F. EXCEPTION FOR PUBLICLY TRADED PARTNERSHIPS.

   a. A publicly traded partnership is a partnership that is traded on an established securities market or is readily tradable on a secondary market.

   b. Publicly traded partnerships are sometimes referred to as master limited partnerships.

   c. Income from a publicly traded partnership:

      i. Cannot be used to offset losses from non-publicly-traded partnerships or other activities.

      ii. Cannot be used to offset losses from other publicly traded partnerships.

   d. Losses from a publicly traded partnership that are disallowed can be carried forward and allowed as a deduction in a year when the same publicly traded partnership has net income or is disposed of.

Example

Dana purchased an interest in a non-publicly traded partnership that had a loss in the current year of $15,000. She also purchased an interest in a master limited partnership with $20,000 of passive income. Since income from a publicly traded partnership cannot offset losses from non-publicly traded partnerships, the flow through income of $20,000 from the master limited partnership will be fully taxable to Dana this year, and the $15,000 of losses will be disallowed this year (and carried forward).

G. EXCEPTION FOR REAL ESTATE ACTIVITIES.

1. Real estate trade/business.

    a. Losses are not considered passive for certain real estate professionals provided that:

        i. Real estate is >50% of their personal services for the year, and

        ii. The taxpayer performs >750 hours of service in real property trades or business in which the taxpayer materially participates.

    b. Real estate professionals that meet the participation test above will treat losses from real estate rental activities as nonpassive and can offset those losses against active and portfolio income.

2. Real estate rental activities for non-real estate professionals.

    a. Individuals can deduct up to $25,000 of rental real estate losses against active and portfolio income.

    b. Two tests must be met to qualify for this exception:

        i. Active participation in the activity (participates in management decisions, an easier hurdle to clear than material participation), and

        ii. Ownership of 10% or more (in value) of all interests in the activity during the taxable year.

    c. The $25,000 offset allowance is reduced by 50% of AGI in excess of $100,000 (complete phaseout at $150,000 AGI). Therefore, there is a loss of $1 for every $2 of AGI greater than $100,000. The loss is deducted from the $25,000 maximum available. Note: If you are required to calculate this, there are two steps:

    1. Determine the maximum allowable loss after phaseout.

    2. Limit #1 by actual rental real estate losses incurred.

H. SUSPENDED LOSSES/CARRYOVERS.

The at-risk rules are applied before the passive loss rules. If a loss is not allowed because of the at-risk limitations, it is not a suspended loss under the passive loss rules. Rather, it is suspended under the at-risk rules.

Examples

- Ronnie, who earned a salary of $180,000, invested $30,000 for a 15% interest in a passive activity in the current year. Operations of the activity resulted in a loss of $300,000, of which Ronnie's share was $45,000. $15,000 of Ronnie's loss is suspended under the at-risk rules, which leaves a potential deduction of $30,000. The $30,000 loss is suspended under the passive loss rules because Ronnie does not have any passive income.

- Larry has the following income and losses for the current year:

Salary for managing an S corporation	$50,000
Dividend income from ABC Company stock	$1,000
Loss from a 20% limited partnership interest in Realty Capital Partners, a limited partnership	($4,000)
Loss from a 10% interest in an S corporation, in which he works full time managing one of the branches	($3,000)

His AGI is calculated as follows:

Salary	$50,000
Dividend Income	$1,000
Limited partnership interest (passive loss cannot be deducted because limited partners are not material participants)	0
S corporation interest (works full time, and is therefore a material participant)	($3,000)
Adjusted Gross Income	$48,000

XIV. EMPLOYEE EXPENSES

A. TYPE OF DEDUCTION.

1. Section 162 allows employees who incur expenses while performing their job duties a deduction for these amounts.

2. Most unreimbursed employee expenses are miscellaneous itemized deductions subject to the 2% of AGI floor. Exceptions include impairment-related work expenses of handicapped individuals (miscellaneous itemized deductions not subject to the 2% floor) and moving expenses (deduction for AGI).

3. For a self-employed taxpayer, job-related expenses are deductions <u>for</u> AGI (typically reported on Schedule C).

B. TRANSPORTATION.

1. Expenditures Allowed.

   a. Taxpayer may deduct unreimbursed expenditures related to transportation from one place to another while on company business as deductions from AGI (2% miscellaneous itemized deduction).

   b. Employee cannot be in travel status.

   c. Examples are automobile expenses, parking, and taxi fares.

2. Commuting.

   a. Normally disallowed (personal expense).

   b. Exceptions that allow a deduction.

      i. Transporting heavy tools (incremental cost only).

      ii. A commute to a second job (based on distance between jobs; location of taxpayer home is irrelevant).

      iii. Employer requires employee to travel between work stations (expenses between work stations only are deductible).

      iv. Taxpayer commutes to a temporary work location (generally defined as less than one year).

EXHIBIT 17: WHEN ARE LOCAL TRANSPORTATION EXPENSES DEDUCTIBLE?

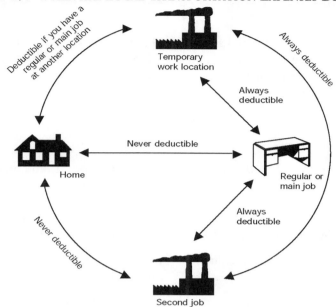

Publication 17; Figure 28-B

3. Computation of auto expenses.

  a. Actual operating cost method.

    i.   Include depreciation, gas, licenses, maintenance, insurance, etc.

    ii. Must be prorated between business and personal use.

  b. Automatic mileage method – A fixed amount of money per business mile plus tolls, parking, etc. The mileage rate for 2006 is .445 cents per mile.

  c. General rules – Either method is acceptable with the following constraints:

    i.   Vehicle must be owned or leased by the taxpayer claiming the deduction.

    ii. Only one vehicle can be used at any given time.

    iii. If standard mileage rate is used in Year 1, then MACRS cannot be used later.

    iv. If election to expense under Section 179 or MACRS is used in Year 1, then no change to the automatic mileage method is allowed.

C. TRAVEL.

1. Must be away from tax home.

  a. To deduct travel expenses, the taxpayer must determine the location of the tax home. Generally, the taxpayer's tax home is the regular place of business or post of duty regardless of where the taxpayer maintains the family home.

  b. If the taxpayer does not maintain a residence or have a regular place of business, the taxpayer is considered a transient (an itinerant). The tax home is wherever the taxpayer is currently working. As a transient, the taxpayer cannot claim a travel expense deduction because the taxpayer is never considered away from home.

Example

Tiffany lives in Cincinnati where she has a seasonal job for 8 months and earns $15,000. She works the remaining 4 months in Miami, also at a seasonal job, and earns $4,000. Cincinnati is her main place of work because she spends most of her time there and earns most of her income there.

---

2. Description of deduction.

   a. Transportation, meals, lodging, and incidentals while away from home on business.

   b. Expenditures are unreimbursed expenses and are miscellaneous itemized deductions subject to the 2% of AGI floor.

   c. An overnight stay is required. Overnight is defined as substantially longer than a work day.

   d. Meals and lodging are not deductible if the travel is a single day trip. Meals are limited to a 50% deduction.

3. The employee's absence from home must be temporary in nature.

   a. A temporary assignment must be 1 year or less. If assignment is more than 1 year, the tax home changes, and the away-from-home requirement is not met.

   b. The taxpayer's household cannot be moved to the new location.

4. Restrictions on certain types of business travel.

   a. Conventions must be related to the trade or business to be classified as deductible travel.

   b. Spousal travel is disallowed unless it is for a bona fide business purpose.

   c. Deductions for travel on cruise ships are limited to twice the highest per diem amount allowed for a day of domestic travel by employees in the executive branch of the federal government.

   d. While expenses related to attending a meeting or seminar related to income-producing activities are not allowed, they are deductible if connected with the taxpayer's trade or business. If the meeting is on a U.S. cruise ship, the maximum deductible amount is $2,000.

5. Combined business and pleasure travel.

   a. Domestic travel.

      i. A domestic trip must be primarily for business purposes in order to deduct transportation expenses. If primarily business, taxpayer can deduct 100% of transportation expenses. If not primarily business, taxpayer cannot deduct any transportation expenses.

      ii. Other expenses must be allocated between business and personal.

Example

Marleen works in Atlanta, and takes a business trip to New Orleans. On her way home, she stops in Mobile to visit her parents. She spends $630 for the 9 days she was away from home for travel, meals, lodging, and other travel expenses. If she had not stopped in Mobile, she would have been gone only 6 days and her total cost would have been $580. She can deduct $580 for her trip, including the cost of round-trip transportation to and from New Orleans. The cost of her meals is subject to the 50% limit on meal expenses.

---

    b.   Foreign travel.

        i.   An allocation of transportation expenses is required between business and personal travel unless:

           A)   The total time is 7 days or less, or

           B)   Less than 25% of the time was spent on personal travel, or

           C)   The taxpayer has no control over the schedule, or

           D)   The desire for vacation is not a major factor in deciding to take the trip.

Examples

- Victor traveled to Paris primarily for business. He left Denver on Tuesday and flew to New York. On Wednesday, he flew from New York to Paris, arriving the next morning. On Thursday and Friday, he had business discussions, and from Saturday until Tuesday, he was sightseeing. He flew back to New York, arriving Wednesday afternoon. On Thursday, he flew back to Denver. Although Victor was away from his home in Denver for more than a week, he was not outside the United States for more than a week because the day of departure does not count as a day outside the United States. He can deduct his cost of the round-trip flight between Denver and Paris. He can also deduct the cost of his stay in Paris for Thursday and Friday while he conducted business. However, he cannot deduct the cost of his stay in Paris from Saturday through Tuesday because those days were spent on nonbusiness activities.

- Jody flew from Seattle to Tokyo. She spent 14 days on business and 5 days on personal matters and then flew back to Seattle. She spent one day flying in each direction. Because only 5 of the 21 days (less than 25%) of her total time abroad was for nonbusiness activities, she can deduct as travel expenses what it would have cost her to make the trip if she had not engaged in any nonbusiness activity. The amount she can deduct is the cost of the round-trip plane fare and 16 days (14 days plus the 2 days of travel) of meals (subject to the 50% limit), lodging, and other related expenses.

Example

Allison took a trip from Montgomery, Alabama to London, England. She was away from home for 10 days. She spent 2 days vacationing and 8 days on business (including the 2 travel days). Her expenses are as follows:

Airfare	$1,200
Lodging (10 days × $150)	$1,500
Meals (10 days × $90)	$900

Allison's deduction is $2,760. [$1,200 + (8 × $150) + 1/2 (8 × $90) = $2,760]. Less than 25% of the time was personal so no allocation of transportation expenses is required.

EXHIBIT 18: DEDUCTIBLE TRAVEL EXPENSES

Expense	Description
Transportation	The cost of travel by airplane, train, or bus between your home and your business destination. If you were provided with a ticket or you are riding free as the result of a frequent traveler or similar program, your cost is zero.
Taxi, Commuter Bus, and Limousine	Fares for these and other types of transportation between the airport or station and your hotel, or between the hotel and your work location away from home.
Baggage and Shipping	The cost of sending baggage and sample or display material between your regular and temporary work location.
Car	The costs of operating and maintaining your car when traveling away from home on business. You may deduct actual expenses or the standard mileage rate, including business-related tolls and parking. If you lease a car while away from home on business, you can deduct business-related expenses only.
Lodging	The cost of lodging if your business trip is overnight or long enough to require you to get substantial sleep or rest to properly perform your duties.
Meals	The cost of meals only if your business trip is overnight or long enough to require you to stop to get substantial sleep or rest. Includes amounts spent for food, beverages, taxes, and related tips. Only 50% of meal expenses are allowed as a deduction.
Cleaning	Cleaning and laundry expenses while away from home overnight.
Telephone	The cost of business calls while on your business trip, including business communication by fax machine or other communication devices.
Tips	Tips you pay for any expenses in this chart.
Other	Other similar ordinary and necessary expenses related to your business travel such as public stenographer's fees and computer rental fees.

IRS Publication 334

D. EDUCATION EXPENSES.

1. General requirements for deductibility.

   a. To maintain or improve existing skills in the present job – Nondegree classes are allowed as long as they maintain or improve existing skills.

   b. To meet legally imposed or employer requirements to retain current job, such as continuing education requirements.

2. Nondeductible expenses.

   a. To meet minimum requirements of the current job (education degree to become a teacher).

   b. To qualify the taxpayer for a new job (law degree).

   c. For review classes or exams for items such as the CPA or bar exam.

3. Allowable expenditures.

   a. Direct expenses.

      i. Books.

      ii. Tuition.

      iii. Typing, photocopying, etc.

   b. Indirect expenses.

      i. Transportation (i.e., from office to school).

      ii. Travel.

         A) Meals subject to 50% reduction.

         B) Lodging.

      iii. Laundry while in travel status.

Example Question

Dawn, who holds a Bachelors degree in Art History, is a middle school teacher in New Orleans. She wants to further her education in Art History, believing this will allow her become a better teacher. Dawn spent her summer break attending the University of Hawaii taking art history courses. Her expenses are as follows:

Books and tuition	$2,000
Meals	1,000
Lodging	700
Laundry while in travel status	200
Transportation	700
Total	**$4,600**

What is Dawn's education expense deduction?

Answer: $4,100. [2,000 + 0.5 (1,000) + (700 + 200 + 700)] = 4,100. The shortcut would be to take the total and deduct 50% of the meals. Before taking this approach, it would be wise to check each category and make sure each category is deductible.

EXHIBIT 19: DEDUCTIBLE EDUCATIONAL EXPENSES FLOW DIAGRAM

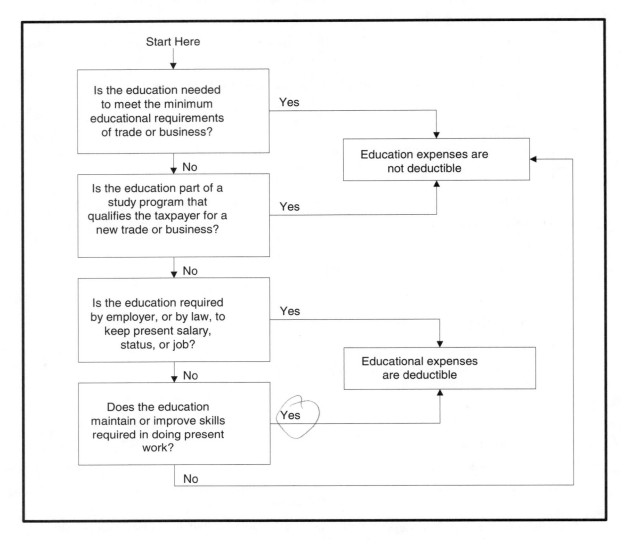

IRS Publication 17

E. MEALS AND ENTERTAINMENT (ONLY 50% DEDUCTIBLE).

1. Entertainment expenses are subject to the 50% reduction.

    a. Meals – Including taxes and tips.

    b. Entertainment – Including cover charges, parking, and entertainment room rentals.

2. There are exceptions to the 50% reduction.

    a. Transportation (e.g., cab fare).

    b. If the full value of expenditure is included in employee's compensation.

    c. If the value is de minimis.

    d. If it is a company event (e.g., parties or picnics).

3. Classification of expenses.

   a. Directly related to business.

      i. Entertainment precedes or follows an actual business meeting.

      ii. Not necessary for actual benefit to occur but must have expectation of benefit.

      iii. The expenditure should be in a clear business setting.

   b. Associated with business.

      i. Promoting goodwill and maintaining customer relations.

      ii. There must be intent to obtain new business or to continue existing business.

4. Restrictions.

   a. Business meals.

      i. Directly related to or associated with a business meeting.

      ii. Must be reasonable cost.

      iii. Taxpayer must be present at the meal.

   b. Club dues.

      i. No deduction allowed.

      ii. Entertainment costs at club may still qualify (subject to 50% deductibility).

   c. Tickets for entertainment.

      i. Eligible amount is limited to face value of the tickets plus tax (but not fees).

      ii. Skybox amount limited to number of seats available (even if all are not used) times price of regular seats.

      iii. Subject to 50% deductibility.

   d. Business gifts.

      i. Limited to $25 per donee per year.

      ii. Gifts less than $4 and promotional items (e.g., pens with business name) are excluded from limits.

      iii. Additional deductions allowed for incidental costs (e.g., engraving, delivery, gift wrapping).

      iv. No deduction allowed for gifts to superiors or employers.

      v. Employee achievement awards based on length of service or safety under $400 are excluded.

Examples

- Kay entertains one of her clients and incurs the following:

Taxi	$30
Door cover fee	25
Dinner	128
Tips to waitress	25
Total	**$208**

Assuming proper substantiation, Kay's deduction is $119. [30 + 1/2 (25 + 128 + 25)] = 119.

- Chelsea, the sales director for a software company, pays $2,000 to obtain a skybox for an evening production of "Cats." The skybox holds 15 seats and Chelsea invites 14 clients. Nonluxury seats sell for $25 each. The refreshments served to Chelsea and her clients cost $455. A substantial business discussion was held before and after the show and Chelsea has all necessary substantiation. Chelsea's deduction is $415. 50% [(15 seats × $25) + 455] = $415.

- Elizabeth made the following gifts during the current year:

To Candace, a key client ($4 of the amount listed was for gift wrapping)	$104
To Kathy, Elizabeth's secretary, on Kathy's birthday	24
To Jan, Elizabeth's boss, at Christmas	28
Total Gifts	**$156**

Assuming proper substantiation, Elizabeth's deduction is $53. $29 ($25 + $4) + $24 = $53. The cost of gift wrapping is allowed. No deduction is available for a gift to a superior. $25 per person limit.

F. HOME OFFICE.

1. Must be exclusively and regularly used for business, and must also be one of the following:

   a. Must be principal place of business.

      i. A home office will be considered a principal place of business if it is used exclusively and regularly by the taxpayer for administrative or management activities of a trade or business, and there is no other fixed location where these activities are performed to a substantial extent.

   b. Place of business used by clients, patients, or customers.

2. Deductions and limits.

   a. Requires allocation of total household expenses.

   b. Cannot exceed net income of business (i.e., cannot create a loss).

   c. Must first deduct expenses that would be allowed anyway (i.e., taxes, mortgage interest).

   d. For self-employed individuals, the deduction is for AGI.

   e. For employees, the deduction is from AGI (2% miscellaneous itemized deduction).

   f. Disallowed expenses can be carried forward.

3. Coordination with personal residence gain exclusion.

   a. When an individual taxpayer sells a principal residence, he or she can exclude up to $250,000 of gain ($500,000 if married) if he or she owns the home and uses it as a principal residence for at least two out of five years preceding the sale.

   b. In general, when a personal residence is also used for business purposes, such as a home office, the home must be divided into two properties when sold.

      i. The portion of the gain attributable to the personal use is generally eligible for the gain exclusion.

      ii. The portion of the gain attributable to the business use may be taxable as a sale of a business asset.

         A) If the home office portion was used as a principal residence for two of the five years preceding the sale, the taxpayer can exclude gain on the entire residence. However, gain attributable to depreciation deductions occurring after May 6, 1997 will still be taxable.

         B) If the home office portion was NOT used as a principal residence for two of the five years preceding the sale, the taxpayer will be taxed on the business portion of the residence.

Example

Jerry, an unmarried individual, purchased a residence on May 1, 2001. He originally used the entire home as a personal residence. On June 1, 2003, he began using 15% of the home as a home office. He continued to use the home office until May 1, 2005, when he sold the home.

Because he used his entire home as a personal residence for 25 months during the five year period prior to sale, he will qualify for the maximum exclusion of $250,000. However, any gain attributable to depreciation claimed will be taxable to Jerry.

G. JOB HUNTING EXPENSES.

1. Seeking new employment in the same trade or business is deductible whether the taxpayer gets the job or not.

2. Seeking employment in different trade or business is not deductible under any circumstances.

3. Deductible expenses include travel, printing, postage, and employment agency fees.

4. No deduction is allowed if you are seeking employment for the first time.

H. OTHER EMPLOYEE EXPENSES.

1. Classified as Miscellaneous Itemized Deductions, subject to the 2% of AGI floor.

    a. Professional dues and subscriptions.

    b. Union dues and work uniforms.

    c. Malpractice insurance premiums.

2. Miscellaneous expenses not subject to 2% floor.

    a. Impairment-related work expenses of handicapped individuals.

    b. Gambling losses to the extent of gambling winnings.

I. REIMBURSED EMPLOYEE EXPENSES.

1. Accountable plans.

    a. Requires adequate accounting of all expenditures.

    b. Employee must return any unused allowance.

    c. Requires substantiation.

        i. Amount of expenditure.

        ii. Time and place of expenditure.

        iii. Business purpose.

        iv. Relationship to person entertained.

        v. Itemized receipts for all lodging.

        vi. Itemized receipts for all expenditures $75 or more.

        vii. Not required if a per diem method is used.

    d. Reimbursements are excluded from employee's gross income and expenses are not deductible from gross income.

    e. If employee does not comply, the nonaccountable plan rules are used.

2. Nonaccountable plans.

    a. If you are not in an accountable plan, then you are in a nonaccountable plan.

    b. All reimbursements are income to the employee.

        i. Expenses related to the reimbursement are deductible as miscellaneous itemized deductions subject to the 2% of AGI floor.

    c. Unreimbursed employee expenditures.

        i. 50% deductibility applies for meals and entertainment.

        ii. Expenses are deductible as miscellaneous itemized deductions subject to the 2% floor.

        iii. If reimbursement is available and not sought, no deduction is allowed.

3. Per diem allowances for meals and lodging.

   a. Simplifies record keeping.

   b. The IRS publishes tables that provide per diem amounts for lodging and for meals and incidental expenses (based on city location).

XV. ITEMIZED DEDUCTIONS

A. ITEMIZED DEDUCTIONS – IN GENERAL.

1. Major itemized deductions.

   a. Medical expenses.

   b. Taxes.

   c. Interest.

   d. Charitable contributions.

   e. Casualty losses.

2. Miscellaneous itemized deductions.

   a. Deductions not subject to the 2% floor.

      i. Impairment related work expenses.

      ii. Gambling losses.

      iii. Annuity contract basis recovery.

      iv. Pro rata portion of estate taxes paid with respect to income in respect of decedent.

   b. Deductions subject to the 2% floor.

      i. Employee business expenses.

      ii. Home office expenses.

      iii. Investment expenses.

      iv. Tax return preparation fees.

      v. All other miscellaneous itemized deductions.

B. MEDICAL EXPENSES.

1. In general.

   a. Includes expenditures for taxpayer, spouse, and any dependents.

   b. Must not be reimbursed expenditures.

   c. Subject to 7.5% of AGI floor.

   d. Must be paid on behalf of taxpayer, spouse, or dependent.

2. What is covered.

   a. Diagnosis, cure, mitigation, treatment, or prevention of disease.

   b. Transportation primarily for and essential to the medical expenses in (a) above.

   c. Qualified long-term care services (subject to certain limits).

   d. Insurance premiums covering all of the above (subject to certain limits).

3. What is not covered.

   a. Unnecessary cosmetic surgery.

   b. Funerals.

4. Diagnosis, cure, mitigation, treatment, or prevention of disease.

   a. Examples: hospital charges, doctor's fees, glasses, insurance premiums, stop-smoking programs, surgery to correct vision, legal abortion, and weight loss programs.

   b. Prescription medicines and insulin.

   c. Nursing home expenditures (including meals) may be allowed if medical care is primary reason for admittance.

   d. Cost of lead-based paint removal.

   e. Surgery to correct a congenital deformity or disfiguring disease.

   f. Tuition for a special school may be allowed if the school has special facilities or medical care related to the infirmity is received.

   g. Capital expenditures – allowable with some restrictions.

      i. Expenditures are of a medical nature.

      ii. Expenditures are on the advice of a physician.

      iii. Facilities are used primarily by patient alone.

      iv. Facilities are built at a reasonable expense.

      v. Operating and maintenance expenditures are also allowable.

      vi. Appraisal costs for determining the change in value are also allowable (miscellaneous itemized deduction subject to 2% of AGI floor).

      vii. Capital expenditure deduction is allowed in the year incurred, not in the year paid.

      viii. Limited to the amount that the expenditures exceed any increase in the value of the property.

      ix. Deduction is only allowed while the medical condition exists.

      x. The 7.5% AGI floor applies to capital expenditures.

5. Transportation and lodging.

   a. These expenditures are allowed as medical expenses (subject to 7.5% AGI floor).

   b. Includes: fares, ambulance, personal car, tolls, parking, etc. Personal car allowance can be actual expenses or standard rate ($0.18/mile plus parking and tolls for 2006).

   c. Includes the travel costs of parent with a minor child.

   d. Includes the travel costs of any person necessary to travel with the patient.

    e.   Lodging also included with some restrictions.

        i.   Must be primary and essential for medical care.

        ii.   Must be in a licensed medical care facility.

        iii.   Accommodations must be reasonable.

        iv.   No significant element of personal pleasure can be involved.

        v.   Limited to $50 per night for each person.

    f.   No meal deduction is allowed with one exception.

        i.   If meals are provided on site and are part of the medical care.

        ii.   The 50% meal deductibility does not apply to this exception.

6.   Qualified long-term care expenses.

    a.   Medical services for a chronically ill person which are provided under a prescribed plan of care.

        i.   Chronically ill is defined as being unable to perform (without substantial assistance from another individual) at least 2 activities of daily living (e.g., eating, dressing, bathing) for a period of at least 90 days due to a loss of functional capacity.

    b.   Includes expenditures for diagnostic, therapeutic, preventive, rehabilitative and personal care services.

7.   Health insurance premiums.

    a.   Expenditures for accident and health insurance premiums are deductible (subject to 7.5% AGI floor).

        i.   Individual and group policies are covered.

        ii.   Any premiums paid by the employer are not deductible.

        iii.   Special rules for self-employed persons.

            A)   100% of the health insurance premiums can be deducted for AGI.

            B)   No deduction is allowed for premiums paid by an employee if an employer-paid plan is available.

    b.   The premiums paid for long-term care are qualifying medical expenses subject to the 7.5% AGI floor. The maximum deductible premium depends on the taxpayer's age.

EXHIBIT 20: 2006 MAXIMUM DEDUCTIBLE LONG-TERM CARE PREMIUMS
(SUBJECT TO 7.5% OF AGI FLOOR)

Attained Age Before Close of Taxable Year	Annual Maximum Deductible Premiums
40 or less	$280
More than 40 but not more than 50	$530
More than 50 but not more than 60	$1060
More than 60 but not more than 70	$2,830
More than 70	$3,530

8. Year of deduction.

   a. A deduction is available in the year paid for both cash-basis and accrual-basis taxpayers.

   b. A deduction is available in the year incurred for deceased taxpayers.

   c. If a payment is made on a credit card, the payment is deemed to have been made at the time of the charge.

   d. A current deduction is not allowed for prepayment of future medical care unless the taxpayer is under an obligation to make the payment.

9. Reimbursements.

   a. Expected reimbursements are disregarded in determining the amount of deduction.

   b. Tax benefit rule applies if a reimbursement occurs in a future year.

   c. Reimbursement is considered part of gross income if a tax benefit resulted.

Example

Mae, an employee of XYZ Company, has an AGI of $20,000. She incurred the following medical expenses (she itemizes her deductions):

Health insurance premiums	$850
Dental expenses	$500
Unreimbursed medical	$450 ($1,000 medical expenses less $550 reimbursement)

Her total medical expenses are $1,800 ($850 + $500 + $450). She must reduce this amount by 7.5% of her AGI. Therefore, deductible medical expenses are $300 ($1,800 – $1,500 (7.5% of $20,000)).

C. TAXES.

1. General.

   a. Taxes defined.

      i. An enforced contribution.

      ii. Purpose is to raise revenue (i.e., not payment for special use or privilege).

        iii. Certain taxes are deductible as an itemized deduction.

    b. Fees defined.

        i. Purpose is to collect payment for a special use or privilege.

        ii. Only deductible as a business expense (ordinary and necessary).

2. Summary of deductible taxes.

    a. State, local, and foreign real property taxes.

    b. State and local personal property taxes (if tax is based on value of property).

    c. State, local, and foreign income taxes.

    d. State and local sales taxes (in lieu of deduction for state and local income taxes).

3. Property taxes, assessments, and apportionment of taxes.

    a. Property taxes.

        i. Deductible for the person the taxes are imposed on regardless of who pays them.

        ii. Must be based on the value of the property (ad valorem).

    b. Assessments.

        i. Imposed for purposes of local benefit (e.g., roads, schools, etc.), actions that typically increase the value of the property.

        ii. Usually not deductible but added to the basis of the property.

    c. Apportionment for real estate transfers.

        i. Based on the number of days each held the property during the tax year.

        ii. Apportionment rules govern the deduction – not the purchase agreement.

        iii. Based on the date of the transfer.

        iv. If purchase agreement does not apportion, then basis adjustment is required.

            A) If buyer pays all the tax:

                1) Seller's portion is added to the amount realized by the seller.

                2) Buyer's basis is increased by the same amount.

            B) If seller pays all the tax:

                1) Buyer's portion is deducted from the amount realized by seller.

                2) Buyer's basis is reduced by the same amount.

4. State and local income taxes.

    a. These taxes paid are itemized deductions only.

    b. For cash-basis taxpayers the amount included is the withheld amount.

    c. Estimated tax payments are also allowed as deductions.

    d. Refunds occurring in future years are included in Gross Income at that time, to the extent a tax benefit was received.

    e. Any state income taxes that are paid, whether for the previous, current, or future year, are deducted in the year paid.

5. Remember that property taxes and state/local income taxes incurred in a trade or business or on production of income property are deductions for AGI.

6. State and local general sales taxes.

    a. Individual taxpayers may elect to deduct either state and local income taxes, or state and local sales taxes as an itemized deduction.

        i.   Each year, individuals should consider whether or not to make this election, depending upon their relative amounts of state and local income taxes compared to sales taxes.

        ii. This election would especially be appropriate for taxpayer's residing in a state that does not impose a state income tax.

    b. Amount of deduction.

        i.   The taxpayer can deduct the actual amount of general sales taxes paid. This would require the taxpayer to accumulate receipts showing sales taxes paid.

        ii. Alternatively, the taxpayer may determine their deduction using standardized IRS tables. If the standard IRS tables are used, the taxpayer can claim an additional deduction for sales taxes paid for the purchase of a motor vehicle or boat.

    c. The deduction for sales taxes is subject to the phase-out limitation on itemized deductions for taxpayers with adjusted gross income exceeding specified amounts.

Examples

- Robin's employer withheld $4,200 in state income taxes in 2005, and she paid an additional $1,200 in estimated state income tax payments. She filed her 2004 state income tax return in April 2005, and received a state tax refund of $700 in 2005. She claimed the standard deduction on her federal return for 2004. If she itemizes, she can deduct $5,400 ($4,200 + $1,200) in state income tax on her 2005 federal income tax return. The $700 refund is not offset against the itemized deduction and is not taxable income because Robin claimed the standard deduction for 2004.

- Sherry generally itemizes deductions and is a resident of a state that imposes income tax. Information regarding Sherry's state income tax transactions for 2005 is as follows:

State taxes withheld in 2006	$7,200
Refund received in 2006 from overpayment of 2005 state tax liability	1,500
Deficiency assessed as paid for 2004 (as a result of audit by the state)	3,000
Interest paid on the tax deficiency	500

The 2004 deficiency and interest thereon were paid by Sherry in 2006. If she elects to itemize deductions for 2006, she can deduct $10,200. (7,200 + 3,000) = 10,200. The interest on the deficiency is personal interest and is not deductible. The refund is reported as income under the tax benefit rule. It does not affect the amount deductible.

EXHIBIT 21: WHICH TAXES CAN YOU DEDUCT?

	You Can Deduct	You Cannot Deduct
Income Taxes	State and local income taxes. Foreign income taxes. Employee contributions to state funds listed under contributions to state benefit funds. One-half of self-employment tax paid.	Federal income taxes. Employee contributions to private or voluntary disability plans. State and local general sales taxes (if you choose to deduct state and local income taxes).
General Sales Taxes	State and local general sales taxes.	State and local income taxes (if you choose to deduct state and local general sales taxes).
Real Estate Taxes	State and local real estate taxes. Foreign real estate taxes. Tenant's share of real estate taxes paid by cooperative housing corporation.	Taxes for local benefits (with exceptions). Trash and garbage pickup fees (with exceptions). Rent increase due to higher real estate taxes. Homeowners' association charges.
Personal Property Taxes	State and local personal property taxes.	Import duties.
Other Taxes	Taxes that are expenses of your trade or business or of producing income. Taxes on property producing rent or royalty income. Occupational taxes.	State and local sales and use taxes. Federal excise taxes, such as telephone taxes. (see Taxes and Fees You Cannot Deduct). Per capita taxes.
Fees and Charges	Fees and charges that are expenses of your trade or business or of producing income.	Fees and charges that are not expenses of your trade or business or of producing income, such as fees for driver's licenses, car inspections, parking, or charges for water bills (see Taxes and Fees you Cannot Deduct). Fines and penalties.

IRS Publication 17; Table 24-1

D. INTEREST.

1. Investment interest.

   a. Interest on funds borrowed to acquire investment assets.

   b. Deduction for investment interest is limited to net taxable investment income.

      i. Investment income.

         A) Gross income from interest, dividends, annuities, royalties, etc.

B) Dividends taxed at the JGTRRA reduced rates are not included in investment income.

C) Capital gains, taxed at the capital gain rate, are not included in investment income.

D) Cannot be derived in the ordinary course of business.

E) Does not include tax-exempt interest income.

    ii. Investment expenses.

        A) Must be directly connected with the production of income.

        B) Do not include interest expense in investment expenses for this calculation.

        C) Includes subscriptions to professional newsletters, safe deposit box rentals, etc.

  c. Net investment income = investment income – investment expenses.

  d. Carryover of disallowed investment interest allowed indefinitely.

Example

Mario had the following items of income and expense for the current year:

Interest income from Inron Company bonds	$5,000
Interest income from State of Louisiana bonds	$1,000
Margin interest expense (investment interest expense)	($7,000)

If he itemizes, Mario can only deduct $5,000 of the investment interest expense. His taxable investment income is $5,000 ($5,000 TAXABLE interest). The State of Louisiana bonds are municipal bonds, and the interest is tax exempt.

---

2. Qualified residence interest.

  a. Interest paid or incurred on debt for a qualified residence of the taxpayer is deductible.

    i. Qualified residence includes a primary residence and one other residence.

    ii. May include a condo, trailer, boat with living quarters, and mobile homes.

    iii. The debt must be secured by the property.

    iv. Maximum allowable acquisition indebtedness is $1,000,000 ($500,000 for married filing separately).

    v. Acquisition indebtedness also includes construction and substantial improvements.

  b. Home equity loans are also covered. Interest is deductible on the indebtedness to the lesser of:

    i. FMV less acquisition indebtedness.

    ii. $100,000.

Example

Mary owned a home with a FMV of $400,000. The first mortgage had a balance of $320,000. Mary takes out a home equity loan of $90,000. How much of the debt will be qualified residence interest? All of Mary's first mortgage (acquisition indebtedness) will qualify, but only $80,000 ($400,000-$320,000, the actual equity in the home) will qualify on the home equity loan since total indebtedness cannot exceed FMV.

---

3. Interest paid for services.

    a. Points on a home loan are deductible in the year paid (principal residence loans only).

        i. Borrower is treated as paying any points seller paid for borrower's mortgage.

        ii. Can deduct points up to funds provided plus seller-paid points.

        iii. Buyer must reduce basis in home by points paid by seller. Seller reduces amount realized by this amount.

    b. Points on other loans must be capitalized and amortized.

    c. Must be compensation for use of money.

    d. Points on refinancing must be capitalized and amortized over the life of the loan. However, if refinancing is incurred for home improvements, and the points are paid from separate funds, the points are currently deductible.

Examples

- When Gary took out a $100,000 mortgage loan to buy his home in the current year, he was charged one percentage point ($1,000). He met all the tests for deducting points except the only funds he provided were a $750 down payment. Of the $1,000 charged for points, he can deduct $750 in the current year.

- When Stephanie took out a $100,000 mortgage loan to buy her home in the current year, she was charged one percentage point ($1,000). Tim, who sold her the home also paid one point ($1,000) to help her get her mortgage. Stephanie met all the tests for deducting points, except the only funds she provided were a $750 down payment. In the current year, Stephanie can deduct $1,750 ($750 of the amount she was charged plus the $1,000 paid by Tim). She must reduce the basis of her home by the $1,000 paid by Tim.

---

4. Prepayment penalty – Considered to be interest paid and is deductible (if the interest itself is eligible).

5. Interest paid to related parties.

   a. Deductible according to normal interest rules.

   b. Refer to rules on loans to related parties.

6. Other restrictions.

   a. Cannot deduct interest paid on behalf of another (e.g., child, parent).

   b. Prepaid interest deduction is based on accrual-basis rules for all taxpayers.

7. Classification.

   a. If interest is paid for a business use or the production of income, then it is deductible for AGI.

   b. If interest is paid for personal use (investment interest and qualified residence interest), then it is deductible from AGI.

8. Personal Interest – Personal interest is not deductible (e.g., bank cards, consumer loans).

Example

During the current year, Albert paid the following interest charges:

Home mortgage	$9,000
On loan to purchase household furniture (personal)	800
On loan to purchase State of Louisiana general obligation bonds (tax exempt)	750

If Albert itemizes his deductions for the current year, the amount deductible as interest expense is $9,000. The interest on the loan to purchase household furniture is nondeductible consumer interest. The interest on the loan to purchase State of Louisiana bonds is not deductible.

Example

Rowena, a single taxpayer, purchased an airplane for $130,000. In order to obtain financing for the purchase, Rowena issued a lien on her personal residence in the amount of $130,000. At the time, the residence had a fair market value of $400,000 and a first mortgage of $320,000. For the plane loan, Rowena may claim the interest on $80,000 as deductible home mortgage interest. Home equity loans are limited to the lesser of:

- The fair market value of the residence, reduced by acquisition indebtedness, or

- $100,000.

Thus, $400,000 (fair market value) – $320,000 (first mortgage) provides a limit of $80,000. Interest on the remaining $50,000 of the loan will be treated under the consumer interest rules (i.e., not deductible).

---

9. Certain taxpayers may deduct up to $2,500 (for 2006) of interest paid on a higher education loan.

    a. AGI phaseout for 2006:

        • Joint return $105,000 – 135,000

        • All others $50,000 – 65,000

E. CHARITABLE CONTRIBUTIONS.

1. Donations to what kind of organizations qualify for a deduction?

    a. Must be made to a qualified organization.

        i. U.S. District of Columbia, a state or possession of the U.S., or a political subdivision of a state or possession.

        ii. Organizations located in U.S. that are organized and operated exclusively for religious, charitable, scientific, literary, or educational purposes or for the prevention of cruelty to children or animals.

        iii. Veterans' organizations.

        iv. Cemetery companies.

        v. IRS Publication 78 lists qualified charitable organizations. This information can also be obtained from www.irs.gov.

EXHIBIT 22: EXAMPLES OF CHARITABLE CONTRIBUTIONS – A QUICK CHECK

Use the following lists for a quick check of contributions you can or cannot deduct. See *Publication 17; Section 26* for more information and additional rules and limits that may apply.

Deductible as Charitable Contributions	Not Deductible as Charitable Contributions
Money or property you give to:	Money or property you give to:
• Churches, synagogues, temples, mosques, and other religious organizations	• Civic leagues, social sports clubs, labor unions, and chambers of commerce
• Federal, state, and local governments, if your contribution is solely for public purposes (for example, a gift to reduce the public debt)	• Foreign organizations (except certain Canadian, Israeli, and Mexican charities)
• Nonprofit schools and hospitals	• Groups that are run for personal profit
• Public parks and recreation facilities	• Groups whose purpose is to lobby for law changes
• Salvation Army, Red Cross, CARE, Goodwill Industries, United Way, Boy Scouts, Girl Scouts, Boys and Girls Clubs of America, etc.	• Homeowners' associations
• War veterans' groups	• Individuals
Costs you pay for a student living with you, sponsored by a qualified organization	• Political groups or candidates for public office
Out-of-pocket expenses when you serve a qualified organization as a volunteer	Cost of raffle, bingo, or lottery tickets
	Dues, fees, or bills paid to country clubs, lodges, fraternal orders, or similar groups
	Tuition
	Value of your time or services
	Value of blood given to a blood bank

IRS Publication 17; Table 26-1

2. Qualifying organizations are also classified as:

   a. Public charities.

      i. Receive broad public support.

      ii. General examples – churches, educational institutions, hospitals, medical research organizations.

      iii. Specific examples – American Red Cross, Girl Scouts, United Way, Goodwill, Mercer University.

   b. Private foundations.

      i. Not defined directly in the Code but, rather, by reference to a list of the types of organizations that are not private foundations.

      ii. Typically funded by large contributions from a small number of contributors and income from investments and businesses unrelated to the foundation's charitable purposes.

      iii. Usually functions as a charity by making grants to organizations that conduct charitable activities, instead of performing the activities itself.

3. Deduction is allowed in year paid for both cash and accrual-basis taxpayers.

4. Consequences of a benefit received by donor.

   a. If benefit is inconsequential, may deduct in full.

   b. If a consequential benefit is received, the contribution deduction must be reduced by the fair market value of the benefit.

   c. There is a special rule for contribution related to the right to buy athletic tickets from universities – 80% of donation qualifies as deductible charitable contribution.

5. No deductions allowed for volunteering of services, but related personal expenses are deductible.

   a. Mileage for charitable use of an automobile is 18 cents per mile (for 2006) or actual unreimbursed expenses for oil and gas.

   b. Rental value of property used by a qualified charity is not deductible.

   c. Cost of child care while performing charity-related activities is nondeductible.

   d. Donating blood is considered to be a nondeductible personal service.

6. Record keeping.

   a. Must have written receipt for gifts over $250.

      i. Receipt must have amount of cash or description of property.

      ii. Taxpayer must have receipt by due date of return or when return is filed.

   b. Noncash property over $500 and less than or equal to $5,000.

      i. An appraisal is not required. However, taxpayers may wish to get an independent appraisal to support the deduction claimed.

   c. Noncash property over $5,000 ($10,000 for nonpublic stock).

    i.   Noncash contributions with a value over $5,000 must be substantiated by a qualified appraisal of the property. A summary of the appraisal must be attached to the donor's income tax return for the year in which the deduction is first claimed.

    ii.   The appraisal requirement will also apply if a taxpayer donates, to one or more charities, a number of similar items (such as coins) with a total value exceeding $5,000.

    iii.   An appraisal is not required for contributions of publicly traded securities for which market quotes are readily available on an established securities market.

    iv.   The costs of an appraisal are not deductible as a charitable contribution. However, these costs are deductible by individuals as miscellaneous itemized deductions, subject to the 2% of AGI floor.

d.   Valuation.

    i.   Generally, fair market value at the date of gift.

    ii.   Taxpayer must keep records of terms of agreement, basis, appraisals, etc.

7. Limits.

a.   General.

    i.   Depending on the type of property and the type of charity, there is a limit on the amount of deductible contribution.

    ii.   There is an overall 50% of AGI limit for <u>all</u> charitable contributions during a year.

    iii.   Carryover up to five years is available for disallowed amounts.

b.   Ordinary income property – property that, if sold, gives rise to ordinary income.

    i.   Includes inventory, taxpayer-created art and short-term capital assets.

    ii.   Deduction is the lesser of the FMV or adjusted basis.

c.   Capital gain property – Property that, if sold, gives rise to long-term capital gain or Sec. 1231 gain.

    i.   Stocks, bonds, real estate, etc.

    ii.   Deduction amount equals FMV.

        A)   Exception for capital gain portion of property given to some private foundations (do not receive funding from the general public, e.g., Ford Foundation).

            1)   If operating foundation (spends its income on charitable purpose) – fully deductible.

            2)   If nonoperating foundation – only adjusted basis is deductible.

        B)   Exception for capital gain portion of tangible personalty (to any organization).

            1)   If the donee puts property to unrelated use – adjusted basis only.

            2)   Fully deductible if donor believes that property will be put to a related use.

d.   Contributions made to the following organizations cannot exceed 50% of AGI.

    i.   Religious, public, education, governmental institutions.

    ii.   Private operating foundations.

      iii. Some private nonoperating foundations.

         A) If they distribute within 2½ months of the beginning of the following year to public charities and private operating foundations.

         B) If they pool donations and distribute.

   e. The following contributions are limited to 30% of AGI.

      i. Cash and ordinary income property to private nonoperating foundations (that do not qualify as 50% organizations).

      ii. Applies to LTCG property donated to 50% organizations.

      iii. If donor elects to forego deduction of capital gain, property moves to 50%.

      iv. If donor elects to forego capital gain, deduction is lost – not carried over.

      v. Donations to 50% organizations are applied to limits before 30% gifts.

   f. 20% Ceiling – Applies to LTCG property given to nonoperating foundations (not 50% organizations).

EXHIBIT 23: CHARITABLE CONTRIBUTION DEDUCTIONS

Types of Property	Amount of Deduction	Limit for Public Charities, Private Operating Foundations and Certain Private Nonoperating Foundations	Limit for Other Private Nonoperating Foundations
Cash	FMV	50% of AGI	30% of AGI
Ordinary Income Property and ST Capital Gain Property	Lesser of the adjusted basis or the FMV	50%	30%
Long-Term CG Property:			
• Intangibles	FMV	30%	20%
	Basis election	50%	20%
• Tangible Property (related use)	FMV	30%	20%
	Basis election	50%	20%
• Tangible Property (unrelated use)	Basis	50%	20%
• Real Property	FMV	30%	20%
	Basis election	50%	20%

Example

Gina graduated from Mumford University. She donated $2,000 to the athletic department of the University to guarantee priority to purchase two premium season tickets to home football games. In addition, Gina purchased two season tickets for the regular price of $500 ($250 each). Gina's charitable contribution for the current year is $1,600. 80% of $2,000 is deductible since Gina is paying for the right to purchase tickets. The $500 expenditure for the tickets cannot be claimed since it provided Gina with a benefit.

---

8. Bargain Sale to Charity.

    a. In General.

        i.   A bargain sale to charity occurs when a donor/seller transfers property to a charity (or other tax-exempt organization) in exchange for a sum that is less than the FMV of the property.

        ii. Considered part sale and part charitable contribution.

    b. Income and estate tax ramifications.

        i.   The difference between the sales price of the asset and the seller's basis allocated to the asset will be a capital gain to the seller for income tax purposes.

        ii. The difference between the fair market value of the asset and the consideration received is considered the allowable FMV for the charitable contribution. The basis not allocated to the sale of the asset is the basis for the consideration of the charitable contribution.

        iii. The buyer's tax basis is equal to the price paid plus the carryover basis from the donor of the gifted portion.

        iv. The property sold will not be included in the seller's gross estate upon death.

    c. Basis allocation.

        i.   The basis of the property sold in a bargain sale to charity must be allocated between the portion of the property sold and the portion donated to charity.

        ii. The formula to calculate the basis of the property sold is: [(Amount realized on sale to charity / Fair market value of entire property) × Adjusted basis of entire property].

Example

Steve owns property with a basis of $60,000 and a current value of $120,000, which he sells to charity for $100,000. Steve must first allocate basis between the sale and the charitable gift.

Basis for property sold = [($100,000 / 120,000) × $60,000] = $50,000

Therefore, Steve will have a capital gain of $50,000 computed as follows:

Cash received from charity	$100,000
Less: Adjusted basis allocated to asset sale	(50,000)
Equals: Capital gain	$ 50,000

He will also have a FMV for calculation of the charitable income tax deduction of $20,000, computed as follows:

Fair market value of property transferred to charity	$120,000
Less: Sales price	(100,000)
Equals: FMV for the charitable contribution	$ 20,000

The adjusted taxable basis for the calculation of the charitable income tax deduction will be calculated as follows:

Total adjusted taxable basis (ATB)	$ 60,000
Less: Allocated to sale	(50,000)
Equals: ATB for charitable purposes	$ 10,000

Example

- Clarence makes the following charitable donations:

	Basis	Fair Market Value
Inventory held for resale in Clarence's business (a sole proprietorship)	$8,000	$6,000
Stock in Roth Corp. held as an investment (acquired 2 years ago)	10,000	40,000
Coin collection held as an investment (acquired 10 years ago)	1,000	7,000

[handwritten: Ordinary Income Property →]

[handwritten: Intangible Property →]

The inventory was given to a local public school. The Roth Corp. stock was given to Clarence's church, and the coin collection was given to the Boy Scouts. Both donees promptly sold the property for the stated fair market value. Ignoring percentage limitations, Clarence's charitable contribution for the current year is $47,000.

Inventory is ordinary income property, but the fair market value ($6,000) must be used if lower than the basis ($8,000). Stock is intangible property and is not subject to the tangible personal property "use related" rules. Since a sale of the Roth Corp. stock would have yielded a long-term capital gain, the full fair market value qualified for the deduction ($40,000). The coin collection comes under the tangible personal property "use related" exception (unrelated use), and therefore the adjusted basis ($1,000) must be used. ($6,000 + 40,000 + 1,000) = $47,000.

- Colleen, a calendar-year taxpayer, made the following charitable contributions:

	Basis	Fair Market Value
Cash to church	$5,000	$5,000
Unimproved land to the city of Violet, Louisiana	40,000	70,000

The land had been held as an investment and was acquired 5 years ago. Shortly after receipt, the city of Violet sold the land for $90,000. Colleen's AGI is $120,000. She has two options with respect to the contribution deduction. First she can deduct the FMV of the land limited to 30% of her AGI. In this case the total deduction would be $41,000 ($5,000 (cash) + $36,000 ($70,000 FMV limited to 30% × $120,000)). The carryover for the next five years is $34,000 ($70,000 FMV − $36,000 current year deduction). Alternatively, she can deduct the adjusted basis, limited to 50% of AGI. In this case, the total deduction would be $40,000 for the land plus $5,000 cash for a total of $45,000.

d. Charitable contributions by business entities.

    i. Partnerships and S corporations – the charitable contributions are deducted by the partners and shareholders on their individual income tax returns. The amount of the deduction is reported to the partners and S corporation shareholders on Schedule K-1.

    ii. C corporations – the charitable deduction is reported on the corporation's income tax return (Form 1120). The deduction is based on the type of property donated, the type of organization to which the property is donated, and the corporation's taxable income before taking into account the charitable deduction.

        A) Ordinary income property (inventory, etc.) – generally, a corporation may deduct the basis of ordinary income property donated to charity. However, the corporation will receive a deduction equal to basis plus half of the unrealized appreciation (not to exceed twice the basis) in the following situations:

            1) The property is used by the charitable organization to care for the ill or infants.

            2) The property is scientific equipment that will be donated to a college or university for research or experimentation.

            3) The property is computer equipment that will be donated to a primary or secondary school (grades K – 12).

        B) Capital-gain property – generally, the corporation may deduct the fair market value of the capital-gain property donated to charity. However, the deduction will be limited to the property's adjusted basis in the following situations:

            1) The property is tangible personal property that is use-unrelated. Use-unrelated means that the property is put to a use that is not related to the charity's exempt purpose.

            2) The property is donated to certain private foundations.

        C) Limit on charitable deduction.

            1) The maximum charitable deduction a corporation can take in a taxable year is limited to 10% of the corporation's taxable income before certain deductions.

                a) The deductions that are not taken into account include the charitable-contribution deduction, the dividends-received deduction, and net operating loss and capital loss carrybacks.

Example

In the current year, XYZ Corporation had net income from operations of $60,000 and received a dividend of $4,000, which is eligible for the 70% dividends-received deduction. During the year, the corporation donated $8,000 in cash to the University of New Jersey.

The maximum charitable contribution deduction that XYZ is entitled to is $6,400 ($60,000 + $4,000 = $64,000 × 10% = $6,400).

XYZ will have taxable income of $54,800 ($60,000 + $4,000 – $2,800 dividends-received deduction – $6,400 charitable-contribution deduction).

---

            2) Any disallowed deduction may be carried forward for up to five years.

Example

Assume the same facts as the previous example. XYZ Corporation may carry forward the disallowed deduction of $1,600 ($8,000 donation – $6,400 deduction) for up to five years.

F. CASUALTY LOSSES FOR INDIVIDUALS.

1. Section 165.

   a. Losses of nonbusiness property are limited to losses from fire, storm, shipwreck, or other casualty or theft.

   b. Casualties refer to losses meeting three criteria:

      i. Identifiable event.

      ii. Property damage results.

      iii. Event is sudden, unusual, and unexpected.

Examples

- Car accident (unless willful negligence or willful act caused it).

- Fires (unless taxpayers set it or paid someone else to).

- Earthquake.

- Flood.

- Tornado.

- Vandalism.

---

2. Events that are not casualties.

   a. Termite damage is an example of something that is not expected and is identifiable but is not considered "sudden" by the IRS. However, the courts have allowed casualty loss treatment for a sudden Southern Pine Beetle attack since these insects can destroy a tree in 5-10 days.

   b. Also not allowed are property devaluations caused by storm damage to neighboring houses, but not to the taxpayer's property.

      i. The Tax Court denied neighbors of O.J. Simpson a casualty loss deduction resulting from a 30% decline in the market value of their house as a result of the murder trial. The ruling centered on the fact that there was no physical damage (Chamales v. Commr., TC Memo 2000-33).

      ii. Similarly, taxpayers were denied a casualty loss deduction for buyer resistance to the sale of their house due to an earthquake in the area (Palos v. Commr).

   c. Most drought-related losses are considered progressive deterioration and are not casualties.

3. Theft losses.

   a. Includes larceny, embezzlement and robbery, but excludes misplaced items.

   b. Theft losses are deducted in the year of discovery not the year of theft. The deduction is only allowed to the extent that the loss exceeds the expected recovery from any insurance.

   c. If the insurance claim is greater than the adjusted basis, a gain is recognized.

4. When to deduct casualty losses.

   a. General rule – Loss is deductible in the year the loss occurs (except theft losses). If a reasonable chance of recovery from insurance exists, no loss is allowed.

   b. Disaster area losses.

      i. When the President declares a disaster area, the losses may be deducted in the year preceding the actual loss.

      ii. If previous year's taxes have already been filed, the taxpayer may file an amended return.

      iii. Disaster loss rules also apply to a personal residence if the disaster causes the residence to be unsafe, and, within 120 days of the President's declaration, local authorities order the structure demolished.

5. Measuring the amount of loss.

   a. Amount of loss.

      i. The amount of the loss is the lesser of:

         A) The adjusted basis, or

         B) The difference between the FMV before the event less the FMV after the decline in FMV.

      ii. Losses from property held for partial business and partial personal use is determined separately for each portion.

      iii. Losses are reduced by any insurance recovery.

      iv. Appraisal or cost of repairs is generally required to determine the extent of the loss.

   b. Reduction for $100 and 10% of AGI floor – The deduction for casualty losses on personal use property is reduced by both the $100 floor and by 10% of AGI. The $100 floor applies to each incident, but the 10% floor is applied to the aggregate casualty loss amount for the year.

   c. Personal use property losses are itemized deductions.

Example

Larry had art worth $10,000 (basis of $15,000) stolen from his apartment. During the year, he had a salary of $30,000 and no other deductions. Larry's itemized deduction from the theft of the art.

Loss	$10,000	(lesser of basis or reduction in FMV)
Less: 10% AGI (10% × $30,000)	(3,000)	
$100 floor	(100)	
Itemized deduction	$6,900	

---

6. Personal casualty gains and losses – If the taxpayer has both losses and gains, they are netted. If gains exceed losses, both gains and losses are treated as gains and losses from sale of capital assets and may be short term or long term. The different types of property are not netted together. If losses exceed gains, all items are ordinary income and losses.

G. MISCELLANEOUS ITEMIZED DEDUCTIONS.

1. Deductions subject to 2% of AGI floor (some of these were discussed in Employee Business Expense section).

   a. Job search costs.

      i. Only deductible if looking for job in present occupation.

      ii. Not necessary to get the job in order to get the tax deduction.

      iii. Includes employment agency fees, travel, resume expenses.

   b. Work clothes and uniforms.

      i. Wearing must be a condition of employment.

      ii. Must not be suitable for everyday wear.

      iii. Full-time military uniforms are usually not deductible.

   c. Professional organization dues.

   d. Hobby expenses (to extent of hobby income).

   e. Work tools if expected to last ≤1 year.

   f. Expenses to produce or collect income (e.g., safe deposit box used to store securities).

   g. Expenses related to paying any tax (e.g., appraisal fees, tax preparation fees).

   h. Other unreimbursed employee business expenses.

2. Deductions not subject to 2% AGI floor.

   a. Federal estate tax on income in respect of decedent (IRD).

   b. Gambling losses to extent of gambling winnings.

   c. Unrecovered investment in annuity contract when annuity ceases because taxpayer died.

   d. Impairment-related work expenses of handicapped taxpayer.

H. OVERALL LIMITATION ON CERTAIN ITEMIZED DEDUCTIONS.

1. When AGI exceeds $150,500 for 2006 ($75,250 for Married Filing Separate), a taxpayer will begin to lose the benefit of some itemized deductions.

   a. Does not apply to medical expenses, investment interest, casualty losses or gambling losses.

   b. Adjustment is 3% of AGI above the threshold.

   c. Maximum reduction is 80% of covered itemized deductions.

   d. Reduction is made after other code provisions (e.g., 2% AGI floor for miscellaneous items).

   e. Per EGTRRA 2001, for years 2006 and 2007, the reduction is reduced by one-third. For 2008 and 2009, the reduction is reduced by two-thirds.

2. The overall limitation is eliminated for tax years after 2009.

XVI. ALTERNATIVE MINIMUM TAX

A. GENERAL.

1. This tax is a backup to the income tax to ensure that no taxpayer with substantial economic income can avoid significant tax liability using deductions and exclusions.

B. INDIVIDUAL ALTERNATIVE MINIMUM TAX.

1. This tax parallels the federal income tax in many ways. For example, both allow depreciation deductions, but the amount used in the calculation will be different.

2. A taxpayer may have to pay the AMT if their taxable income for regular tax purposes, combined with any adjustments and preference items, exceeds:

   a. $45,000 (for 2006) if married filing a joint return or a qualifying widower with dependent child.

   b. $33,750 (for 2006) if filing status is single or head of household.

   c. The exemptions are phased out at upper income levels.

3. Calculating Alternative Minimum Taxable Income (AMTI):

	Regular taxable income
+	Positive AMT adjustments
-	Negative AMT adjustments
+	Tax preferences
=	Alternative Minimum Taxable Income

4. Calculating Alternative Minimum Tax (AMT):

	AMTI
-	AMT exemption
=	Minimum tax base
X	AMT rate
=	Tentative AMT
-	Regular income tax on taxable income
=	AMT

5. Adjustments.

   a. Adjustments made to taxable income in the formula can be either positive or negative.

   b. Most adjustments relate to timing differences because of separate income tax and AMT calculation procedures/rules. A positive adjustment is made when the deduction allowed for income tax purposes exceeds the deduction allowed for AMT purposes. The opposite is true for a negative adjustment.

   c. If the income received for AMT purposes exceeds the income reported for regular income tax, the adjustment is positive. A negative adjustment is made when the income for regular tax is more than for AMT.

EXHIBIT 24: ALTERNATIVE MINIMUM TAX

Adjustment	Regular Tax	AMT	Positive/Negative
Personal and Dependency Exemptions	Allowed	Disallowed	Positive
Standard Deduction	Allowed	Disallowed	Positive
Itemized Deduction – Medical	> 7.5% of AGI	>10% of AGI	Positive
Itemized Deduction – Taxes (state income taxes and property taxes)	Allowed	Disallowed	Positive
Miscellaneous Itemized Deductions	Allowed >2% of AGI	Disallowed	Positive
Interest on Student Loans	Allowed	Disallowed	Positive
Difference between home mortgage interest and qualified-residence interest	Allowed	Disallowed	Positive
Investment Interest Expense as limited for AMT purposes (related to qualified-residence interest and private-activity-bond interest)	Allowed	Disallowed	Positive
Exercise of Incentive Stock Options	Not taxed	Bargain element (spread) is an addback	Positive
Tax benefit rule for state income tax refund	Included in income	Not included in income	Negative
Reduction of itemized deductions	Some deductions disallowed	No reduction	Negative
Depreciation of post-86 property	MACRS allowed	ADS allowed	Both*
Mining Exploration and development costs			Both*
Pollution control facilities			Both
Research and experimental expenses			Both
Completed contract method	Small businesses can use the completed contract method	Small businesses must use the percentage-of-completion method	Both
Passive activity losses			Both
Adjusted gain/loss			Both

*Both means the adjustment could be positive or negative depending upon circumstances.

6. Tax preferences are always positive.

    a. The AMT is designed to take back all or part of the tax benefits derived through the use of these tax preferences (remember that all tax preferences are positive). These items include:

        i. The part of deduction for certain depletion that is more than the adjusted basis of the property.

        ii. Tax-exempt interest on certain private activity bonds (e.g., stadiums).

        iii. 50% exclusion of gain on sale of certain small business stock (Section 1202).

            A) 7% of excluded amount of gain (3.5% of total gain) is a tax preference item for Alternative Minimum Tax (AMT) purposes for stock disposed of on or after March 6, 2003 and before tax year beginning in 2008.

            B) For tax years ending after May 6, 1997, the AMT preference is 42% of excluded amount.

            C) For qualified stock acquired after 2000, the AMT preference will be 28% of excluded amount.

        iv. Accelerated depreciation on certain property placed in service before 1987.

7. Other components of the AMT formula (exemption amount) – Different exemption amounts are used depending on the status of the taxpayer. The exemption is phased out across the board at a rate of $0.25 for each dollar over the threshold amount.

Filing Status	Exemption Amount	Phaseout Range
Married, Joint	$45,000	$150,000 – $382,000
Single	$33,750	$112,500 – $273,500
Head of Household	$33,750	$112,500 – $273,500
Married, Separate	$22,500	$75,000 – $191,000

8. AMT credit – A minimum tax credit may be generated when AMT is paid. If not fully utilized, it may be carried forward indefinitely. It is applicable only from the AMT that occurs due to timing differences (i.e., it is not applicable to exclusions such as the standard deduction, personal exemptions, etc.).

C. MINIMUM TAX CREDIT FOR INDIVIDUALS.

    a. In General.

        i. Generally, the alternative minimum tax paid in one year may be used as a credit against regular tax in a future year.

        ii. The credit may be carried forward (not back) indefinitely.

        iii. For individual taxpayers, the credit is claimed on Form 8801.

    b. Exclusion vs. deferral items.

        i. For noncorporate taxpayers, the credit is only available to the extent the alternative minimum tax was attributable to deferral items, which are timing differences. The alternative minimum tax attributable to exclusion items is not available as a credit.

ii. The minimum tax credit is determined by calculating the adjusted net minimum tax. The adjusted net minimum tax is the difference between the actual alternative minimum tax paid and the alternative minimum tax that would have been paid taking into account only exclusion items.

iii. The following AMT adjustments/preferences are considered exclusion items:

   A) Standard deduction.

   B) Itemized deduction.

   C) Personal exemption.

   D) Exclusion of gain from qualified small business stock (Section 1202).

   E) Tax-exempt interest treated as a tax preference for AMT.

   F) Percentage depletion treated as a tax preference for AMT.

iv. Any adjustment/preference that is not an exclusion item is a deferral item.

Example

Dave Myers, a single taxpayer, just filed his income tax return for the year 2006. With the return, Dave had to pay $35,000 of alternative minimum tax, resulting from the exercise of incentive stock options (deferral item) and some tax-exempt interest from private-activity bonds (exclusion item). If Dave had taken into account only the exclusion items (tax-exempt interest), his AMT liability would have only been $20,000. Therefore, his minimum tax credit is $15,000, calculated as follows:

Alternative Minimum Tax (AMT) paid with return	$35,000
Less: AMT based on exclusion items only	(20,000)
AMT based on deferral items (minimum tax credit)	$15,000

D. CORPORATE ALTERNATIVE MINIMUM TAX.

1. Corporations may have to pay the AMT if taxable income for regular tax purposes, combined with any adjustments and preference items, exceeds $40,000. The exemption is phased out at a rate of $0.25 for each dollar of AMTI in excess of $150,000.

2. Exemption from AMT for small businesses.

   a. Certain small businesses are exempt from the AMT.

   b. In their first year of existence, all corporations are exempt.

   c. In the second year of existence, the corporation will be exempt if its gross receipts were less than $5,000,000 in the prior year.

   d. In the third year (and going forward), the corporation will be exempt if its average annual gross receipts for all prior three-year periods are less than $7,500,000.

   e. Once the corporation fails the gross receipts test, the corporation becomes subject to AMT prospectively.

3. Adjustments applicable only to corporations.

   a. The Adjusted Current Earnings (ACE) adjustment applies only to corporate taxpayers. This adjustment was designed to ensure that all corporations pay some minimum tax on economic income.

   b. The ACE adjustment is equal to 75% of the difference between adjusted current earnings (ACE) and alternative minimum taxable income (AMTI). Adjusted current earnings is essentially economic income.

Example

XBA Corp has AMTI of $200,000 before any ACE adjustment. The corporation has adjusted current earnings of $300,000. Therefore, the ACE adjustment is $75,000 [($300,000 − $200,000) × 75%]. The $75,000 would be added to the AMTI before the ACE adjustment in arriving at Alternative Minimum Taxable Income.

---

4. Some AMT adjustments are not applicable to corporations (only applicable to individuals).

   a. Adjustments for itemized deductions, standard deductions, and personal exemptions of individuals are not applicable to corporations.

   b. Adjustments for Incentive Stock Options (ISOs) are not applicable to corporations.

   c. Adjustments for circulation and research expenditures are not applicable to corporations.

   d. Adjustments for qualified small business (Section 1202) stock are not applicable to corporations.

5. Calculation of Alternative Minimum Taxable Income (AMTI for a corporation):

	Taxable Income
+	Positive AMT adjustments
-	Negative AMT adjustments
+	Tax preferences
=	Alternative Minimum Taxable Income before ACE Adjustment
+	ACE Adjustment
=	Alternative Minimum Taxable Income

6. Calculation of Alternative Minimum Tax (AMT for corporations):

	AMTI
-	AMT exemption ($40,000)
=	Minimum tax base
x	AMT rate (20%)
=	Tentative AMT
-	Regular income tax on taxable income
=	AMT

E. THE TICKET TO WORK AND WORK INCENTIVES ACT OF 1999.

1. The Ticket to Work and Work Incentives Act of 1999 permits personal nonrefundable credits (e.g., dependent care credit, adoption expense credit, HOPE credit) to offset both the regular tax and the AMT.

2. This is done by limiting the amount of nonrefundable credits by the sum of the taxpayer's regular tax liability less any allowable foreign tax credit plus the amount of AMT liability.

XVII. TAX CREDITS

A. TAX CREDITS.

Provide benefits on a more equitable basis than tax deductions; credits are not affected by the tax rate of the taxpayer.

B. OVERVIEW AND PRIORITY OF CREDITS.

1. Refundable tax credits – These are paid to the taxpayer even if the amount exceeds the taxpayer's tax liability.

2. Nonrefundable tax credits – At best, your tax liability can be reduced to zero. If the taxpayer has multiple nonrefundable tax credits, they must be offset using the priority list defined in the Code. Some credits are subject to carryover provisions (e.g., foreign tax credit).

C. GENERAL BUSINESS CREDITS.

1. Rehabilitation expenditures credit.

    a. Tax credit allowed to rehabilitate industrial and commercial buildings and certified historic sites. It is set up to discourage businesses from moving to newer locations.

    b. To qualify for the rehabilitation credit, the expenditures must exceed either the adjusted basis of the property or $5,000.

    c. The basis of the building is reduced by the full rehabilitation credit. The residual investment amount is added to the basis of the property.

2. Energy credit -- 10% credit on qualified energy property (generates energy from a solar or geothermal source).

3. Reforestation credit -- 10% of basis of qualified timber property.

4. Work Opportunity Tax Credit allows a credit of 40% of the first $6,000 paid during the first year of work to each targeted group employee hired before January 1, 2006. For summer youth employees, the credit is 40% of the first $3,000 for any 90-day period between May 1 and September 15. The maximum credit is $2,400 per employee ($1,200 for summer youth).

5. Research activity credit.

    a. This credit is the sum of the incremental research credit and the basic research credit.

    b. Incremental research credit – The Code does not specifically list what research activities qualify. However, it does state what is not allowed.

    c. Basic research credit – This credit applies to C corporations but not S corporations or Personal Service Corporations. It allows qualifying corporations to take an additional 20% credit for basic research payments.

6. Low-income housing credit.

    a. This credit is available to qualified low-income housing projects. One requirement for qualification is to have the property certified under such a title.

    b. If the property continues to qualify, the credit has a 10-year life.

7. Disabled access credit.

a. This credit is 50% of the "eligible access" expenditures over $250 but not more than $10,250 [maximum credit equals ($10,250 – 250) × 50% or $5,000].

b. Only eligible small businesses can claim the disabled access credit. An eligible small business is a business with $1 million or less in gross receipts and 30 or fewer full-time employees.

c. The credit applies to any qualifying project (installation of ramps, raised markings on routine usage items, etc.).

d. If the credit is used, the adjusted basis for that piece of property is reduced by that same amount.

D. PERSONAL CREDITS.

1. Earned income credit (EIC).

a. The credit is designed to encourage economically disadvantaged individuals to join the work force.

b. Earned income equals the summation of employee compensation and/or self-employment earnings less one-half of self-employment tax. It excludes from income such things as interest, dividends, and alimony.

c. The earned income credit is calculated by multiplying a maximum income by a credit percentage.

EXHIBIT 25: EARNED INCOME CREDIT FOR TAX YEARS BEGINNING IN 2006

Qualified Individuals with	Credit Percentage (A)	Earned Income Level (B)	Phaseout Percentage	Phaseout Level Range*	Max Credit (A × B)
No qualifying children	7.65%	$5,380	7.65%	$6,740-12,120 (MFJ $8,740-14,120)	$412
1 qualifying child	34%	$8,080	15.98%	$14,810-32,001 (MFJ $16,810-34,001)	$2,747
2 or more qualifying children	40%	$11,340	21.06%	$14,810-36,348 (MFJ $16,810-38,348)	$4,536

Greater of modified adjusted gross income or earned income.

d. Two types of nontaxable income are included in the AGI phaseout amount. They are tax-exempt interest and amounts received from a pension or annuity, and any distributions or payments received from an individual retirement plan to the extent not included in income.

e. In addition, each child must meet all 3 of the following tests: relationship, residency, and age.

f. The earned income credit is also available to certain workers without children.

Examples

- Jim and Helen have one child, Bo, who turns 18 in 2006 and has been living with them since his birth. In 2006, their combined income was $18,000 and Bo did not work. Jim and Helen plan to file a joint income tax return for 2006. Their earned income credit for 2006 is: ($8,080 × 34% = $2,747), $2,747 − (($18,000 − $16,810) × 15.98%) = $2,557.

- Ann and her daughter, Stephanie, lived with her mother, Joy, in 2006. Ann is 25 years old. Her only income was $9,100 from a part-time job. Joy's only income was $35,000 from her job.

  Stephanie is a qualifying child of both Ann and Joy. Since Ann and Joy both have the same qualifying child, only one can take the credit. Only Joy can take the credit because her adjusted gross income is higher than Ann's. However, Joy cannot take the earned income credit because her adjusted gross income is above the phaseout level. Even though Joy cannot take the earned income credit, neither can Ann take the credit, because her mother's adjusted gross income is more than Ann's.

- Diane and Suzanne are sisters. They shared a house for all of 2006. Diane has 3 young children who lived in the household all year. Suzanne does not have any children. However, she cares for Diane's children as if they were her own. Diane earns $12,000 and Suzanne earns $13,000.

  The children meet the age and residency test for both Diane and Suzanne. They meet the relationship test for Diane because they are her children. They also meet the relationship test for Suzanne because they lived with her in the same household for the whole year. She cared for them as if they were her own children. Therefore, they qualify as her eligible foster children.

  Diane's children are qualifying children for both Diane and Suzanne. However, because Suzanne's adjusted gross income is higher than Diane's, she is the only one who can take the credit.

2. Credit for the elderly or disabled.

    a. This limited, nonrefundable credit applies to taxpayers 65 and older or those under 65 who are retired and permanently or totally disabled. If married, the couple must file a joint return.

    b. The maximum credit is 15% of $5,000 for all filers except MFJ ($7,500 for MFJ) and MFS ($3,750 for MFS).

    c. The $5,000/$7,500/$3,750 amounts are reduced by Social Security not included in gross income and one-half of AGI in excess of $7,500 ($10,000 for married/joint).

Example

Ricky and Regina are husband and wife, both age 69. During the current year, they receive Social Security benefits of $4,000, have adjusted gross income of $12,000, and file a joint return. Their credit for the elderly is $375 ($7,500 (base amount) − $4,000 (Social Security benefits) − $1,000 (one-half of adjusted gross income in excess of $10,000) = $2,500 × 15% = $375).

---

3. Foreign tax credit.

    a. The foreign tax credit is a means of avoiding double taxation by granting a tax credit for taxes paid or accrued to a foreign country or a U.S. possession.

    b. A taxpayer may not take advantage of both the foreign tax credit and the foreign earned income exclusion.

    c. If the tax in the foreign jurisdiction is more than the U.S. tax, it is generally more advantageous to take the tax credit.

4. Child and Dependent Care Credit.

    a. The credit is allowed for a portion of child or dependent care expenses paid for the purpose of allowing the taxpayer to be gainfully employed.

    b. For eligibility, the taxpayer must have earned income, must be paying the expenses in order to work or look for work, and must keep a home for a qualifying individual. A qualifying individual is:

        i.   A dependent under age 13 for whom a dependency exemption may be claimed.

        ii. Any other person who is physically or mentally incapable of caring for himself or herself. In this case, the taxpayer must either (1) be able to claim the person as a dependent, or (2) be able to claim the person as a dependent except for the fact that the person had income exceeding the exemption amount.

        iii. The taxpayer's spouse who is physically or mentally incapable of self-care.

        iv. Certain dependent children of divorced parents.

    c. Household services, in addition to expenses for the care of the children, can be included to determine the credit amount.

    d. For 2006, the employment-related expenses eligible for the credit are limited to $3,000 for one qualifying child and $6,000 for two or more qualifying children.

e. To calculate the credit, multiply the work-related expenses by a percentage (which depends upon gross income).

EXHIBIT 26: CHILD AND DEPENDENT CARE CREDIT FOR 2006

Adjusted Gross Income		Applicable Percentage
Over	But not over	
$0	$15,000	35%
15,000	17,000	34%
17,000	19,000	33%
19,000	21,000	32%
21,000	23,000	31%
23,000	25,000	30%
25,000	27,000	29%
27,000	29,000	28%
29,000	31,000	27%
31,000	33,000	26%
33,000	35,000	25%
35,000	37,000	24%
37,000	39,000	23%
39,000	41,000	22%
41,000	43,000	21%
43,000	No Limit	20%

Example

Billy and Jo have two preschool children, ages 3 and 5. They claim their children as dependents and file a joint income tax return. Billy earned $10,000 and Jo earned $28,000. During the current year, they paid $7,500 for child care expenses at Elmwood Street Nursery.

They figure their credit as follows:

AGI	$38,000
Applicable % for credit	23%
Total work-related expenses	$7,500
Maximum expenses that can be taken into account in calculating credit	$6,000
Amount of credit ($6,000 × 23%)	**$1,380**

This credit level is reduced dollar-for-dollar by the amount of reimbursement from a dependent care assistance plan.

5. Adoption credit.

   a. The adoption credit is a nonrefundable credit for qualified adoption expenses. The maximum credit is $10,960 (for 2006) per eligible child, including special needs children.

   b. The credit is taken in the year the adoption becomes final. Any unused credit may be carried forward up to five years.

   c. The credit is phased out beginning at modified AGI of $164,410 with complete phaseout at $204,410.

6. Child tax credit.

   a. For 2006, a $1,000 credit is given for each qualifying child under the age of 17. The credit will decrease in future years based on the following schedule:

Year	Credit Per Child
2005-2009	$1,000
2010 and later	$500

   b. Qualifying child includes child, stepchild, grandchild, or eligible foster child. In any case, the child must be a dependent.

c.   Credit is reduced $50 for each $1,000 above threshold.

Status	AGI Threshold
Married filing jointly	$110,000
Single or head of household	$75,000
Married filing separately	$55,000

d.   The child tax credit is a refundable credit.

   i.   The child tax credit is refundable to the extent of 10% (for 2006) of the taxpayer's earned income in excess of $11,300 (for 2006).

7.   Tax Credit for Employer-Provided Child Care Facilities

   a.   In General.

      i.   Taxpayers are eligible to receive a tax credit for certain qualified employee child care expenses.

      ii.   Qualified child care expenses include costs paid or incurred:

         A)   To acquire, construct, rehabilitate or expand property that is to be used as part of the taxpayer's qualified child care facility.

         B)   For the operation of the taxpayer's qualified child care facility, including the costs of training and certain compensation for employees of the child care facility, and scholarship programs.

         C)   Under a contract with a qualified child care facility to provide child care services to employees of the taxpayer.

      iii.   To be a qualified child care facility, the principal use of the facility must be for child care (unless it is the principal residence of the taxpayer), and the facility must meet all applicable state and local laws and regulations, including any licensing laws.

   b.   Amount of Credit.

      i.   The credit is equal to 25% of qualified expenses for employee child care and 10% of qualified expenses for child care resource and referral services.

      ii.   The maximum total credit that may be claimed by a taxpayer cannot exceed $150,000 per taxable year.

      iii.   Any amounts for which the taxpayer may otherwise claim a tax deduction are reduced by the amount of these credits.

8.   HOPE Scholarship Credit.

   a.   Available for tuition and fees incurred and paid in the first two years of postsecondary education for taxpayer, spouse, or dependent.

      i.   Books, room and board are not qualifying expenses.

      ii.   Qualifying expenses must be reduced by any tax-free income, and taxpayers cannot use the same educational expense for figuring more than one benefit.

    b.   The credit is 100% of first $1,100 of qualified expenses paid in the tax year plus 50% of the next $1,100. Maximum of $1,650 for the tax year.

    c.   Calculated on a per student basis.

    d.   Student must carry at least half of normal load during one term.

    e.   A convicted drug felon is not eligible.

9.   Lifetime Learning Credit.

    a.   Available for tuition and fees (undergraduate, graduate, or professional degree programs).

    b.   May claim 20% of qualified expenses up to $10,000.

    c.   Maximum of $2,000 credit per year per tax return. Note that maximum is family based unlike the HOPE credit.

    d.   Student must be enrolled at least half time in a degree/certificate program.

    e.   If courses are taken to acquire or improve job skills, student can be enrolled less than half time.

    f.   Credit can be claimed an unlimited number of years.

    g.   Cannot claim both the HOPE Scholarship Credit and Lifetime Learning Credit for the same individual in the same year. However, it would be possible to take the HOPE Scholarship Credit and the Lifetime Learning Credit on the same return if there are two students in the family (each qualifying individually).

    h.   Taxpayers may claim a HOPE Scholarship Credit or Lifetime Learning Credit for a taxable year and exclude from their gross income any amounts distributed (both the contributions and the earnings portions) from a Coverdell Education Savings Account on behalf of the same student, as long as the distribution is not used for the same educational expenses for which a credit was claimed.

EXHIBIT 27: MAGI* PHASEOUT FOR HOPE AND LIFETIME LEARNING CREDITS FOR 2006

Married filing joint	$90,000 – $110,000
All other taxpayers	$45,000 – $55,000

*MAGI – AGI and foreign earned income exclusion and
U.S. possessions and Puerto Rico income exclusions.

EXHIBIT 28: HIGHLIGHTS OF TAX BENEFITS FOR HIGHER EDUCATION FOR 2006

	HOPE Scholarship Credit	Lifetime Learning Credit	Coverdell Education Savings Account[1]	Traditional, Roth, SEP & SIMPLE IRAs[1]	Student Loan Interest	Qualified Tuition Programs[2] (Section 529 Plans)	Education Savings Bond Program[1]	Employer's Educational Assistance Program[1]
What is your benefit?	Credits can reduce the amount of tax you must pay		Earnings are not taxed	No 10% additional tax on early withdrawal	You can deduct the interest	Earnings are not taxed	Interest is not taxed	Employer benefits are not taxed
What is the annual limit?	Up to $1,650 per student	Up to $2,000 per family	$2,000 contribution per beneficiary	Amount of qualifying expenses	$2,500	Determined by Sponsor	Amount of qualifying expenses	$5,250
What expenses qualify besides tuition and required enrollment fees?	None		Books Supplies Equipment Room & board if at least a half-time student Payments to state tuition program	Books Supplies Equipment Room & board if at least a half-time student	Books Supplies Equipment Room & board Trans-portation Other necessary expenses	Books Supplies Equipment Room & board if at least a half-time student	Payments to Coverdell ESAs Payments to qualified tuition program	Books Supplies Equipment
What education qualifies?	1st 2 years of under-graduate	All undergraduate and graduate[3]						
What are some of the other conditions that apply?	Can be claimed only for 2 years Must be enrolled at least half-time in a degree program		Can contribute to Coverdell Education Savings Accounts and qualified tuition program in the same year Must withdraw assets by age 30		Must have been at least half-time student in a degree program	Distribution is excluded from gross income HOPE and Lifetime Learning Credit are permitted in the same year but not for the same expenses	Applies only to qualified series EE bonds issued after 1989 or series I bonds	
In what income range do benefits phase out?	2006: $45,000 - $55,000; $90,000 - $110,000 for joint returns		$95,000 - $110,000; $190,000 - $220,000 for joint returns	No phaseout[5]	$50,000 – $65,000 $105,000 – $135,000 for joint returns	No phaseout	2006: $63,100 - $78,106; $94,700 - $124,700 for joint returns	No phaseout

[1] Any nontaxable withdrawal is limited to the amount that does not exceed qualifying educational expenses.

[2] Exclusion is extended to distributions from Qualified Tuition programs established by an entity other than a State after December 31, 2003.

[3] For Coverdell Education Savings Accounts, qualified elementary and secondary school expenses are also permitted (Grades K-12).

[4] Phaseouts exist at the time of contribution. They are not relevant for withdrawals.

XVIII. PROPERTY TRANSACTIONS – CAPITAL GAINS AND LOSSES

A. TYPES OF ASSETS.

1. Capital Assets.

    a. Capital assets are personal-use assets and most investment assets. Losses from personal-use assets are not deductible but losses from investment assets are.

    b. Section 1221 in the Code defines what is <u>not</u> a capital asset as follows (the Code does not have a list defining capital assets, only those that are <u>not</u> capital assets).

        i. Accounts and notes receivable – This refers to receivables acquired from the sale of inventory or services associated with a business.

        ii. Copyrights and creative works – These types of assets are usually considered ordinary assets and not capital assets.

        iii. Inventory – This refers to inventory held for sale to customers – mainly for business use.

        iv. Depreciable property or real estate – If these assets are used by a business, they are not considered capital assets.

        Note: Remember A-C-I-D.

2. Ordinary Assets.

    a. Property which, if sold, results in the recognition of ordinary income.

    b. Examples.

        i. Inventory.

        ii. Accounts and notes receivable.

        iii. Works of art in the hands of the creator.

        iv. Copyright for the person who applied for and received it.

3. Section 1231 Assets.

    a. Depreciable personal or real property used in business or for the production of income.

    b. By statute, specifically includes:

        i. Timber, coal or iron ore.

        ii. Livestock.

        iii. Unharvested crops.

        iv. Goodwill, intangibles.

B. RATES.

1. Long-term capital gains generally receive preferential tax treatment.

2. Taxpayers use the capital gains rate only when it is advantageous to do so.

3. Assets held more than one year are long term. Assets held one year or less are considered short term. The day of disposition (but not the day of acquisition) is included in the holding period.

EXHIBIT 29: CAPITAL GAINS RATES

Type	Holding Period	Tax Rate
Long-term capital gains	More than one year	15%/5%*
Short-term capital gains	One year or less	Ordinary Income
Qualifying Dividend Income	Received after 12/31/02	Taxed at individual capital gains rate.
Section 1250 Gain (depreciable real property)	More than one year	25%
Collectibles	More than one year	28%
Section 1202 Qualifying Small Business Stock	Five years or more	28% (on 50% of gain)

* The 5% rate applies to a taxpayer in the 10% or 15% marginal ordinary income tax bracket. The 15% rate applies to taxpayers in all other upper brackets.

4. Capital gains taxation was changed under JGTRRA 2003. The rates were reduced, and the five-year property rule was repealed. This new law affects any assets sold after May 6, 2003.

    a. The changes to capital gains taxation include:

        i. The previous 10% long-term capital gains rate used for taxpayers in <u>lower</u> brackets was reduced to 5%. This rate will drop to <u>0%</u> in 2008, then return to <u>10%</u> in 2009.

        ii. The previous 20% long-term capital gains rate used for taxpayers in <u>higher</u> brackets was reduced to 15%. The 20% rate will return in 2009.

        iii. The taxation of short-term capital gains is not changed; it is taxed as ordinary income.

    b. Qualifying Dividend Income for Individuals – Dividend income may be taxed as a capital gain if it meets the following requirements:

        i. Received from a domestic corporation or a "qualified foreign corporation."

        ii. The stock must be held for more than 61 days during the 121-day period beginning 60 days before the ex-dividend date.

        iii. Regular dividends from real estate investment trusts will not qualify for a reduced rate, but long-term distribution dividends will be taxed at a reduced rate.

        iv. Dividends from a regulated investment company will qualify for the reduced rate to the extent they resulted from a long-term capital gain. Also the long-term gain on the sale of the shares will qualify.

Example

For the past four years, Rob Marley has received periodic dividends from the Blue Chip stock he owns. Last week, he received a rather large dividend. Since Rob is in the 35% tax bracket, that large dividend will be taxed at 15% rather than 35% because the stock is from a domestic corporation, and he has held the stock for the required amount of time.

C. CAPITAL GAINS NETTING PROCEDURE.

1. Net STCG and STCL. If there is a NSTCL, it reduces any net LTCG from the 28% group, then 25% group, and then 15% group.

2. Net gains and losses from the 28% group. If there is a net loss, use first to reduce gain from 25% group, then the 15%.

3. Net gains and losses from 15% group. If there is a net loss, use first to reduce gain from 28% group, then 25% group.

4. If there exists a net STCG and any LTCL, net them first against 28%, then 25%, then 15% LTCLs.

Examples.

		Example 1		Example 2		Example 3	
ST	STCG	$4,000		$3,000		$1,000	
	STCL	2,000		9,000		5,000	
		$2,000	Gain (STCG)	$6,000	Loss (STCL)	$4,000	Loss (STCL)
28% LT	Gain	$3,000		$4,000		$2,000	
	Loss	9,000		1,000		1,000	
		$6,000	Loss (LT)	$3,000	Gain (LT)	$1,000	Gain (LT)
25% LT		$0		$1,000	Gain (LT)	$2,000	Gain (LT)
15% LT	Gain	$13,000		$4,000		$2,000	
	Loss	9,000		1,000		1,000	
		$4,000	Gain (LT)	$3,000	Gain (LT)	$1,000	Gain (LT)
Net	Net	$2,000	STCG	$6,000	STCL	$4,000	STCL
		$2,000	LTCL (28%)	$7,000	LTCG	$4,000	LTCG
Final Net		$0	Gain or loss	$1,000	LTCG (15%)	$0	Gain or loss

Note: It is not possible to end up with both gains and losses.

D. DETERMINING GAIN OR LOSS – SUMMARY.

1. The realized gain or loss is the economic result of the transaction. It is calculated by reducing the amount realized by the adjusted basis of the property.

   a. If the amount realized exceeds the adjusted basis, then gain results.

   b. If the amount realized is less than the adjusted basis, then loss occurs.

2. The recognized gain/loss is the gain/loss that is reported on the tax return.

   a. Any gain or loss that is not currently recognized, is either deferred (postponed) or excluded (disallowed).

E. DETERMINING GAIN OR LOSS.

1. Realized gain or loss.

   a. The difference between the amount realized from the sale or other disposition of property and the property's adjusted basis. A realized gain indicates the amount realized exceeded the property's adjusted basis and a realized loss indicates the excess of the adjusted basis over the amount realized.

   b. Sale or other distribution – One must determine whether a sale or distribution occurred as opposed to a fluctuation in property value. Trade-ins, casualties, condemnations, thefts, and bond retirements are treated as dispositions of property.

   c. Amount realized.

      i. This is the sum of any money received, plus the FMV of other property received, plus real property taxes owed by the seller but paid by the buyer, plus any liability on the property assumed by the buyer (e.g., mortgage or some other liability – 2nd mortgage, lien, etc.).

      ii. The fair market value of property received in a sale or other disposition has been defined by the courts as the price at which property will change hands between a willing seller and a willing buyer, both with knowledge of relevant facts, when neither is compelled to buy or sell.

2. Adjusted basis.

   a. Adjusted basis is the property's original basis adjusted to the date of disposition (cost + capital additions – capital recoveries) = adjusted basis.

Example

Harold bought a building for $20,000 cash and assumed a mortgage of $80,000. Harold's basis in the building is $100,000.

---

3. Capital recoveries. There are many forms of capital recoveries but the most widely known are depreciation, casualties, and theft.

4. Capital additions – Cost of capital improvements made to the property by the taxpayer (this does not include ordinary repair and maintenance).

5. Sales, exchange, or condemnation of personal-use assets. Realized losses associated with personal-use assets are not recognized. Exception: casualty or theft losses. In contrast, realized gains may be fully taxable.

F. RECOVERY OF CAPITAL DOCTRINE.

1. This doctrine allows taxpayers to recover the cost or other original basis of property acquired, free from tax. For example, the cost or other basis of depreciable property is recovered through annual depreciation deductions.

2. Rule 1 – A realized gain that is never recognized (tax-free or excluded gain) results in the permanent recovery of more than the taxpayer's cost or other basis for tax purposes. For example, under Section 121, up to $500,000 of realized gain on the sale of a personal residence may be excluded from income.

3. Rule 2 – A realized gain where recognition is postponed (deferred gain) results in the temporary recovery of more than the taxpayer's cost or other basis for tax purposes. For example, a like-kind exchange under Section 1031 or an involuntary conversion under Section 1033 are all eligible for postponement treatment.

4. Rule 3 – A realized loss that is never recognized (disallowed loss) results in the permanent recovery of less than the taxpayer's cost or other basis for tax purposes. For example, a loss on the sale of a personal-use asset is not deductible.

5. Rule 4 – A realized loss where recognition is postponed (postponed loss) results in the temporary recovery of less than the taxpayer's cost or other basis for tax purposes.

G. DETERMINATION OF BASIS OF PROPERTY RECEIVED FROM A SALE.

This is generally the property's cost – the amount paid for in cash or other property. Exception: A bargain purchase has a cost basis equal to its FMV (Logic: bargain purchase element would have been included in income).

1. Lump-sum property purchases – The lump-sum cost is allocated between the properties based on their respective fair market values.

Example

Scott bought a tract of land for $20,000 and subdivided the land into 10 building lots of equal size. If Scott sells all 10 lots individually his basis in each would be $2,000.

H. DETERMINATION OF BASIS AND HOLDING PERIOD WHEN PROPERTY IS RECEIVED BY GIFT

1. A gift indicates that there is no cost to the recipient. However, a basis to the gifted property is still assigned and depends on the following:

    a. The date of the gift.

    b. The donor's adjusted tax basis of the property gifted.

    c. The amount of the gift tax paid (if any) by the donor.

    d. The fair market value of the property on the date of the gift.

2. Gift of appreciated property.

a. When the donor gives appreciated property to the donee, generally the basis to the donee is the carryover basis of the donor. The donee's basis is the donor's old basis.

b. The donor's holding period also carries over to the donee.

c. A realized gain occurs if the donee subsequently sells the gifted property at a higher price than the property's adjusted basis.

d. If the donor paid gift tax at the time the appreciated property is gifted, the donee can increase his or her basis by a portion of the gift taxes paid. The following formula is used to determine a donee' basis when the donor has paid gift taxes:

$$\text{Donee's Adjusted Basis} = \text{Donor's Adjusted Basis} + \frac{(\text{unrealized appreciation}}{\text{FMV}} \times \text{gift tax paid})$$

Example

Chelsea gave Virginia stock with a FMV of $60,000, and paid gift tax of $15,000. Chelsea had originally acquired the stock two years ago for $20,000. Virginia's basis in the gift is $30,000, calculated as follows:

Answer:

$$\$20,000 + \left[\frac{40,000 \times 15,000}{60,000}\right] = \$30,000 \text{ Basis}$$

Basis includes $20,000 of carryover basis, plus $10,000 of the gift tax paid. Virginia immediately has a holding period of two years, which is the carryover holding period from Chelsea.

---

3. Gift of loss property.

   a. When the donor gives loss property to the donee, the double basis rule applies.

   b. Basis cannot be determined until the donee subsequently disposes of the gifted property.

      i. Gain Basis.

         A) If the donee subsequently disposes of the property at a higher price than the donor's adjusted tax basis, the donee determines the gain based on the donor's basis (carryover basis).

         B) The donor's holding period also carries over to the donee in determining whether the gain is short-term or long-term.

         C) If the donor paid gift tax at the time of the gift, the gift tax is NOT allocated to the donee's basis when the property is subsequently disposed of.

      ii. Loss Basis.

         A) If the donee subsequently disposes of the property at a lower price than the fair market value of the property at the time of the gift, the donee determines the loss based on the fair market value at the time of the gift.

         B) The donor's holding period does NOT carryover to the donee in determining whether the loss is short-term or long-term. The donee's holding period begins on the date of the gift.

      C) If the donor paid gift tax at the time of the gift, the gift tax is NOT allocated to the donee's basis when the property is subsequently disposed of.

    iii. If the donee sells the gifted property at a price between the donor's adjusted tax basis and the fair market value at the date of the gift, no gain or loss is recognized at the time of the sale.

Example

Bill received an acre of land as a gift from his father. At the time of gift, the land had a fair market value of $700,000. His father purchased the land four years ago for $800,000, and paid gift tax of $100,000 as a result of the gift. Assuming Bill sold the land one week after receiving the gift:

If Bill sold the land for $850,000, he would have a long-term capital gain of $50,000 ($850,000 – $800,000) on the sale. Bill will use his father's carryover basis of $800,000 (gain basis), and will use his father's carryover holding period of four years. Gift tax paid by the father will NOT be allocated to Bill's basis, because this was a gift of loss property.

If Bill sold the land for $550,000, he would have a short-term capital loss of $150,000 ($550,000 – $700,000) on the sale. Bill's basis will be the $700,000 fair market value on the date of the gift (loss basis), and Bill's holding period will begin on the date of the gift. Gift tax paid by the father will NOT be allocated to Bill's basis, because this was a gift of loss property.

If Bill sold the land for $730,000, there will be no gain or loss, because he sold the land at a price between the father's adjusted tax basis and the fair market value at the date of the gift. Holding period is irrelevant, since there is no gain or loss.

I. BASIS OF PROPERTY RECEIVED FROM A DECEDENT.

1. When receiving property from a decedent, the basis of such property is the FMV at the date of death or, if the alternate valuation date is properly elected, the FMV up to six months after the date of death. However, there are restrictions on electing the alternate valuation date.

2. Alternate valuation date limitations.

    a. An estate tax return must be filed.

    b. Both the value of the gross estate and the estate tax liability must be reduced below what the primary valuation date would have yielded.

    c. The alternate valuation date is six months after the date of death unless the property is disposed of prior to six months after the date of death, in which case the valuation is the disposition value.

3. Deathbed gifts.

a. If appreciated property is given to a donee who then dies within one year and bequeaths it back to the donor, the basis of the inherited property will be the donor's adjusted basis at the time of the gift. No stepped-up basis is received.

Example

Joey gives property to his father in 2006 that on the date of the gift has a FMV of $7,000. No gift taxes were paid. Joey has an adjusted basis in the property of $2,300. Joey's father dies at the end of 2006 and bequeaths the property back to Joey, within one year of the date of the gift. Hence, Joey's basis in the property is $2,300 (donor's basis).

---

4. Survivor's share of property (JTWROS).

a. The basis of such property is the FMV at the date of the decedent's death for the portion related to decedent. This is added to the basis of survivor.

Example

Martin and Mary owned, as joint tenants, land that they purchased for $60,000. At the date of Mary's death, the property had a FMV of $100,000. Local law states that joint tenants each have a half-interest in the income for jointly held property. Martin figures his basis in the property as follows:

Interest Martin bought up front	$30,000
Interest Martin received @ Mary's death	$50,000
Martin's basis @ Mary's death	$80,000

Common law states don't allow an adjustment to the surviving owner's interest in the property.

---

5. The holding period of property acquired from a decedent – The holding period of property acquired from a decedent is always deemed to be long term. This provision applies regardless of whether the property is disposed of at a gain or loss.

6. Community property – Community property receives an adjustment in basis to FMV on both halves at the death of the first spouse.

J. HOLDING PERIOD EXCEPTIONS.

1. Generally, property must be owned over a year to be treated as long-term property.

2. Gift property – If the donor's basis carries over to the donee, then the donor's holding period is added (tacked on) to the donee's holding period.

3. Inherited property – The property is treated as long term regardless of the actual original holding period.

4. Capital asset or Section 1231 asset – In a like-kind exchange between a capital asset or Section 1231 asset, the newly acquired property includes the holding period of the former property.

5. Mark to market rules.

a. Apply to Section 1256 contracts.

        i.   Regulated futures contracts.

        ii.   Foreign currency contracts.

        iii. Nonequity options, such as S&P 500 Index Option.

        iv. Dealer equity options.

   b.   Any Section 1256 contracts must be marked to market at year-end and gain/loss must be reported. The effect is to treat the contract as if it were sold on the last day of the taxable year.

   c.   Capital gain/loss is treated as if 40% short term and 60% long term. Gain is adjusted by any amounts considered in previous years and is reflected in adjustment to basis.

K. DISALLOWED LOSSES.

1.   Related taxpayers – Losses from sales to related parties are disallowed.

   a.   Related parties include brothers, sisters, and lineal descendants (it stops at and does not include cousins); corporations in which the taxpayer has a 50% or greater interest; and several other complex relationships.

   b.   However, if the subsequent sale of the property by the recipient results in a gain, this gain can be reduced by the previously disallowed loss. The related buyer's holding period begins on the date of the purchase from the related party.

Example

Dad sells stock to Son for $70 on January 1, 2006. Dad's ATB was $100 and Dad had purchased the stock on February 4, 1998. Dad's loss of $30 is disallowed and Dad will never benefit from the loss.

On June 2, 2006, Son sells the stock to an unrelated party for $115. His gain is $15 ($115 – $70 = $45 – $30 = $15). Son was able to allocate Dad's disallowed loss to his gain.

---

2. Wash sales.

    a. A wash sale occurs if the taxpayer sells or exchanges stock/securities for a loss and, within 30 days <u>before or after</u> the date of the sale or exchange, acquires relatively identical/similar stock/securities.

    b. If such an event occurs, the basis of the new stock/securities will include the unrecovered portion of the basis of the formerly held stock/securities.

Example

Tiffany purchased 100 shares of Ace Corporation stock for $28,000 on January 1, 2005. In the current tax year, she sells 30 shares of the 100 shares purchased on January 1, 2005, for $8,000. Twenty-nine days earlier, she purchased 30 shares for $7,500.

Tiffany's recognized loss is $0, calculated as follows:

Amount realized	$8,000
Adjusted basis (30 × $280)	(8,400)
Realized loss	(400)
Recognized loss	$0 (Loss postponed because of wash sale rule.)

Her basis in the new shares is $7,900:

Basis in old shares	$7,500
Add: postponed loss	400
Basis in new shares	$7,900

---

3. Conversion of personal property to business property or income-producing property.

    a. If converted, the basis for loss is the lower of the property's FMV on the date of conversion or the adjusted basis.

    b. The basis for gain is the property's adjusted basis.

    c. The basis for depreciation is the same as the basis for loss, explained above.

L. INSTALLMENT SALES.

1. In General.

    a. The general rule of taxation is that all gains are recognized in the year of sale or exchange. An exception to this rule applies to the installment sale method of accounting.

    b. An installment sale is any sale of property (see exceptions below) in which the seller will receive at least one payment after the close of the tax year in which the sale occurs.

    c. The installment-sale method allows the taxpayer to spread out the gain as the payments are received.

    d. The installment method is automatic for sales that qualify. However, the taxpayer is allowed to elect out of the installment method by reporting the entire gain in the year of sale.

2. Installment treatment is not available for:

   a. Property held for sale in ordinary course of business (inventory).

   b. Gains on stocks/securities traded in an established market.

3. Tax ramifications of installment sales.

   a. The gain is reported based on the amount of cash received and the gross-profit percentage resulting from the sale.

      i. The gross-profit percentage is calculated by subtracting the seller's adjusted tax basis from the total contract price, and dividing that by the contract price.

Example

Mike Orentlich sold a 40-acre tract of land for $500,000 on January 1, 2005. The land had an adjusted basis of $300,000. The agreement specified a down payment of $100,000, with the remaining $400,000 sales price paid over a 5-year-note term at 10% interest. The gross profit from the sale is $200,000 ($500,000 − $300,000), and the gross-profit percentage is 40% ($200,000 profit ÷ $500,000 sales price).

---

      ii. Down payment – the down payment received from an installment sale is partially a capital gain and partially a return of capital. The capital gain portion is based on the amount of cash received and the gross-profit percentage calculated above.

Example

Assume the same facts as above. The down payment of $100,000 received by Mike is reported as a $40,000 capital gain and a $60,000 return of capital. The capital-gain portion is calculated by multiplying the down payment by the gross-profit percentage ($40,000 = $100,000 down payment × 40% gross-profit percentage). The remaining $60,000 of the down payment will be considered a nontaxable return of capital.

---

      iii. Note payments – the note payments received from the buyer are partially ordinary income, partially capital gain, and partially a return of capital.

Example

Assume the same facts as above. Mike received a note payment of $120,000 in the first year, of which $40,000 represented accrued interest. Therefore, the note payment represented $40,000 of interest and $80,000 of principal repayment. The note payment would be reported as $40,000 ordinary income, $32,000 capital gain ($80,000 principal payment × 40% gross-profit percentage), and $48,000 nontaxable return of capital ($120,000 note payment − $40,000 interest − $32,000 capital gain).

---

4. Other provisions of installment sales.

    a. Gains recaptured as ordinary income under Sections 1245 and 1250 (depreciable property) are not eligible for installment-sale treatment. These amounts are fully recognized as ordinary income in the year of the sale.

    b. If the selling price is more than $3,000 and the contract does not have a reasonable rate of interest, interest will be imputed.

    c. If property is sold to a related party and the related party sells the property to a third party within two years, the deferred gain must be recognized in full by the original seller.

    d. If an installment obligation is sold or otherwise disposed of, any unreported gain must be reported in the year the note was transferred.

M. SALES OR EXCHANGES – SPECIAL ISSUES.

1. Worthless securities – If the securities are capital assets, they will be treated as being disposed of/sold on the last day of the tax year. This extends the holding period.

2. Options – If the option is a capital asset, the grantee will realize a capital gain or loss upon sale/exchange. If the grantee fails to exercise the option, the sale/exchange will be considered to have occurred on the expiration date.

3. Patents.

    a. When all substantial rights to a patent are transferred by the holder, it is treated as a sale/exchange of a long-term capital asset.

        i. Substantial rights – This means that no contingencies or limitations exist. For example, the holder cannot put restrictions on the transfers to certain geographic locations.

        ii. Definition of holder – Must be an individual (usually the creator of the patent).

    b. Exception: Authors, artists, and composers cannot obtain capital gain treatment when transferring their works (usually treated as ordinary gain or loss).

4. Franchises, trademarks, trade names.

    a. When transferring a franchise, trademark, or trade name, if the transferor retains significant power, the transferred asset is not considered to be a capital asset under Section 1253. A franchise transfer is not considered the sale/exchange of a capital asset.

    b. Relinquish significant power – This means that the transferor will not have control over assignments, advertisings, product quality, and supply and equipment purchases, to name a few.

    c. Noncontingent payments – If the transferor retains a significant power, the periodic noncontingent transfer payments will be considered ordinary income. The franchisee must capitalize and amortize the payments over 15 years.

5. Contingent payments – These are treated as an ordinary deduction for the franchisee and ordinary income for the franchisor.

6. Short sales.

    a. Taxpayer anticipates a decline in the price of stock and sells it short.

b. Taxpayer sells stock she has borrowed and repays it with substantially identical property (either already owned or purchased after the sale).

Example

Ginna has been watching the market carefully and decides that Pear Computer is not going to make its target quarterly income. In anticipation that the stock price will decline, Ginna sells 100 shares of Pear (borrowed from her broker) for $10,000. In 60 days, Ginna purchases 100 shares for $8,000 and repays her broker, closing the short sale. Ginna made $2,000 on the transaction.

---

c. The term "short sale against the box" refers to a short sale where the seller borrows stock but actually already owns the same stock.

Example

Ginna already owned 100 shares of Pear but borrowed 100 shares from her broker. To close the short sale, she delivers the shares she already owns. The advantage is that she has more flexibility in reporting when the sale occurs.

---

d. The nature of the gain. If the stock is a capital asset to the taxpayer, then the gain/loss is capital.

   i.   If the taxpayer has not held substantially identical securities for the required long-term holding period at the date of the short sale or the substantially identical property is acquired between the short-sale date and the closing date, any gain/loss is short term.

   ii. If substantially identical property has been held for the long-term holding period on the short-sale date and it is used to close the sale, the gain is long term.

   iii. If substantially identical property has been held for the long-term holding period on the short-sale date and a loss occurs, it is considered long term whether the substantially identical property was used to close the sale or not.

e. Constructive sale rules to reduce the reporting flexibility for short sales against the box. If a taxpayer does not close a short position by January 31st in the year following the short sale, a constructive sale is deemed to have been made on the earlier of (1) the short-sale date (if the taxpayer owned substantially identical securities at that time) or (2) when the taxpayer acquired substantially identical securities during the year of the short sale.

XIX. PROPERTY TRANSACTIONS: NONTAXABLE EXCHANGES

A. GENERAL.

1. The tax law recognizes that nontaxable exchanges result in a change in the form but not in the substance of the taxpayer's relative economic position. The replacement property received in the exchange is viewed as substantially a continuation of the old investment.

2. In a nontaxable exchange, realized gains or losses are not recognized. However, the nonrecognition is usually temporary because the gain or loss is postponed. This is accomplished by assigning a carryover basis to the replacement property.

B. LIKE-KIND EXCHANGES – SECTION 1031.

1. In General.

   a. Section 1031 provides for nontaxable exchange treatment if the following requirements are satisfied:

      i. The form of the transaction is an exchange.

      ii. Both the property transferred and the property received are held either for productive use in a trade or business or for investment.

      iii. The property is like-kind property.

2. Like-kind property.

   a. The words "like-kind" refer to the nature or character of the property and not to its grade or quality. One kind or class of property may not be exchanged for property of a different kind or class.

   b. The following properties/exchanges are NOT considered like-kind:

      i. Personal-use assets (personal auto).

      ii. Ordinary assets (inventory).

      iii. Securities.

      iv. Personalty exchanged for realty. Depreciable tangible personal property must be within the same general business asset class or the same product class (e.g., office furniture, information systems, automobiles, and trucks).

      v. Livestock of different sexes.

      vi. Foreign real estate for domestic real estate.

3. Exchange requirement – The transaction must actually involve an exchange of property to qualify as a like-kind exchange.

4. Boot.

   a. Boot is property received in an exchange that is not like-kind property.

   b. Boot includes:

      i. Cash received.

      ii. Liabilities assumed from the taxpayer by the other party.

iii. Other non-like-kind property, such as personal property received in an exchange involving real property.

c. The receipt of boot will:

i. Result in the recognition of gain if there is a realized gain.

ii. Result in no recognition if there is a realized loss.

d. Exception: If the boot is appreciated or depreciated property, the gain or loss is recognized to the extent of the difference between the FMV and adjusted basis of the boot.

Examples

Bob exchanged investment land with an adjusted basis of $35,000, receiving another parcel of investment land with a fair market value of $50,000 plus $12,000 in cash. As a result of this exchange, Bob will have a realized (economic) gain of $27,000 and a recognized (taxable) gain of $12,000.

Fair market value of property received	$50,000
Cash (boot) received	$12,000
Amount realized	$62,000
Less: Adjusted basis in asset surrendered	(35,000)
Equals: Realized Gain	$27,000
Recognized gain (lesser of realized gain or boot received	$12,000

Bob exchanged investment land with an adjusted basis of $55,000, receiving another parcel of investment land from Steve with a fair market value of $50,000. Bob's land was subject to a $15,000 mortgage, which was assumed by Steve. As a result of this exchange, Bob will have a realized (economic) gain of $10,000 and a recognized (taxable) gain of $10,000.

Fair market value of property received	$50,000
Cash (boot) received	$15,000
Amount realized	$65,000
Less: Adjusted basis in asset surrendered	(55,000)
Equals: Realized Gain	$10,000
Recognized gain (lesser of realized gain or boot received	$10,000

The mortgage assumed by Steve represents boot to Bob.

---

5. Multiple properties.

a. An exchange may involve more than one property.

b. When multiple properties are involved, such as in the exchange of businesses, the various business assets are matched with those of the same kind.

6. Basis and holding period of property received.

a. The basis of like-kind property received in the exchange is the property's FMV less deferred gain or plus postponed loss. If the exchange partially qualifies for nonrecognition (if recognition is associated with boot), the basis of like-kind property is the property's FMV less postponed gain or plus postponed loss. The basis of any boot received is the boot's FMV.

b. The Code provides an alternative approach for determining the basis of like-kind property received:

> Adjusted basis of like-kind property surrendered
>
> + Adjusted basis of boot given
>
> + Gain recognized
>
> - FMV of boot received
>
> - Loss recognized
>
> = Basis of like-kind property received

Example (Like-Kind Exchange)

Pat exchanges real estate (adjusted basis $50,000, FMV $80,000) held for investment for other real estate (FMV $80,000) held for investment. Pat's basis in the new property is $50,000.

Example (Partially Nontaxable Exchange)

Craig trades in a truck (adjusted basis $6,000) for a new truck (FMV $5,200) and receives $1,000. Craig's basis in the new truck is:

Adjusted basis of old truck	$6,000
Cash received	($1,000)
Gain recognized ($6,200 – $6,000)	$200
Basis of new truck	$5,200

---

c. The holding period of the property surrendered in the exchange carries over and tacks on to the holding period of the like-kind property received.

d. The boot's holding period starts from the date of exchange rather than a carryover holding period.

7. Other requirements.

a. If like-kind property is exchanged with a related party, the taxpayer and related party must not dispose of the like-kind property received in the exchange within a 2-year time period following the exchange. Exception: death and involuntary conversions.

b. The property to be received in an exchange must be identified in a written agreement within 45 days after the transferred property is surrendered.

c. Property in the exchange must be received on or before the earlier of:

   i.   180 days after the transfer of the property given up, or

   ii. The due date of the tax return (including extensions) for the year the property was given up.

C. INVOLUNTARY CONVERSIONS – SECTION 1033.

1. An involuntary conversion results from the destruction (complete or partial), theft, seizure, requisition, condemnation, or sale or exchange under threat or imminence of requisition or condemnation of the taxpayer's property.

2. Section 1033 allows a taxpayer who incurs an involuntary conversion to postpone recognition of gain realized from the conversion (remember: this is the exception to the two-year holding period under like-kind exchanges). The rules for nonrecognition are as follows:

   a. If the amount reinvested in replacement property equals or exceeds the amount realized, realized gain is not recognized.

   b. If the amount reinvested in replacement property is less than the amount realized, realized gain is recognized to the extent of proceeds not reinvested.

3. Computing the amount realized – Typically the amount realized from the condemnation of property is equal to the amount received as compensation for the property. Severance damages are usually not included in the amount realized.

4. Replacement property.

   a. The general requirement is that the replacement property is similar in service or use to the involuntarily converted property. For an owner-user, the functional use test applies, and for an owner-investor, the taxpayer use test applies.

      i.   Functional use test – The taxpayer's use of the replacement property and of the involuntarily converted property must be the same. For example, an office building used as an office building by the owner is subject to an involuntary conversion. The replacement property must be an office building used as an office building.

      ii. Taxpayer use test – The owner-investor's properties must be used in similar endeavors as the previously held properties. There is more flexibility with this test than the functional use test. For example, if the owner had held the office building as an investment property, then the replacement property can be any realty investment property.

5. Time limitation on replacement.

   a. Normally the taxpayer has a 2-year time period at the end of the taxable year in which any gain is realized from the involuntary conversion to replace the property. Exception: Condemnation of real property used in a trade or business or held for investment has a 3-year period.

   b. The earliest date for replacement is typically the date the involuntary conversion took place.

6. Nonrecognition of gain – This can be either mandatory or elective depending upon the disposition/conversion of the replacement property (was it money or similar property).

a.   Direct conversion – If converting to replacement property, nonrecognition of realized gain is mandatory. The basis of the converted property is the same as the replacement property. Direct conversion is rare in practice.

b.   Conversion into money – If the conversion is into money, nonrecognition is elective. The basis of the replacement property is the property's cost less postponed (deferred) gain. If postponement is elected, the holding period of the replacement property includes the holding period of the converted property.

c.   Section 1033 applies only to gains, not losses.

Example

Bill had some property condemned by the State of Louisiana. The property had an adjusted basis of $26,000. Bill received $31,000 from the state for the property. Bill just realized a gain of $5,000 ($31,000 – $26,000) and bought new property that was similar in use to his old property for $29,000. He must recognize a gain of $2,000 ($31,000 – $29,000). Bill's basis in his new property is as follows:

Cost of new property	$29,000
Gain not recognized (deferred gain)	($3,000)
Bill's basis in the new property	$26,000

---

7.   Involuntary conversion of a personal residence.

a.   The tax consequences depend on whether a casualty or condemnation occurred, and if it produced a realized loss or gain.

b.   Loss circumstances.

i.   If the conversion is a condemnation, the realized loss is not recognized.

ii.   If the conversion is a casualty, the realized loss is recognized subject to the personal casualty loss limitations.

c.   Gain circumstances.

i.   If the conversion is a condemnation, the gain may be postponed under either Section 1033 or if qualifying, excluded under Section 121.

ii.   If the conversion is casualty, the gain is only postponed under the involuntary conversion provisions.

D.   SALE OF A PERSONAL RESIDENCE – SECTION 121.

1.   Section 121 gives a universal exclusion of up to $250,000 (married filing joint, $500,000) to any taxpayer who meets certain use tests.

a.   Home must have been owned and used as a principal residence for at least 2 of the 5 years before the sale (do not have to be consecutive years).

b.   Either spouse can meet the ownership requirement, but both must meet the use requirement. Neither spouse can be ineligible because of the once-every-two-year limit in (c).

c. Exclusion can be used once every two years.

d. If taxpayer fails to meet (a) and (b) because of a change in employment or health, taxpayer may be entitled to a partial exclusion based on the shorter of either the use or ownership.

e. If one spouse can take a full exclusion and one cannot, then the exclusion is the sum of the amounts calculated on a separate basis as if they had not been married.

f. The exclusion does not apply to gain attributable to post May 6, 1997 depreciation for business/rental use of the house.

g. Taxpayers who deferred gain under the older Section 1034 provisions may tack on the old residence's use and ownership period to the new residence.

Examples

- Gloria, a single taxpayer, sold her condominium in Seattle because she has a new job in Detroit. On the sale date, she had owned the condo for only 18 months. Since Gloria failed to meet both the use and ownership tests due to a change in employment, she can get a partial exclusion: 18 months/24 months × $250,000 = $187,500.

  If Gloria had lived in the condo for two years, but had only owned it for one year (she rented for a year before she purchased it), proposed Regs specify that the shorter of the two periods should be used. Her partial exclusion would then be: 12 months/24 months × $250,000 = $125,000.

- Merrily and Wallace get married and Wallace moves into the house that Merrily has been using as her principal residence for six years. Nine months later, Wallace gets a big promotion and the newlyweds move to another city. They realized a $700,000 gain on the sale of their residence. Merrily meets the ownership and use tests. She gets a full exclusion of $250,000. Wallace does not need to meet the ownership test (since his wife did), but he is held to the use test. He has only been there 9 months, so his exclusion is 9/24 × $250,000 = $93,750. Their total exclusion is $250,000 + $93,750 = $343,750.

- If Wallace and Merrily had just moved to a larger house in the same city, Merrily gets her $250,000 exclusion (she has met all tests, and it has been at least two years since she claimed an exclusion), but Wallace does not get any exclusion. Remember that the partial exclusion is only allowed if the sale is necessitated by a change in employment, health.

---

2. When selling a personal residence, like any other personal asset, losses are not recognized.

XX. SECTION 1231 AND RECAPTURE PROVISIONS

A. SECTION 1231 ASSETS.

1. Relationship to capital assets – If a business is disposing of depreciable and/or real property, any loss is treated, as per Section 1231, as an ordinary loss (deductible for AGI). Gains are given capital gain treatment (see exception under look-back rules in this section).

2. Section 1231 property.

   a. Included.

      i. Depreciable personal or real property used in business (see below) or for the production of income (e.g., machinery, equipment, and buildings).

      ii. Timber, coal, or domestic ore.

      iii. Livestock held for breeding, dairy, or sport.

      iv. Unharvested crops on land used in a business.

      v. Certain nonpersonal-use assets.

   b. Excluded.

      i. Property not held for the long-term holding period (12 months or less).

      ii. Property where casualty losses exceed casualty gains.

      iii. Inventory/property held for sale to customers.

      iv. Intangible assets.

      v. Capital assets.

3. Special rules for certain Section 1231 assets.

   a. Timber – If the taxpayer elects to treat cut timber as being held for sale or business, the transaction qualifies under Section 1231.

   b. Livestock – There is a 24-month holding period for cattle and horses and a 12-month holding period for other livestock to qualify for Section 1231 treatment.

   c. Select nonpersonal use capital assets – These are assets held for the production of income (land, investment painting, etc.). If subject to by casualty or theft, they may fall under Section 1231.

B. SECTION 1245 RECAPTURE.

1. Requires any recognized gain to be treated as ordinary income to the extent of depreciation taken on the property disposed of up to the gain recognized. It does not apply if the property is disposed of at a loss. Any remaining gain will usually be Section 1231 gain.

2. Section 1245 property.

   a. Includes all depreciable personal property, patents, copyrights, and leaseholds.

Example

Blaine bought a depreciable business asset for $75,000. Before selling it for $60,000, he was able to write off $45,000 in depreciation. Following Section 1245, Blaine has to treat the entire gain on the sale of the business asset as ordinary income.

Purchase price	$75,000
Depreciation deduction taken	(45,000)
Basis in asset before sale (adjusted basis)	$30,000
Selling price	$60,000
Basis in asset (adjusted basis)	(30,000)
Gain on sale (ordinary income)	$30,000
Recapture depreciation to extent of gain realized	($30,000)
Net 1231 Gain	$0

---

3. This section does not apply to losses – Section 1231 rules are used, resulting in ordinary loss treatment.

C. SECTION 1250 RECAPTURE.

1. This provision prevents taxpayers from receiving benefits of both accelerated depreciation and long-term capital gain treatment. It requires the recapture of the depreciation deducted by the taxpayer over what it would have been using straight line.

2. Section 1250 property is depreciable real property (typically buildings and structural components).

3. Losses do not have any depreciation recapture and are usually treated as Section 1231 losses (i.e., if a business loss, then deducted for AGI, other losses are deducted from AGI).

4. Gain attributable to straight-line depreciation is taxed at 25% maximum capital-gains rate.

5. Any gain not attributable to depreciation is subject to 15% rate.

Example

Mark sold a building on June 15, 2006 for $100,000. He had originally acquired the building in 2001 for $75,000. Straight-line depreciation taken was $30,000. Mark is in a 35% marginal tax bracket. The character of his gain is $30,000 at 25% rate; $25,000 at 15% rate. The unrecaptured Section 1250 gain (i.e., depreciation) is taxed at 25% while the remaining long-term capital gain receives a 15% tax rate.

D. CONSIDERATIONS TO SECTIONS 1245 AND 1250.

1. Exceptions – Recapture under Sections 1245 and 1250 do not apply to the following:

    a. Gifts – The recapture potential carries over to the donee.

    b. Death – When owner of asset dies, asset receives step to fair market value in basis; therefore, no recapture to heir.

    c. Charitable transfers – Recapture potential reduces the amount of charitable contribution deduction in the case basis is used.

    d. Certain nontaxable transactions – Recapture potential carries over to the transferee.

    e. Like-kind exchanges – Any remaining recapture potential carries over to the property received.

    f. Involuntary conversions – Any remaining recapture potential carries over to the property received.

2. Other applications (installment sales) – Recapture gain is recognized in the year of sale and is treated as ordinary income until the recapture potential is fully netted out.

E. SPECIAL RECAPTURE PROVISIONS.

1. When sale/exchange of depreciable property occurs between certain related parties, any gain recognized is ordinary income.

F. LOOK-BACK RULE.

1. If a taxpayer has a net Section 1231 gain for the current year, they must report the gain as ordinary income to the extent of any Section 1231 losses reported within the past five taxable years.

Example

Davis, Inc. sold some business equipment during the current year, realizing a $15,000 gain on the sale. The equipment was originally purchased 3 years ago, and this was the only asset sale for this year. Last year, Davis, Inc. had an $8,000 net Section 1231 loss.

For the current year, the net Section 1231 gain is treated as a $7,000 long-term capital gain and an $8,000 ordinary gain. When the taxpayer has a net Section 1231 gain for the year, the lookback rules may recapture some or all of the net gain as ordinary income.

XXI. TAXATION OF INVESTMENT TRANSACTIONS

EXHIBIT 30: SUMMARY OF TAXATION OF INVESTMENT TRANSACTIONS

		Income	Sale at Gain	Sale at Loss	Adjusted Taxable Basis
A	Stocks	Taxable*	Capital Gain	Capital Loss	Generally Cost
B	Bonds – Corp. or Treasury	Taxable	Capital Gain	Capital Loss	Generally Cost
C	Municipal Bonds	Not Taxable	Capital Gain	Capital Loss	Generally Cost
D	OID Bonds – Corp. or Treasury	Taxable	Capital Gain	Capital Loss	Generally Cost
E	Options on Stocks	See NQSOs & ISOs			Cost + Income Recognized
F	Exchanges (Tax-free)	N/A	Capital Gain to extent of boot	Postponed	Generally Carryover
G	Installment Sales	Taxable Interest	Capital Gain	N/A	Cost
H	Property Inherited	Taxable	Long-Term Capital Gain	Long-Term Capital Loss	FMV @ Death or Alternate Date
I	Mutual Funds	Taxable	Capital Gain	Capital Loss	Cost + Income Reinvested
J	Gifts	Taxable	Capital Gain	Capital Loss	Double-Basis Rule
K	Personal Residence	N/A	Exempt to $250,000 or $500,000	Disallowed	Cost
L	Personal-Use Property	N/A	Capital Gain	Disallowed	Cost
M	1244 Stock	Taxable	Capital Gain	Ordinary Loss (limited)	Cost
N	Exchange of Series E/EE bonds	Deferred	Capital Gain	Capital Loss	Generally Cost
O	1202 Stock	Taxable	Capital Gain (exclude 50% of gain, gain recognized is taxed at 28%)	Capital Loss	Cost

> **Note 1:** Income refers to proceeds from the investment after acquisition.
> **Note 2:** Capital gains are long term or short term depending on the holding period.
> **Note 3:** Basis depends on how acquired.
> **Note 4:** Cost includes purchase price and transaction costs.

*Dividends may be taxed at long-term capital gains rates.

A. SALES OF STOCK.

1. The basis will be the purchase price of the stock plus any commissions or fees associated with the purchase. Basis may be subsequently adjusted for nontaxable stock dividends, stock splits, or nontaxable distributions that are a return of capital.

2. Basis options when selling.

   a. FIFO (default).

   b. Specific identification (only if indicated at the time of the sale).

3. Gain will be calculated as net sales proceeds less adjusted basis.

4. Follow capital-gain rules.

5. Cash dividends are includible in taxable income.

6. A sale will result in capital gain or loss unless sold for basis.

7. Reinvested dividends are currently taxed and taxpayers will add dividends reinvested to the basis of stock.

B. BONDS – CORPORATE OR TREASURY.

1. Income (interest) is taxable.

2. The sale of a bond creates a capital gain or loss if disposed of at an amount different from basis.

3. If a corporate bond is bought at a premium, then the taxpayer will reduce the basis by the amount of amortization taken (if elected).

4. Treasury bond interest is not subject to state income tax.

C. MUNICIPAL BONDS.

1. The interest on municipal bonds is tax exempt for federal tax purposes.

2. The sale of a municipal bond creates a capital gain or loss if disposed of at an amount different from basis.

3. Premiums on municipal bonds must be amortized and the basis must be reduced by the amortized amount. No deduction is taken for the amortization on municipal bonds.

D. ORIGINAL ISSUE DISCOUNT (OID) BONDS – CORPORATE OR TREASURY.

1. OID typically applies to zero-coupon or deep-discount bonds.

2. Interest is usually accrued and includible in income in spite of an absence of cash flow.

3. The sale of an OID will result in capital gain or loss if the sale proceeds are different from the adjusted tax basis.

4. The accrued interest reported each year by the taxpayer is added to the basis.

E. STOCK OPTIONS.

1. Usually given by employer as a form of compensation.

2. Gives taxpayer right to buy company's stock at a certain price within a specific time frame.

3. Generally, no income is recognized when the option is granted.

4. The amount and timing of income recognition depends upon the type of stock option awarded.

    a. Nonqualified stock options (NQSOs).

        i. Individual will recognize income when NQSO is granted, if the option is traded on an exchange and there is not a substantial risk of forfeiture, such as cannot exercise for a year.

        ii. Individual is taxed when the option is exercised on the difference between FMV of the stock on the date of exercise and the option price (bargain element).

        iii. The bargain element is taxed at ordinary income rates and will be included in the employee's W-2.

        iv. Any appreciation that occurs after the date of exercise is taxed as capital gain (basis is the FMV at date of exercise, holding period calculated since the date of exercise determines if long term or short term).

    b. Incentive stock options (ISOs).

        i. No income is recognized when option is granted.

        ii. No regular tax is due when option is exercised.

        iii. Tax is due when stock is sold. If taxpayer does not dispose of stock within two years after option grant and holds the stock for more than one year (after exercise), any gain over the exercise price will be capital gain. If taxpayer sells stock within one year after exercise date, gain is treated as ordinary income. If within the calendar year, then it is W-2 income and there is no AMT positive adjustment if the taxpayer sells stock acquired with options exercised before October 23, 2004. Stock acquired with options exercised after October 22, 2004 and sold in a disqualifying disposition in the same calendar year does not require income or employment tax withholding but is reported as ordinary income.

        iv. AMT may require earlier recognition of income because the difference between the option price and the FMV at date of exercise is an addback for AMT purposes.

Example

- John's employer grants him a nonqualified stock option (NQSO) with an exercise price of $25. John exercises the NQSO when the market value is $40. The $15 difference is included in John's W-2 income and is subject to FICA and FUTA. If John sells the stock two years later for $60, his basis in the stock is $40 and he has a long-term capital gain of $20. The gain will be taxed at 15%.

- George's employer grants him an incentive stock option (ISO) on January 1, 2005, with an exercise price of $25. George exercises the ISO on January 1, 2006, when the market price is $40. No ordinary income recognition is triggered (but $15 will be an AMT adjustment). George sells the stock two years later for $60, his basis is $25 and he has a $35 long-term capital gain (15%) for regular tax.

  Note: His AMT basis is $40, and AMT gain is $20.

F. MUTUAL FUNDS.

1. Mutual funds usually distribute income and capital gains on an annual basis.

2. Taxation of mutual funds:

   a. Capital gains earned by mutual fund.

      i. If the capital gain is distributed to the shareholder in cash, the shareholder will be taxed on the capital gain, and will not be permitted to adjust his or her tax basis in the mutual fund shares.

      ii. If shareholder elects to automatically reinvest the capital gain, the shareholder will still be taxed on the capital gain, but is permitted to increase his or her adjusted tax basis in the mutual fund shares.

      iii. Short-term capital gain distributions are taxed at ordinary income tax rates, and long-term capital gain distributions are taxed at favorable long-term capital gain rates.

   b. Dividends earned by mutual fund.

      i. If the dividend is distributed to the shareholder in cash, the shareholder will be taxed on the dividend, and will not be permitted to adjust his or her tax basis in the mutual fund shares.

      ii. If shareholder elects to automatically reinvest the dividend, the shareholder will still be taxed on the dividend, but is permitted to increase his or her adjusted tax basis in the mutual fund shares.

      iii. Mutual fund dividends may be taxed at favorable capital gain rates if the dividend is considered a qualified dividend.

         A) The following requirements must be met for a dividend to be considered a qualified dividend.

            1) The dividends must have been paid by a U.S. corporation or a qualified foreign corporation.

            2) The shareholder must have held the stock for more than 61 days during the 121-day period that begins 60 days before the ex-dividend date (holding period requirement)

         B) Mutual funds that pass through dividend income to their shareholders must meet the holding period requirement for the dividend-paying stocks that they hold, in order for corresponding amounts that they pay out to be reported as qualified dividends to the shareholders.

   c. Sale of mutual fund shares by shareholder.

      i. When a shareholder sells his or her mutual fund shares, a capital gain or loss will result.

         A) The gain or loss is determined by taking the sales price less the shareholder's adjusted tax basis.

         B) The shareholder has the following options in determining basis of shares sold:

            1) First-in, first-out.

            2) Average cost per share.

            3) Specific identification (must identify shares before the sale).

C) If a shareholder recognizes a capital gain from the sale of mutual fund shares, the capital gain can be offset by any capital losses from the sale of other securities. Conversely, if a shareholder recognizes a capital loss from the sale of mutual fund shares, the capital loss can offset by any capital gains from the sale of other securities.

Example

Tommy purchased a mutual fund with a $10,000 lump-sum amount two years ago. He elected to reinvest all dividends and capital gains. Last year, the mutual fund paid a dividend of $500 and had a capital gain distribution of $200. During the current year, the mutual fund paid a dividend of $700 and had capital gain distribution of $300. Today, Tommy sold all of the mutual fund shares for $20,000.

This year, Tommy will report dividend income of $700 and capital gains of $300 on his personal income tax return, even though the dividend and capital gain were reinvested. The dividend income may be taxed at favorable capital gain rates, if the dividend is a qualified dividend.

Tommy's basis in the mutual fund shares is $11,700 ($10,000 original cost + $500 + $200 + $700 + $300). Since he was taxed on the dividends and capital gains over the two-year holding period, he will be entitled to increase his basis in the mutual fund shares.

Tommy will have a capital gain of $8,300 ($20,000 sales price less $11,700 basis) resulting from the sale of the mutual fund shares. This capital gain can be offset by any capital losses Tommy incurs from the sale of other securities.

G. PERSONAL-USE PROPERTY.

1. The sale of personal-use property at a gain will generally be a capital gain.

2. The loss on a sale of personal-use property is nondeductible.

H. SECTION 1244 STOCK.

1. Gains from the sale of Section 1244 stock are capital gains.

2. Losses on Section 1244 stock are ordinary losses up to $50,000 per year for single taxpayers and up to $100,000 for married filing jointly taxpayers.

3. Any excess losses beyond the $50,000 or $100,000 as applicable in the year are capital losses (subject to offsetting other capital gains and limited to $3,000).

I. EXCHANGE OF E OR EE BONDS FOR HH BONDS.

1. If a cash-basis taxpayer did not make the election to report interest currently on Series E or EE bonds held, he may have exchanged these bonds for Series HH bonds without recognizing any of the deferred interest on the E/EE bonds.

2. The basis of the E/EE bonds carries over, and when the HH bonds are redeemed, the deferred interest is then recognized.

XXII. BUSINESS ORGANIZATIONS

> **Note:** Only a basic understanding of these concepts is usually tested on the exam. Additional information is in Appendix 4.

A. LEGAL FORMS OF BUSINESS ORGANIZATIONS.

1. Sole proprietorship – A business owned by an individual, who is personally liable for the obligations of the business.

2. General partnership – An association of two or more persons, who jointly control and carry on a business as co-owners for the purpose of making a profit. The partners are personally liable for the obligations of the business.

3. Limited partnership – A partnership in which at least one partner is a general partner and at least one other is a limited partner, who does not participate in management and has limited liability.

4. Limited liability partnership (LLP) – Usually a professional partnership (CPAs, attorneys) wherein the partners have limited liability to the extent of investment except where personally liable through malpractice. This form protects the individual assets of the nonmalpracticing partners.

5. Limited liability company (LLC) – An entity where the owners (members) have limited liability for debts and claims of the business even while participating in management. The governing document is called an operating agreement. Some states prohibit single member LLCs.

6. Corporation – A separate legal entity that is created by state law and operates under a common name through its elected management. Owners (shareholders) have limited liability.

7. S Corporation – A corporation with = 100 shareholders, all individuals other than resident aliens, certain estates or trusts, and no more than one class of stock.

B. SOLE PROPRIETORSHIPS.

1. A sole proprietorship is a business owned and controlled by one person who is personally liable for all debts and claims against the business.

2. Advantages of sole proprietorships:

   a. No separate entity (simplicity).

   b. Not costly to establish.

   c. Can respond quickly to business opportunity.

   d. Easy to terminate business.

3. Disadvantages of sole proprietorships:

   a. Not easy to raise capital.

   b. Unlimited liability.

   c. Proprietorship will probably terminate upon death or incapacity of proprietor.

4. Taxation of sole proprietorships.

   a. Income from the sole proprietorship is taxed directly to the proprietor, who must include a Schedule C in his or her individual tax return (Form 1040).

    b.   Neither the formation nor the termination of a proprietorship are taxable events.

C. GENERAL PARTNERSHIPS.

1.   Characteristics of a general partnership are found in partnership law (the law of agency).

    a.   The elements of a general partnership:

       i.   A common ownership interest in an ongoing business.

       ii.   A sharing of profits and losses of the business.

       iii.   A right to participate in the management and operation of the business.

    b.   A partnership is treated as an entity, separate and apart from its individual members for limited purposes:

       i.   The partnership has the capacity to sue and be sued in the name of the partnership (state laws vary).

       ii.   Judgments can be entered against a partnership in its partnership name.

       iii.   The partnership is subject to liquidation proceedings under Federal Bankruptcy Laws.

       iv.   The partnership can participate in transfers and ownership of personal and real property (state laws vary).

    c.   A partnership may be treated as an aggregate under federal laws and some state laws.

2.   Formation of partnership.

    a.   No special state filings are required in forming a general partnership.

    b.   The contribution of money or property to a partnership, in exchange for a partnership interest, is a non-taxable transaction.

    c.   Basis in partnership interest.

       i.   A partner's basis in the partnership interest begins with contributions and is subsequently adjusted by earnings and losses.

         A)   Cash contribution – basis equal to the value of the cash contributed.

         B)   Property contribution – carryover basis.

       ii.   Distributions to partners will reduce basis.

       iii.   A partner's basis is also decreased by any share of his/her liabilities assumed by the partnership.

3.   Taxation of partnerships.

    a.   Partnerships are flow-through entities for purposes of federal income taxation.

    b.   Items of income and deduction, which occur at the partnership level, will not be taxed to the partnership. Instead, those items of income and deduction will be reported to the partner on his or her individual federal income tax return (Form 1040).

    c.   Income and deductions will flow-through to the partner and retain their character. Items which flow-through separately and retain their character include the following:

       i.   Income and loss items (such as ordinary income, rental income, capital gain income, etc.).

       ii.   Deductions (such as charitable contributions, Section 179 expense, etc.).

      iii.   Credits (such as low-income housing, rental real estate, etc.).

      iv.   Investment interest.

      v.   Self-employment.

      vi.   Adjustments and tax preference items (such as depreciation, depletion, etc.).

      vii.   Foreign taxes.

      viii. Other (such as tax-exempt interest income, distributions of property or money, nondeductible expenses, etc.).

  d.   These items of income and deduction are reported on Schedule K of the Federal Partnership Return (Form 1065) and will be reported to the partners on Schedule K-1. Each partner will receive a Schedule K-1 that includes his share or allocation of each item of income and deduction. The sum of all Schedule K-1's will equal the amount reported on Schedule K.

  e.   Each of the separately stated items on Schedule K-1 will be reported in the appropriate place on the partner's individual federal income tax return (Form 1040). For example, interest and dividends are reported on Schedule B.

D. LIMITED PARTNERSHIPS.

1. Formation.

  a.   The partners sign a certificate that sets forth the firm name, nature and duration of business, names of partners, etc.

  b.   The certificate is filed with the designated state or local official.

  c.   The contribution of money or property to the partnership, in exchange for a partnership interest, is a non-taxable transaction.

  d.   Basis in partnership interest.

      i.   A partner's basis in the partnership interest begins with contributions and is subsequently adjusted by earnings and losses.

         A)   Cash contribution – basis equal to the value of the cash contributed.

         B)   Property contribution – carryover basis.

      ii.   Distributions to partners will reduce basis.

      iii.   A partner's basis is also decreased by any share of his/her liabilities assumed by the partnership.

2. Liability of partners to creditors.

  a.   A limited partner is liable to creditors only to the extent of that partner's contributed or promised capital.

  b.   A general partner is liable to creditors in the way of unlimited personal liability.

3. Rights of a partner.

  a.   A limited partner (member) has no authority to bind the partnership; however, a general partner has such authority.

    b. A limited partner and general partner have the same rights as partners in a general partnership with respect to suing, examining books, accounting, the return of partner's capital contribution, the assignments of rights to partner's interest, etc.

4. Taxation of limited partnerships.

    a. Limited partnerships are taxed under the same concepts as a partnership.

    b. See Taxation of Partnerships.

E. FAMILY LIMITED PARTNERSHIP (FLP).

1. Introduction.

    a. A Family Limited Partnership ("FLP") is a partnership with a general partner and at least one limited partner. FLPs are generally designed to address several purposes: convenient administration of investments, while retaining control, as a vehicle for annual gifts for transfer tax planning purposes. In addition, FLPs provide for creditor protection for limited partners.

    b. A typical FLP is instituted by a senior family member who transfers business or investment assets to the partnership. The general partner has significant control over the business activities of the partnership, makes investment and management decisions and determines when distributions should be made to the limited partners. This determination is based upon the general partner's evaluation of the needs of the partnership operations. Often, the senior family member serves as general partner.

    c. The partnership agreement will govern how partnership income is divided among the partners. Generally, both general and limited partners share income and cash flow based on their percentage interest in the partnership. The taxable income of the FLP is reported annually and allocated to each partner on the basis of that partner's percentage interest. The allocation is noted on the Schedule K-1 issued to each partner. Usually, the general partner annually distributes at least enough cash to pay the income tax liability attributable to each partner.

    d. Distributions are not taxable to the extent the partner has basis in the partnership interest. The partnership itself (unlike a corporation) is not subject to tax, because it passes through all items of income and deduction to the partners. Limited partners also have restrictions on their ability to transfer their partnership units to others, so that the general partners can prevent the units from being transferred outside of the family.

2. Advantages.

    a. The principal benefit of an FLP is its significant impact in reducing a transferor's gift and estate tax. By using an FLP, the owner can take advantage of gift and estate tax valuation rules relating to "minority interests" and "marketability" that can reduce transfer taxes. Due to the significant restrictions imposed on the limited partnership units, the partnership units typically will have a value that is approximately 30 percent less than the value of the assets that originally were transferred to the partnership. Actual discounts can range from 25% to 60%. Besides reduced asset values for estate and gift tax purposes through significant valuation discounts, other benefits include:

        i. Ability of the general partners to make substantial gifts yet maintain control of the partnership assets.

        ii. Continuing control of income from transferred assets since distributions from an FLP must be authorized by general partners.

    iii. Identification of partnership assets as separate assets and not marital assets. This would be important in the event of a divorce.

    iv. Control the future investment of family assets and retain a critical mass to enhance future investment opportunities.

    v. Reduced probate costs with respect to real estate located in other states. No ancillary administration is required.

    vi. Institutionalization and enhancement of family communication on family business and investment matters.

F. CORPORATIONS.

1. Nature of corporations.

    a. Business corporations are artificial, legal entities whose creation and operations are controlled by state statutes.

    b. A corporation is regarded as a person who is separate from the shareholders. The owners of interests in corporations, for most purposes under federal and state constitutions and statutes, are not restricted to natural persons.

        i. The capacity of a corporation to sue and be sued in the name of the corporation.

        ii. The protection against self-incrimination (restricted to natural persons).

        iii. Criminal liability.

        iv. Licensing statutes.

    c. Shareholders.

        i. Shareholders are generally the holders of ownership interests in the corporation. Their interests are freely transferable.

        ii. Death of a shareholder does not dissolve or otherwise affect the corporation.

        iii. Shareholders enjoy limited liability (amount of their investment) and are not personally liable for the debts of the corporation.

        iv. Shareholders have equitable interests in, but not legal title to, corporate property.

        v. Shareholders do not represent the corporation but vote for the board of directors which determines corporate policy and appoints officers. The officers represent the corporation.

        vi. Shareholders may sue and be sued by the corporation, and they may deal with the corporation in an "arm's length" transaction.

    d. Tax considerations (double taxation of profits).

        i. The profits of a corporation are taxed to the corporation at special corporate rates.

        ii. Distributions of profits, in the form of dividends, are treated as taxable income to the recipients.

        iii. If shareholders sell their shares, they are taxed on any gains, but perhaps at a rate lower than the rate imposed on ordinary income.

    e. Classifications.

        i. Common stock.

A) The owners of common stock are entitled to a pro rata share of properly declared dividends out of corporate profits without any preferences (e.g., after payment of taxes and interest to lenders and bondholders). They are entitled to any specified dividends required to be paid to preferred shareholders, if any preferred stock has been issued.

B) Common stock shareholders have a right to vote.

C) Common stock shareholders have rights to ultimate distribution of assets of corporation upon dissolution.

ii. Preferred stock – Holders of preferred stock have a preference that usually entails rights to receive dividends or distribution upon liquidation of the corporation. Corporations may issue different classes and/or series of preferred stock.

A) Cumulative preferred – If the corporation fails to pay a dividend, the dividend is carried over and paid in a subsequent year before the holders of common stock receive dividends.

B) Participating preferred – Preferred shareholders share in distribution of additional dividends after payment of dividends to holders of preferred and common stock if there are additional distributions of corporate profits.

C) Convertible preferred – Preferred shares may be exchanged for common stock or other preferred stock at a specified rate.

D) Redeemable (callable) preferred – The corporation has the right to purchase, reacquire and cancel shares at a specified price.

2. Special taxes applicable to C corporations.

  a. In general.

    i. The following special taxes apply exclusively to C corporations:

      A) Personal holding company tax.

      B) Personal service corporation tax.

      C) Accumulated earnings tax.

    ii. These taxes are paid by the C corporation.

  b. Personal holding company tax.

    i. The objective of the personal holding company tax is to discourage individual taxpayers from using the corporate entity solely for tax avoidance.

    ii. The personal holding company tax applies only if the corporation is considered a personal holding company, and the corporation has undistributed personal holding company income.

      A) A corporation will be considered a personal holding company if it meets both of the following tests:

        1) Ownership test – During the last half of the taxable year, greater than 50% of the value of the outstanding stock of the corporation is owned by five or fewer individuals, and

2) Passive income test – At least 60% of the corporation's adjusted ordinary gross income consists of personal holding company income.

    a) Adjusted ordinary gross income is the company's gross income, with several adjustments. Adjustments include reductions for property taxes, depreciation, and interest expense.

    b) Personal holding company income is generally defined as passive income and certain income from services.

B) Undistributed personal holding company income is the corporation's adjusted taxable income, less the dividends paid deduction.

iii. The tax is computed by multiplying the undistributed personal holding company income by the highest individual income tax rate (currently 15% for 2006).

A) The personal holding company tax is levied in addition to the regular tax.

B) Corporations not subject to the personal holding company tax:

1) S corporations.

2) Life insurance companies.

3) Banks.

4) Certain other financial institutions.

c. Personal service corporation tax.

i. Personal service corporations are corporations that meet the following requirements:

A) Involved in fields of health, law, engineering, architecture, accounting, actuarial science, performing arts, or consulting.

B) At least 95% of the stock is held by active or retired employees.

ii. Income earned by a personal service corporation is taxed to the corporation at a flat 35% rate.

d. Accumulated earnings tax.

i. The objective of the accumulated earnings tax is to discourage individual taxpayers from using the corporate entity solely for tax avoidance.

ii. The tax applies whenever a corporation accumulates earnings beyond its reasonable needs, unless the corporation can prove to the contrary by a preponderance of evidence.

3. Taxation at Liquidation.

a. In General.

i. For tax purposes, a liquidation occurs when a corporation is no longer a going-concern.

ii. A complete liquidation is taxed as a sale or exchange to the shareholder. This treatment is similar, but not identical, to the tax treatment of a qualified stock redemption.

b. Effect on Shareholder.

i. In general, the shareholders are treated as having sold their stock to the liquidating corporation. As a result, the shareholders may recognize gain or loss.

  ii. The gain or loss recognized is calculated as the difference between the fair market value of the property received from the corporation and the adjusted basis of the shareholder's stock.

 c. Effect on Corporation.

  i. A liquidating corporation may or may not be required to recognize gain or loss, depending on the nature of the transaction.

  ii. Generally, the corporation is required to recognize gain or loss upon complete liquidation.

   A) The gain or loss is calculated as if the corporation's assets were sold at fair market value.

   B) Losses may be disallowed in certain circumstances.

    1) If the distribution is made to certain related parties, the loss may be disallowed.

    2) If the distribution is made with certain built-in loss property, the loss may be disallowed.

G. S CORPORATIONS.

1. Taxation of S corporation shareholders.

 a. In general, the IRS treats S corporation shareholders as partners. Shareholders of S corporations are required to report pro-rata shares of corporate items that flow through.

 b. It should be noted that while partnerships have great flexibility in the allocation of income and deductions, this advantage is not available to S corporations. All items of income are reported based on the ownership percentage of each shareholder.

 c. The principal advantage of S corporation status is the avoidance of the double taxation scheme associated with C corporation status.

 d. Generally an S corporation must be a calendar year taxpayer unless they can establish a business purpose to the satisfaction of the IRS for the deviation.

 e. For purposes of the Code's fringe benefit provisions, an S corporation is treated as a partnership, and a shareholder-employee who owns more than 2 percent of its stock is treated as a partner. Thus, the value of benefits provided to a more-than-2-percent shareholder-employee must be included in that shareholder's gross income unless the Code specifically allows exclusion of the benefit by a partner.

 f. Accident and health insurance premiums paid by an S corporation for a more-than-two-percent shareholder-employee are deductible by the corporation and are included in the shareholder's gross income. For 2006, 100 percent of the amount included in income may be deducted by the shareholder-employee.

2. Election.

 a. Requirements for S corporation election – must be deemed a "small business corporation."

  i. The entity must be organized under the laws of any U.S. state or territory.

  ii. Shareholders may be individuals, estates, certain trusts or certain tax-exempt organizations. Partnerships and corporations may not be shareholders.

      A) A grantor, voting trust, or a testamentary trust may be an eligible shareholder for two years after the deemed owner's death.

      B) Exempt organizations such as qualified pension plans, profit-sharing plans, stock bonus plans, and charitable organizations may be shareholders.

   iii. Only citizens or residents of the U.S. may be shareholders.

   iv. The entity may only have one class of stock issued and outstanding.

      A) The rights of the holders must be identical with regards to profits and assets of the corporation.

      B) However, two classes are permitted if the only difference is voting rights.

   v. The entity may have no more than 100 shareholders.

      A) A husband and wife (as well as certain families) are considered one shareholder regardless of how they hold their shares.

  b. How to make the election.

   i. S corporation status is elected by having all shareholders consent and file Form 2553 by the 15th day of the 3rd month of the tax year in which the shareholders wish the election to take effect.

   ii. The corporation must meet all of the eligibility requirements in the pre-election period of the tax year in which the shareholders want the election to take effect.

3. Special taxes applicable to S corporations.

  a. In general.

   i. Although S corporations are flow-through entities, they may be required to pay one of the following taxes:

      A) Built-in gains tax.

      B) LIFO recapture tax.

      C) Excess net passive income tax.

   ii. These taxes are paid by the S corporation, not by the shareholders.

  b. Built-in gains tax.

   i. The built-in gains tax applies to S corporations that used to be C corporations.

   ii. The tax is imposed on any unrealized built-in gain that is recognized on the disposition of any asset by the S corporation.

      A) The unrealized built-in gain is the difference between the fair market value and the basis of an asset, as of the date the C corporation converts to an S corporation (conversion date).

      B) The recognized built-in gain is any gain recognized from the sale of an asset within the 10-year period following the S election.

      C) Any assets acquired by the S corporation after the conversion date are not subject to the built-in gains tax.

D) Any appreciation of the asset after the date of conversion is not subject to the built-in gains tax.

Example

Parrish Industries, a former C corporation, elected S corporation status last year (conversion date). On the conversion date, Parrish owned land with a fair market value of $75,000 and an adjusted basis of $50,000. Therefore, the unrealized built-in gain is $25,000 ($75,000 − $50,000). In the current year, Parrish sells the land for $80,000, resulting in a $30,000 gain on sale. Parrish will be subject to built-in gains tax on $25,000, the unrealized built-in gain as of the conversion date.

---

     iii. The tax is computed by applying the highest corporate income tax rate (currently 35%) to the S corporation's net recognized built-in gain for the tax year.

     iv. The amount of recognized built-in gain passed through and taxed to shareholders is reduced by the built-in gain tax paid by the S corporation.

  c. LIFO recapture tax.

     i. The LIFO recapture tax applies to S corporations that used to be C corporations.

     ii. A C corporation that uses the LIFO (last-in, first-out) method of inventory valuation in its last taxable year before making an S corporation election must include in income a LIFO recapture amount.

       A) The LIFO recapture amount is the excess of the inventory valuation under the FIFO (first-in, first-out) method over the inventory valuation under the LIFO method.

       B) The recapture amount is reported in the taxable income of the C corporation in its last tax year.

       C) The inventory's basis is increased by the LIFO recapture amount.

Example

StaceCo converted from a C corporation to an S corporation. On the date of the conversion, StaceCo had inventory with a LIFO basis of $90,000. The FIFO value of the inventory was $140,000. StaceCo must add $50,000 ($140,000 − $90,000) LIFO recapture amount to its last C corporation tax return.

---

     iii. The LIFO recapture tax is the tax on the LIFO recapture amount.

       A) The tax is calculated based on the corporation's ordinary income tax rate.

       B) The tax is payable by the corporation in four installments.

         1) The first installment is due with the C corporation's final income tax return (Form 1120).

2) The remaining three installments are due with the S corporation's income tax returns (Form 1120S) for the three subsequent tax years.

Example

Assume the same facts as in the previous example. If StaceCo is taxed at the 35% corporate income tax rate, its year 2000 tax liability will increase by $17,500 (35% × $50,000 LIFO recapture amount). StaceCo must pay $4,375 (one-fourth of $17,500) of the LIFO recapture tax with its year 2000 corporate income tax return (Form 1120). The remaining three installments of $4,375 must be paid with StaceCo's next three tax returns (Form 1120S).

    C) No interest is due if the required installments are paid on a timely basis.

    D) There is no requirement that estimated tax payments be made with respect to any LIFO recapture tax due.

    E) Any additional appreciation attributable to the inventory (over its FIFO basis) will be subject to the built-in gains tax as the inventory is sold.

d. Excess net passive income tax.

    i. The excess net passive income tax applies to S corporations that used to be C corporations.

    ii. The S corporation must pay a tax on its excess net passive income if passive investment income exceeds 25% of its gross receipts during the year.

        A) Passive investment income is generally gross receipts derived from royalties, rents, dividends, interest, annuities, and gains from sales of securities.

        B) Net passive income is passive investment income reduced by any allowable deduction directly connected with the production of such income.

        C) The tax is imposed on the excess net passive income (ENPI). ENPI is calculated as follows:

$$\text{ENPI} = \text{Net passive income} \times \frac{\text{Passive investment income less 25\% of gross receipts}}{\text{Passive investment income}}$$

        D) The tax only applies if the S corporation has accumulated earnings and profits at the end of its taxable year.

    iii. Tax on excess passive income.

    A) The tax is based on the maximum corporate income tax rate (currently 35%).

Example

In the current year, SAP Company, an S corporation that was formerly a C corporation, had gross receipts of $200,000. Gross receipts included $75,000 of passive rental income. Rental expenses were $30,000 for the year. Therefore, SAP Company has excess net passive income (ENPI) of $15,000 for the taxable year. The ENPI is calculated as follows:

$$\$15,000 = \$45,000 \times \frac{[\$75,000 - (25\% \times \$200,000)]}{\$75,000}$$

The excess net passive income tax is $5,250 (35% × $15,000).

    B) The tax on excess net passive income paid by the S corporation reduces the amount of each item of passive investment income that flows through to the shareholders.

4. Revocation and termination of S corporation status.

    a. This election may be revoked by the consent of more than half of the corporate shareholders (including non-voting) and may specify a particular date, but if not, revocation is effective the first of the following tax year unless made effective in the first 15 days of tax year in which case it relates back to the beginning of the tax year.

    b. S corporation status is terminated on the day a terminating event occurs (any event which causes the S corporation to no longer meet the requirements of S corporation status).

      i. If a corporation has accumulated earnings and profits as well as passive investment income that exceeds 25% of gross receipts for three consecutive years, its election will be terminated beginning with the following year.

    c. Taxation at Liquidation.

      i. S corporations are subject to many of the same liquidation rules applicable to C corporations.

      ii. In general, the distribution of property to shareholders in complete liquidation is treated as if the property was sold to the shareholders.

      iii. The S corporation incurs no tax on liquidation gains.

H. LIMITED LIABILITY COMPANIES (LLCs).

1. LLCs are one of the most versatile types of entities. An LLC provides limited liability to its members and allows great flexibility regarding the taxation of the entity.

2. Formation of LLCs.

    a. To form a new LLC, the members file an article of organization with the state.

      i. Costs of forming an LLC may be higher than with other business entities because LLCs are new and there is unfamiliarity.

      ii. Operating agreement is created.

    b.   A partnership or corporation can be converted to an LLC.

    c.   No limit on the number of members allowed.

    d.   The formation of an LLC is a non-taxable event.

3.   Taxation of LLCs.

    a.   An LLC can be taxed as any of the following:

        i.   Sole proprietorship – only available for single owned LLCs. The owner will disregard the LLC for tax purposes and simply file a Schedule C on the individual return (Form 1040) to report the activity of the LLC.

        ii.   Partnership – available for LLCs with 2 or more owners (members). A partnership return (Form 1065) will be filed to report the income of the LLC. The members will each receive a Schedule K-1 with their apportioned income and will report this income on the appropriate schedule on their individual federal income tax returns (Form 1040).

        iii.   Corporation – available for any LLC. A corporate return (Form 1120) will be filed to report income of the LLC. Just as a corporation, the LLC will have two levels of taxation.

        iv.   S Corporation – available for those LLCs that elect to be treated as a corporation (association) and file Form 2553 to elect small business treatment. This form must be filed by the 15th day of the third month after the beginning of the LLC. As with shareholders of S Corporations, members will report income on their individual federal tax returns based on the Schedule K-1 they receive from the S Corporation return (Form 1120S).

EXHIBIT 31: DIFFERENCES BETWEEN TYPES OF BUSINESS ORGANIZATIONS

	Type of Business Organization					
	Sole Proprietor	Partnership*	LLP	LLC**	S-Corp	Corporation
What type of liability do the owners have?	Unlimited	General Partnership – Unlimited; Limited Partnership – Limited	Limited	Limited	Limited	Limited
What federal tax form is required to be filed for the organization?	Form 1040, Schedule C	Form 1065	Form 1065	Form 1040, Schedule C or Form 1065 or Form 1120 or Form 1120S	Form 1120S	Form 1120
Under what concept is the organization taxed?	Individual Level	Flow-through	Flow-through	LLCs can be taxed as sole proprietorships, partnerships, corporations, or S-corporations	Flow-through	Entity Level
On what tax form is the owner's compensation reported?	Form 1040, Schedule C	Schedule K-1	Schedule K-1	Form 1040, Schedule C, or Schedule K-1, or Form W-2 and Schedule K-1, or W-2	W-2 and Schedule K-1	W-2 (dividends are reported on Form 1099-div)
What is the nature of the owner's income from the organization?	Self-employment income	Self-employment Income*	Self-employment income	Self-employment income, or W-2 income and ordinary income, W-2 income	W-2 income and ordinary income	W-2 income and dividend income
What is the basis for determining tax-advantaged retirement plan contributions?	Net Schedule C income (less ½ SE tax)	Self-employment Income* (less ½ SE tax)	Self-employment Income (less ½ SE tax)	Self-employment income (less ½ SE tax) or W-2 income	W-2 income	W-2 income

Flow-through: All items of income will flow from the entity to the individual partners/owners/members return while retaining the character of the income at the entity level.

* Limited Partners will generally not have self-employment income.

** The LLC will have the same tax characteristics and attributes as the type of entity it has elected to be taxed as.

Note: Family Limited Partnerships (FLPs) have the same treatment for general partners as general partnerships and for limited partners the same treatment as limited partnerships.

XXIII. TAXATION OF TRUSTS AND ESTATES

A. IN GENERAL.

1. A trust is a legal arrangement whereby an individual transfers legal ownership of property to a trustee.

2. Trusts are generally treated as separate taxable entities subject to taxation under Subchapter J of the Internal Revenue Code.

3. An estate is a legal entity that comes into existence upon the death of an individual and remains in existence until the decedent's assets pass to the heirs.

   a. The estate consists of the probate estate.

   b. The estate holds and protects the assets, collects income from those assets, and satisfies obligations of the estate until all the assets are distributed.

4. Trusts and estates are referred to as fiduciaries.

5. Trust income can be taxed to:

   a. Trust – if income is accumulated in the trust.

   b. Beneficiary – if income is distributed from the trust.

   c. Grantor – if the trust is a grantor trust (discussed below).

B. TYPES OF TRUSTS.

1. Simple trust.

   a. Required to distribute all income to beneficiaries each year.

   b. Charitable donations are prohibited.

   c. Principal distributions are prohibited.

   d. Allowed a personal exemption of $300.

2. Complex trust.

   a. A trust in which income can be accumulated.

   b. Principal can be distributed.

   c. The trust pays tax on accumulated income.

   d. Allowed a personal exemption of $100.

3. Grantor trust.

   a. If a trust is a grantor trust, the grantor pays tax on all trust income.

   b. Trust is ignored for income tax purposes.

   c. A trust will be a grantor trust if the grantor retains the power to control enjoyment. These powers include the power to:

      i. Add or remove beneficiaries.

      ii. Determine the timing of distributions.

      iii. Alter the beneficiary's share of principal or income.

C. FIDUCIARY ACCOUNTING INCOME.

1. The accounting income of a fiduciary is determined by the decedent's will (in the case of an estate), or the trust instrument (in the case of a trust).

2. Every fiduciary may have its own unique set of rules for the computation of accounting income.

3. A common difference between fiduciary accounting income and fiduciary taxable income is the treatment of capital gains.

   a. For accounting purposes, capital gains generally represent an increase in the value of the principal and are not available for distribution to the income beneficiaries.

   b. For tax purposes, the capital gains represent taxable income.

4. Trustee fees are generally deductible for tax purposes, but may be treated as either income or principal for trust accounting purposes.

D. FIDUCIARY TAXABLE INCOME AND DISTRIBUTION DEDUCTION.

1. The taxable income of a trust is similar to the calculation of taxable income for an individual taxpayer.

2. Major differences between trust taxable income and individual taxable income:

   a. A trust is entitled to a deduction for distributions made to beneficiaries.

   b. A trust is not entitled to a standard deduction.

   c. A trust is entitled to a personal exemption of $300 for a simple trust and $100 for a complex trust.

3. If an administrative expense is claimed as a deduction on the estate tax return of a decedent, it may not also be claimed as a deduction on the income tax return of the decedent's estate. However, the deduction can be prorated between the two returns.

4. Medical expenses paid for the care of the decedent before his or her death:

   a. If paid within one year after death, the medical expenses can be deducted either on the final income tax return (Form 1040) of the decedent or the estate tax return of the decedent (Form 706), but not both.

   b. If paid more than one year after death, the expenses can only be deducted on the estate tax return.

5. Deduction for distributions made to beneficiaries.

   a. The fiduciary is allowed a deduction for the amount of distributions made to beneficiaries during the year. The amount deductible by the fiduciary is the same amount that is taxable to the beneficiaries.

   b. The distribution deduction is calculated as the lesser of Distributable Net Income (DNI) or the amount actually distributed to the beneficiaries.

   c. Distributable Net Income (DNI).

      i. DNI is similar to fiduciary accounting income.

      ii. Includes most normal income/expense items.

      iii. Excludes items relating to corpus such as capital gains, stock splits, and depreciation of business assets.

E. FIDUCIARY TAX RATES AND FILING REQUIREMENTS.

1. Fiduciaries file Form 1041 on or before the 15th day of the fourth month after the close of the tax year. Grantor trusts may also file a Form 1041.

2. A trust must adopt a calendar year.

3. Estates may adopt either a calendar year or fiscal year. The first taxable year begins on the day following the decedent's death.

4. Estates and trusts are subject to the following rate schedule (a very highly progressive structure).

Trust and Estate Tax Rates (Year 2006)

If taxable income is:			
Over --	But not over --	The tax is:	Of the amount over --
$0	$2,050	---------------15%	$0
$2,000	$4,850	$307.50 + 25%	$2,050
$4,700	$7,400	$1,007.50 + 28%	$4,850
$7,150	$10,050	$1,721.50 + 33%	$7,400
$9,750	------------	$2,596.00 + 35%	$10,050

5. Any component of fiduciary taxable income consisting of long-term capital gain is taxed at a maximum rate of 15%.

6. Trusts may be subject to alternative minimum tax.

F. TAX TREATMENT OF DISTRIBUTIONS TO BENEFICIARIES.

1. Beneficiary is taxed on an amount equal to the distribution deduction.

2. The fiduciary receives a deduction for the distribution.

3. Income distributed to the beneficiary maintains its character (capital gain, ordinary income, etc.).

4. A beneficiary who receives a distribution from a fiduciary will receive a Schedule K-1 each year. The K-1 summarizes the amounts and character of the various items of income that constitute the taxable portion of the distribution.

5. A beneficiary who receives a distribution from a fiduciary with both taxable and nontaxable DNI will only be taxed on a portion of the distribution received.

Example

ABC Trust has DNI of $100,000, of which $40,000 is nontaxable. The beneficiary received a distribution of $20,000 during the year. The distribution received will be taxable in the amount of $12,000 [$20,000 distribution × ($60,000 taxable DNI divided by $100,000 total DNI)] and nontaxable for the remaining $8,000.

---

6. Because a simple trust is required to distribute all trust income to its beneficiaries, the entire amount of taxable DNI will be taxed to the beneficiaries each year.

XXIV. AUDIT, PENALTIES, AND TAXPAYER'S RIGHTS

A. IN GENERAL.

1. A Taxpayer Compliance Measurement Program (TCMP) randomly selected returns used for statistical purposes of the IRS to develop discriminate analysis standards (presently indefinitely suspended).

2. Audit probability varies with income level and type of income.

3. Situations that might trigger an audit.

   a. Significant investment losses.

   b. Business expenses that produce significant losses.

   c. Operating a cash business.

   d. Deductions that are larger than the average deduction taken by taxpayers at a similar income level.

B. TYPES OF AUDITS.

1. A correspondence audit is one in which the issue is generally minor and is performed through the mail.

2. An office audit is usually restricted in scope to specific item(s) and is performed at the IRS office.

3. A field audit is an examination of numerous items and is performed on the premises of the taxpayer.

C. STATUTE OF LIMITATIONS.

1. Three years from the filing date of the return or due date if later.

2. Six years if 25% of gross income is unreported.

3. No statute of limitations for failure to file or if a fraudulent return is filed.

D. INTEREST AND PENALTIES.

1. Interest – Interest runs from unextended due date.

2. Penalties.

   a. Failure to file: 5.0% per month up to 25%. If failure-to-file penalty is fraudulent, the penalty is increased to 15% per month up to a 75% maximum.

   b. Failure to pay: 0.5% per month up to 25%. If both a failure-to-file penalty and a failure-to-pay penalty apply, the failure-to-file penalty is reduced by the failure-to-pay penalty.

   c. Accuracy-related penalty: 20% of underpayment for intentional disregard of rules and regulations without intent to defraud.

Example

Taxpayer files a timely tax return but fails to pay an amount of $15,000 in additional tax. $6,000 is attributable to the taxpayer's negligence. The negligence penalty will be $1,200. A 20% penalty is applied to the $6,000.

      d.   There are various fraud penalties for deliberate actions (deceit, misrepresentation, and concealment).

Example

Taxpayer files tax return 39 days after the due date. Along with the return he remits a check for $6,000, which is the balance of the tax owed. Disregarding any interest element, the total failure-to-file and failure-to-pay penalties are $600.

Calculated as follows:

Failure-to-pay penalty:

[1/2% × $6,000 × 2 (two months, any fraction counts as a full month)]	$60	
Plus: Failure-to-file penalty [5% × $6,000 × 2 months]	600	
Less: Failure-to-pay penalty (they run concurrently)	(60)	540
Total penalties (failure-to-file and failure-to-pay)		$600

The failure-to-file penalty of $600 is reduced by the failure-to-pay penalty of $60 making the adjusted failure-to-file penalty $540. Adding the failure-to-pay penalty of $60 (it reduced the failure-to-file, but it did not go away) makes a total penalty of $600.

E. BURDEN OF PROOF.

1.   The IRS has the burden of proof on factual matters if the taxpayer has creditable evidence supporting his or her position.

    a.   The taxpayer must have records and must cooperate with IRS.

    b.   Corporations, trusts, and estates must have a net worth of $7 million or less to qualify.

F. INNOCENT SPOUSE RELIEF.

1.   If a married couple files jointly, both spouses are jointly and individually responsible for the tax and any interest or penalty due on the joint return.

    a.   One spouse may be held responsible for all the tax due even if all the income was earned by the other spouse.

    b.   However, a spouse may be relieved of the tax, interest, and penalties on a joint tax return in some cases.

2.   To receive relief, an individual must file Form 8857, Request for Innocent Spouse Relief.

    a.   Only one Form 8857 needs to be filed, even if the spouse is requesting relief for more than one tax year.

    b.   An individual should file Form 8857 as soon as they become aware of a tax liability for which they believe only their spouse should be held liable.

    c.   An executor may also file Form 8857 on behalf of a decedent, provided the decedent satisfied the eligibility requirements while alive.

3.   Types of relief available:

    a.   Innocent spouse relief.

        i.   By requesting innocent spouse relief, an individual can be relieved of responsibility for paying tax, interest, and penalties if their current or former spouse improperly reported (or omitted) items from the joint tax return.

        ii.   An individual must meet all of the following conditions to qualify for innocent spouse relief:

            A)   An individual filed a joint return which has an understatement of tax due as a result of erroneous items (unreported income, erroneous deductions, etc.) of the individual's current or former spouse.

            B)   The individual can establish that, at the time they signed the joint return, they did not know that there was an understatement of tax.

            C)   After taking into account all of the facts and circumstances, it would be unfair to hold the individual liable for the understatement of tax.

    b.   Relief by separation of liability.

        i.   When requesting relief by separation of liability, an individual can allocate any understatement of tax between themselves and their spouse.

        ii.   The individual is only responsible for their own portion of any underpayment.

        iii.   An individual must meet both of the following conditions to qualify for relief by separation of liability:

            A)   The individual must have filed a joint return.

            B)   The individual must meet one of the following requirements:

                1)   The individual is no longer married to (or separated from) the spouse with whom they filed the joint return.

                2)   The individual was not a member of the same household as the spouse with whom they filed the joint return.

    c.   Equitable relief.

        i.   If an individual does not qualify for innocent spouse relief or relief by separation of liability, they can still be relieved of responsibility for tax, interest, and penalties through equitable relief.

        ii.   An individual must meet all of the following conditions to qualify for equitable relief:

            A)   The individual does not qualify for innocent spouse relief or relief by separation of liability.

  B) The individual and the spouse (or former spouse) did not transfer assets to one another as a part of a fraudulent scheme.

  C) The individual did not file the return with the intent to commit fraud.

  D) After taking into account all the facts and circumstances, it would be unfair to hold the individual liable for the understatement of tax.

  E) The income tax liability from which the individual seeks relief must generally be attributable to an item of the spouse (or former spouse) with whom the individual filed the joint return.

G. REPRESENTING CLIENTS BEFORE THE IRS.

1. In General.

 a. Only a recognized representative can represent a client before the Internal Revenue Service.

 b. A representative can act on the client's behalf at conferences, hearings, or meetings with the IRS.

 c. The representative must be granted authority to act on behalf of the client. Authority is granted through a Power of Attorney.

2. Recognized Representative.

 a. A recognized representative must file a written declaration with the IRS that states he or she is qualified and authorized to represent the client.

 b. Recognized representatives can include:

  i. Attorneys.

  ii. CPAs.

  iii. Enrolled agents or enrolled actuaries.

  iv. Certain unenrolled individuals, such as an unenrolled tax return preparer.

   A) Unenrolled individuals typically have limited authority to represent the client.

   B) Unenrolled individuals must present satisfactory identification and proof of authority to represent the client.

 c. Recognized representatives do not include:

  i. Individuals convicted of a criminal offense.

  ii. Individuals under disbarment or suspension from practicing as attorneys, CPAs, or actuaries.

  iii. Individuals who are suspended from practice before the IRS.

  iv. Officers or employees of the U.S. government or of the District of Columbia.

  v. Members of Congress, if receiving compensation regarding the IRS issue.

  vi. CFP® Practitioners.

3. Power of Attorney.

 a. A power of attorney is a written authorization for an individual to act on one's behalf.

 b. With a power of attorney, any representative (other than an unenrolled preparer) can usually perform the following acts:

      i.   Represent the client before the IRS.

      ii.   Record the interview.

      iii.   Sign on the client's behalf:

         A)   Waiver of restriction on assessment or collection of a tax deficiency.

         B)   Consent to extend the statutory time period for assessment or collection of a tax.

         C)   Closing agreement.

      iv.   Receive (but not cash) a refund check.

  c.   A representative generally cannot sign a client's income tax return, except as preparer.

H. REFORM OF IRS'S PROCEDURES.

  1.   Extensive reform of the IRS's procedures relating to audit:

    a.   There must be a reasonable notice on third-party summons.

    b.   The Act limits use of financial status and economic reality techniques.

    c.   The criteria for audit selection must be disclosed.

    d.   The attorney-client privilege is extended to tax advisers who are authorized to practice before the IRS.

    e.   Due process must be followed for tax collection levies.

APPENDIX 1: HOW TO PROVE CERTAIN BUSINESS EXPENSES

If you have expenses for:	THEN you must keep records that show details of the following elements.			
	Amount	Time	Place or Description	Business Purpose and Business Relationship
Travel	Cost of each separate expense for travel, lodging, and meals. Incidental expenses may be totaled in reasonable categories such as taxis, daily meals for traveler, etc.	Dates you left and returned for each trip and number of days spent on business.	Destination or area of your travel (name of city, town, or other designation).	Purpose: Business purpose for the expense or the business benefit gained or expected to be gained. Relationship: N/A
Entertainment	Cost of each separate expense. Incidental expenses such as taxis, telephones, etc., may be totaled on a daily basis.	Date of entertainment. (Also see Business Purpose).	Name and address or location of place of entertainment. Type of entertainment if not otherwise apparent. (Also see Business Purpose.)	Purpose: Business purpose for the expense or the business benefit gained or expected to be gained. For entertainment, the nature of the business discussion or activity. If the entertainment was directly before or after a business discussion; the date, place, nature, and duration of the business discussion, and the identities of the persons who took part in both the business discussion and the entertainment activity. Relationship: Occupations or other information (such as names, titles, or other designations) about the recipients that shows their business relationship to you. For entertainment, you must also prove that you or your employee was present if the entertainment was a business meal.
Gifts	Cost of the gift.	Date of the gift.	Description of the gift.	
Transportation (cars)	Cost of each separate expense. For car expenses, the cost of the car and any improvements, the date you started using it for business, the mileage for each business use, and the total miles for the year.	Date of the expense. For car expenses, the date of the use of the car.	Your business destination (name of city, town, or other designation).	Purpose: Business purpose for the expense. Relationship: N/A

IRS Publication 17; Table 28-2

Note: While it is unlikely that the exam will test substantiation requirements in this detail, the chart is provided for your convenience.

APPENDIX 2: TRAVEL, ENTERTAINMENT, AND GIFT EXPENSES AND REIMBURSEMENTS

Type of Reimbursement (or Other Expense Allowance) Arrangement	Employer Reports on Form W-2	Employee Shows on Form 2106[1]
Accountable		
Actual expense reimbursement. Adequate accounting and excess returned.	Not reported.	Not shown if expenses do not exceed reimbursement.
Actual expense reimbursement. Adequate accounting and return of excess both required but excess not returned.	Excess reported as wages in box 1.[2] Amount adequately accounted for is reported only in box 13 -- it is not reported in box 1.	All expenses (and reimbursements reported on Form W-2, box 13) only if some or all of the excess expenses are claimed.[3] Otherwise, the form is not filed.
Per diem or mileage allowance (up to federal rate). Adequate accounting and excess returned.	Not reported.	All expenses and reimbursements only if excess expenses are claimed.[3] Otherwise, form is not filed.
Per diem or mileage allowance (exceeds federal rate). Adequate accounting up to the federal rate only and excess not returned.	Excess reported as wages in box 1.[2] Amount up to the federal rate is reported only in box 13 -- it is not reported in box 1.	All expenses (and reimbursements equal to the federal rate) only if expenses in excess of the federal rate are claimed.[3] Otherwise, form is not filed.
Nonaccountable Either adequate accounting or return of excess, or both, not required by plan.	Entire amount is reported as wages in box 1.	All expenses.[3]
No Reimbursement	Normal reporting of wages, etc.	All expenses.[3]

IRS Publication 334

[1] Employees may be able to use Form 2106-EZ. The qualifications are listed on the form.

[2] Excess is also reported in boxes 3 and 5, if applicable.

[3] Any allowable business expense is carried to line 20 of Schedule A (Form 1040) and deducted as a miscellaneous itemized deduction.

APPENDIX 3: ARE MY POINTS FULLY DEDUCTIBLE THIS YEAR?

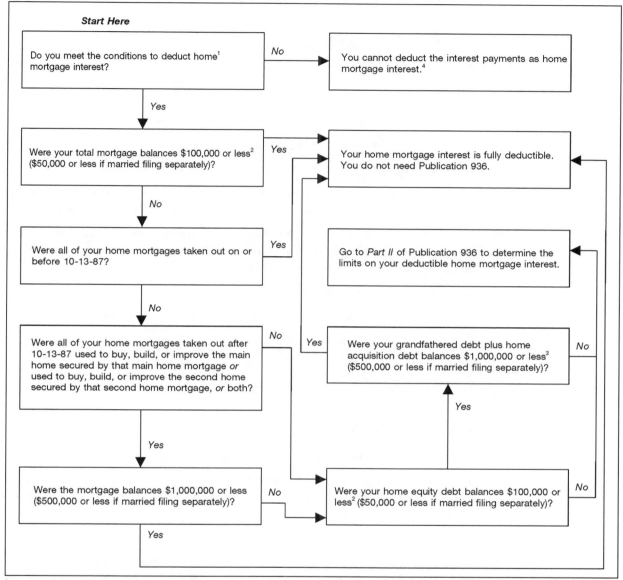

[1]You must itemize deductions on Schedule A (Form 1040) and be legally liable for the loan. The loan must be a secured debt on a qualified home. See *Home Mortgage Interest*.

[2]If all mortgages on your main or second home exceed the home's fair market value, a lower limit may apply. See *Home equity debt limit* under *Home Equity Debt* in *Part II* of Publication 936.

[3]Amounts over the $1,000,000 limit ($500,000 if married filing separately) qualify as home equity debt if they are not more than the total home equity debt limit. See Publication 936 for more information about grandfathered debt, home acquisition debt, and home equity debt.

[4]See *Table 25-1* for where to deduct other types of interest payments.

IRS Publication 17; Figure 25-B

> **Note:** While this is unlikely to be tested in this detail on the exam, the chart is provided for your convenience.

APPENDIX 4: BUSINESS ORGANIZATIONS

> **Note:** Only a basic understanding of these concepts is usually tested on the exam.

I. GENERAL PARTNERSHIPS.

1. Formation of a partnership.

   a. No special formality is ordinarily necessary to create a partnership.

   b. A partnership may be expressly created by contract.

      i. Partnership agreement may be either a verbal contract or a written contract.

         A) A partnership agreement must be in writing in order to be enforceable, under the Statute of Frauds, if it authorizes partners to deal in transfers of real property.

         B) If a partnership is formed for a term of more than one year under a verbal agreement, it is treated as a partnership at will, which may be terminated by any party without liability. A partnership for term requires the assent of all partners for dissolution.

         C) Usual contents of articles of partnership:

            1) Name – State law may restrict use of certain names and/or words.

            2) Nature of business and duration.

            3) Contributions to be made by individual partners.

            4) Manner of dividing profits and losses – Unless otherwise specified, partners share profits and losses equally.

            5) Salaries and drawing accounts, if any.

            6) Restrictions on the authority of any partners.

            7) Conditions for withdrawal from partnership and provisions for the continuation of the business if the partnership is dissolved (partnership buy and sell agreement).

      ii. Capacity of partners.

         A) Minors – Partnership agreement is voidable by a partner who is a minor. However, if rights of creditors are involved, the minor cannot withdraw his or her original investment in the partnership.

         B) If a partner is adjudicated to be mentally incompetent or insane after the partnership is formed, the partnership is not automatically dissolved.

         C) Corporations – State laws vary.

            1) Traditionally, a corporation could not be a partner.

            2) If that corporation's charter (certificate or articles of incorporation) so provides, it may be a partner.

      iii. Consent to formation of partnership by all partners is necessary.

   c. Partnership may be implied if parties intended to be co-owners of a business.

      i. Factors to be considered:

A) Joint ownership of business property.

B) Sharing management responsibilities.

C) Contributing capital or investing jointly.

D) Sharing profits or losses.

    ii. It does not, however, necessarily mean that a group of people has formed a partnership if they are co-owners of property or share gross income.

    iii. A person will not be treated as a partner merely because he or she receives a share of profits in payment of a debt, wages, interest on a loan, annuity to a widow or representative of a deceased partner, or consideration for the sale of goodwill or other property.

2. Partnership property includes:

    a. Real and personal property contributed by individual partners at the time of formation of the partnership or subsequently for the permanent use of the partnership.

    b. Property subsequently acquired with partnership funds on account of the partnership.

    c. Any realized appreciation in the value of partnership property.

3. Rights and duties of partners.

    a. Each partner has a right and a duty to share in the management of the partnership. Unless otherwise provided in the partnership agreement:

        i. Each partner has one vote, regardless of his or her interest in the firm.

        ii. In connection with ordinary business decisions, majority vote controls.

        iii. Unanimous consent is required for changing the partnership agreement, for altering the scope of the business or the capital structure, and in matters significantly affecting the nature, liability, or existence of the partnership.

        iv. Each partner is expected to devote full time and exclusive service to the partnership absent of a contrary agreement.

        v. Unless otherwise agreed, partners do not receive remuneration for their partnership services, except that surviving partners are entitled to reasonable compensation for services rendered in winding up the affairs of the dissolved partnership.

        vi. Each partner has the right to examine the books and records of the partnership, which should be maintained at the place of business of the firm, and has the right to information concerning the partnership's business from co-partners.

    b. Property rights.

        i. Rights with respect to specific partnership property.

           A) Partners are tenants in partnership, which means they are co-owners of partnership property with the right to possession for partnership purposes.

           B) Upon the death of a partner, rights in specific partnership property vest in the remaining partners.

           C) A partner may not assign rights to specific partnership property nor subject it to marital rights, attachment or execution by the partner's individual creditors, etc.

    ii.   Rights to an interest in the partnership.

        A) Each partner has a right to a share of the profits and surplus (considered to be personal property).

        B) A partner's interest in the partnership is subject to assignment, attachment, and other charging orders. An assignment does not dissolve the partnership or permit an assignee to interfere with management.

  c. Fiduciary duties.

    i.   Each partner is an agent for co-partners and is, therefore, accountable as a fiduciary.

    ii. A partner must act in good faith with loyalty and honesty for the benefit of the partnership and make full disclosure to co-partners of matters relating to the partnership.

    iii. A partner will be liable for any personal gain or profits derived from using the partnership property or the exercise of power as a partner.

4. Relationship between partners and third persons.

  a. In dealing with third persons on behalf of the partnership, each partner acts as an agent for the partnership and its members.

  b. A partner's authority to bind the partnership contractually may be based upon:

    i.   Express actual authority provided for in the partnership agreement.

    ii. Implied actual authority.

        A) Necessary for the conduct of the ordinary business of the partnership.

        B) Usually, partners have broad implied authority, which will vary with the nature of the particular business of each partnership, unless limited by agreement.

    iii. Apparent authority.

        A) A third person who deals with a partner may assume that the partner has authority to bind the firm in a transaction relating to the usual business of the firm.

        B) Unless the third person knows that the partner lacks authority, the partnership and co-partners will be liable to the third party for any damage.

    iv. Partners may ratify unauthorized acts of a partner.

  c. Admissions and representations concerning partnership affairs made by an authorized partner bind the partnership if they are made while conducting the ordinary business of the partnership.

  d. Knowledge of or notice to a partner of facts concerning matters relevant to the partnership's affairs will be imputed to the partnership and other partners.

  e. The partnership and the co-partners are liable for breaches of trust and for torts committed by a partner or employee while acting within the scope of his or her authority in the ordinary course of business of the partnership.

  f. Liability of partners to third persons – Partners are jointly liable in contract. In most states, actions based upon contract must be brought against all the partners jointly (together).

5. Termination of partnership – Occurs following the dissolution and winding up (liquidation) of a partnership.

a.   Dissolution – Occurs when a partner ceases to be associated with the partnership business, resulting in a change in the relation of the partners.

   i.   By acts of the partners:

   A)   If the partnership agreement provided for a partnership for term and the term has elapsed or the purpose for which it was formed has been accomplished, the partnership is dissolved.

   B)   Partners may mutually agree to dissolution.

   C)   If the partnership is a partnership at will, a partner's good faith withdrawal or expulsion dissolves the partnership without liability.

   D)   If the partnership was for a specified term, withdrawal of a partner without cause will subject the withdrawing partner to liability; expulsion without cause subjects other partners to liability.

   E)   Admission of a new partner results in dissolution of the former partnership and the creation of a new one. The new partnership is liable for the obligations of the old partnership.

   F)   Voluntary or involuntary transfer of a partner's interest for the benefit of creditors does not automatically dissolve a partnership.

   ii.   Dissolution by operation of law:

   A)   Death of a partner.

   B)   Bankruptcy of the partnership or a partner (in most cases).

   C)   Illegality, which makes it unlawful to continue the business or continue with one of the partners.

   iii.   Dissolution by judicial decree:

   A)   Upon application of a partner.

   1)   A partner has been judicially declared mentally incompetent.

   2)   A partner is permanently incapable of participating in management.

   3)   The business of the partnership can only be operated at a loss.

   4)   Improper conduct of a partner.

   5)   Serious personal dissension among partners.

   B)   Upon application of a third party.

   1)   Assignee of a partner if it was a partnership at will.

   2)   Judgment creditor of a partner who obtained a charge on the interest of the partner's debtor in the partnership.

b.   Winding up.

   i.   Dissolution terminates the authority of partners, except the authority to complete unfinished business. Unfinished business is that which is necessary for winding up, including collecting, preserving, and selling partnership assets, discharging liabilities, collecting debts owed to the partnership, allocating current income, and accounting to each other for the value of their interests in the partnership.

ii. Distribution of assets.

A) Distribution is made out of partnership assets and any additional contributions by partners necessary to pay liabilities of the partnership.

B) Order of payment:

1) Payment to outside creditors.

2) Payment to partners who have made advances or incurred liabilities on behalf of the partnership.

3) Return of capital contributions to partners.

4) Payment of any surplus to partners in accordance with ratios fixed by agreement or, if none, equally.

C) Concept of marshaling of assets arises when the partnership and/or an individual partner is insolvent.

1) If the partnership is insolvent, partnership's creditors have priority over individual's creditors with respect to partnership assets. The partnership's creditors may then look to partners' assets.

2) If a partner is insolvent, the order of payment is:

a) Partner's creditors.

b) Partnership creditors.

iii. Taxation at Dissolution.

A) In General.

1) When dissolution occurs, the partnerships taxable year closes with respect to all its partners.

2) If partners use different taxable years than the partnership, a bunching of income may occur.

B) Liquidating Distributions.

1) When a partnership liquidates, the liquidating distributions made to a partner usually consist of an interest of several partnership assets.

2) The partner may be required to recognize gain on the distribution. The calculation of gain is based on a set of distribution ordering rules.

a) Cash is considered distributed first. The partner will recognize gain to the extent the cash received exceeds his or her basis in the partnership interest.

b) The partner's remaining basis is then allocated to inventory and receivables.

c) Any additional basis is then allocated to the other assets received by the partner.

3) If the partner received only money, receivables, or inventory, the partner will be allowed to recognize a loss if the partner's basis in the partnership interest exceeds the partner's basis in the assets distributed.

4) The partnership itself typically does not recognize gain or loss on liquidating distributions.

J. LIMITED PARTNERSHIPS.

1. Dissolution.

   a. By acts of parties.

      i. Expiration of term in which the partnership was formed.

      ii. If the partnership is not formed for a specified term, the will of a general partner.

      iii. Withdrawal or expulsion of a general partner unless otherwise provided in the certificate or unless members consent to continuation.

   b. By operation of law.

      i. Death or insanity of a general partner if the business cannot be continued in accordance with certificate or consent of other members.

      ii. Illegality.

      iii. Bankruptcy of firm or a general partner.

   c. Limited partner's withdrawal, death, assignment of interest or bankruptcy (unless it causes the bankruptcy of the firm) does not result in the dissolution of the firm.

   d. Winding up and liquidation procedure, following dissolution, is the same as that for a general partnership except for the priorities in distribution.

      i. The Uniform Limited Partnership Act specifies the following order for distribution of the partnership's assets:

         A) Outside creditors.

         B) Limited partners' shares of profit and any other compensation.

         C) Limited partners' return of capital contributions.

         D) Advances, loans, etc. made by general partners.

         E) General partners' shares of profits.

         F) General partners' return of capital contributions.

      ii. The Revised Uniform Limited Partnership Act changes the order by including claims of partners, who are creditors, with outside creditors and combining limited and general partners together.

K. CORPORATIONS.

1. Classifications of corporations.

   a. Based upon location.

      i. Domestic corporation – Conducts business in the state of its incorporation.

      ii. Foreign corporation – Conducts business outside of the state of its incorporation.

      iii. Alien corporation – Incorporated in a country other than the United States.

   b. Based upon sources of funds (or revenue), function and ownership arrangements.

      i. Public corporation – Formed by legislative bodies for governmental purposes.

      ii. Private corporation – Created for private benefit.

        A) Issues shares of stock.

        B) May be a closely held corporation – Shares of stock are held by one individual or by a small group.

    iii. Nonprofit corporation – Organized for charitable, religious, educational, social, etc., purpose under special state statute.

    iv. Professional corporation – A private corporation, the members of which engage in a profession, organized in order to gain advantages relating to taxes, pension, and insurance plans, etc.

  c. Subchapter S corporation – A corporation that meets certain qualifications, provided for in Subchapter S of the Internal Revenue Code, may elect to be treated in a manner similar to a partnership for federal tax purposes. Corporate income is not taxed but is allocated among the shareholders for income tax purposes.

2. Incorporation procedure.

  a. The corporation's charter, articles of incorporation, or certificate of incorporation generally must contain:

    i. A corporate name.

        A) Must use the word "corporation" or "incorporated" or an abbreviation, such as "corp." or "inc."

        B) The name cannot be misleading or subject to confusion with the name of another organization.

    ii. General nature and purpose.

    iii. Duration – Usually perpetual.

    iv. Capital structure.

    v. Internal organization – May be described in articles of incorporation or in bylaws.

    vi. Location of registered office and agent to receive service of process within the state.

    vii. Names, addresses, and signatures of incorporators.

        A) Usually, incorporators need not have any interest in the corporation, nor must they be subscribers.

        B) The number of incorporators varies from one to three; statute may provide that incorporators need not be natural persons.

  b. Articles of incorporation are filed with the appropriate state official (typically the secretary of state), necessary fees are paid, and notice of the filing is given.

  c. Organizational meetings.

    i. Incorporators elect the board of directors, adopt bylaws, authorize the board to issue stock, etc.

    ii. The board of directors adopts minutes of meetings of incorporators (if required), preincorporation contracts, a seal, and a form for stock certificates, accepts subscriptions, etc.

iii. Bylaws are internal rules for governing and regulating the conduct of corporate affairs. Bylaws cannot conflict with articles of incorporation or statutes.

3. Disregarding the corporate entity.

   a. In unusual situations, a court may ignore the legal fiction of the corporation as an entity (pierce the corporate veil) when the corporation has been used to perpetuate fraud, circumvent law, accomplish an illegal purpose, or otherwise evade law.

   b. Courts will disregard the corporate entity, even though technically a corporation exists, and hold directors, officers, or shareholders personally liable for the transactions conducted in the corporate name.

   c. Courts will disregard the corporate entity if a corporation is not maintained as an entity, separate from its shareholders, in order to prevent abuse of the corporate privilege for personal benefit.

      i. Records and funds have been commingled, and the enterprise has not been established on an adequate financial basis (e.g., thin capitalization).

      ii. This arises occasionally in the case of a close corporation with only one or a few shareholders or in the case of parent-subsidiary corporations.

4. Corporate financing.

   a. Debt securities.

      i. In general, bonds are evidences of obligations to pay money. The term "bond" is often used; although, technically, this particular obligation may be a debenture.

         A) Bonds are secured by a lien or other security interest in assets.

         B) Debentures are secured by the general credit of the borrower rather than by specific property.

         C) Bonds are issued by business firms, governments, and others to investors with a designated maturity date when the principal, or face amount, is to be paid.

         D) Bonds provide fixed income because interest is paid at specified times and at specified rates.

         E) Discount – Bonds may be sold for less than their face value.

         F) Premium – Bonds may be sold for more than their face value.

      ii. Corporate bonds – Agreement is termed the bond indenture. Bondholders do not participate in corporate affairs.

         A) Debentures are unsecured obligations – If the issuing corporation defaults, holders of debentures can look only to assets in which other creditors or bondholders have no security interests.

         B) Mortgage bonds – Secured by real property.

         C) Equipment trust bonds – Secured by equipment, legal title is vested in a trustee.

         D) Collateral trust bonds – Secured by intangible corporate property such as shares of stock in other corporations or accounts receivable.

         E) Convertible bonds – Bonds that may be exchanged for other bonds or stock at a specified rate.

      F) Callable bonds – The issuing corporation has the right to repay the principal prior to maturity.

  b. Equity securities – Every corporation issues common stock and may be authorized to issue preferred stock.

    i. Authorized shares – Stock which the corporation is empowered by its charter to issue.

    ii. Issued shares – Authorized shares that have been sold.

      A) Outstanding shares – Shares that have been issued and are in the hands of shareholders.

      B) Treasury shares – Issued shares that have been reacquired by the corporation.

    iii. Par value shares – Shares that have been assigned a stated dollar value.

      A) May be originally issued for an amount greater than par (premium).

      B) In most states, par value shares cannot be originally issued for less than par value (discounted).

    iv. No par shares – Shares that are not assigned any specific fixed price. No par shares are usually issued for a price that is fixed by the board of directors.

    v. Stated capital.

      A) Sum of par value of all issued par value shares and consideration received for all no par value shares.

      B) Includes outstanding and treasury shares.

5. Corporate purpose – Defines the nature of the business in which the corporation engages.

  a. The purpose must be legal and may be broadly stated in the charter.

  b. Every corporation "has the purpose of engaging in any lawful business unless a more limited purpose is set forth in its articles of incorporation."

6. Corporate management – Shareholders.

  a. Shareholders' position in the corporation – Shareholders have limited powers.

    i. The shareholders' approval is necessary in order to make fundamental changes that affect the corporation (i.e., amending the charter, merging with another corporation or dissolving).

    ii. The shareholders have power to elect and remove members of the board of directors for cause.

    iii. With some limitations, the shareholders have the right to inspect books, records, and shareholders' lists.

    iv. The shareholders do not participate in the management of the corporation.

  b. Meetings of the shareholders.

    i. Annual meeting.

      A) Usually, the date and place are fixed in the bylaws.

      B) Written notice must be given within the specified statutory period of time, but may be waived.

      ii.   Special meetings may be called.

      iii.   Quorum (minimum number of shares that must be represented at a meeting) – Fixed in the corporate charter within specified statutory range.

7.   Corporate management – Directors.

   a.   Qualifications, election, and tenure.

      i.   There are few statutory requirements for qualification as a director.

      ii.   The number of directors is specified in the charter or bylaws.

      iii. The initial board of directors is named in the charter or elected by the incorporators. Subsequent directors are elected by the shareholders.

      iv. The term of a director is usually one year but may be longer; directors may be divided into classes with staggered terms.

      v.   Provisions in the charter and/or statute determine the method of filling vacancies.

      vi. Shareholders have power to remove directors, with or without cause, in accordance with the charter or bylaws. Directors may have power to remove a director for cause.

   b.   Functions of board of directors – Responsible for the management of the corporation.

      i.   The board must act as a body at a meeting. The Model Business Corporation Act (MBCA) does, however, provide for signed, written unanimous consent in lieu of a meeting.

           A)   Regular meetings are provided for in the bylaws. Notice is not necessary.

           B)   Special meetings may be called, but notice is required.

           C)   Quorum requirements vary from state to state (usually a majority) and are established by the bylaws.

           D)   Directors may not vote by proxy.

           E)   Ordinarily, a majority vote is necessary for board action.

           F)   Directors may participate in meeting through conference telephone communications.

      ii.   Corporate powers are exercised by the board of directors. Management responsibilities are:

           A)   Declare dividends.

           B)   Make policy decisions concerning the scope of business, initiate major changes in corporate financing, structure, etc.

           C)   Appoint, supervise, and remove officers.

           D)   Fix compensation of officers and directors.

      iii. Delegation of powers of board of directors.

           A)   Functions relating to ordinary, interim managerial decisions may be delegated to an executive committee.

           B)   Functions relating to daily operations are normally delegated to officers, who as agents carry out the transactions on behalf of the corporation.

8. Role of directors and officers.

   a. Directors manage the corporation and establish general policies and the scope of the business within the purposes and powers stated in the corporate charter.

      i. Directors may not act individually; they must act convened as a board.

      ii. The board of directors has power to authorize actions that are legal exercises of the corporation's powers.

      iii. The board supervises and selects officers, defines their duties and authority, and fixes their compensation if not otherwise provided for in the bylaws.

      iv. Dividends are declared by the board of directors.

   b. The business judgment rule.

      i. Directors are normally not liable for poor business judgment or honest mistakes if they act in good faith in what they consider to be the best interests of the corporation, and with the care that an ordinarily prudent person would exercise under similar circumstances.

      ii. The directors are not insurers of business success.

   c. Duties of directors.

      i. If there is a breach of these duties, directors are liable to the corporation. The corporation may sue in its own name, or a derivative suit may be brought by shareholders or a representative, such as a trustee in bankruptcy.

      ii. Standards of conduct for directors are owed to the corporation.

      iii. Fiduciary duties of directors are owed to the corporation. As fiduciaries, directors are required to perform their duties in good faith, acting in the best interests of the corporation. Directors must use the same amount of care as an ordinary prudent person in a like position under similar circumstances.

         A) Directors should supervise officers to whom they have delegated responsibilities.

         B) Directors should not use their positions to secure personal advantages.

         C) Directors who deal with the corporation must make full disclosure.

      iv. Directors are liable to the corporation if they:

         A) Compete with the corporation.

         B) Usurp a corporate opportunity.

         C) Fail to disclose an interest conflicting with that of the corporation.

         D) Engage in insider trading in buying or selling shares by using confidential information that they possess because of their position.

         E) Improperly issue a dividend or other distribution.

         F) Make an improper stock issue.

         G) Fail to comply with provisions of law, the corporate charter, or bylaws of the corporation.

      v. Contracts between a corporation and a director of a corporation that has one or more common directors may be scrutinized by the courts.

   d. Rights of directors.

      i. Participate in meetings of the board of directors; notice of special meetings must be given.

ii.   Inspect the books and records of the corporation.

iii. Indemnification for expenses, judgments, fines, costs, etc., incurred in corporate-related criminal or civil actions, other than actions brought by or on behalf of the corporation.

iv.   Compensation may be fixed in the charter or by the board of directors.

e. Rights and duties of corporate officers and managers who deal with third persons as agents of, and on behalf of the corporation.

i.   Usually, officers include a president, one or more vice presidents, a secretary, and a treasurer selected by the board of directors.

ii.   The board may also select other officers and agents.

iii. Law of agency and employment applies. The authority of officers, other agents, and employees may be expressed (in the charter, bylaws, or resolutions of the board of directors) or implied (customary and incidental power of such officers); actual authority or apparent authority (because the corporation holds out that its officers have the usual power of similar officers of other corporations); or the board may ratify acts of its officers.

iv.   Officers have fiduciary duties similar to those of directors.

9. Shareholder rights.

a. Right to have a stock certificate evidencing rights of an owner of a proportionate interest in the corporation according to the total number of shares issued.

i.   Intangible personal property.

ii.   A shareholder whose ownership interest is recorded has the right to:

A) Receive notice of meetings and participate in meetings.

B) Dividends when declared.

C) Participate in the distribution of assets upon dissolution.

D) Receive operational and financial reports.

iii. Certifies that the named person is the owner of the stated number of fully paid and nonassessable shares.

iv.   In some states shares of stock may be issued with certificates.

b. Right to transfer shares (may be restricted).

i.   A stock certificate is usually transferred by negotiation.

A) It has physical delivery and an endorsement on the certificate itself so that a good faith purchaser for value is the owner of the shares represented by the certificate, free of adverse claims. The purchaser is entitled to be registered as a shareholder and receive a new certificate.

B) Until the corporation is notified of the transfer, it recognizes the record holder (transferor) as entitled to all shareholder rights.

ii.   Restrictions on transferability are enforceable if noted on the certificate. Such limitations are usually provided for in the case of a small closely held corporation, in order to maintain ownership within the group.

A) Consent of the group is necessary in order to transfer shares, or

   B) The corporation or shareholders have the right of first refusal.

  iii. A provision has been made for transfers of uncertificated securities in the 1977 revisions of Article 8 of the Uniform Commercial Code (UCC), which has been adopted in a few states.

 c. Preemptive rights.

  i. The right of current shareholders to purchase or subscribe to newly issued stock in proportion to the amount of stock currently owned before it is offered to the public.

  ii. Preserve prior relative power of each shareholder.

  iii. Statutes vary.

  iv. Stock warrants are issued to the shareholders of record so that they can purchase the shares in accordance with their preemptive rights.

 d. Right to dividends and other distributions.

  i. Dividends are distributions of cash or other property, including shares of stock, to shareholders in proportion to their respective number of shares or interests in the corporation.

  ii. Dividends are payable to record holders on a specified record date.

  iii. Shareholders do not have rights to dividends (distributions of profits) until declared by the board of directors.

  iv. Cash dividends – Once declared, dividends are corporate debts and cannot be rescinded.

  v. Stock dividends – May be revoked before actually issued to shareholders.

  vi. Statutes impose restrictions on issuance of dividends that will result in the corporation's insolvency or in impairment of its capital.

   A) Dividends may only be paid out of legally available funds of a corporation, in accordance with state law.

   B) Dividends cannot be declared if it will result in insolvency of the corporation or impair its capital. Directors may be liable to the corporation and/or shareholders for improper issuance of dividends, especially if they acted in bad faith.

  vii. Directors must act diligently, prudently, and in good faith and may be liable civilly and criminally for improperly or illegally declaring dividends.

  viii. Ordinarily, directors are not required to declare dividends unless a refusal to do so is an abuse of discretion.

 e. Right to vote. Normally common and preferred stockholders have the right to vote, unless the right is denied in the charter.

  i. Usually, preferred shareholders are denied the right to vote.

  ii. Treasury shares cannot be voted.

 f. Inspection right. A shareholder (for more than six months or of more than five percent of the outstanding shares) has a right to obtain information and examine a copy of relevant books, records and minutes for proper purposes in person or by an agent, attorney, etc.

10. Shareholder liabilities – Shareholders are not normally personally liable to creditors of the corporation. They may, however, be liable in the following situations:

   a. In some cases, majority shareholders are treated as also owing a fiduciary duty to the corporation and minority shareholders.

   b. A shareholder is liable for illegally or improperly paid dividends if he or she had knowledge that the dividends were improper.

   c. A shareholder is liable if he or she received shares that were issued for no consideration or consideration that did not satisfy the statutory requirements (water stock).

   d. A shareholder is liable for any unpaid stock subscriptions.

L. S CORPORATIONS.

   1. Revocation and termination of S corporation status.

      a. This election may be revoked by the consent of more than half of the corporate shareholders (including nonvoting) and may specify a particular date; but if not, revocation is effective the first of the following tax year unless made effective in the first 15 days of tax year, in which case, it relates back to the beginning of the tax year.

      b. S corporation status is terminated on the day a terminating event occurs (any event which causes the S corporation to no longer meet the requirements of S corporation status).

         i. If a corporation has accumulated earnings and profits as well as passive investment income that exceeds 25% of gross receipts for three consecutive years, its election will be terminated beginning with the following year.

      c. Taxation at Liquidation.

         i. S corporations are subject to many of the same liquidation rules applicable to C corporations.

         ii. In general, the distribution of property to shareholders in complete liquidation is treated as if the property was sold to the shareholders.

         iii. The S corporation incurs no tax on liquidation gains.

Taxation Theory	Proprietorship	Partnership	LLP	LLC	S Corporation	C Corporation
Aggregate Theory	Schedule C			Single owner LLC can file as proprietor-ship		
Hybrid Theory		Form 1065	Form 1065	Form 1065		
Entity Theory				1120 or 1120S by elec-tion		Form 1120
Other Notes					Property dis-tribution, stock redemp-tion, and liq-uidation are like Subchap-ter C	

Aggregate Theory – The entity is not a separate taxable entity from the owners. Contributions to and distributions from are not taxable events.

Hybrid Theory – The income is taxed under an aggregate concept, but the entity must file and report the taxable income (Subchapter K).

Entity Theory – The entity is a separate taxable entity, and must determine its tax liability and file on an annual basis. Contributions to and distributions from are generally taxable events (Subchapter C).

APPENDIX 5: BUSINESS CYCLE THEORIES

M. EXTERNAL AND INTERNAL FACTORS.

a. The external theories find the root of the business cycle in the fluctuations of something outside the economic system such as wars, revolutions, political events, rates of growth of population and migrations, discoveries of new lands and resources, scientific and technological discoveries, and innovations.

b. The internal theories look for mechanisms within the economic system itself that give rise to self-generating business cycles. Thus, every expansion will breed recession and contraction, and every contraction will in turn breed revival and expansion in a quasi-regular, repeating, never-ending chain. However, each peak and valley is higher than the last, leading to growth in the economy over the long-term, despite the business cycle.

Actual Business Cycle

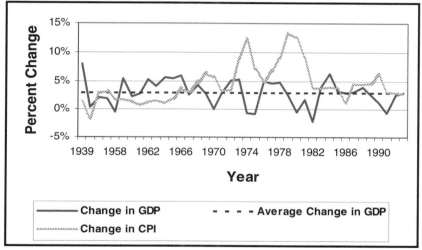

1. Actual business cycle.

a. The actual business cycle has averaged growth of approximately 2.9% per year.

b. The business cycle will exceed the average in some years while in other years the growth will be less than the average.

c. Decreases in interest rates are often accompanied by economic expansions while increases in interest rates are accompanied by economic contractions.

INCOME TAX PLANNING

Problems

Income Tax Planning

TAX LAW – LEGISLATIVE, ADMINISTRATIVE, AND JUDICIAL

1. Ed lost his tax case in the U.S. District Court. He may appeal to the:

   a. U.S. Supreme Court.

   b. U.S. Tax Court.

   c. U.S. Court of Federal Claims.

   d. U.S. Court of Appeals.

2. From which court is there no appeal?

   a. U.S. Court of Appeals.

   b. U.S. District Court.

   c. U.S. Tax Court.

   d. Small Cases Division of the U.S. Tax Court.

3. Which of the following is/are true regarding audits, procedures, and appeals for a taxpayer?

   1. The taxpayer must pay any tax deficiency assessed by the IRS and sue for a refund to bring suit in the U.S. District Court.

   2. A taxpayer can obtain a jury trial in the U.S. Tax Court.

   3. The IRS makes private letter rulings available for publication.

   4. The IRS or the taxpayer can appeal to the U.S. Tax Court for a decision rendered by the Small Cases Division of the Tax Court.

   a. 1 only.

   b. 1 and 2.

   c. 1 and 3.

   d. 2, 3, and 4.

   e. 1, 2, 3, and 4.

4. Which of the following is the highest primary authority on tax law?

   a. Revenue Rulings.

   b. Tax Court Decisions.

   c. Technical Advice Memorandums.

   d. IRS Publications.

---

5. Which entity is never subject to federal income tax?

  a. Partnership.

  b. S corporation.

  c. C corporation.

  d. Individual.

  e. Trust.

GROSS INCOME – INCLUSIONS

6. Mary is single and has one dependent. Her financial records show the following items in the current year: $6,000 gift received from her uncle; $1,000 dividends received on domestic common stock; $12,000 prize won in state lottery; $50,000 salary from her employer; $6,000 child support received and $7,500 alimony received from ex-spouse; and a $5,000 short-term capital loss. What is Mary's adjusted gross income for the current year?

    a. $76,500.

    b. $70,500.

    c. $67,500.

    d. $65,500.

7. Ken, age 23, a full-time student at State University, is claimed as a dependent by his parents. He earned $1,600 from a summer job this year. In addition, he received $1,350 of interest income from a savings account established with funds inherited from his grandmother. He had total itemized deductions of $150 in the current year. What is Ken's taxable income this year?

    a. $0.

    b. $1,050.

    c. $2,200.

    d. $2,950.

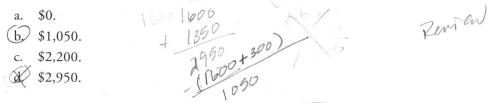

8. Arlene, who is 75 years old and single, is claimed as a dependent on her son's tax return. During the current year, she received $1,700 interest on a savings account, $1,000 of interest income from municipal bonds, and $4,000 of Social Security benefits. She also earned $1,250 from a part-time job. What is Arlene's gross income?

    a. $1,250.

    b. $2,950.

    c. $5,700.

    d. $6,350.

    e. $7,950.

9. In October 2006, Michele, a cash-basis CPA, contracted to perform an audit during the month of December 2006. At the time the contract was being negotiated, the client offered to pay for the services in December 2006. However, Michele wanted to defer the income until 2007. Therefore, the final agreement called for a $2,000 payment in January 2007. Michele also prepared a corporate tax return in November 2006. When she completed the tax return on December 1, 2006, the client offered to pay the $450 charge, but Michele refused to accept payment until 2007. What amount must Michele report on her 2006 return?

    a. $0.

    b. $450.

    c. $2,000.

    d. $2,450.

    e. None of the above.

10. Steve, an accrual-basis taxpayer, performed services for a customer and collected the amount due, $2,000 in 2006. Later that year the customer told Steve that he had not performed the services properly and the customer wanted a refund. The dispute was still in process at the end of 2006. Steve paid the customer $100 in 2007 to settle the suit. Which of the following is correct?

    a. Steve is not required to recognize any income until 2007, when the suit is settled.

    b. Steve is required to recognize $1,900 income in 2006.

    c. Steve is required to recognize the $2,000 in 2006 as income received under a claim of right.

    d. Steve is required to recognize as income in 2006 his best estimate of the amount he will have left after satisfying the customer's claim.

    e. None of the above.

11. Pete Johns operates a printing business. In the past, the business has used the cash method of accounting. This year, Pete decided to switch to the accrual method of accounting. At the beginning of the year, he had accounts receivable of $50,000. Assuming Pete's request for a change in accounting method is approved by the IRS, what adjustment to taxable income will be required in the taxable year?

    a. Positive adjustment of $50,000.

    b. Negative adjustment of $50,000.

    c. Positive adjustment of $25,000.

    d. No adjustment will be required.

12. Which of the following cannot use the cash method of accounting?

    a. Solely owned personal service corporation in the actuarial science business.

    b. C corporation with gross receipts of $25 million.

    c. Sole proprietor whose annual gross receipts for all prior years exceed $10 million.

    d. Partnership that has gross receipts of $3 million.

13. Stacy Whitten owns and operates three clothing stores. She opened the stores four years ago, after receiving a $50,000 loan from the local bank. Currently, the three stores are located in different parts of the same city and have combined gross receipts of $16 million. However, she eventually wants to expand the franchise to include different cities and states. Which statement best reflects the accounting requirements for the businesses?

    a. The cash method must be used for all items of revenue, cost, and expense.

    b. Either the cash or accrual method may be used for all items of revenue, cost, and expense.

    c. The accrual method must be used for inventory but the cash method may be used in accounting for other expenses.

    d. The long-term contract method may be used for the inventory, if the inventory is sold on the installment basis.

14. In which of the following situations may the taxpayer use the Completed Contract method of accounting for long-term contracts? Assume the taxable year is the calendar year in all cases.

    a. A contract to construct a road, estimated to be completed in 18 months. The contractor has average annual gross receipts of $16 million.

    b. A contract to construct a bridge in Boston, estimated to be completed in 3 years. The contractor has average annual gross receipts of $9 million.

    c. A contract signed on September 14 to build the residence of Scott Dalton. It is estimated that it will take six months to complete the job. The contractor has gross receipts of $12 million.

    d. A contractor with annual gross receipts averaging $25 million just signed an agreement to construct a highway. The highway should be completed in approximately 4 years. *unit cost*

15. Cable TV Co., an accrual-basis taxpayer, allows its customers to pay by the month ($30 each month), by the year ($300 per year), or two years in advance ($600). In December of 2006, the company collected the following amounts applicable to future services:

January 2007 services (monthly contracts)	$15,000
January 2007 – December 2007 services (annual contracts)	$38,000
January 2007 – December 2008 services (two-year contracts)	$19,000

    The income from the above that must be reported as gross income for 2006 is:

    a. $15,000.
    b. $19,000.
    c. $34,000.
    d. $38,000.
    e. $72,000.

16. Ron and Marge, residents of a community property state, were married in 2005. Late that same year they separated (began living apart) and were divorced in 2006. Each earned a salary and together they received income from community-owned investments in all relevant years. They filed separate returns in 2006 and 2007. Which of the following is correct?

    a. In 2006 and 2007, Marge must report only her salary and one-half of the income from community property on her separate return.

    b. In 2006, Marge must report on her separate return one-half of Ron and Marge's salaries and one-half of the community property income.

    c. In 2007, Marge must report on her separate return one-half of Ron and Marge's salaries for the period they were married as well as one-half of the community property income and her income earned after the divorce.

    d. In 2006, Marge must report only her salary on her separate return.

    e. None of the above.

17. Vicki, age 70, retired from Austin Industries several years ago. While at the company, she contributed to the 401(k) plan, which now has a balance of $50,000. Vicki also has a Traditional IRA with a balance of $15,000. In the current year, Vicki purchased an annuity for $26,000 to provide her with an additional source of retirement income. Under the contract, Vicki will receive $300 each month for the rest of her life. According to actuarial estimates, Vicki will live to receive 100 payments and will receive a 3% return on her original investment. Which of the following statements is correct regarding payments received under the annuity?

   a. If Vicki collects $3,000 in the current year, the $3,000 is treated as a recovery of capital and, thus, is not taxable.

   b. If Vicki dies after collecting a total of 50 payments, she has an economic loss that is not deductible.

   c. If Vicki lives to collect more than 100 payments, she must amend her prior years' returns to increase her taxable portion of each payment received in the past.

   d. If Vicki lives to collect more than 100 payments, all amounts received after the 100th payment must be included in her gross income.

   e. None of the above.

18. Kathy, age 70, is single and an employee of Expo Corporation. Her only sources of income this year are $80,000 of W-2 wages, $6,000 in Social Security benefits, and $1,000 interest on State of Alabama bonds. Based on the above, Kathy's adjusted gross income for the current year is:

   a. $80,000.

   b. $81,000.

   c. $83,000.

   d. $85,100.

   e. $86,100.

19. Ruby, a widow, elected to receive the proceeds of a $100,000 face value insurance policy on the life of her deceased husband in ten annual installments of $11,900 each (beginning last year). In the current year, she received $11,900, which included $1,900 interest. Ruby dies in December of the current year after collecting the current year's payment. What is the amount subject to income tax on her final tax return?

   a. $0.

   b. $1,900.

   c. $5,000.

   d. $6,900.

   e. None of the above.

20. During the current year, a taxpayer collected $400 interest on U.S. Treasury bills, $750 interest on Baldwin County school bonds, and $100 from a state income tax refund (she itemized her deductions last year). She also received $200 in dividends from a U.S. common stock. Her gross income from the above is:

    a. $0.
    b. $300.
    c. $700.
    d. $1,350.
    e. $1,450.

21. Robert retired on May 31, 2006, and receives a monthly annuity of $1,200 payable for life. His life expectancy at the date of retirement was 10 years (120 months). The first payment was received on June 15, 2006. During his life, Robert contributed $24,000 towards the cost of the annuity. How much of the payments received may Robert exclude from taxable income for the years 2006, 2007, and 2008?

	2006	2007	2008
a.	$0	$0	$0
b.	$1,400	$2,400	$2,400
c.	$8,400	$8,400	$8,400
d.	$8,400	$14,400	$14,400
e.	$14,400	$14,400	$14,400

22. Thomas named his wife, Kim, the beneficiary of a $120,000 (face amount) insurance policy on his life. The policy provided that upon his death, the proceeds would be paid to Kim with interest over her remaining life expectancy (which was calculated at 20 years). Thomas died and Kim began receiving a regular annual payment of $15,000 from the insurance company. How much of each payment must Kim include in her gross income each year?

    a. $0.
    b. $3,000.
    c. $6,000.
    d. $9,000.
    e. $15,000.

23. Kate was recently diagnosed with lung cancer and was certified by her doctor on June 1st of the current year as terminally ill. On July 1st of the current year, Kate sold her life insurance policy with a face value of $500,000 to a viatical settlement provider for $340,000. Assuming she had paid $50,000 in premiums, how much of the $340,000 proceeds must she include in her gross income for the current year?

    a. $0.
    b. $34,000.
    c. $50,000.
    d. $290,000.
    e. $340,000.

24. Scott is terminally ill and has a life expectancy of 9 months. He sold his $600,000 ($100,000 basis) life insurance policy to a viatical settlement provider for $250,000. What are the tax implications?

    a.   The tax treatment will be determined upon Scott's death.

    b.   Scott will not be taxed on this transaction.

    c.   Scott will be required to include $350,000 in his gross income.

    d. $150,000 is taxable to Scott.

    e.   None of the above.

25. Which of the following death benefits would be included in the gross income of the decedent or the decedent's spouse?

    1. $30,000 death benefit paid by the decedent's employer to the decedent's spouse.

    2.   Proceeds from a life insurance policy on the decedent's life, paid to the decedent's spouse.

    3.   A bonus attributable to the decedent, but paid to the decedent's spouse.

    4.   A $10,000 lump-sum distribution from a qualified pension plan paid to the decedent's spouse.

        a.   1 and 2.

        b.   1, 2, and 3.

        c.   3 and 4.

        d.   1, 3, and 4.

        e.   1, 2, 3, and 4.

26. David Jones is covered by a $180,000 group term life insurance policy and his daughter is the beneficiary. Jones' employer pays the entire cost of the policy for which the uniform annual premium is $8 per $1,000 of coverage. How much of this premium is taxable to Jones?

    a. $0.

    b. $640.

    c. $1,040.

    d. $1,440.

    e. $12,480.

27. Carol and Jack were divorced in January of the current year. In accordance with the divorce decree, Jack transferred title of their home to Carol in the current year. The home, which had a fair market value of $150,000, was subject to a $70,000 mortgage to be retired after 240 more monthly payments (20 more years). Monthly mortgage payments are $1,000. Under the terms of the settlement, Jack is obligated to make the mortgage payments on the home for the remaining 20-year term of the indebtedness, regardless of how long Carol lives. Jack made 12 mortgage payments in the current year totaling $12,000. What amount is taxable as alimony to Carol for her current year tax return?

    a. $0.

    b. $12,000.

    c. $80,000.

    d. $92,000.

    e. $162,000.

28. With regard to the alimony deduction related to a post-1984 divorce, which one of the following statements is correct?

    a. Alimony is deductible by the payor spouse, and includible in income by the payee spouse, to the extent that payment is contingent on the status of the divorced couple's children.

    b. The divorced couple may be members of the same household at the time alimony is paid, provided that the persons do not live as husband and wife.

    c. Alimony payments must terminate upon the death of the payee spouse.

    d. Alimony may be paid either in cash or in property.

29. Jon and Bonnie were divorced. Their only marital property was a personal residence with a value of $300,000 and cost of $125,000. Under the terms of the divorce agreement, which did not include the word "alimony," Bonnie would receive the house. She would pay Jon $20,000 each year for five years. If Jon died before the end of the five years, the payments were to be made to his estate. Bonnie and Jon lived apart when Jon received the payments.

    a. Jon does not recognize any income from the above transaction.

    b. Jon must recognize a $87,500 [½ × ($300,000 – $125,000)] gain on the sale of his interest in the house.

    c. Bonnie can deduct $20,000 a year for alimony paid.

    d. Bonnie can deduct $25,000 as alimony paid.

    e. None of the above.

30. Which of the following are requirements for deductions for alimony under post-1984 decrees and agreements?

    1. The agreement specifies that the payments are alimony.

    2. The payor and payee are not members of the same household at the time the payments are made.

    3. There is no liability to make the payments after the payee's death.

    4. The payments are not for the support of the payor's children.

      a. 1 and 2.

      b. 1, 2, and 3.

      c. 2 and 3.

      d. 2, 3, and 4.

      e. 1, 2, 3, and 4.

31. Assume the following payments meet the tax requirements for deductible alimony. Which of the following alimony payment streams will result in alimony recapture to the payer?

	Year 1	Year 2	Year 3
a.	$100,000	$120,000	$150,000
b.	$0	$10,000	$50,000
c.	$50,000	$40,000	$30,000
d.	$20,000	$30,000	$15,000
e.	$60,000	$45,000	$25,000

32. John is single, with no dependents. For the past few years, he has worked as a teller at Second Bank. The bank does not offer a retirement plan to employees, but John has contributed approximately $1,800 per year to a Traditional IRA over the last three years. Unfortunately, during the current year, John was laid off due to a slowing economy. John received salary of $11,000 for the portion of the year he worked. When he was laid off from the bank, he filed for unemployment, and received a total of $3,000 of state unemployment compensation benefits for the year. He had no other source of income. The amount of state unemployment compensation benefits that should be included in John's current year adjusted gross income is:

    a. $3,000.

    b. $2,000.

    c. $1,500.

    d. $1,000.

    e. $0.

33. Clark, age 25, bought a Series EE U.S. savings bond in 1996. Redemption proceeds will be used for payment of college tuition for Clark's dependent child. One of the conditions that must be met for tax exemption of accumulated interest on these bonds is that the:

    a. Purchaser of the bonds must be the sole owner of the bonds (or joint owner with his or her spouse).

    b. Bonds must be bought by a parent (or both parents) and put in the name of the dependent child.

    c. Bonds must be bought before the owner of the bonds reaches the age of 24.

    d. Bonds must be transferred to the college for redemption by the college rather than by the owner of the bonds.

34. Lois is single and has two dependents. Financial records show the following items in the current year:

Gift from a friend	$12,000
Dividends received on stock	$1,200
Prize won in state lottery	$1,000
Salary from employer	$35,000
Child support received from ex-spouse	$6,000
Alimony received from ex-spouse	$12,000
Long-term capital loss	$5,000

How much is Lois' adjusted gross income for the current year?

    a. $43,200.

    b. $44,200.

    c. $46,200.

    d. $48,200.

    e. $58,200.

35. Kent, age 28, spent the first six months of the current year working as a financial planner for Question Capital Management. He took a new job out-of-state with Investments R' Us, a smaller financial planning firm. He feels as though he can become a partner at the new firm within five years. His only regret is that he was required to move from Texas, his home state, to New Jersey. Kent had the following items of income and loss in the current year:

Salary (combined for both jobs)	$60,000
Long-term capital loss	$500
Short-term capital loss	$4,500
Qualified moving expenses (paid by Kent)	$4,000

What is Kent's adjusted gross income for the current year?

a. $51,500.
b. $52,000.
c. $53,000.
d. $56,000.
e. $57,000.

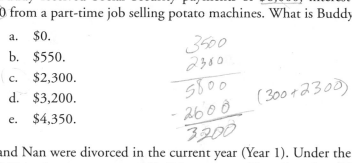

36. Buddy is age 62, single, and claimed as a dependent by his daughter on her tax return. During the current year, Buddy received Social Security payments of $6,000, interest on a bank account of $3,500, and $2,300 from a part-time job selling potato machines. What is Buddy's taxable income?

a. $0.
b. $550.
c. $2,300.
d. $3,200.
e. $4,350.

37. Nick and Nan were divorced in the current year (Year 1). Under the divorce agreement, Nan is to receive $100,000 in the current year, $60,000 next year (Year 2) and nothing thereafter. The payments were to cease upon Nan's death or remarriage. How much, if any, should Nick have to claim as alimony recapture in Year 3?

a. $0.
b. $30,000.
c. $115,000.
d. $122,500.
e. $130,000.

38. On January 1, Dennis loaned his daughter, Betty, $90,000 to purchase a new personal residence. There were no other loans outstanding between Dennis and Betty. Betty's only income was $30,000 salary and $4,000 interest income. Dennis had investment income of $200,000. Dennis did not charge Betty interest. The relevant federal rate was 9%. For the current year:

   a. Betty must recognize $8,100 (0.09 × $90,000) imputed interest income on the loan.

   b. Dennis must recognize imputed interest income of $4,000.

   c. Dennis must recognize imputed interest income of $8,100.

   d. Betty is allowed a deduction for imputed interest of $8,100.

   e. None of the above.

39. John, the majority shareholder in XYZ, Inc., received an interest-free loan from the corporation. Which of the following is/are correct?

   a. If the loan is classified as an employer-employee loan, the corporation's taxable income will not be affected by the imputation of interest.

   b. If the loan is classified as a corporation-shareholder loan, the corporation's taxable income will increase as a result of the imputation of interest.

   c. If John uses the funds to take a vacation, the imputation of interest will cause a net increase to his taxable income.

   d. All of the above.

40. Which of the following benefits provided by an employer to its employees is taxable?

   a. Employees of the ABC Department Store are allowed a 5% discount on store merchandise. ABC's normal gross profit percentage is 20%.

   b. Undergraduate tuition is waived by State University for the dependent children of employees.

   c. Crash Test Airline provides free standby flights to its employees.

   d. Incidental personal use of the company car.

41. A client purchased a mutual fund with a $10,000 lump-sum amount four years ago. During the holding period, $4,000 of dividends was reinvested. Today the shares are valued at $20,000 (including any shares purchased with dividends). If the client sells shares equal to $13,000, which statement(s) is/are correct? (CFP® Certification Examination, released 11/94)

   1. The taxable gain can be based on an average cost per share.

   2. The client can choose which shares to sell, thereby controlling the taxable gain.

   3. To minimize the taxable gain today, the client would sell shares with the higher cost basis.

   4. The client will **not** have a gain as long as he/she sells less than what he/she invested.

      a. 1, 2, and 3.

      b. 1 and 3.

      c. 2 and 4.

      d. 4 only.

      e. 2, 3, and 4.

GROSS INCOME – EXCLUSIONS

42. Scott, age 22, is a full-time student at State University and a candidate for a bachelor's degree. During the current year, he received the following payments:

State scholarship for ten months (tuition and books)	$5,000	Q Scholarship
Loan from college financial aid office	$2,000	
Cash support from parents	$5,000	
Cash dividends	$500	Tax
Total	**$12,500**	

What is Scott's adjusted gross income?

   a. $500.
   b. $800.
   c. $5,800.
   d. $12,800.
   e. None of the above.

43. Which of the following is excluded from gross income?

   a. Damages received from a sexual harassment lawsuit.
   b. Unemployment compensation.
   c. Hobby income.
   d. Workers compensation benefits.
   e. Compensatory damages related to damaged reputation.

44. Rick has been a night watchman at INVEST, Inc. for 10 years. During the current year, he received the following from his employer:

Salary	$20,000
Hospitalization insurance premiums paid directly to provider	$3,660
Value of lodging on company premises for employer's convenience as a condition of Rick's employment	$3,000
Cash reward for discovering and preventing burglary	$1,000

What amount is includible in Rick's adjusted gross income for the current year?

   a. $20,000.
   b. $21,000.
   c. $23,000.
   d. $23,660.
   e. $27,660.

45. During this year, Matt was injured on his job. As a result of the injury, he received the following payments during this year:

Workers compensation	$2,600
Reimbursement from his employer for medical expenses paid by Matt (nondiscriminating medical plan)	$1,200
Damages for physical injuries	$10,000

What is the amount to be included in Matt's gross income for the current year?

 a. $0.

b. $12,000.

c. $10,000.

d. $13,800.

46. Ron is the manager of a hotel. To be available in emergency situations, Ron's employer requires that he live in one of the hotel rooms (without charge). The value of the room is $1,500 per month if occupied each night. The hotel is ordinarily 70% occupied. If Ron did not live there, he would live in an apartment that would rent for $900 per month. The monthly gross income includible for federal income tax purposes attributable to living in the hotel room is:

a. $0.   *Condition*

b. $900.

c. $1,350.

d. $1,500.

47. Tracy is employed by a large corporation with 500 employees. The corporation has an exercise facility within its office for the exclusive use of the employees. A health club membership at a similar public facility would cost Tracy $1,200 per year. How much of this benefit must Tracy include in her adjusted gross income?

 a. $0.

b. $500.

c. $600.

d. $1,200.

48. Under the Franklin Company, Inc. cafeteria plan, all full-time employees are allowed to select any combination of the benefits below. The total value of benefits received by the employee cannot exceed $8,000 a year.

1. Whole life insurance, $2,000.

2. Group medical and hospitalization insurance for the employee only, $4,000 a year.

3. Group medical and hospitalization insurance for employee's dependents, $2,000 a year.

4. Child-care payments, actual cost but not more than $3,000 a year if one child or $6,000 if 2 or more children.

5. Cash required to bring the total value of benefits and cash to $8,000.

Which of the following statements is true?

a. Becky, a full-time employee, selects choices 1 and 2 and $2,000 cash. Her gross income must include the $2,000 cash and the $2,000 from the life insurance.

b. Bob, a full-time employee, elects to receive $8,000 cash because his wife's employer provided benefits for him. Bob is not required to include the $8,000 in gross income.

c. Vicki, a full-time employee, elects to receive choices, 1, 2, and 3. She is not required to include any amount from such benefits in gross income.

d. Don, a full-time employee, selects options 2 and 3 and $2,000 in child care (4). Don must include $2,000 in gross income.

e. None of the above.

49. Which of the following fringe benefits would be excluded from an employee's gross income?

1. Business magazine subscriptions paid for by an employer in the names of various employees.

2. Season tickets to football games.

3. Parking provided near its business by an employer for its employees.

4. On-premises athletic facilities provided by an employer to its employees.

a. 1 only.

b. 2 only.

c. 2 and 4.

d. 1, 3, and 4.

e. 1, 2, 3, and 4.

50. Which of the following fringe benefits received by an employee would be excluded from the employee's gross income?

1. Employer-provided parking of $100.

2. Dues to a public athletic club paid for by the employer.

3. Tickets to the basketball game tonight.

4. Employer-provided interior decorating for a new personal residence.

a. 1 and 2.

b. 1 and 3.

c. 2 and 4.

d. 1, 3, and 4.

e. 1, 2, and 4.

51. Crescent Company offers a 10% discount to all nonofficer employees. Officers, all highly compensated, are allowed a 30% discount on company products. Crescent's gross profit rate is 35%. Which of the following is true?

    a. An officer who takes a 30% discount must include the extra 20% (30%-10%) in gross income.

    b. All discounts taken by employees are includible in their gross income because the plan is discriminatory.

    c. All discounts taken by officers (30%) are includible in their gross income because the plan is discriminatory.

    d. None of the discounts are includible in income because the discount in all cases is less than the company's gross profit percentage.

    e. None of the above.

52. Romig Company was experiencing financial difficulties, but was not bankrupt or insolvent. Shelby, the holder of a mortgage on Romig's building, agreed to accept $60,000 in full payment of the $90,000 due. Shelby had sold the property to Romig for $200,000 five years ago. Peoples Bank, which held a mortgage on other real estate owned by Romig, reduced the principal from $75,000 to $35,000. The bank had made the loan to Romig when it purchased the real estate from Roper, Inc. As a result of the above, Romig must:

    a. Include $70,000 in gross income.

    b. Reduce the basis in its assets by $70,000.

    c. Include $130,000 in gross income and reduce its basis in its assets by $40,000.

    d. Include $40,000 in gross income and reduce its basis in the building by $30,000.

    e. None of the above.

53. Brian, an employee of Duff Corporation, died on July 25 of the current year. Under the terms of Duff Corporation's Death-Benefit-Only (DBO) plan, Duff Corp. made payments of $10,000 to his widow and $10,000 to his 17-year-old son. What amounts should be excluded from gross income of the widow and son in their respective tax returns for the current year?

	Widow	Son
a.	$0	$0
b.	$2,500	$2,500
c.	$5,000	$5,000
d.	$7,500	$7,500
e.	$10,000	$10,000

54. During the current year, Bill Hill sustained a serious injury in the course of his employment. As a result of this injury, Bill received the following payments:

Workers Compensation	$3,000
Reimbursement from his employer's accident and health plan for medical expenses paid by Bill	$2,400
Compensatory damages for physical injuries	$6,000
Punitive damages for physical injuries	$5,000

The amount to be included in Bill's gross income should be:

    a. $0.

    b. $3,000.

    c. $5,000.

    d. $11,000.

    e. $16,400.

55. On January 1 of the current year, David was awarded a post-graduate fellowship grant of $6,000 by a tax-exempt educational organization. David is not a candidate for a degree and was awarded the grant to continue his research. The grant was awarded for the period August 1 of the current year through July 31 of the following year. On August 1 of the current year, David elected to receive the full amount of the grant. What amount should be included in his gross income for the current year?

    a. $0.

    b. $2,500.

    c. $3,000.

    d. $4,500.

    e. $6,000.

56. Which of the following distributions would usually create taxable income for a taxpayer?

    a. Taking a loan against the cash value of an insurance policy.

    b. Taking a loan against a modified endowment contract.

    c. Taking a loan against a depreciable asset.

    d. Both a and b.

57. Which of the following statements about employer-provided insurance is false?

    a. Group term life insurance premiums paid by an employer may cause an increase in the employee's W-2 income.

    b. If medical reimbursements exceed medical expenses under an employer-provided health plan, the employee may have taxable income.

    c. Disability insurance premiums paid by an employer are deductible by the employer and not taxed to the employee.

    d. The portion of disability insurance premiums paid for by an employee is a deductible medical expense.

58. Julie's earns $40,000 and her employer provides a flexible spending account (FSA). Julie and her husband incur $5,000 in child care expenses for their two children each year. Julie's husband, Joe, has a $300,000 salary. If Julie and Joe file as married filing jointly, which of the following statements comparing the child-care tax credit and an FSA is true?

    a. Julie would be better off using her FSA to pay child-care expenses.

    b. Julie would be better off using the child-care credit.

    c. Julie can use FSA to pay child-care expenses and still claim the child-care credit.

    d. The maximum amount of child-care expenses that can be paid from a flexible spending account is $3,000.

    e. You cannot pay child-care expenses from a flexible spending account.

59. Which of the following statements regarding Coverdell Education Savings Accounts is/are true?

    1. Maximum contribution per account beneficiary is $2,000 per year.

    2. Contributions can only be made for an individual under the age of 21.

    3. When distributed for educational expenses, only the interest earned is taxable.

    4. Room and board for a less-than-half-time student is a qualified education expense.

    a. 1, 2, and 4.

    b. 1, 3, and 4.

    c. 2, 3, and 4.

    d. 1 and 4.

    e. 1 only.

60. Steven, age 49, is an executive for a Fortune 500 company. He is currently taxed at the highest marginal income tax rate due to a large bonus he receives at the end of the year. He is becoming increasingly concerned with his growing tax liability each year, and would like to start investing in assets that will allow him to defer taxes. Which of the following would not be a good purchase for Steven?

    a. Rare coins.

    b. Variable annuity.

    c. 12-month CDs with daily compounding.

    d. Ocean-front property.

DEDUCTIONS FOR ADJUSTED GROSS INCOME

61. Which of the following is/are deductible <u>for</u> adjusted gross income?

    1. Alimony paid to the taxpayer's ex-spouse.
    2. Capital losses.
    3. Ordinary and necessary expenses incurred in a business.
    4. Contribution to a Roth IRA.
    5. Child support paid to ex-spouse.

    a. 3 and 5.
    b. 1, 3, and 5.
    c. 2, 3, and 5.
    d. 1, 2, and 3.
    e. 1, 2, 3, 4, and 5.

62. Which of the following is not a deduction for AGI?

    a. Maintenance expense for a rental property actively managed by the taxpayer.
    b. Qualified moving expenses of a taxpayer.
    c. Professional dues of an employee, not reimbursed by the employer.
    d. One-half of self-employment tax paid.

63. Which of the following types of deductions can be claimed in arriving at an individual's adjusted gross income?

    a. Unreimbursed business expenses if the individual is an outside employee-salesperson.
    b. Personal casualty losses.
    c. Charitable contributions.
    d. Alimony payments.
    e. Union dues.

64. In the current year, Kim is transferred by her employer from New Orleans to Houston. Her expenses are not reimbursed and are as follows:

Costs of moving household furnishings	$1,600
Transportation costs	$300
Meals in route	$400
Lodging in route	$250
	$2,550

    Her qualified moving expenses are:

    a. $1,850.
    b. $2,150.
    c. $2,350.
    d. $2,550.

65. Joel, a self-employed individual, has the following items related to his tax return:

Gross receipts from his business	$50,000
Operating expenses for business	$30,000
Self-employment tax paid	$3,060
Health insurance premiums	$1,200
Mortgage interest	$5,000

What is Joel's AGI?

a. $16,220.

b. $16,940.

c. $17,160.

d. $17,270.

e. $19,280.

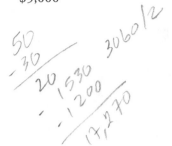

66. Jimmy and Dee Dee, both age 35, are married and filed a joint return for 2006. Jimmy earned a salary of $90,000 and was covered by his employer's pension plan. Also, Jimmy and Dee Dee earned interest of $5,000 on their joint savings account. Dee Dee was not employed and the couple had no other income. On June 15, Jimmy contributed $4,000 to an IRA for himself and $4,000 to an IRA for Dee Dee. The allowable IRA deduction on Jimmy and Dee Dee's year 2006 joint return is:

a. $0.

b. $250.

c. $4,000.

d. $6,000.

e. $8,000.

67. Thad and Debra Claiborne, both age 48, are married and filed a joint return for the current year. Their adjusted gross income was $100,000, including Thad's $95,000 salary. Debra had no income of her own. Neither spouse was covered by an employer-sponsored pension plan. What amount could the Claiborne's contribute to IRAs for 2006 to take advantage of their maximum allowable IRA deduction in their return?

a. $0.

b. $2,000.

c. $3,000.

d. $6,000.

e. $8,000.

68. Judy Martin, who is age 45 and divorced, received taxable alimony of $30,000 in 2006. In addition, she received $900 in earnings from a part-time job. Judy is not covered by a qualified pension plan. What was the maximum deductible regular IRA contribution that Judy could have made for 2006?

    a. $0.

    b. $250.

    c. $900.

    d. $2,125.

    e. $4,000.

69. For 2006, Mary Sue (age 40) and Bob White (age 42) reported the following items of income:

	Mary Sue	Bob	Total
Salary	$40,000	$35,000	$75,000
Interest income	1,000	200	1,200
Cash prize won on TV game show	-0-	10,000	10,000
Total	$41,000	$45,200	$86,200

Mary Sue is not covered by a qualified retirement plan, but Bob is covered. She and Bob established Individual Retirement Accounts (IRAs) during the year. Assuming a joint return was filed for the current year, what is the maximum that they can deduct for any contributions made to their IRAs for 2006?

    a. $0.

    b. $1,200.

    c. $4,000.

    d. $6,000.

    e. $8,000.

70. A single taxpayer, age 54, retired two years ago and is receiving a pension of $600 per month from her previous employer's qualified pension plan. She has recently taken a position in a small CPA firm that has no pension plan. She will receive $10,000 in compensation from the CPA firm as well as the $7,200 from her pension. What amount, if any, can she contribute to a deductible IRA for 2006?

    a. $0.

    b. $1,500.

    c. $4,000.

    d. $5,000.

    e. $5,500.

71. Which of the following statements is true regarding a health savings account?

    a. Amounts within the health savings account that are not used within the calendar year must be forfeited.

    b. Dental expenses are not qualified medical expenses under a health savings account.

    c. Individuals age 55 and older who are covered by a high-deductible health plan can make additional catch-up contributions to the health savings account.

    d. A health savings account can only be established by an individual, not an employer.

72. Which of the following statements is/are correct regarding a health savings account?

    1. A health savings account is not subject to COBRA continuation coverage.

    2. Distributions from a health savings account used for qualifying medical expenses will be both income tax-free and penalty-free.

    3. Individual contributions made to a health savings account are deductible as a medical expense itemized deduction.

    4. Catch-up contributions are allowed for those participants age 50 or older.

        a. 1 and 2.

        b. 3 and 4.

        c. 1, 2 and 3.

        d. 1, 2 and 4.

        e. 2, 3 and 4.

73. Which of the following individuals can contribute to a deductible IRA for 2006?

Person	Filing Status	AGI	Covered by Pension Plan
1. Jane	Single	$30,000	Yes
2. Joe	MFJ	$100,000	No (and neither is spouse)
3. Barbie	MFJ	$120,000	No (but spouse is covered)
4. Maggie	MFJ	$40,000	Yes

        a. 3 only.

        b. 3 and 4.

        c. 2, 3, and 4.

        d. 1, 3, and 4.

        e. 1, 2, 3, and 4.

74. Which of the following is a deduction for adjusted gross income?

        a. Charitable contributions.

        b. Student loan interest.

        c. Taxes on a principal residence.

        d. Foreign taxes.

        e. Personal casualty loss deduction.

PERSONAL AND DEPENDENCY EXEMPTIONS

75. Angie and Buddy, both age 55, filed a joint return for the current year. They provided all the support for their son who is 19 and had no income. Their daughter, age 23, and a full-time student at a university, provided 70% of her own support during the current year. How many exemptions should Angie and Buddy claim on their current year joint income tax return?

    a. 5.
    b. 4.
    c. 3.
    d. 2.

76. John, age 50, filed a joint return with his wife Joan, age 24. Their son, Chip, was born December 16 of the current year. John provided 60% of the support for his 73-year-old widowed mother until May 1, when she died. His mother's only income was from Social Security benefits totaling $3,000. How many exemptions should John and Joan claim on their joint tax return?

    a. 2.
    b. 3.
    c. 4.
    d. 5.

77. Steve provided more than one-half of the support for the following relatives and none of them were members of Steve's household: cousin, nephew and a foster parent. None of these relatives had any income, nor did any of them file an individual or joint return. All of the relatives are U.S. citizens. Which of these relatives could be claimed as a dependent on Steve's return?

    a. Cousin.
    b. Nephew.
    c. Foster parent.
    d. None of the above.

78. Mary Sue and Bob, who are married and file a joint return, provided over 50% of the support for Becky, Rachel and Vicki during the year. Their 22-year old daughter, Becky, a college student, earned $3,300 during the year. Mary Sue and Bob's married daughter, Rachel, filed a joint return with her husband. Vicki, who is Mary Sue's mother, lives with Mary Sue and Bob. Vicki's only income during the year was $5,200 of Social Security benefits, and she used that entire amount for her own support. Which of the following statements is/are _incorrect?_

    1. Mary Sue and Bob can claim Becky as a dependent.

    2. Mary Sue and Bob may claim Rachel as a dependent if neither Rachel nor her husband was required to file a return.

    3. Mary Sue and Bob may not claim Vicki as a dependent because Vicki's gross income is too high.
        a. 1 only.
        b. 2 only.
        c. 3 only.
        d. 1 and 3.
        e. 1, 2, and 3.

79. Mike and Pam, ages 67 and 65, respectively, filed a joint tax return for the current year. They provided all of the support for their 18-year-old son, who had $2,200 of gross income. Their 23-year-old daughter, a full-time student until her graduation on June 25 of this year, earned $4,000, which was 40% of her total support during the year. Her parents provided the remaining support. Mike and Pam also provided total support for Pam's father, who is a Colombian citizen and life-long resident of Colombia. How many personal and dependency exemptions can Mike and Pam claim on their income tax return?

        a. 2.
        b. 3.
        c. 4.
        d. 5.
        e. None of the above.

80. Thomas and Cecilia Martinez are married and filed a joint income tax return for the current year. During this year they properly claimed a personal exemption for their dependent 17-year-old daughter, Hazel. Since Hazel earned $5,400 in the current year from a part-time job at the college she attended full-time, Hazel was also required to file an income tax return. What amount was Hazel entitled to claim as a personal exemption on her individual income tax return for the current year?

        a. $0.
        b. $1,200.
        c. $2,450.
        d. $2,900.
        e. $5,800.

TAX DETERMINATION

81. William, who is covered by a qualified retirement plan and is age 30 and single, provided the following information for his 2006 income tax return:

Salary	$30,000
Contribution to a Roth Individual Retirement Account	$3,000
Total itemized deductions	$6,000
Number of exemptions claimed	1

William should report taxable income for 2006 of:

   a. $17,950.
   b. $19,800.
   c. $20,700.
   d. $24,000.
   e. None of the above.

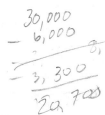

```
30,000
-  6,000
           0,
-   3,300
   20,700
```

82. Calculate the taxable income for a single taxpayer, age 66 with no dependents, provided the following information for his 2006 income tax return:

Gross income	$46,000
Capital loss	$5,000 (3000)
Total itemized deductions	$4,950 (5150+1250)

Personal Exemption 3,300

   a. $33,300.
   b. $33,950.
   c. $34,100.
   d. $35,050.
   e. $36,150.

```
46,00
-  6400 std + special
-  3000 cap loss
-  3300 personal
   33,300
```

83. Peter, a single taxpayer, age 62, had adjusted gross income of $42,000 in 2006. He paid the cost of maintaining his dependent mother, age 90, in a home for the aged for the entire year. His itemized deductions totaled $5,400. What amount should Peter report as taxable income for 2006?

   a. $27,850.
   b. $30,400.
   c. $31,750.
   d. $34,600.

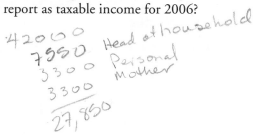

```
42000   Head of household
 7550   Personal
 3300   Mother
 3300
 27,850
```

84. Which of the following children have income subject to federal income tax at his/her parents' highest marginal rate?

- Brittany, age 12, earns $5,000 in salary.
- Kate, age 7, has $1,800 in dividends from a mutual fund.
- Tony, age 3, has $850 in interest from a savings account.
- Amanda, age 14, has $1,900 in dividends and interest.

    a. Brittany.

    b. Kate and Tony.

    c. Kate.

    d. Kate, Tony, and Amanda.

    e. All of the children will have income subject to tax at the parents' highest marginal rate.

85. Michael Christen, age 13 in 2006, has the following income: $3,000 investment income from mutual funds and $5,000 earned income from a paper route. His parents claim him as a dependent. How much of Michael's income is taxed at the parents' highest marginal rate?

    a. $0.

    b. $1,300.

    c. $2,600.

    d. $3,000.

    e. $3,500.

86. Which of the following statements regarding the "kiddie tax" is/are correct?

    1. It only applies to unearned income from property transferred to a child from the child's parents.

    2. It applies to all children under the age of 15.

    3. A child's earned and unearned income may be subject to the tax.

    4. It is based on the additional tax the parents would have paid assuming the child's net unearned income had been included in the parents' taxable income.

    a. 4 only.

    b. 1 and 4.

    c. 1, 2, and 3.

    d. 1, 2, and 4.

    e. 1, 2, 3, and 4.

87. Allison, who is 12 years old, is claimed as a dependent on her parents' tax return. During 2006, she earned $2,200 from a summer job. She also earned $1,800 in interest and dividends from investments that were given to her by her maternal grandfather, Michael, five years ago. How much of Allison's income will be taxed at her parents' highest marginal rate in 2006?

    a. $0.

    b. $100.

    c. $1,250.

    d. $1,800.

    e. $4,000.

88. Which of the following are true regarding personal service corporations?

    1. Employee fringe benefits cannot be offered.

    2. Unreasonable compensation may be reclassified as a constructive dividend.

    3. Dividend received deduction is not available.

    4. Income is taxed at a 35% flat rate.

    a. 1 only.

    b. 4 only.

    c. 1 and 3.

    d. 2 and 4.

    e. 1, 2, and 4.

FILING STATUS/FILING LEVELS

89. George, whose wife died last November, filed a joint tax return for last year. He did not remarry and has continued to maintain his home for his two dependent children. In the preparation of his tax return for this year, what is George's filing status?

    a. Single.

    b. Qualifying widower.

    c. Head of household.

    d. Married filing separately.

    e. None of the above.

90. Beth Brown's husband died in 2006. Assume Beth does not marry, and continues to maintain a home for herself and her dependent infant child during 2007, 2008, and 2009, providing full support for herself and her child during these 3 years. For 2006, Beth properly filed a joint return. For 2009, Beth's filing status is expected to be:

    a. Single.

    b. Married filing joint return.

    c. Head of household.

    d. Qualifying widow with dependent child.

    e. None of the above.

91. Mary's husband died in March of the current year. What filing status should Mary use in the current year?

    a. Single, if she has a dependent child.

    b. Married Filing Joint.

    c. Married Filing Separate, if she has a dependent child.

    d. Head of Household.

DEDUCTIONS AND LOSSES

92. John is the sole shareholder of River Rafting, Inc., a C corporation. In the current year, he receives a salary of $150,000 and dividends of $60,000 from River. River's taxable income for the current year is $400,000. On his audit, the IRS reduces John's salary by $60,000 to $90,000 because it was determined to be unreasonable. Which of the following statements is correct?

    a. John's gross income will increase by $60,000 as a result of the IRS adjustment.
    b. River's taxable income will not be affected by the IRS adjustment.
    c. John's gross income will decrease by $60,000 as a result of the IRS adjustment.
    d. River's taxable income will increase by $60,000 as a result of the IRS adjustment. *John is not effected*
    e. None of the above.

93. Sylvia, a real estate broker, files a Schedule C and had the following income and expenses in her business:

Commissions received	$120,000
Expenses:	
Commissions paid to nonbrokers for referrals (illegal under state law)	$30,000
Commissions paid to other real estate brokers for referrals (legal under state law)	$15,000
Travel and transportation	$16,000
Supplies	$4,200
Office, phone, and fax	$3,500
Parking tickets for illegal parking	$400

    38,700

    How much Schedule C net income must Sylvia report from this business?

    a. $50,900.
    b. $51,300.
    c. $81,300.
    d. $96,300.
    e. $96,700.

94. Randy, a calendar-year, cash-basis taxpayer, owns and operates furniture rental outlets in Georgia. He wants to expand to other states. He spends $20,000 investigating furniture stores in Alabama and $12,000 investigating stores in Florida. He acquires the Alabama stores but not the stores in Florida. Regarding the above expenses, Randy should:

    a. Capitalize $20,000 and not deduct $12,000.
    b. Expense $32,000.   *similar business → deduct*
    c. Expense $12,000 and capitalize $20,000.
    d. Capitalize $32,000.

95. Bill Jackson lives with his family in Fort Worth. He drives to work in Austin each day, a distance of 110 miles. He eats at the nearest local restaurant each night and often stops overnight at a hotel in Austin when he works late. Bill has paid $900 in hotel rentals for the past year. Which of the following is true?

   a. The maximum expense Bill can deduct for meals is $75.

   b. Bill can deduct hotel costs, since the commute is greater than 50 miles.

   c. Bill can deduct hotel costs and 50% of the cost of meals.

   d. Bill cannot deduct any of these expenses on his tax return because commuting expenses are nondeductible.

96. Sara pursued a hobby of selling antique furniture in her spare time. During the year she sold furniture for $3,000. She incurred expenses as follows:

Cost of goods sold	$2,000
Supplies	$1,200
Interest on loan to get business started	$800
Advertising	$750

   Assuming that the activity is a hobby, and that she cannot itemize this year, how should she report these items on her tax return?

   a. Include $3,000 in income and deduct $4,750 for AGI.

   b. Ignore both income and expenses since hobby losses are disallowed.

   c. Include $3,000 in income and deduct nothing for AGI since hobby expenses must be itemized.

   d. Include $3,000 in income and deduct interest of $800 for AGI.

   e. None of the above.

97. Bob and Teddi own a house at the beach. The house was rented to unrelated parties for 8 full weeks during the current year. Bob and Teddi used the house 16 days for their vacation during the year. After properly dividing the expenses between rental and personal use, it was determined that a loss was incurred as follows:

Gross rental income			$6,400
Less:	Mortgage interest and property taxes	$7,000	
	Other allocated expenses	1,000	(8,000)
	Net rental loss		($1,600)

What is the correct treatment of the rental income and expenses on Bob and Teddi's joint income tax return for the current year?

    a. A $1,600 loss should be reported.

    b. The $7,000 rental portion of interest and taxes can be deducted.

    c. The rental expenses (other than interest and taxes) are limited to the gross rental income in excess of deductions for interest and taxes allocated to the rental use.

    d. Since the house was used only 20% personally by Bob and Teddi, all expenses allocated to personal use may be deducted.

    e. Include none of the income or expenses related to the beach house in their current year income tax return.

98. Chris owns a vacation home which he plans to rent for 190 days this year. He also plans to live in the house during the year. What is the maximum number of days he can live in the home without jeopardizing the property's status as a rental property?

    a. 14 days.

    b. 19 days.

    c. 95 days.

    d. 140 days.

    e. 190 days.

99. Frank paid the following expenses for his dependent son, Mitch, during the current year:

Principal payments on automobile loan	$15,000
Interest on the automobile loan	$1,500
Payment of Mitch's medical expenses	$4,000
Payment of Mitch's property taxes (ad valorem)	$1,000

How much of the above may Frank deduct (ignoring any hurdles or thresholds) in computing his itemized deductions?

    a. $4,000.

    b. $5,000.

    c. $5,500.

    d. $6,500.

    e. $21,500.

100. On January 10 of last year (Year 1), Todd sold stock with a cost of $6,000 to his son, Trey, for $4,000 (its fair market value). On July 31 of the current year (Year 2), Trey sold the same stock for $5,000 in a bona fide arms length transaction to Mary, who is unrelated to Trey or Todd. What is the proper treatment of these transactions?

    a. Neither Todd nor Trey has a recognized gain or loss in either Year 1 or Year 2.

    b. Todd has a recognized loss of $2,000 in Year 1.

    c. Trey has a recognized gain of $1,000 in Year 2.

    d. Trey has a recognized gain of $2,000 in Year 2.

    e. Todd has a recognized loss of $2,000 in Year 1 and Trey a recognized gain of $1,000 Year 2.

101. Versa, Inc. is an accrual-basis taxpayer. Versa uses the accounts receivable aging approach to calculate their accounting allowance for bad debts. The following information is available for the current year related to bad debts.

Credit sales	$450,000
Collections on credit sales	$375,000
Amount added to the allowance account	$60,000
Beginning balance in the allowance account	$25,000
Bad debts written off in the current year	$32,000

The tax deduction for bad debt expense for Versa for the current year is:

    a. $32,000.

    b. $35,000.

    c. $53,000.

    d. $92,000.

102. Three years ago, Eric loaned Robin $5,000 (Year 1) with the understanding that the loan would be repaid in two years. Last year, in Year 3, Robin filed for bankruptcy, and Eric learned that he would receive $0.10 on the dollar. In the current year, Year 4, the final settlement was made, and Eric received $300. Assuming the loan is a nonbusiness bad debt, how should Eric account for the loan?

    a. $4,700 ordinary loss in the current year.

    b. $3,000 ordinary loss last year and $1,700 ordinary loss in the current year.

    c. $4,700 short-term capital loss in the current year.

    d. $3,000 short-term capital loss last year and $1,700 short-term capital loss in the current year.

    e. $5,000 ordinary loss last year.

5,000

103. Two years ago, Kevin loaned his friend, Randy, $5,000. In the current year, Randy paid Kevin $1,500 in final settlement of the loan. Kevin has $100,000 of salary and $5,000 of capital gains for the current year. What amount of the loss <u>may he use</u> in the current year?

   a. $0.
   b. $1,500.
   c. $3,000.
   d. $3,500.
   e. $5,000.

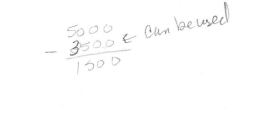

104. On October 15, 2005, Erin purchased stock in Glennan Irish Ale Corporation (the stock is not small business stock) for $2,000. On June 15, 2006, the stock became worthless. How should Erin treat the loss in 2006?

   a. $1,000 long-term capital loss.
   b. $2,000 short-term capital loss.
   c. $2,000 long-term capital loss.
   d. $1,000 short-term capital loss.
   e. $2,000 ordinary loss.

105. On January 15 of last year, Pat, a single taxpayer, purchased stock in Fisher Corporation (the stock is §1244 small business stock) for $10,000. On January 10 of the current year, he sold the stock for $70,000. How should Pat treat the gain on his current year tax return?

   a. $60,000 ordinary income.
   b. $60,000 long-term capital gain.
   c. $50,000 ordinary income, $10,000 long-term capital gain.
   d. $50,000 ordinary income, $10,000 short-term capital gain.
   e. $60,000 short-term capital gain.

106. On September 19, 2005, an investor purchases 5,000 shares of Tenor Corporation for $5,000. On March 31, 2006, the stock became worthless. What is the recognized gain or loss in 2006 and how is it classified?

   a. $3,000 STCL.
   b. $5,000 STCL.
   c. $3,000 LTCL.
   d. $5,000 LTCL.

107. Buddy Short, CPA, is a cash-basis taxpayer. In April of last year, Buddy billed a client $4,500 for the following professional services:

Estate planning	$3,000
Personal tax return preparation	$1,000
Compilation of business financial statements	$500

No part of the $4,500 was ever paid. In April of the current year, the client declared bankruptcy, and the $4,500 obligation became totally uncollectible. What loss can Buddy deduct on his current year tax return for this bad debt?

a. $0.

b. $500.

c. $1,500.

d. $3,000.

e. $4,500.

108. Kurt, who worked as a manager for Review Corp., loaned Review Corp. $4,000 two years ago. Kurt did not own any of Review's stock, and the loan was not a condition of Kurt's employment by Review. This year, Review declared bankruptcy and Kurt's note receivable from Review became worthless. What loss can Kurt claim on his income tax return for this year assuming no other capital gains or losses?

a. $2,000 ordinary loss.

b. $2,000 long-term capital loss.

c. $3,000 short-term capital loss.

d. $4,000 business bad debt.

e. $4,000 short-term capital loss.

DEPRECIATION, COST RECOVERY, AMORTIZATION, AND DEPLETION

109. Last year, Black had a §179 deduction carryover of $8,000. In the current year, he elected §179 for an asset acquired at a cost of $10,000. Black's net income for the current year is $15,000. Determine Black's §179 deduction for the current year (assume no other income).

    a. $8,000.

    b. $10,000.

    c. $15,000.

    d. $17,500.

    e. $18,000.

110. During the year, SAW Furniture purchased the following assets:

Date	Asset	Cost
February 20	Saws	$50,000
October 30	Lathes	$100,000

In computing depreciation of these assets, which of the following conventions will be used?

    a.   Half-year.

    b.   Mid-quarter.

    c.   Mid-month.

    d.   Mid-week.

111. Which one of the following assets is eligible for either a depreciation or amortization deduction for federal income tax purposes?

    a.   Raw land used in a trade or business.

    b.   Copyright.   Amortizable

    c.   Personal residence.

    d.   Clothing owned by John's Clothes, a clothing store.

112. All of the following properties listed below are used in a trade or business or held for the production of income. which one of the following properties is not depreciable or amortizable for federal income tax purposes?

    a.   Computer.

    b.   Rental real estate.

    c.   Sports Utility Vehicle.

    d.   Land.

PASSIVE ACTIVITY LOSSES

113. In the current year, Bob invested $50,000 for a 20% interest in a partnership in which he was a material participant during the year. The partnership incurred a loss, and Bob's share was $75,000. Which of the following statements is <u>false</u>?

    a. Since Bob has only $50,000 of capital at risk, he cannot deduct more than $50,000 against his other income.

    b. Bob's nondeductible loss of $25,000 can be carried over and used when the at-risk provisions allow.

    c. If Bob has taxable income of $45,000 from the partnership in the following year and no other transactions that affect his at-risk amount, he can use all of the $25,000 loss carried over from the current year.

    d. Bob's $75,000 loss is nondeductible in the current year and the following year under the passive loss provisions.

114. Joseph, age 54 and single, earns a salary of $180,000 working for a manufacturing company. He is an avid saver, and over the years has amassed an investment portfolio of $2,000,000. He expects the portfolio to appreciate in value at an average rate of 8% per year. Last year he received dividends and interest from the portfolio of $40,000. After speaking with a financial planner, Joseph decided to invest $30,000 for a 15% interest in a passive activity in the current year. Operations of the activity resulted in a loss of $300,000, of which Joseph's share was $45,000. How is his loss for the current year characterized?

    a. $15,000 is suspended under the at-risk rules, and $30,000 is suspended under the passive loss rules.

    b. $30,000 is suspended under the at-risk rules, and $15,000 is suspended under the passive loss rules.

    c. $45,000 is suspended under the passive loss rules.

    d. $45,000 is suspended under the at-risk rules.

    e. None of the above.

115. In the current year, George invested $100,000 for a 20% partnership interest in an activity in which he is a material participant. The partnership reported a loss of $400,000 in the current year and a loss of $200,000 in the following year. George's share of the partnership's loss was $80,000 in the current year and $40,000 in the following year. How much of the loss from the partnership can George deduct?

	Current Year	Following Year
a.	$80,000	$40,000
b.	$80,000	$20,000
c.	$0	$0
d.	$80,000	$0
e.	None of the above.	

116. In the current year, Fred invested $25,000 for a 25% interest in a real estate rental partnership where he was a general partner and a material participant. Fred's AGI was $125,000 and his allocated loss from the real estate activity was $30,000. Fred has no passive income this year. What is Fred's deductible loss on his federal tax return from the above transaction for the current year?

   a. $0.

   b. $12,500.

   c. $15,000.

   d. $25,000.

   e. $30,000.

117. Philip, a professor, earned a salary of $140,000 from a university in the current year. He received $35,000 in dividends and interest during the year. In addition, he incurred a loss of $25,000 from an investment in a passive activity. His at-risk amount in the activity at the beginning of the current year was $15,000. What is Philip's adjusted gross income for the current year?

   a. $115,000.

   b. $150,000.

   c. $160,000.

   d. $175,000.

   e. None of the above.

118. Arthur, an attorney, owns and participates in a separate business (not real estate) during the current year. He has one employee who works part-time in the business. Which of the following statements is correct?

   a. If Arthur participates for 500 hours and the employee participates for 520 hours during the year, Arthur qualifies as a material participant.

   b. If Arthur participates for 600 hours and the employee participates for 1,000 hours during the year, Arthur qualifies as a material participant.

   c. If Arthur participates for 120 hours and the employee participates for 125 hours during the year, Arthur qualifies as a material participant.

   d. If Arthur participates for 95 hours and the employee participates for 5 hours during the year, Arthur probably does not qualify as a material participant.

   e. None of the above.

119. Carter, an unmarried individual, had an adjusted gross income of $180,000 in the current year before any IRA deduction, taxable Social Security benefits, or passive activity losses. Carter, incurred a loss of $30,000 from rental real estate in which he actively participated. What amount of loss (attributable to this rental real estate) can be used in the current year as an offset against income from nonpassive sources?

   a. $0.

   b. $12,500.

   c. $25,000.

   d. $30,000.

   e. None of the above.

120. Which of the following activities is/are treated as a "rental activity" under the passive activity rules?

    1. Property rental where average customer use is 6 days.

    2. Property rental where average customer use is 30 days and no significant services are provided.

    3. Property rental where extraordinary services are provided on behalf of the owners.

    4. Property rental where the property is customarily made available during defined business hours for the nonexclusive use of customers.

    a. 1 only.

    b. 2 only.

    c. 2 and 3.

    d. 2, 3, and 4.

    e. 1, 2, 3, and 4.

121. Paula purchased an interest in a publicly traded partnership with a current loss of $7,000. If she purchased a nonpublicly traded partnership with $10,000 of passive income, how much of the passive loss can be used to offset income in the current year?

    a. $0.

    b. $3,000.

    c. $5,000.

    d. $7,000.

    e. $10,000.

122. Under the passive activity rules, income is generally classified as active income, portfolio income, or passive income for tax purposes. The classification of income is instrumental in determining whether certain passive losses are deductible. Which of the following types of income is/are generally considered passive income for tax purposes?

    1. Interest income.

    2. Royalty income.

    3. Rental income.

    4. Dividend income.

    a. 3 only.

    b. 3 and 4.

    c. 2 and 3.

    d. 2, 3, and 4.

    e. 1, 2, and 4.

EMPLOYEE EXPENSES

123. Jenny holds two jobs – a full-time job with Continental Corporation and a part-time job with Delta Corporation. Jenny uses her car to get to work, and the mileage involved is as follows: from Jenny's home to Continental is 60 miles; from Continental to Delta is 10 miles; and from Delta to Jenny's home is 60 miles. Jenny's deductible mileage for each work day is:

   a. 0 miles.

   b. 10 miles.

   c. 60 miles.

   d. 70 miles.

   e. 120 miles.

124. When travel includes both business and pleasure:

   a. No transportation expenses can be deducted if foreign travel is included.

   b. Transportation expenses must be allocated if domestic travel is included.

   c. For foreign travel, no allocation between business and pleasure of transportation expenses is required if the taxpayer was away from home for seven days or less.

   d. For foreign and domestic travel, no allocation between business and pleasure of transportation expenses is required if the taxpayer spends at least 75 percent of the time on business.

125. In the current year, Ashley took a trip from Montgomery, Alabama, to London, England. She was away from home for ten days. Two midweek days were spent vacationing and eight days were spent on business (including the two travel days). Her expenses are as follows:

Airfare	$1,200
Lodging (10 days × $150)	$1,500
Meals (10 days × $90)	$900
	$3,600

Ashley's deduction is:

   a. $2,760.

   b. $2,880.

   c. $2,700.

   d. $3,600.

126. Melinda, who holds a Bachelor of Arts degree in Art History, is a middle school teacher in New Orleans. She wants to further her education in Art History, believing this will help her become a better teacher. Melinda spent her summer break attending the University of Hawaii taking art history courses. Her expenses are as follows:

Books and tuition	$2,000
Meals	$1,000
Lodging	$700
Laundry while in travel status	200
Transportation	700
	$4,600

Her education expense deduction before the 2% of AGI floor taken into consideration is:

   a. $0.

   b. $2,500.

   c. $4,100.

   d. $4,400.

   e. $4,600.

127. Steve entertains one of his clients on January 1 of the current year. Expenses paid by Steve are:

Taxi	$30
Door cover charge	$25
Dinner	$128
Tips to waitress	$25
Total	$208

Assuming proper substantiation, Steve's current year deduction is:

   a. $119.

   b. $162.

   c. $183.

   d. $208.

128. Robbins, the sales director for a software company, pays $2,000 to obtain a skybox for an evening production of "Cats." The skybox holds 15 seats, and Robbins invites nine clients. Nonluxury seats sell for $25 each. The refreshments served to Robbins and her clients cost $455. A substantial business discussion was held before and after the show and Robbins has all necessary substantiation. Robbins' deduction is:

   a. $375.00.

   b. $415.00.

   c. $830.00.

   d. $2,227.50.

   e. $2,455.00.

129. Lance made the following gifts during the current year:

To Jack, a key client ($4 of the amount listed was for gift wrapping)	$104 → 29
To Vernon, Lance's secretary, on Vernon's birthday	$24 → 24
To Steve, Lance's boss, at Christmas	$28
Total	$156

53

Assuming proper substantiation, Lance's deduction is: ~~D2807~~

    a. $49.

    b. $53.

    c. $75.

    d. $79.

    e. $156.

130. At Thanksgiving of the current year, Delle Corp. gave business gifts to 15 individual customers. These gifts, which were not of an advertising nature, had the following fair market values:

3 gifts at $12 each	36
4 gifts at $25 each	100
4 gifts at $60 each	100
4 gifts at $100 each	100

Of the total gifts given, how much was deductible as a business expense for the current year?

    a. $0.

    b. $336.

    c. $375.

    d. $575.

    e. $776.

131. Foster, a corporate executive, incurred the following business-related, unreimbursed expenses in the current year:

Entertainment	$4,000
Travel	$2,000
Education	$1,000 for work

Assuming that Foster does not itemize deductions, how much of these expenses can he deduct on his current year tax return?

    a. $0.

    b. $1,000.

    c. $3,000.

    d. $4,000.

    e. $6,000.

ITEMIZED DEDUCTIONS

---

132. Dave, a single, calendar year, cash-basis taxpayer, has the following transactions for the current year:

Salary from job	$60,000
Alimony paid to ex-wife	$5,000
Medical expenses	$7,500

Based on this information, Dave has which of the following?

   a. Adjusted Gross Income of $60,000.

   b. Medical expense deduction of $3,000.

   c. Medical expense deduction of $3,375.

   d. Medical expense deduction of $4,125.

   e. Medical expense deduction of $4,500.

133. Which, if any, of the following expenses qualify for deductibility under miscellaneous itemized deductions, subject to a 2% of AGI floor?

   a. Cost of regular uniforms of U.S. Marine officer on active duty.

   b. Job-hunting expenses of a recent college graduate looking for his first job.

   c. Job-hunting expenses of an art history professor seeking employment as a chef.

   d. Cost of local service for a taxpayer's residential phone which is also used for business.

   e. None of the above.

134. Which of the following miscellaneous itemized deductions are not subject to the 2% of AGI floor?

   a. Gambling losses to the extent of gambling gains.

   b. Union dues.

   c. Work uniforms (not suitable for street wear).

   d. Home office expenses of an employee (the employer does not provide a regular office).

135. A friend of yours has asked you to prepare her federal income tax return for last year. She has given you a box of receipts, cancelled checks, W-2s, and other miscellaneous documentation. In preparing her return, you notice that she incurred several types of taxes during the year. She incurred real property taxes on a home that she purchased two years ago, personal property taxes on her Ford Explorer (based on the value of the car), New Jersey income taxes, and a penalty tax for underpayment of a previous year's tax liability. Which of these taxes is not deductible as an itemized deduction?

   a. State income taxes.

   b. Real property taxes.

   c. Personal property taxes.

   d. Penalty taxes.

136. Which of the following expenditures may be taken as either a deduction or as a tax credit?

    a. Qualified moving expenses.
    b. Health insurance premiums for self-employed individuals.
    c. Foreign taxes.
    d. Professional dues for an employee.

137. Which of the following, if any, qualify for the medical expense deduction?

    a. Cremation expenses for dependent mother.
    b. Nonprescribed cold remedy purchased at a drug store.
    c. Nonprescribed vitamin supplements purchased from a mail-order catalogue.
    d. Liposuction to reduce double chin due to aging and excess weight.
    e. None of the above.

138. During the current year, Abe incurred and paid the following expenses:

Psychiatrist bills for Alex (Abe's stepson)	$1,400
Tuition, room and board for Alex at the Dalton School	$12,000
Doctor bills for Cynthia (Alex's mother, Abe's spouse)	$2,000
Charges at Memorial Nursing Home for Cynthia	$24,000

Alex qualifies as Abe's dependent. Alex's psychiatrist recommended the Dalton School because of its small class sizes and rigorous discipline control. The school provides no special medical facilities or care. Cynthia has been diagnosed as having deteriorating brain disease. Memorial offers the proper care Cynthia needs. For these expenses, the amount that qualifies for the medical deduction is:

    a. $0.
    b. $1,400.
    c. $27,400.
    d. $38,000.
    e. $39,400.

139. Upon the recommendation of a physician, Sidney has an air filtration system installed in his personal residence since he suffers from severe allergy problems. Sidney incurs and pays the following amount during the current year:

Filtration system and cost of installation	$10,000
Increase in utility bills due to the system	$1,000
Cost of certified appraisal of property	$500

The system has an estimated useful life of 15 years. The appraisal was to determine the value of Sidney's residence with and without the system. The appraisal states that the system increased the value of Sidney's residence by $2,000. Expenses qualifying for the medical expense deduction in the current year total:

    a. $1,500.

    b. $8,000.

    c. $9,000.

    d. $11,000.

    e. $11,500.

140. Donna's employer withheld $4,200 in state income taxes from her salary in the current year. Donna also paid an additional $1,200 in estimated state income tax payments. She filed her previous year's state income tax return in April of the current year, and received a state tax refund of $700 in the current year. She claimed the standard deduction on her federal return for the previous year. Which of the following statements is correct?

    a. If she itemizes, she can deduct $4,700 in state income tax on her current year federal income tax return.

    b. If she itemizes, she can deduct $5,400 in state income tax on her current year federal income tax return.

    c. She is required to report the $700 state income tax refund as income in the current year.

    d. Statements B and C are correct.

141. During the current year, Ginny paid the following taxes:

Taxes on residence (for period January 1 through August 31 of current year)	$2,000
State motor vehicle tax (based on the value of the automobile)	$120

Ginny sold the residence on June 30 of the current year, and the real estate taxes were not prorated between the buyer and the seller. How much of the above taxes qualify as a deduction from AGI for the current year (rounded to nearest dollar)?

    a. $1,480.

    b. $1,601.

    c. $1,800.

    d. $2,000.

    e. $2,120.

142. Taxpayer is a resident of a state that imposes income tax. Information regarding Taxpayer's state income tax transactions is as follows:

Taxes withheld in the current year	$7,200
Refund received in the current year from overpayment of prior year tax liability	$1,500
Deficiency assessed on return filed two years ago (as a result of audit by the state)	$3,000
Interest on the tax deficiency	$500

The deficiency and interest thereon were paid by Taxpayer in the current year. If Taxpayer elects to itemize deductions for the current year, how much of the above transactions can be deducted?

    a. $7,700.

    b. $9,700.

    c. $10,200.

    d. $10,700.

    e. None of the above.

143. During the current year, Horace paid the following interest charges:

On home mortgage loan	$9,000
On loan to purchase household furniture (personal)	$800
On loan to purchase state of Louisiana general obligation bonds (tax-exempt)	$750

If Horace itemizes his deductions from AGI for the current year, the amount deductible as interest expense is:

    a. $800.

    b. $1,550.

    c. $9,000.

    d. $9,800.

    e. $10,550.

144. In the current year, Helen (a single taxpayer), purchases an airplane for $130,000. In order to obtain financing for the purchase, Helen issues a lien on her personal residence in the amount of $130,000. At the time, the residence had a fair market value of $400,000 and a first mortgage of $320,000. For the plane loan, Helen may claim as qualified home mortgage interest the interest on what amount?

    a. $30,000.

    b. $80,000.

    c. $100,000.

    d. $130,000.

    e. None of the above.

145. George graduated from Ball University. In the current year, he donated $2,000 to the athletic department of the university to guarantee priority to purchase two premium season tickets to home football games. In addition, George purchased two season tickets at the regular price of $500 ($250 each). George's charitable contribution for the current year is:

    a. $1,000.

    b. $1,600.

    c. $2,000.

    d. $2,500.

    e. None of the above.

146. In the current year, Jeff makes the following charitable donations:

	Basis	Fair Market Value
Inventory held for resale in Jeff's business (a sole proprietorship)	$8,000	$6,000
Stock in Hetzer Co. held as an investment (acquired two years ago)	$10,000	$40,000
Coin collection held as an investment (acquired ten years ago)	$1,000	$7,000

The Hetzer Co. stock was given to Jeff's church, and the coin collection was given to the Boy Scouts. Both donees promptly sold the property for the stated fair market value. Ignoring percentage limitations based on AGI, Jeff's charitable contribution for the current year is:

    a. $19,000.

    b. $47,000.

    c. $53,000.

    d. $55,000.

    e. None of the above.

147. A calendar-year taxpayer made the following charitable contributions in the current year:

	Basis	Fair Market Value
Cash to church	$5,000	$5,000
Unimproved land to the city of Kenner, Louisiana	$40,000	$70,000

The land had been held as an investment and was acquired 5 years ago. Shortly after receipt, the city of Kenner sold the land for $90,000. If the taxpayer's AGI is $120,000, the allowable charitable contribution deduction is:

    a. $25,000 if the reduced deduction election is not made.

    b. $75,000 if the reduced deduction election is made.

    c. $37,000 if the reduced deduction election is not made.

    d. $45,000 if the reduced deduction election is made.

    e. None of the above.

148. John, who resided in New Jersey, was unemployed for the last six months of last year. In January of the current year, he moved to Florida and obtained a full-time job in February. He kept this job for the balance of the year. John paid the following expenses in the current year in connection with his move:

Rental of truck to move his personal belongings to Florida	$1,200
Penalty for breaking the lease on his New Jersey apartment	500
Total	$1,700

How much can John deduct in the current year for moving expenses?

    a. $0.

    b. $500.

    c. $1,200.

    d. $1,450.

    e. $1,700.

149. Tom is the owner of a rare postage stamp worth $1,000. He purchased the stamp several years ago for $100. If Tom donates the stamp to the local university, which of the following is true?

    a. He will receive a deduction of $100 because the stamp is considered a collectible.

    b. He will receive a deduction of $1,000 because the stamp is capital gain property.

    c. He will receive a deduction of $100 because the property is use-unrelated.

    d. He will receive a deduction of $100 because the stamp was held long term.

150. Last year, Marsha charged $3,000 on her credit card for her dependent son's medical expense. Payment to the credit card company had not been made by the time she filed last year's income tax return. Also, Marsha paid a physician $3,000 last year for the medical expenses of her mother, (qualified as a dependent) who died the previous year. What amount qualifies for Marsha's medical expense deduction for last year?

    a. $0.

    b. $3,000.

    c. $4,500.

    d. $6,000.

    e. None of the above.

151. Which of the following are casualty losses for income tax purposes?

    1. Erosion due to rain or wind.

    2. Termite infestation.

    3. Damages to personal automobile resulting from a taxpayer's negligent driving.

    4. Misplaced or lost items.

        a. 1 only.

        b. 3 only.

        c. 4 only.

        d. 1 and 3.

        e. 1, 2, 3, and 4.

152. Rick had art worth $10,000 (basis of $15,000) stolen from his apartment. During the year, he had a salary of $30,000 and no other deductions. Compute Rick's itemized deduction (after adjustments) from the theft of the art.

    a. $6,900.

    b. $9,900.

    c. $10,000.

    d. $15,000.

    e. None of the above.

153. Nona Ivey sustained $20,000 of termite damage to her house in Dallas. Assuming no insurance reimbursement and an AGI of $60,000, what is the amount of her casualty loss deduction?

    a. $0.

    b. $6,900.

    c. $7,000.

    d. $13,900.

    e. $15,000.

154. Paul, a CPA, donated two hours of service to a charity for an auction. The CPA normally charges $200 per hour. Mona purchased his package at the auction for $500. How much can the CPA take as a charitable contribution deduction?

    a. $0.

    b. $100.

    c. $200.

    d. $400.

    e. $500.

155. Jorge is single and owns $30,000 of stock he originally purchased 4 years ago for $7,000. His adjusted gross income (AGI) is $40,000. If Jorge donates the stock to his church, which of the following is the maximum amount he can deduct as a charitable contribution for this gift on his federal income tax return this year? (CFP® Certification Examination, released 8/2004)

    a. $12,000.

    b. $15,000.

    c. $20,000.

    d. $30,000.

ALTERNATIVE MINIMUM TAX

156. The alternative minimum tax applies to which of the following?

    1. Individuals.
    2. Trusts.
    3. Partnerships.
    4. Corporations.
        a. 1 only.
        b. 1 and 2.
        c. 1, 2, and 3.
        d. 1, 2, and 4.
        e. 2, 3, and 4.

157. Which one of the following is *not* an adjustment for individuals in computing the alternative minimum tax?

        a. Standard deduction.
        b. Personal and dependency exemptions.
        c. Research and experimental expenditures.
        d. Casualty losses.
        e. MACRS depreciation deductions.

158. Which one of the following is/are tax preference item(s) used in computing the alternative minimum tax for an individual?

    1. Tax-exempt income from a state of Louisiana general obligation municipal bond.
    2. Percentage depletion in excess of basis on a mining property.
    3. Tax-exempt interest on a private activity bond.
    4. Exclusion of gain on the sale of certain qualified small business corporation stock.
        a. 1 and 2.
        b. 1 and 3.
        c. 1, 2, and 3.
        d. 2, 3, and 4.
        e. 1, 2, 3, and 4.

159. Scott received incentive stock options (ISOs) from his employer. The option allows Scott to purchase 100 shares of company stock at $50 per share. Scott exercises the option five years later when the FMV of the stock is $125 per share. Scott holds the stock for three more years and then sells it for $175 per share. In the year of exercise, Scott has reportable amounts for regular tax purposes and for AMT purposes, respectively, of:

    a. $0 and $0.

    b. $0 and $7,500.

    c. $7,500 and $5,000.

    d. $12,500 and $5,000.

    e. $5,000 and $7,500.

160. Which of the following statements is true regarding the alternative minimum tax credit for noncorporate taxpayers?

    1. The credit can be carried forward indefinitely.

    2. The credit can offset future AMT liability.

    3. The credit can offset future regular tax liability.

    4. The credit can be carried back to prior years.

    5. The credit available is based on the total AMT liability, even if some of the adjustments/preferences causing the AMT liability are exclusion items.

        a. 1 and 3.

        b. 1, 2, and 5.

        c. 2, 3, and 4.

        d. 1, 3, and 5.

        e. 1, 2, 4, and 5.

161. Your client, who has a taxable income of $180,000, is concerned about being subject to the alternative minimum tax (AMT). The following itemized deductions were deducted in computing your client's taxable income. Which of the following itemized deductions would be an adjustment to regular taxable income in arriving at Alternative Minimum Taxable Income (AMTI)?

    1. Casualty losses.

    2. State income taxes paid.

    3. Employee business expenses in excess of 2% of the employee's AGI.

    4. Donation made to the local university.

        a. 1 and 2.

        b. 2 and 3.

        c. 1 and 4.

        d. 2, 3, and 4.

162. Which of the following is a tax preference item for the purpose of calculating the alternative minimum tax?

    1. Tax exempt interest from a private activity bond.
    2. Cash contributions to charitable organizations.
    3. Cash flows from limited partnerships.
    4. Personal-service income in excess of tax losses.
        a. 1 only.
        b. 2 only.
        c. 1 and 2.
        d. 1, 3, and 4.
        e. 1, 2, 3, and 4.

163. Which of the following statements regarding alternative minimum tax (AMT) are true? (**CFP®** **Certification Examination, released 8/2004**)

    1. AMT reduces the tax benefits from certain types of deductions and tax preferences allowable for regular tax purposes.
    2. Depreciation allowable for AMT can never be the same as that allowable for regular tax purposes.
    3. It is generally advantageous to accelerate ordinary income into years when AMT will be paid.
    4. It is generally advantageous to defer to a future year the payment of state income and real estate taxes when AMT will be paid in the current year.
        a. 1 and 3 only.
        b. 3 and 4 only.
        c. 1, 2 and 4 only.
        d. 1, 3 and 4 only.

TAX CREDITS

164. Which, if any, of the following properly describes the earned income credit (EIC) for the current year?

    a. Is available regardless of the amount of the taxpayer's adjusted gross income.

    b. Is not available to a surviving spouse.

    c. To take advantage of the credit, a taxpayer must have a qualifying child.

    d. The EIC is a refundable credit and may be received from an employer.

165. To be eligible for the earned income credit, a taxpayer may be required to have a qualifying child. A qualifying child must meet which of the following test(s)?

    a. Relationship.

    b. Residency.

    c. Age.

    d. All of the above tests must be met.

166. Cynthia and Ted Skeckel are married and file a joint return. They report $50,000 of adjusted gross income ($15,000 salary earned by Ted and $35,000 salary earned by Cynthia). They claim two exemptions for their dependent children. During 2006, they paid the following amounts to care for their 5-year-old son, Alex, and 7-year-old daughter, Tedra, while they worked:

Day care center	$3,000
Housekeeping services provided by Mrs. Skeckel, Ted's mother, while she is baby sitting	$1,000
Mrs. Skeckel for baby sitting	$4,000

They may claim a credit for child and dependent care expenses of:

    a. $1,200.

    b. $1,500.

    c. $1,600.

    d. $6,000.

    e. $8,000.

167. Guidry, unmarried, pays Hellen Smith (a housekeeper) $7,000 to care for his physically incapacitated mother so that he can remain gainfully employed. He has adjusted gross income of $48,000 and claims his mother as a dependent. Guidry's credit for dependent care expenses for 2006 is:

    a. $0

    b. $600.

    c. $1,200.

    d. $1,400.

    e. $2,400.

168. A widow maintains a home for herself and her two dependent preschool children. In 2006, she had adjusted gross income of $51,000 (all earned income). She paid work-related expenses of $4,000 for a housekeeper to care for her children. How much can she claim as a child-care credit in 2006?

    a. $0.

    b. $480.

    c. $600.

    d. $800.

    e. $900.

169. Which of the following statements are true regarding the HOPE Scholarship Credit?

    1. The credit is only available for the first two years of post-secondary education.

    2. The credit has a $1,650 lifetime cap. *per year*

    3. The credit is calculated as 100% of the first $1,100 and 50% of the next $1,100 of eligible expenses.

    4. The credit may be applied towards eligible expenses including tuition and books.

        a. 1, 3, and 4.

        b. 2 and 3.

        c. 1 and 3.

        d. 1 only.

        e. None of the statements are true.

170. The Lifetime Learning credit:

    a. Is available for a maximum of five years.

    b. Will vary according to the number of students in the taxpayer's family.

    c. Can be elected in conjunction with the HOPE scholarship credit for the same student.

    d. Must be elected.

    e. None of the above statements is correct.

171. George has returned to school to take a course that will allow him to become a real estate broker. The course fee was $1,300. His wife, Phyllis, a schoolteacher, has enrolled in a massage school with a goal of becoming a massage therapist. Tuition at the school totaled $9,000. George and Phyllis' AGI for the year is $75,000. Assuming both schools are accredited, what is the amount of Lifetime Learning credit they can elect?

    a. $0.

    b. $1,000.

    c. $2,000.

    d. $5,000.

    e. $10,300.

172. A client has an income tax liability of $20,000 before payments and credits. He made estimated payments of $6,000 and had $13,000 of taxes withheld from his paycheck. He is also eligible for a nonrefundable credit of $3,000 this year. Which statement is correct regarding this client's income tax situation for the current year?

    a. The client will receive a refund of $2,000 after filing his federal income tax return.

    b. The client will file a federal income tax return, and will owe no tax and will not receive a refund.

    c. The client will owe $1,000 of additional tax when he files his federal income tax return.

    d. The client will owe $4,000 of additional tax when he files his federal income tax return.

PROPERTY TRANSACTIONS – CAPITAL GAINS AND LOSSES

173. Last year, John purchased the following lots of FinPlan, Inc. stock.

Purchased Date	No. of Shares	Basis
April 24	100	$5,000
June 25	100	$6,000
August 3	200	$13,000

(handwritten: 50, 60, 65)

On December 15 of the current year, John sold 100 shares for $5,500. John did not specifically identify the shares of stock sold. What is his recognized gain or loss?

    a. No gain or loss.

    b. $1,000 STCL.

    c. $500 STCG.

    d. $500 LTCG.

    e. $500 STCL.

174. Which of the following assets is *not* generally considered a capital asset?

    a. XYZ Corporation stock held for investment.

    b. A personal residence.

    c. A computer used in a business.

    d. U.S. government securities held for investment.

    e. A personal auto.

175. Jerry has the following capital gains and losses for the current year:

LTCG	$20,000	STCG	$20,000
LTCL	$15,000	STCL	$7,500

(handwritten: 5,000 ; 12,500)

What are Jerry's net long-term and short-term gains?

    a. NSTCG = $17,500 NLTCG = $0.

    b. NLTCG = $15,000 NSTCG = $20,000.

    c. NLTCG = $5,000 NSTCG = $20,000.

    d. NLTCG = $5,000 NSTCG = $12,500.

    e. None of the above.

176. This year, Mary has short-term capital losses of $6,000, short-term capital gains of $11,000, and long-term capital losses of $6,000. How much may Mary deduct against her ordinary income this year?

   a. $0.
   b. $1,000.
   c. $3,000.
   d. $6,000.
   e. None of the above.

177. Cathy sold 100 shares of GlassCo stock for $5,200. She paid $4,000 for the stock two years ago. Commissions of $80 on the sale and $50 on the purchase were paid. What is the amount realized and the gain recognized, respectively, on this sale?

   a. $1,200 and $1,070.
   b. $5,120 and $1,070.
   c. $5,070 and $1,070.
   d. $5,200 and $1,200.

178. Dean Rett, a single taxpayer in the highest marginal income tax bracket, bought some baseball cards three years ago. If he sells the cards today at a gain, what is the maximum rate at which the gain will be taxed?

   a. 5%.
   b. 10%.
   c. 15%.
   d. 28%. ← collectibles
   e. 35%.

179. The basis for property received as a dividend is:

   a. Zero.
   b. The property's basis in the hands of the paying corporation.
   c. The fair market value of the property on the date of distribution.
   d. Undeterminable until the property is subsequently sold to a third party.

180. A capital asset was acquired on March 15, 2005. To meet the long-term holding period, what is the earliest date the asset could be sold?

   a. August 16, 2005.
   b. December 31, 2005.
   c. March 15, 2006.
   d. March 16, 2006.

181. Five years ago, Mario purchased stock in YoGulp, a publicly traded company that manufactures drinkable yogurt. He purchased the stock for $10,000, and the fair market value is now $17,000. Yesterday, he gifted the stock to his 16-year-old son, Larry, who is currently taxed at the 15% ordinary income tax rate. What would be the income tax consequences to Larry if he sold the stock tomorrow and recognized a gain on the sale of $7,000?

    a.   Short-term capital gain taxed at a rate of 15%.

    b.   Short-term capital gain taxed at a rate of 10%.

    c.   Long-term capital gain taxed at a rate of 5%.

    d.   Long-term capital gain taxed at a rate of 10%.

    e.   Long-term capital gain taxed at a rate of 15%.

182. The following assets were used in John's business:

Asset	Holding Period	Gain/Loss
Equipment	4 years	$2,100
Truck	6 months	($1,200)
Common stock (capital assets)	3 years	$2,000

The equipment had a zero adjusted basis and was purchased for $8,000. The truck was purchased for $3,000 and sold for $1,800. The stock was purchased for $3,000 and sold for $5,000. In the current year (the year of the sale), John should report what amount of net capital gain and net ordinary income?

    a. $2,100 LTCG.

    b. $800 LTCG and $900 ordinary gain.

    c. $2,000 LTCG and $900 ordinary gain.

    d. $4,100 LTCG and $1,200 ordinary loss.

    e.   None of the above.

183. In the current year, Cecily had taxable income of $30,000 not considering capital gains and losses and her personal exemption. In the current year, she incurred a $5,000 net short-term capital loss and a $5,000 net long-term capital loss. What is her long-term capital loss carryover to the following year?

    a. $0.

    b. $2,000.

    c. $4,000.

    d. $5,000.

    e.   None of the above.

184. Gift property (no gift tax was paid by the donor):

    a. Has a zero basis to the donee because the donee did not pay anything for the property.

    b. Has the same basis to the donee as the donor's adjusted basis if the donee disposes of the property at a gain.

    c. Has the same basis to the donee as the donor's adjusted basis if the donee disposes of the property at a loss and the fair market value on the date of gift was less than the donor's adjusted basis.

    d. Has a zero basis to the donee if the fair market value on the date of gift is less than the donor's adjusted basis.

    e. None of the above.

185. Craig gives Scott (his son) stock with a basis of $80,000 and a fair market value of $70,000. No gift tax is paid. Scott subsequently sells the stock for $78,000. What is his recognized gain or loss?

    a. No gain or loss.

    b. $2,000 loss.

    c. $8,000 gain.

    d. $78,000 gain.

    e. None of the above.

186. Christine purchased 100 shares of Romig Corporation stock for $28,000 ten years ago. In the current tax year, she sells 30 shares of these shares for $8,000. Twenty-nine days earlier, she had purchased 30 shares for $7,500. What is Christine's recognized gain or loss on the sale of the stock, and what is her basis in the 30 shares purchased 29 days earlier?

    a. $400 recognized loss, $7,500 basis in new stock.

    b. $0 recognized loss, $7,500 basis in new stock.

    c. $0 recognized loss, $7,900 basis in new stock.

    d. $0 recognized loss, $8,250 basis in new stock.

    e. None of the above.

187. William Barnhill gave his son, Simon, a house on August 1 of this year. No gift tax was paid. The fair market values of the house on January 1, August 1, and December 31 of the current year were as follows: $130,000, $140,000, and $150,000. Mr. Barnhill purchased the property five years ago for $60,000 and used it as rental property the entire time he held it. He took cumulative straight-line depreciation through July 31 of the current year of $10,000. What is Simon Barnhill's initial tax basis?

    a. Simon's initial tax basis is zero because he did not pay anything for the house.

    b. Simon's initial tax basis is the same as William's cost.

    c. Simon's initial tax basis is the same as William's cost, less depreciation, regardless of what Simon does with the property.

    d. Simon's initial tax basis is the fair market value on the date of the gift.

    e. Simon's initial tax basis is the fair market value as determined on the last day of the year in which the gift was given.

188. Tommy inherited 200 shares of ACME Inc stock from his uncle, who died three months ago. His uncle originally bought the stock at a total cost of $5,300. The value of the 200 shares of ACME Inc stock was $6,000 on the date of his uncle's death. Its value rose to $6,500 as of yesterday, and Tommy sold it for $6,500. Tommy's taxable gain on the sale would be:

    a. $500 short-term capital gain.

    b. $500 long-term capital gain.

    c. $1,200 short-term capital gain.

    d. $1,200 long-term capital gain.

189. Nicole, a single taxpayer, made the following gift in the current year to her son, Scott: Securities costing $50,000, FMV at date of gift is $90,000. Which statement is correct?

    a. Scott has taxable income of $40,000.

    b. Scott's basis in the securities is $50,000.

    c. Scott's basis in the securities is $90,000.

    d. None of the above.

190. An individual received a bequest of 100 shares of XYZ stock from a relative who died on March 1 of this year. The relative bought the stock at a total cost of $5,500. The value of the 100 shares of XYZ stock was $5,750 on March 1. Its value rose to $6,250 on July 1 of this year, on which day the individual sold it for $6,250, incurring expenses for the sale of $250. The taxable gain on the sale would be a: (CFP® Certification Examination, released 8/2004)

    a. $250 long-term capital gain.

    b. $250 short-term capital gain.

    c. $500 long-term capital gain.

    d. $500 short-term capital gain.

PROPERTY TRANSACTIONS: NONTAXABLE EXCHANGES

191. Which of the following types of business or investment property is eligible for like-kind exchange treatment?

    a. Securities.

    b. Different sex livestock.

    c. Inventory held for sale.

    d. Business equipment.

192. Which statement below is true with regard to property transactions?

    a. Gain realized represents the economic gain received by the taxpayer.

    b. Gain recognized represents the economic gain received by the taxpayer.

    c. A recognized loss generally is deferred to later tax years.

    d. A recognized gain may be more than a realized gain.

193. Which of the following statements regarding like-kind exchanges is/are true?

    1. Like-kind exchange treatment is automatic, not elective.

    2. A realized loss resulting from a like-kind exchange can only be recognized if boot is received.

    3. Liabilities discharged generally are treated as boot received.

    4. Prior depreciation deductions must be recaptured as ordinary income in the year of the exchange, even if no boot is received.

    a. 2 only.

    b. 1 and 3.

    c. 2 and 3.

    d. 1, 3, and 4.

    e. 1, 2, and 4.

194. Taxpayer exchanges a machine (A) and building for another machine (B) in a like-kind exchange. The (A) machine had an adjusted taxable basis of $40,000 and a fair market value of $30,000. The building had an adjusted basis of $20,000 and a fair market value of $35,000. The large machine (B) has a fair market value of $65,000. What is the taxpayer's recognized gain or loss? There were no mortgages and no cash exchanged.

    a. $0.

    b. $10,000 loss.

    c. $5,000 gain.

    d. $15,000 gain.

    e. None of the above.

195. On February 2 of the current year, taxpayer exchanged a bank building, having an adjusted taxable basis of $600,000 and subject to a mortgage of $275,000 for another bank building with a fair market value of $800,000 and subject to a mortgage of $275,000. Transfers were made subject to outstanding mortgages. What amount of gain should taxpayer recognize in the current year?

    a. $0.
    b. $75,000.
    c. $200,000.
    d. $275,000.

196. An office building with an adjusted taxable basis of $120,000 was destroyed by fire on January 2 of last year. On January 15 of the current year, the insurance company paid the owner $200,000. The owner reinvested $190,000 in a new office building. What is the basis of the new building if §1033 (nonrecognition of gain from an involuntary conversion) is elected?

    a. $110,000.
    b. $120,000.
    c. $180,000.
    d. $190,000.

197. John owned business property that was destroyed by a fire. His adjusted taxable basis in the property was $10,000, and AllFarm insurance company just sent him a check for $15,000 to cover the loss. If John timely buys qualified replacement property for $12,000, what is his realized and recognized gain?

    a. $0 gain realized, $0 gain recognized.
    b. $3,000 gain realized, $15,000 gain recognized.
    c. $5,000 gain realized, $3,000 gain recognized.
    d. $10,000 gain realized, $5,000 gain recognized.
    e. $15,000 gain realized, $15,000 gain recognized.

198. Which of the following is not a requirement for a nontaxable exchange?

    a. The form of the transaction is an exchange.
    b. Both the property transferred and the property received are held either for productive use in a trade or business or for investment.
    c. The property is like-kind property.
    d. The exchange cannot involve related parties.

199. Taxpayer's office building was condemned by a local government authority on May 10, 2004. The adjusted basis was $300,000. Condemnation proceeds of $500,000 were received on February 1, 2005. The taxable year is the calendar year. What is the latest date that the taxpayer can replace the office building to qualify for §1033 (nonrecognition of gain from an involuntary conversion) treatment?

    a. May 10, 2006.
    b. February 1, 2007.
    c. December 31, 2007.
    d. December 31, 2008.

200. Mike exchanged the following old machine in a like-kind exchange. What gain is recognized, and what is the adjusted taxable basis in the new asset?

1. Adjusted basis of old machine $5,000
2. Fair market value of new machine $10,000
3. Fair market value of boot received $0
4. Fair market value of boot given $0

	Gain Recognized	Basis of New Asset
a.	$0	$5,000
b.	$0	$10,000
c.	$5,000	$5,000
d.	$5,000	$10,000
e.	$5,000	$0

201. Mike exchanged the following old machine in a like-kind exchange. What gain is recognized, and what is the adjusted taxable basis in the new asset?

1. Adjusted basis of old machine $5,000
2. Fair market value of new machine $10,000
3. Fair market value of boot received $0
4. Fair market value of boot given $4,000

	Gain Recognized	Basis of New Asset
a.	$0	$5,000
b.	$0	$9,000
c.	$0	$10,000
d.	$4,000	$5,000
e.	$4,000	$10,000

202. Mike exchanged the following old machine in a like-kind exchange. What gain is recognized, and what is the adjusted taxable basis in the new asset?

1.	Adjusted basis of old machine	$5,000
2.	Fair market value of new machine	$10,000
3.	Fair market value of boot received	$0
4.	Fair market value of boot given	$6,000

	Gain Recognized	Basis of New Asset
a.	$0	$5,000
b.	$0	$10,000
c.	$0	$11,000
d.	$5,000	$11,000
e.	$6,000	$11,000

203. Mike exchanged the following old machine in a like-kind exchange. What gain is recognized, and what is the adjusted taxable basis in the new asset?

1.	Adjusted basis of old machine	$5,000
2.	Fair market value of new machine	$10,000
3.	Fair market value of boot received	$4,000
4.	Fair market value of boot given	$0

	Gain Recognized	Basis of New Asset
a.	$0	$5,000
b.	$4,000	$5,000
c.	$4,000	$10,000
d.	$5,000	$5,000
e.	$5,000	$10,000

204. Mike exchanged the following old machine in a like-kind exchange. What gain is recognized, and what is the basis in the new asset?

1.	Adjusted basis of old machine	$5,000
2.	Fair market value of new machine	$10,000
3.	Fair market value of boot received	$0
4.	Fair market value of boot given	$400

	Gain Recognized	Basis of New Asset
a..	$0	$5,000
b.	$0	$5,400
c.	$0	$10,000
d.	$4,600	$10,000
e.	$5,000	$5,000

205. Which of the following exchanges would qualify for nonrecognition of gain under the like-kind exchange rules? D2876

    a. Common stock for preferred stock.

    b. Inventory for a clothing store.

    c. Land used in a business for a bank building.

    d. A building in Boston for a building in Paris.

206. Which of the following may require John to recognize gain on a like-kind exchange?

    a. Payment of cash to Mary, the other party in the exchange.

    b. Assumption of Mary's liability by John.

    c. Assumption of John's liability by Mary.

    d. Receipt by John of property with a FMV less than John's basis in the property surrendered.

207. Karen bought a personal residence for $130,000 ten years ago. She built an additional room on the house for $20,000. She sells the property for $200,000 in the current year and pays $12,000 in real estate commissions and $3,000 in legal fees in connection with the sale. Six months after the sale of the house, she purchased a condo in a different city for $165,000. What is her recognized gain or loss on the sale of the house?

    a. $0.

    b. $35,000.

    c. $38,000.

    d. $55,000.

    e. $58,000.

208. Which of the following is true about the gain excluded on the sale of a personal residence under Section 121?

    a. The taxpayer can exclude up to $250,000 of gain on the sale of the residence, if the taxpayer is at least 55 years of age on the date of sale.

    b. Any portion of realized gain in excess of the exclusion must be recognized as capital gain.

    c. The home must have been used as the taxpayer's principal residence for at least four of the five years preceding the sale.

    d. Only one residence qualifies for this exclusion during a person's lifetime.

209. Neal and Amy sold their personal residence for a gain of $350,000. Which of the following conditions would prevent them from excluding the full gain from income under Section 121?

    a. Neal has owned the house for 3 years.

    b. Amy moved into the house when she and Neal got married one year ago.

    c. The principal residence was a houseboat.

    d. Neal and Amy are both 40 years old.

    e. None of the above will cause inclusion of the gain.

210. B.J. and Sarah own a house in which they have resided for the past 10 years. B.J. is 60 and Sarah is 58. They sell the house for $420,000 and pay realtor fees of $50,000. Their adjusted basis for the house was $70,000. What is their recognized gain on the sale of the residence if they make any possible election?

    a. $0.

    b. $50,000.

    c. $125,000.

    d. $250,000.

    e. $300,000.

211. As part of their divorce agreement, Ron transfers his ownership interest in their personal residence to Marge. The house had been jointly owned by Ron and Marge, and their adjusted basis was $160,000. At the time of the transfer to Marge, the fair market value is $210,000. What is the recognized gain to Ron, and what is Marge's new tax basis for the house?

    a. $0 and $160,000.

    b. $0 and $210,000.

    c. $25,000 and $185,000.

    d. $25,000 and $210,000.

    e. None of the above.

212. Hugh, age 57, is a single taxpayer. In March of this year, Hugh sold his principal residence for $445,000 net of expenses and moved to a nursing home. Hugh paid $120,000 for the residence 18 years ago and has made no improvements to it. How much of the gain must Hugh include in his gross income this year as a result of the sale?

    a. $0.

    b. $55,000.

    c. $75,000.

    d. $120,000.

    e. $325,000.

213. To take advantage of the $250,000 exclusion of gain on the sale of a principal residence (by a single taxpayer) which of the following requirements must be met?

    1. The taxpayer must have attained age 55.

    2. The taxpayer must have occupied the house as his or her primary residence for at least 2 of the last 5 years.

    3. A new or replacement residence must be purchased no more than 2 years before or 2 years after the sale of the residence.

    4. The exclusion must not have been previously claimed by the taxpayer.

        a. 1 only.

        b. 2 only.

        c. 2 and 3.

        d. 1, 2, and 4.

        e. 1, 2, 3, and 4.

214. On July 1 of the current year, George, age 65, sold his principal residence (in which he lived for the last 20 years) for $300,000. It had an adjusted basis of $100,000. On December 1 of the same year, he purchased a new residence for $160,000. What should the taxpayer recognize as the gain on the sale of his residence in the current year?

    a. $0.

    b. $15,000.

    c. $75,000.

    d. $175,000.

    e. None of the above.

215. Doug has been a confirmed bachelor for 60 years and has lived in his ideal bachelor pad (personal residence) for the last 15 years. Suddenly he meets Cary and falls madly in love. They marry and Cary moves in with Doug. After six months, Cary is sick of the bachelor pad and demands that they move. If they sell the house immediately, what is the maximum gain they can exclude?

    a. $500,000.

    b. $312,500.

    c. $250,000.

    d. $125,000.

216. Janie, single, bought a condo in Philadelphia for $140,000 in July 2005. In July 2006, her company transferred her to Dallas. She sells the condo for $180,000. Because she is worried about being transferred again, she decides not to reinvest the proceeds but to just rent for a while in Dallas. Which of the following statements is true?

   a. Janie has a taxable gain of $40,000.

   b. Janie has taxable gain of $20,000.

   c. Janie has no taxable gain.

   d. If Janie would reinvest at least $140,000 in a new residence within 2 years, she would be able to defer gain.

217. Mary, a single taxpayer, purchased a home for $300,000. She lived in the home for 12 months, then sold the home for $200,000 because her employer relocated her to a new city. What are the tax ramifications?

   a. Mary has a $100,000 deductible ordinary loss.

   b. The deductible loss is limited to $30,000, with a $70,000 carryover.

   c. Mary can take a $3,000 capital loss, and will have a $97,000 capital loss carryforward.

   d. Mary's loss is disallowed because the house is personal use property.

SECTION 1231 AND RECAPTURE PROVISIONS

218. Bradley, Inc. sold some land on June 30th of the current year for a $15,000 gain. The land was originally purchased 3 years ago and was classified as a Section 1231 asset. This was the only asset sale for this year. In the previous year, Bradley, Inc. had an $8,000 net Section 1231 loss. For the current year, Bradley's net Section 1231 gain is treated as:

    a.   A $15,000 ordinary loss.

    b.   A $15,000 ordinary gain.

    c.   A $7,000 long-term capital gain and a $8,000 ordinary gain.

    d.   A $8,000 long-term capital gain and a $7,000 ordinary loss.

    e.   None of the above.

219. Ann purchased a $200,000 business machine and took $140,000 of depreciation (straight-line depreciation would have been $100,000). She sold it for $240,000. Which of the following statements about the nature of her gain is true?

    a.   Ann will have a $180,000 section 1231 capital gain.

    b.   Ann will have a $40,000 section 1231 capital gain.

    c.   Ann will have a $140,000 section 1245 ordinary gain.

    d.   Ann will have a $100,000 section 1245 ordinary gain.

    e.   Both b and c are correct.

220. Which of the following dispositions of IRC Section 1245 property would result in the immediate recapture of some or all of previous depreciation deduction taken by the taxpayer?

    a.   Installment sale.

    b.   Distribution by a partnership to its partners.

    c.   Disposition in a tax-free transaction.

    d.   Disposition by gift.

221. Ginny sold a file cabinet used in her business for $250. She had purchased it for $400 and deducted depreciation of $220. What is the amount and character of Ginny's gain or loss recognized on this sale?

    a. $70 ordinary income.

    b. $70 Section 1231 gain.

    c. $150 Section 1231 loss.

    d. $220 ordinary income and $150 Section 1231 loss.

222. Hank sold several Section 1231 business properties during the current year. His overall gain was $34,000 and his depreciation recapture was $15,000, and he held all of these properties for more than one year. The only other Section 1231 transactions Hank has had were in the the last three years. He had a net gain of 7,500 three years ago and a net loss of $9,000 two years ago. He did not have any Section 1231 transactions last year. How are Hank's gains for the current year treated on his income tax return?

    a. $15,000 ordinary gain; $19,000 long term capital gain.

    b. $16,500 ordinary gain; $17,500 long term capital gain.

    c. $17,500 ordinary gain; $16,500 long term capital gain.

    d. $24,000 ordinary gain; $10,000 long term capital gain.

    e. $34,000 ordinary gain.

TAXATION OF INVESTMENT TRANSACTIONS

223. Which of the following statements about Section 1202 Small Business Stock is incorrect?

   a. The stock must be held for more than 5 years to receive the tax benefit.

   b. It applies only to stock issued after August 10, 1993.

   c. Up to 50% of the gain may be excluded.

   d. The capital gains rate is 15% on any gain.

   e. All of the above are true.

224. Two years ago, Mary Francis, a 45-year old single woman, gifted ABC company stock with a basis of $500,000 and a FMV of $225,000 to her son. Mary Francis paid gift tax of $40,000 on the transaction. Yesterday, the son sold the stock for $550,000. The son's taxable gain or loss would be:

   a. $50,000 long-term capital gain.

   b. $54,000 long-term capital gain.

   c. $90,000 long-term capital gain.

   d. $275,000 short-term capital gain and $10,000 long-term capital gain.

   e. $325,000 short-term capital gain.

225. Your client is contemplating the sale of some of her holdings in her shares of XYZ company stock. The stock was acquired as follows:

Date Purchased	Shares Purchased	Cost/Share	Total Cost
August 1, 1997	200	$11	$2,200
July 15, 1999	200	$19	$3,800
May 25, 2001	300	$13	$3,900
December 1, 2003	100	$21	$2,100

What is the least amount of gain she would be required to report if she sold 500 shares for $10,000.

   a. $500.

   b. $1,500.

   c. $2,500.

   d. $2,700.

226. Jim, recently retired, is 62 years old and expects to be in the maximum federal and state tax bracket. He plans to liquidate three of the investments listed below. Assume that each investment is worth $50,000 and has grown from an original investment of $25,000 over a period of more than 3 years. Liquidation of which three of the following investments, in order of priority, would result in the lowest tax liability for Jim? (CFP® Certification Examination, released 8/2004)

1. 401(k) plan.
2. CD paying 4%.
3. U.S. savings bonds.
4. Traditional IRA (contributions were not deductible).
5. A blue chip stock.

    a. 2, 3 and 1.
    b. 2, 5 and 3.
    c. 2, 5 and 4.
    d. 3, 5 and 1.

BUSINESS ORGANIZATIONS

---

227. Which of the following describes a weakness of the sole proprietorship form of business?

    a.   Owner has too many partners.

    b.   Business is in constant danger of bankruptcy.

    c.   Owner has no control.

    d.   Business depends solely on the owner.

228. A business fails and the owners lose their investment in the company, along with their personal residences, automobiles, and other personal property. What type of business entity does this suggest?

    a.   Common shareholders in a corporation.

    b.   Preferred shareholders in a corporation.

    c.   Limited partners in a limited partnership.

    d.   General partners in a general partnership.

229. Which of the following describes a main strength of the corporate form of business entity?

    a.   Ease of establishment.

    b.   Ease of management.

    c.   Ease of raising capital.

    d.   Freedom from business income taxes.

230. Which of the following describes the corporate form of business entity?

    1.   Limited liability.

    2.   Limited life.

    3.   Proxy.

    4.   Board of Directors.

    a.   1 only.

    b.   2 only.

    c.   3 only.

    d.   1 and 3.

    e.   1, 3, and 4.

231. Which of the following can be considered a strength of the partnership form of business entity?

    1.   Ease of management.

    2.   Ease of establishment.

    3.   Lack of special taxes.

    a.   1 only.

    b.   2 only.

    c.   2 and 3.

    d.   1, 2, and 3.

    e.   None of the above.

---

232. A taxpayer is considering starting a new business. The taxpayer is concerned about liability issues affecting his business and expects to incur losses in the first year. Which of the following forms of organizations would be the most appropriate?

    a. Sole proprietorship.

    b. Partnership.

    c. C corporation.

    d. S corporation.

    e. Personal holding company.

233. In order to elect S corporation status for the current year of a calendar-year, newly incorporated business, the following must be done:

    1. Secure the consent of the board of directors of the corporation.

    2. File the election (Form 2553) before the 15th day of the third month of the year the election is to take place.

    3. Issue two classes of stock.

    4. File the election (Form 2553) at any time before the end of the corporation's tax year.

    5. Elect S corporation status upon filing the corporation's initial tax return.

        a. 1, 3, and 5.

        b. 5 only.

        c. 1 and 2.

        d. 2 only.

        e. 3 and 4.

234. Which of the following is/are disadvantages of electing S corporation status?

    1. Fringe benefits are not tax deductible by the S corporation for shareholders owning more than 2% of the stock of the corporation unless included in the shareholder's W-2.

    2. Individual income tax rates may be higher than corporate tax rates.

    3. Section 179 election to expense certain capital expenditures are not allowed at the corporate or individual level.

    4. The corporation cannot have more than 100 shareholders.

        a. 3 and 4.

        b. 1, 2, and 4.

        c. 1, 2, 3, and 4.

        d. 2 and 3.

        e. 4 only.

235. Which of the following statements regarding partnerships, S corporations, and sole proprietorships is not true?

    a. S corporation earnings are not eligible for Keogh retirement plans.

    b. Sole proprietorships are subject to the self-employment tax at a rate of 15.3% of net earnings from self-employment and adjustments for employer contribution deduction.

    c. Guaranteed payments made by a partnership are taxable to the individual partners.

    d. Passthrough earnings of an S corporation are subject to the self-employment tax.

    e. Salary payments made to S corporation shareholders are subject to FICA taxes at the corporate level.

236. Which of the following is correct with regard to the rights of a limited partner?

    1. Has the right to take part in the management of the partnership.

    2. May assign his or her interest in the partnership to anyone he or she wishes at any time.

    3. Is subject to personal liability for partnership debts.

        a. 1 only.

        b. 2 only.

        c. 3 only.

        d. 1 and 3.

        e. 1, 2, and 3.

237. Which of the following is correct regarding both a corporation and general partnership?

    1. Can hold and convey property.

    2. Are regarded as distinct entities for tax purposes.

    3. Profits are divided equally among the owners.

    4. Pay no federal tax on income.

        a. 1 only.

        b. 2 only.

        c. 1 and 2.

        d. 1 and 4.

        e. 1, 2, 3, and 4.

238. When is a corporation likely to elect S corporation status?

    a. A loss is anticipated especially at the start-up of a business.

    b. Desire to issue preferred stock.

    c. Place personal liability on the shareholders.

    d. Borrow money from shareholders.

    e. All of the above.

239. Your client, a wealthy physician in the top marginal tax bracket, is interested in purchasing a franchise in a fast-growing chain with five of his colleagues. After carefully reviewing the proposal, you have determined that apart from a large up-front investment, the business will <u>not</u> need to retain income and the income generated in subsequent years will be paid out to the investors.

Furthermore, your client wants to be assured that after investing so large an amount, the business would not be disrupted if one of his partners lost interest or encountered personal financial reversals.

What form of business makes the most sense given these circumstances? (CFP® Certification Examination, released 11/94)

    a.   Limited partnership.

    b.   General partnership.

    c.   C corporation.

    d.   Professional corporation.

    e.   S corporation.

240. A minority nonemployee shareholder in an S corporation: (CFP® Certification Examination, released 11/94)

    1.   Receives compensation when the corporation declares a dividend.

    2.   Votes for the Board of Directors at the annual shareholders' meeting.

    3.   Receives a K-1 annually in order to prepare a personal income tax return.

    4.   Reports on a personal income tax return a pro-rata share of corporate profit or loss.

        a.   1, 2, and 3.

        b.   1 and 3.

        c.   2 and 4.

        d.   4 only.

        e.   1, 2, 3, and 4.

241. Bob and his brother, George, are interested in forming a business together. However, they are concerned about the following:

    1.   Whether the business will have losses for the next three years.

    2.   Whether or not the business would continue in the event that one brother would die.

    3.   Whether they will have some limited liability protection.

Based on the concerns of the brothers, which form of business is the most appropriate?

    a.   C corporation.

    b.   S corporation.

    c.   Partnership.

    d.   Limited partnership.

    e.   Trust.

242. Eyeore, Inc. is an S corporation. Bill and Diane are the sole owners and are two of the twenty employees of the firm. Eyeore provides each of its employees $50,000 of group term coverage. The premiums on what amount of insurance coverage are taxable to Bill and Diane?

    a. $0.

    b. $25,000.

    c. $50,000.

    d. $75,000.

    e. $100,000.

243. Which of the following (individual or entity) cannot act as a general partner in a family limited partnership (FLP)?

    a. Individual.

    b. Corporation.

    c. Limited liability company.

    d. Trust.

    e. All of the above can serve as a general partner in a family limited partnership.

244. Which of the following is a correct statement regarding the limited partner in a family limited partnership (FLP)?

    a. A limited partner may receive a distribution to the extent that the distribution will cause partnership liabilities to exceed the fair value of partnership assets.

    b. FLPs seldom restrict a limited partner's ability to transfer an interest.

    c. A limited partner may never withdraw from the partnership upon the occurrence of events specified in the partnership agreement.

    d. If a limited partner participates in the control of the partnership business, the partner may be treated as a general partner and, thus, lose his or her limited liability.

245. Which of the following is not an advantage of a family limited partnership?

    a. Transfers of FLP interests are frequently valued at a discount due to lack of control and lack of marketability outside the family group.

    b. Appraisal fees will never be levied due to the discounting methods that a FLP employs.

    c. The senior family member can retain control of the business, since the senior family member is the only family member with a general partnership interest (limited partners are not allowed to participate in management of the business).

    d. Restrictions can be placed on transfers of limited partnership interests by junior family members.

246. Which of the following taxes would potentially apply to a C corporation?

    1.   Alternative Minimum Tax.

    2.   Accumulated Earnings Tax.

    3.   LIFO Recapture Tax.

    4.   Personal Holding Company Tax.

       a.   1 only.

       b.   1 and 3.

       c.   2 and 4.

       d.   1, 2, and 4.

       e.   2, 3, and 4.

247. Which of the following taxes may an S corporation be required to pay?

    1.   Alternative Minimum Tax (AMT).

    2.   LIFO Recapture Tax.

    3.   Built-in Gains Tax.

    4.   Personal Holding Company Tax.

       a.   1 only.

       b.   1 and 3.

       c.   2 and 3.

       d.   1, 2, and 4.

       e.   2, 3, and 4.

248. Which of the following statements is/are correct regarding the built-in gains tax?

    1.   The built-in gains tax is applicable to all S corporations.

    2.   The tax is computed by applying the highest corporate income tax rate to the net recognized built-in gain for the tax year.

    3.   Any appreciation of the asset after the date of conversion (from a C corporation to an S corporation) is not subject to the built-in gains tax.

    4.   The built-in gains tax is paid by the shareholders of the S corporation.

       a.   1 only.

       b.   1 and 3.

       c.   2 and 3.

       d.   1, 2, and 4.

       e.   2, 3, and 4.

249. Which of the following statements is/are correct regarding the LIFO recapture tax?

1. The LIFO recapture tax is applicable to all S corporations.
2. A C corporation that uses the LIFO (last-in, first-out) method of inventory valuation in its last taxable year before making an S corporation election must include in income a LIFO recapture amount.
3. The LIFO recapture tax is calculated based on the corporation's ordinary income tax rate.
4. The tax is payable by the corporation in four installments.
    a. 1 only.
    b. 1 and 3.
    c. 2 and 3.
    d. 1, 2, and 4.
    e. 2, 3, and 4.

250. Which of the following statements is/are true regarding an S corporation?

1. Shareholders of S corporations receive a Schedule K-1 each year.
2. S corporation shareholders can establish a Keogh plan as a result of the S corporation income.
3. One of the disadvantages of an S corporation is that the dividends paid to shareholders are subject to double taxation.
4. Capital losses incurred by an S corporation will flow through to the shareholders and will be reported on the shareholder's personal income tax return.
    a. 1 only.
    b. 2 and 3.
    c. 1 and 4.
    d. 1, 2, and 4.
    e. 2, 3, and 4.

251. Advantages for incorporating a small retail business as a C corporation include which of the following? (CFP® Certification Examination, released 8/2004)

1. Accumulating income at lower tax rates on the first $75,000
2. Withdrawing accumulated profits at capital gain rates
3. Providing tax-favored fringe benefits to shareholders
4. Changing the form of business with ease once a corporation has been formed.
    a. 2 only.
    b. 3 only.
    c. 1 and 3 only.
    d. 1 and 4 only.

252. Which of the following statements is correct regarding the income tax rules relating to a personal service corporation?

    a. The personal service corporation rules typically apply to manufacturing companies owned by four or fewer individuals.

    b. If a corporation is deemed to be a personal service corporation, losses incurred by the corporation will flow through to and be deductible by the shareholders.

    c. If a non-employee becomes a 10% shareholder of the corporation, income earned by the corporation would be taxed using graduated rates.

    d. The corporation is prohibited from earning passive income.

253. Which of the following statements is correct regarding the personal holding company tax?

    a. The personal holding company tax is imposed at a rate of 50% on the undistributed personal holding company income.

    b. The principal way to avoid this penalty tax is to cause the corporation to distribute dividends to shareholders.

    c. The objective of the personal holding company tax is to reduce the tax benefits from certain types of deductions and tax preferences allowable for regular tax purposes.

    d. Life insurance companies may be subject to this tax based on their reserve levels.

254. Harry Robbins formed and is the sole shareholder of the Robbins Company. The company's only asset is a large corporate bond portfolio. The corporation has a policy of never paying dividends. Which of the following statements is correct with respect to the corporate bond interest income received by the corporation each year?

    a. The interest income will be taxed at a flat 35%.

    b. The corporation will be eligible for a dividends received deduction because the interest income received was from a corporate bond.

    c. Income earned by the corporation will be taxed directly to Harry.

    d. The interest income will be taxed to Robbins Company at graduated corporate tax rates, and will also be subject to personal holding company tax.

TAXATION OF TRUSTS AND ESTATES

255. Trusts and estates may be subject to an annual income tax, which is reported on IRS Form 1041. Which of the following items may not be deducted by an estate or trust on this form?

    a. Charitable contributions made to the United Way.

    b. Capital losses to the extent of capital gains.

    c. A casualty loss already claimed as a deduction on an estate tax return (Form 706).

    d. Current losses from passive activities to the extent of current income from passive activities.

256. A trust whose assets are stocks and bonds generates $20,000 of distributable net income (DNI) for the current taxable year. Of this amount, $5,000 is tax-exempt interest on municipal bonds, while the remaining amount is made up of taxable dividends. During the year, the trustee made a $1,000 discretionary distribution (of trust income) to Steve, the trust beneficiary. What is the taxable portion of this distribution?

    a. $0.

    b. $250.

    c. $500.

    d. $750.

    e. $1,000.

257. XY Trust is a complex trust with two beneficiaries, Kerri and Melody. In the current taxable year, the trust had distributable net income (DNI) of $50,000, $10,000 of which was nontaxable. The trustee made a $15,000 cash distribution to Kerri and a $20,000 cash distribution to Melody. Which of the following is a true statement?

    a. Kerri should report taxable income of $10,000; Melody should report taxable income of $15,000.

    b. Kerri should report taxable income of $3,000; Melody should report taxable income of $4,000.

    c. Kerri should report taxable income of $12,000; Melody should report taxable income of $16,000.

    d. Kerri should report taxable income of $15,000; Melody should report taxable income of $20,000.

    e. The trust will be taxed on all of the income.

258. Billy has established a trust that pays out $2,000 each month to this mother, Wendy. The trust department of Allword Bank acts as trustee. Billy retains the right to borrow assets from the trust without security, and he is the remainder beneficiary of the trust. Which of the following must pay the income tax on the $40,000 earned by the trust?

    a. Billy pays on $40,000.

    b. Wendy pays on $24,000; the trust on $16,000.

    c. Wendy pays on $24,000; Billy on $16,000.

    d. The trust pays on $24,000; Billy on $16,000.

    e. The trust pays on $40,000.

259. Ronald has established a trust that pays out $1,000 each month to his mother, Martha. The trust department of Actual Bank acts as trustee. Ronald retains the right to revoke the trust and is the sole heir of his mother's estate and the remainder beneficiary of the trust. Which of the following must pay the income tax on the $15,000 earned by the trust? (CFP® **Certification Examination, released 8/2004**)

    a.   Ronald pays on $15,000.

    b.   Martha pays on $12,000; the trust on $3,000.

    c.   Martha pays on $12,000; Ronald on $3,000.

    d.   The trust pays on $15,000.

AUDIT, PENALTIES, AND TAXPAYER'S RIGHTS

---

260. Tom, a self-employed individual, had income transactions for last year (duly reported on his return filed in April of this year) as follows:

Gross receipts	$320,000
Less cost of goods sold and deductions	(256,000)
Net business income	$64,000
Capital gains	20,000
Net income	**$84,000**

Suppose that in February of next year, Tom discovers he had inadvertently omitted income on the return filed in April last year and retains a CPA to determine his position under the statute of limitations. The CPA should advise Tom that the <u>six-year statute of limitations</u> would apply to his return only if he omitted from gross income an amount in excess of:

    a. $11,000.

    b. $16,000.

    c. $21,000.

    d. $80,000.

    e. $85,000.

[handwritten: .25 × 320,000 + 20,000]

261. Which of the following is/are correct regarding the chances of a taxpayer return being selected for audit?

    1. Chances of selection increase with the size of refund claimed.

    2. Chances increase for taxpayer who has been audited in the past regardless of the outcome.

    3. Chances increase for people who deduct 10% of salary for charity simply because that is in excess of national norms.

    4. Chances increase for self-employed individuals.

    a. 2 and 4.

    b. 1, 2, and 4.

    c. 3 and 4.

    d. 1, 3, and 4.

    e. 1, 2, and 3.

262. Joan has an error on a past tax return (not prepared by current tax preparer) which Joan refuses to correct. The current tax preparer:

  1. Has a duty to notify the IRS or is subject to preparer penalties.

  2. Should withdraw from engagement if error affects current return and is material in amount.

  3. Must withdraw from engagement.

  4. Should consider the materiality of the error even if it does not affect the current year.

      a. 1 and 4.
      b. 2 and 4.
      c. 1 and 3.
      d. 1, 3, and 4.
      e. 1, 2, and 4.

263. In order to obtain innocent spouse relief, a taxpayer must meet the following conditions:

      a. Have filed a separate return.
      b. The understatement of tax must be attributable to a grossly erroneous item of the other spouse.
      c. Spouse had no reason to know the extent of the understatement.
      d. Be elected by taxpayer and taxpayer's spouse.
      e. None of the above.

264. Bill files his tax return 40 days after the due date. Along with the return, Bill remits a check for $5,000 (the balance of the tax owed). Disregarding the interest element, Bill's combined failure-to-file and failure-to-pay penalties are:

      a. $650.
      b. $600.
      c. $500.
      d. $550.
      e. None of the above.

265. Chip files a timely tax return but is later required to pay an additional $15,000 in tax. Of this amount, $6,000 is attributable to the taxpayer's negligence. The negligence penalty will be:

      a. $0, there is no penalty, the return was filed timely.
      b. $500, there is a maximum $500 penalty.
      c. $1,200, a 20% penalty is applied to the $6,000.
      d. $1,800, a 30% penalty is applied to the $6,000.
      e. $3,000, a 20% penalty is applied to all tax due.

266. Margo files her tax return 39 days after the due date. Along with the return, she remits a check for $6,000 (the balance of the tax owed). Disregarding any interest element, her combined failure-to-file and failure-to-pay penalties are:

    a. $660.

    b. $600.

    c. $400.

    d. $440.

    e. None of the above.

267. Sara filed an extension on April 15. On June 1, she filed her tax return and owed $400 on a tax liability of $4,100. Which one of the following will apply? (CFP® Certification Examination, released 11/94)

    a. Failure to file on a timely basis.

    b. Failure to pay the total amount due.

    c. No penalty because of prepayment of over 90% of liability.

    d. Penalty on $400.

    e. Penalty and interest on $400.

268. A client currently is being audited by the IRS, and the agent has proposed a tax deficiency with which the client does not agree. The client has asked a CFP® certificant to research the issue. Which of the following sources is considered to be the most authoritative and, accordingly, would have the highest precedential value in defending the CFP certificant's position to the IRS? (CFP® Certification Examination, released 8/2004)

    a. Revenue ruling.

    b. Revenue procedure.

    c. Private letter ruling.

    d. Treasury regulations.

INCOME TAX PLANNING

Solutions

Income Tax Planning

ANSWER SUMMARY

1. d	27. a	53. a	79. c	105. e	131. a	157. d	183. d	209. b	235. d	261. d
2. d	28. c	54. c	80. a	106. d	132. c	158. d	184. b	210. a	236. b	262. b
3. c	29. a	55. e	81. c	107. a	133. e	159. b	185. a	211. a	237. a	263. c
4. b	30. d	56. b	82. a	108. c	134. a	160. a	186. c	212. c	238. a	264. c
5. a	31. e	57. d	83. a	109. c	135. d	161. b	187. c	213. b	239. e	265. c
6. c	32. a	58. a	84. c	110. b	136. c	162. a	188. b	214. a	240. e	266. b
7. b	33. a	59. e	85. b	111. b	137. e	163. d	189. b	215. c	241. b	267. e
8. b	34. c	60. c	86. a	112. d	138. c	164. d	190. a	216. c	242. e	268. d
9. b	35. c	61. d	87. b	113. d	139. c	165. d	191. d	217. d	243. e	
10. c	36. d	62. c	88. d	114. a	140. b	166. a	192. a	218. c	244. d	
11. a	37. d	63. d	89. b	115. b	141. b	167. b	193. b	219. e	245. b	
12. b	38. b	64. b	90. c	116. b	142. c	168. d	194. d	220. a	246. d	
13. c	39. d	65. d	91. b	117. d	143. c	169. c	195. a	221. a	247. c	
14. c	40. d	66. c	92. d	118. b	144. b	170. d	196. b	222. d	248. c	
15. b	41. a	67. e	93. c	119. a	145. b	171. c	197. c	223. d	249. e	
16. a	42. a	68. e	94. b	120. b	146. b	172. a	198. d	224. a	250. c	
17. d	43. d	69. c	95. d	121. a	147. d	173. d	199. d	225. b	251. c	
18. d	44. b	70. d	96. c	122. a	148. c	174. c	200. a	226. b	252. c	
19. b	45. a	71. c	97. c	123. b	149. c	175. d	201. b	227. d	253. b	
20. c	46. a	72. d	98. b	124. c	150. d	176. b	202. c	228. d	254. d	
21. b	47. a	73. e	99. a	125. a	151. b	177. b	203. b	229. c	255. c	
22. d	48. a	74. b	100. a	126. c	152. a	178. d	204. b	230. e	256. d	
23. a	49. d	75. c	101. a	127. a	153. a	179. c	205. c	231. d	257. c	
24. b	50. b	76. c	102. c	128. b	154. a	180. d	206. c	232. d	258. a	
25. d	51. c	77. b	103. d	129. b	155. a	181. c	207. a	233. d	259. a	
26. c	52. d	78. c	104. c	130. b	156. d	182. c	208. b	234. b	260. e	

TAX LAW – LEGISLATIVE, ADMINISTRATIVE AND JUDICIAL

Court System

1. d

Appeals from the U.S. District Court go to the taxpayer's home circuit of the U.S. Court of Appeals.

Court System

2. d

Small Case Division of the U.S. Tax Court. In the Small Case Division, the amount in controversy is limited to $50,000, and the proceedings are informal. Proceedings may be quicker and less expensive in the Small Case Division.

Appeals

3. c

Statement 2 is incorrect because the Tax Court is a judge trial (there is no jury). Statement 4 is incorrect because neither side may appeal a decision in the Small Cases Division of the Tax Court. The IRS makes letter rulings available for publication through private vendors.

Tax Authority

4. b

Options (a), (c), and (d) are issuances of the IRS that are lower authorities than decisions of the Tax Court.

Taxable Entities

5. a

Partnerships are not subject to federal income tax. C corporations, individuals, and trusts are all taxed at the entity level. S corporations are a flow-through entity, but certain transactions are taxed at the entity level.

GROSS INCOME – INCLUSIONS

Gross Income

6. c

Mary must report adjusted gross income of $67,500. Gross Income = $70,500 ($1,000 dividends + $12,000 lottery prize + $50,000 salary + $7,500 alimony received). $70,500 gross income – $3,000 capital loss = $67,500. The gift and child support payments are excluded from gross income. The capital loss deduction is limited to $3,000.

Taxable Income

7. b

$1,600 earned income + $1,350 interest income = $2,950 – $1,900 (the standard deduction is limited to earned income + $300). Therefore, taxable income is $1,050.

Because Ken is claimed as a dependent by his parents, he is not entitled to a personal exemption on his own return and his standard deduction is reduced. The standard deduction is limited to the greater of 1) $850, or 2) earned income plus $300 (limited to the regular standard deduction). Since his earned income is $1,600, he will receive a standard deduction of $1,900 ($1,600 + $300).

Taxable Income

8. b

The interest income on the savings account and the earned income from the part-time job will be included in her gross income. The interest income earned on the municipal bond is tax exempt and, therefore, excluded from her gross income. Her gross income is equal to $2,950 ($1,700 + $1,250).

The Social Security benefits will not be included in her gross income because her Modified AGI is not large enough. Modified AGI is calculated by adding tax-exempt interest income to AGI.

Constructive Receipt

9. b

$450. A taxpayer is not permitted to defer income for services in the current year by refusing to accept payment. The doctrine of constructive receipt does not reach income that the taxpayer is not yet entitled to receive by contract. Michele does not have to claim the audit fee because the contract calls for payment in 2007.

Tax Benefit Rule

10. c

The amount received by Steve, even though in dispute, is included in his 2006 gross income because he has received the $2,000. Steve will deduct $100 in 2007 to adjust his income for the settlement.

Change in Accounting Method

11. a

Pete will be required to increase his taxable income (positive adjustment) by $50,000 in the current tax year. Since Pete was on the cash method of accounting in prior years, the $50,000 of accounts receivable was never included in his taxable income (no cash was received). Therefore, when switching to the accrual method of accounting, Pete will be required to make a positive adjustment to his taxable income.

Accounting Method

12. b

Option (b) is correct because a C corporation with gross receipts over $5 million cannot use the cash method of accounting.

A qualified personal service corporation can use the cash method of accounting if services are provided in the fields of actuarial science, accounting, law, engineering, health, consulting, architecture or the performing arts.

Option (c) is incorrect because a sole proprietor can use the cash method of accounting.

Option (d) is incorrect because partnerships with gross receipts that do not exceed $5 million can use the cash method of accounting.

Accounting Method

13. c

Option (c) is correct because the accrual method must be used when gross receipts exceed $5 million.

Accounting Method – Long-Term Contracts

14. c

The completed contract may only be used in two situations:

1. Home construction contracts, or

2. Contracts that will be completed within two years (if the contractor has average annual gross receipts of less than $10 million).

Option (c) is correct because the contract is a home construction contract. Therefore, the completed contract method can be used.

Option (a) is incorrect. Even though the contract will be completed within two years, the contractor's average gross receipts are more than $10 million. Therefore, the percentage-of-completion method must be used.

Option (b) is incorrect. The contract will not be completed within two years and is not a home construction contract. Therefore, the percentage-of-completion method must be used.

Option (d) is incorrect. The contract will not be completed within two years (and the contractor's gross receipts are more than $10 million) and is not a home construction contract. Therefore, the percentage-of-completion method must be used.

Accounting Method

15. b

$19,000. An accrual-basis taxpayer may not defer advance payments for services if any of the services will be performed after the tax year following the year of receipt of the advance payment. Therefore, the $19,000 from the two-year contracts must be included in 2006 gross income since part of that income will be unearned at the end of 2007.

Community Property

16. a

Since Ron and Marge are divorced, they must each file a separate return. Marge will report her own salary on her separate income tax return. Community property is considered owned 50% by Ron and 50% by Marge. Since they are now divorced, Marge will report 50% of the income from the community property on her separate return.

Taxation of Annuities

17. d

If Vicki lives longer than her actuarial life expectancy, the subsequent annuity payments received will be fully taxable as ordinary income.

(a) Is incorrect. A portion of each payment will be taxable as ordinary income. and a portion will be treated as a tax-free return of capital. (b) Is in incorrect. If Vicki dies during her actuarial life expectancy, the unrecovered basis in her annuity can be deducted as a miscellaneous itemized deduction (not subject to the 2% of AGI floor) on her final income tax return. (c) Is incorrect. If Vicki lives longer than her actual expectancy, the subsequent annuity payments received will be fully taxable as ordinary income. There is no need to amend prior tax returns.

Adjusted Gross Income

18. d

Kathy's adjusted gross income is:

W-2 Income	$80,000
Interest on State of Alabama bonds (tax-exempt)	–0–
Social Security benefits (85% × $6,000)	5,100
AGI	$85,100

Her Social Security benefits are 85% taxable because her modified AGI of $84,000 ($80,000 + 3,000 + 1,000) exceeds the limits for the year.

Taxation of Life Insurance

19. b

Ruby's final tax return should include only the interest portion of the $11,900 payment. The payment portion attributable to the face amount of the policy is not taxable.

Gross Income

20. c

Interest on Baldwin County school bonds is excluded because it is interest income from a municipal bond. Gross income is $700 ($400 + $100 + $200). If the taxpayer had taken the standard deduction last year, she would not have included the state tax refund since no benefit would have been received.

Taxation of Annuities

21. b

$24,000 ÷ 144,000 (120 months × $1,200/month) = 0.1666 or ⅙ exclusion ratio or fraction × $1,200 = $200 per month is excluded.

In 2006, June to December = 7 months × $200 (exclusion) = $1,400.

Option (b) is only possible correct answer for 2006.

2007 (12 months × $1,200) × ⅙ = $2,400.

2008 (12 months × $1,200) × ⅙ = $2,400.

Taxation of Life Insurance

22. d

Expected proceeds over life = $15,000 × 20 years = $300,000.

Inclusion ratio = (Proceeds – Basis) ÷ Expected: ($300,000 – 120,000) ÷ $300,000 = 60%.

Annual payment of $15,000 × 60% for inclusion = $9,000.

Viatical Settlements

23. a

A is correct because if an individual is terminally ill (expected to die within 24 months), proceeds received from a viatical settlement are not taxable.

Viatical Settlements

24. b

If an individual is terminally ill (expected to die within 24 months), proceeds received from a viatical settlement are not taxable. Scott's actual date of death is irrelevant.

Death Benefits

25. d

(1) Is correct. Death benefits received by the surviving spouse from a decedent's employer are fully taxable to the surviving spouse. This is a Death Benefit Only (DBO) plan. (2) Is incorrect. Life insurance proceeds received because of the death of the insured are typically income tax free to the recipient. (3) Is correct. The bonus received by the spouse would be would be taxable to the spouse as income in respect of a decedent (IRD). (4) Is correct. A distribution from a qualified plan would be taxable to the recipient, even if received after the participant's death. This is also income in respect of a decedent (IRD). However, the distribution will not be subject to an early withdrawal penalty, because the participant's death will exempt the distribution from the penalty.

Group Term Life Insurance

26. c

The cost of up to $50,000 of coverage is nontaxable.

$180,000 − 50,000 = $130,000 × $8/thousand = $1,040 taxable.

Alimony

27. a

To qualify as a alimony for Federal income tax purposes, the following requirements must be met:

- The payment must be made in cash (not property).
- The ex-spouses cannot live together.
- Payments must be made pursuant to a written divorce agreement.
- The agreement cannot specify that the payments are not alimony for federal income tax purposes.
- The payments must cease upon the death of the recipient.

Since the mortgage payments do not cease at Carol's (the recipient's) death, the payments do not constitute alimony. Therefore, Jack will not receive an income tax deduction, and Carol will not be taxed on the payments received.

Alimony

28. c

For Post-1984 divorce agreements and decrees, payments to former spouses are alimony only if:

- The payments are in cash;
- The agreement or decree does not specify that the payments are not alimony for federal income tax purposes;
- The payee and payor are not members of the same household at the time the payments are made; and
- There is no liability to make the payments for any period after the death of the payee.

Alimony

29. a

To qualify as alimony for Federal income tax purposes, the following requirements must be met:

- The payments must be made in cash (not property).
- The ex-spouses cannot live together.
- Payments must be made pursuant to a written divorce agreement.
- The agreement cannot specify that the payments are not alimony for federal income tax purposes.
- The payments must cease upon the death of the recipient.

The residence transferred to Bonnie is not considered alimony, because property transfers are not considered alimony.

Since the cash payments do not cease at Jon's (the recipient's) death, the payments do not constitute alimony. Therefore, Bonnie will not receive an income tax deduction, and Jon will not be taxed on the payments received.

Alimony

30. d

It is not necessary to specify that payments are alimony. However, the agreement cannot specify that the payments are <u>not</u> alimony. All other statements are true.

Alimony Recapture

31. e

Alimony recapture will occur if there is a more-than-$15,000 decrease in alimony payments between the first and second year, or second and third year. Option (e) is correct because there is a drop of $20,000 from Year 2 to Year 3.

Unemployment Compensation

32. a

Unemployment is fully includible in gross income.

Series EE Bonds

33. a

In addition to Option (a), the other conditions are:

- The savings bonds are issued after December 31, 1989;
- The savings bonds are issued to an individual who is at least 24 years old at the time of issuance;
- The exclusion is limited by a MAGI threshold;
- The exclusion is not available to married couples filing separate returns.

Adjusted Gross Income

34. c

$12,000 gift	Excluded from gross income
$1,200 dividend	Includible in AGI
$1,000 won as prize	Includible in AGI
$35,000 salary	Includible in AGI
$6,000 support	Excluded from gross income
$12,000 alimony	Includible in AGI
$5,000 LTCL	Limited to $3,000 per year

$1,200	Dividend
1,000	Prize
35,000	Salary
12,000	Alimony
(3,000)	Long-term capital loss (carryover $2,000)
$46,200	Adjusted Gross Income (AGI)

Adjusted Gross Income

35. c

$60,000 salary – $3,000 short-term capital loss – $4,000 qualified moving expenses = $53,000.

The $1,500 balance of short-term capital loss is carried over.

The $500 balance of long-term capital loss is carried over.

When a taxpayer has both short-term capital loss and a long-term capital loss, the short-term capital loss is offset against ordinary income first, regardless of when the transaction occurred during the year.

Taxable Income

36. d

$3,500	Interest on bank account
2,300	Salary from part-time job (earned income)
$5,800	Taxable income before standard deduction
(2,600)	Standard deduction (earned income of $2,300 + $300)
$3,200	Taxable income

* Social Security benefits are not taxable at his income (modified AGI) level.

* No personal exemptions can be claimed since he is classified as a dependent on another's return.

* Since he is claimed as a dependent on another's return, his standard deduction is limited to the greater of: 1) $850, or 2) earned income plus $300.

Alimony Recapture Front Loading

37. d

Calculation of Recapture:

$$R_3 = R_2 + R_1$$

$$R_2 = P_2 - (P_3 + \$15,000)$$

$$R_1 = P_1 - \left[\frac{(P_2 - R_2 + P_3)}{2} + \$15,000\right]$$

R_3 = amount recaptured in Year 3

R_2 = amount recaptured in Year 2

R_1 = amount recaptured in Year 1

P_1, P_2, P_3 = payments 1, 2, and 3, respectively

Solve R_2 first:

$$R_2 = \$60,000 - (\$0 + 15,000) = \$45,000$$

$$R_1 = \$100,000 - \left[\frac{(\$60,000 - 45,000 + 0)}{2} + \$15,000\right] = \$77,500$$

$$R_3 = \$45,000 + \$77,500 = \$122,500$$

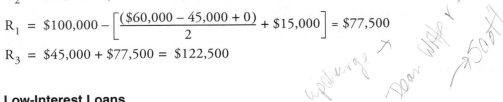

Low-Interest Loans

38. b

Since the loan is not more than $100,000, the imputed interest will be computed using the applicable federal rate less the actual rate, limited to Betty's net investment income. The federal rate would be $8,100 (9% × $90,000). Dennis would impute the lesser of the federal rate or Betty's net investment income. Since Betty's net investment income is $4,000, the imputed interest income to Dennis is $4,000, and the imputed interest expense to Betty is $4,000.

Low-Interest Loans

39. d

If the loan is classified as an employer-employee loan, the corporation will accrue interest income and additional compensation expense. Thus, the corporation's taxable income will not be affected. It follows that Option (a) is correct. Option (b) is also correct because in such a circumstance the corporation will have interest income, and the offsetting adjustment is a dividend paid, which is not deductible by the corporation. If John uses the funds for a vacation, he must recognize either dividend income or compensation income. He will not have an offsetting deduction for the interest on funds used for personal expenditures. Therefore, Option (c) is also correct.

Fringe Benefits

40. d

Personal use of a company car is a taxable fringe benefit. All other fringe benefits listed are excluded from the employee's gross income.

Mutual Funds (CFP® Certification Examination, released 11/94)

41. a

When shares of a mutual fund are sold, the taxpayer can choose from the following methods to calculate basis in the shares sold:

- Specific identification (available for mutual funds and stocks)

- First-in, First-out (FIFO; available for mutual funds and stocks)

- Average cost per share (not available for stocks)

(1) Is correct. The gain can be based on average cost per share, which is an allowed method of basis calculations for mutual fund.

(2) Is correct. The gain can be based on specific identification of shares sold, which would allow the taxpayer to choose the shares sold, thus having some control over the taxable gain.

(3) Is correct. By selling the shares with the highest cost basis (assuming specific identification of shares is used), the client can minimize his or her capital gain.

(4) Is incorrect. Basis must be assigned to the shares sold. Since the fund has appreciated in value, the client will have a gain, even if only some of the shares are sold.

GROSS INCOME – EXCLUSIONS

Inclusion – Exclusion

42. a

$500 dividends. Scholarships for tuition, books, and fees (not room and board) are excluded from adjusted gross income. Loans are not income. The cash support from Scott's parents is a support payment and not includible in gross income.

Inclusion – Exclusion

43. d

Compensatory damages received for physical injury or sickness (medical bill, etc.) are excluded from gross income. Punitive damages are included in gross income.

(a) is incorrect. Compensatory damages received because of personal injury (slander, libel, sexual harassment, etc.) are included in gross income. (b) is incorrect. Unemployment benefits received are included in gross income. (c) is incorrect. Income received from a hobby is included in gross income. Expenses incurred with respect to the hobby are deductible, to the extent of hobby income. (d) is correct. Worker's compensation benefits received are excluded from gross income. (e) is incorrect. Compensatory damages received because of personal injury (slander, libel, sexual harassment, etc.) are included in gross income.

Gross Income Inclusion

44. b

$20,000 salary + $1,000 reward. The hospitalization insurance premiums and lodging are nontaxable fringe benefits (because the lodging is on the employer's premises, and it is a condition of his employment).

Gross Income Inclusion

45. a

None are includible. All payments are to make him whole.

Lodging

46. a

The room is furnished for the convenience of the employer and is required by the employer, so it is not included in gross income.

Employee Benefits

47. a

The value of a health facility or gymnasium provided by the employer, on the employer's premises solely for the use of employees is excluded from gross income by the employee.

Employee Benefits

48. a

The value of the whole life insurance must be included because it is a taxable benefit. (Group term life insurance with face value ≤$50,000 is not taxable.) Health insurance for employees and employees' dependents is a nontaxable benefit. Child-care expense reimbursement is nontaxable. Any cash received is taxable.

Employee Benefits

49. d

Season tickets are includible in the gross income of the employee receiving the tickets. All of the other fringe benefits are excludible. Note: Occasional tickets to sporting events would be excludible.

Employee Benefits

50. b

Statement 1 would be excluded as a qualified transportation fringe benefit.

Statement 2 would be included because club dues paid by the employer must be included in the employee's gross income. The athletic facility must be on a premises owned or leased by the employer to be excluded from the employee's gross income.

Statement 3 is excluded from gross income because occasional tickets to a sporting event would not be included in gross income. However, season tickets would be included in the employee's gross income.

Statement 4 would be included in gross income because it is a personal expense paid for by the employer.

Employee Benefits

51. c

The plan is discriminatory to nonhighly compensated employees; therefore, all discounts actually taken by officers are includible in income, not just the excess of what is available to the nonofficers.

Discharge of Indebtedness

52. d

The $40,000 reduction by the People's Bank is includible in gross income (income from discharge of indebtedness). The $30,000 reduction by Shelby (seller and mortgage holder) is an exception to the general rule, and a $30,000 reduction in basis, in lieu of inclusion in income is taken.

Employee Health Benefits

53. a

The entire payment from a DBO plan is included in the gross income of the recipient.

Gross Income Inclusion

54. c

The question relates to inclusion in gross income. Workers compensation is to make a person whole and is excludable. Compensatory damages for physical injuries are excludable. All punitive damages are includable in income. Reimbursements from an employer medical plan are not includable.

Scholarships

55. e

David is not a candidate for a degree and, therefore, must include all of the grant received. The issue of proration between years is not relevant in this case.

Modified Endowment Contracts

56. b

Ordinarily, withdrawals from an insurance policy receive FIFO tax treatment (basis first). However, withdrawals from a modified endowment contract receive LIFO tax treatment (basis last). Therefore, b is the correct answer, because modified endowment earnings would be drawn out first, even for a loan.

Insurance

57. d

(d) is an incorrect statement. If an employee pays for disability income insurance premiums, the premiums are not deductible by the employee. Note: employer-paid premiums for disability insurance are deductible to the employer. (a) is true. If the employer provides more than $50,000 of group term life insurance protection to an employee, the employee will be taxed on the cost of the excess coverage. (b) is true. If a medical reimbursement exceeds the employee's actual medical expenses, the excess reimbursement will be taxable to the employee. (c) is true. If the employer pays the premium, the employer will receive an income tax deduction. The premiums will not be taxed to the employee. Note: any disability benefit received by the employee will be taxed to the employee, if the employer paid the premiums.

Flexible Spending vs. Child Care Credit

58. a

If Julie is in the 35% bracket because of her husband, paying the expenses out of the flexible spending account will provide a benefit of 35% + 7.65% (FICA) or 42.65% × $5,000 = $2,132.50. If Julie took the child-care credit instead, her tax benefit is 20% × $5,000 or $1,000.

Coverdell Education Savings Accounts

59. e

Statement 1 is correct. The contribution limit is $2,000.

Statement 2 is incorrect because the beneficiary must be under 18.

Statement 3 is incorrect since the contribution is nondeductible (but the earnings are tax free if the distribution is used for qualified education expenses).

Statement 4 is incorrect. A student must be enrolled at least half-time in order for room and board to qualify.

Tax Efficient Investing

60. c

All interest income on the CD would be taxable in the year earned. All of the other choices will result in potential tax-deferred growth/appreciation.

DEDUCTIONS FOR ADJUSTED GROSS INCOME

Adjusted Gross Income

61. d

Child support payments are excluded from income for the parent receiving the support, and the parent paying the support does not get a deduction. Contributions to Roth IRAs are not deductible for adjusted gross income.

Adjusted Gross Income

62. c

Unreimbursed employee business expenses are not deducted in arriving at AGI. These expenses are miscellaneous itemized deductions (subject to the 2% of AGI floor).

Deductions for AGI

63. d

Alimony payments are deductible by the payor for AGI. The other items are itemized deductions (from AGI).

Moving Expense

64. b

($1,600 + $300 + $250) = $2,150. Meals while moving are not deductible. To deduct moving expenses, the new job must be at least 50 miles further from the taxpayer's old residence than the old residence was from the former place of employment. There are additional time requirements about length of employment on the new job.

AGI Calculation

66. d

AGI is calculated by taking the net profit from the business of $20,000 ($50,000 – $30,000) less deductions for AGI of ½ of self-employment tax paid and the medical insurance premiums.

Description	Amount
Gross receipts	$50,000
Operating expenses	(30,000)
Profit from business	$20,000
½ of self-employment tax	(1,530)
Net amount	$18,470
Health insurance premiums	(1,200)
AGI	$17,270

Mortgage interest is an itemized deduction.

IRAs

66. c

Jimmy's IRA is not deductible (phaseout of deductibility of taxpayer that is an active participant). Married filing joint phaseout begins at $75,000 and ends at $85,000 for 2006. Dee Dee's IRA is fully deductible. Active participation in an employer's pension plan by one spouse (Jimmy) does not effect the full deductibility of the other spouse's (Dee Dee) IRA as long as:

- The other spouse (Dee Dee) is not an active participant in an employer-sponsored pension plan, and
- The couple's joint adjusted gross income does not exceed $150,000. Phaseout of deductibility (for the spouse that is not an active participant) is between $150,000 – $160,000.

Therefore, the correct answer is $4,000 (Dee Dee's contribution).

IRAs

67. e

Since the Claibornes are not covered by a pension plan, they are allowed a deductible $4,000 IRA contribution for Thad plus a $4,000 deductible contribution to a spousal IRA. Total deductible IRA contribution of $8,000 is allowed.

IRAs

68. e

Alimony counts as earned income for IRA purposes. Since Judy is not covered by a pension plan and has earned income over $4,000, her maximum deductible IRA contribution is $4,000.

IRAs

69. c

Since both spouses have earned income in excess of $4,000, each can make the maximum contribution to his or her IRA. Bob is covered by a qualified retirement plan, and therefore, his $4,000 deduction is phased out. Married filing joint adjusted gross income phaseout for participants of qualified plans, who want to make contributions to an IRA, begins at $75,000 and ends at $85,000 for 2006. Mary Sue is not covered by a qualified plan, so she can deduct her $4,000 contribution (since the couple's AGI is less than $150,000 for IRA contribution purposes).

IRAs

70. d

She is not currently covered by a qualified pension plan and, therefore, can contribute her earned income up to $5,000 (for 2006) to a deductible IRA.

Note: Since she is age 54, she is eligible for an additional catch-up contribution of $1,000 to her IRA. Therefore, she can contribute up to $5,000 ($4,000 contribution limit for 2006 plus $1,000 catch-up contribution).

HSAs

71. c

Individuals age 55 and older who are covered by a high-deductible health plan can make additional catch-up contributions to the health savings account.

A is incorrect. Amounts not used from the account each year stay in the account and continue to grow on a tax-favored basis.

B is incorrect. Dental expenses (other than cosmetic expenses) are qualified expenses for a health savings account.

D is incorrect. An employer can establish a health savings account for employees.

HSAs

72. d

1 is correct. A health savings account is not subject to COBRA continuation coverage.

2 is correct. Distributions from a health savings account used for qualifying medical expenses will be both income tax-free and penalty-free.

3 is incorrect. The deduction is an above-the-line (for AGI) deduction.

4 is incorrect. Individuals age 55 and older (not 50) who are covered by a high-deductible health plan can make additional catch-up contributions to the health savings account.

IRAs

73. e

Jane can make a contribution to a deductible IRA since she is below the 2006 phaseout range of $50,000-$60,000 for single persons. Joe is not covered by a plan (nor is his spouse) so there is no income limit. Barbie is not covered but her spouse is. Since their income is less than the phaseout of $150,000-$160,000, she can take a deduction. Maggie's income is less than the $75,000-$85,000 phaseout for married filing jointly.

Deductions for AGI

74. b

Only the student loan interest is a deduction for AGI. All of the other deductions are itemized deductions.

PERSONAL AND DEPENDENCY EXEMPTIONS

Exemptions

75. c

Three exemptions are allowed: one each for Angie, Buddy, and their son. No exemption is allowed for their daughter. They did not meet the support test for her.

Exemptions

76. c

The couple is entitled to exemptions for John, Joan, their son, Chip, and John's mother. An exemption is allowed for a dependent who was alive during any part of the taxable year. John's mother's Social Security income is at a level such that it is not included in gross income, thus, it is not considered in applying the gross income test.

Dependents

77. b

Of the potential dependents listed, only the nephew is a qualifying relative. A cousin is not a qualifying person, nor is a foster parent. A foster child can be a dependent if the taxpayer's household is the principal place of residence.

Dependents

78. c

Vicki's Social Security benefits are not included in gross income. Therefore, she does not fail the gross income test and can be claimed by Mary Sue and Bob as a dependent. Statement 1 is correct because Becky is a student and under age 24. Statement 2 is correct because the dependent can file a joint return and qualify as long as neither Rachel nor her husband had to file a return.

Exemptions

79. c

Exemptions are allowed for Mike, Pam, their son, and their daughter. They are not entitled to an exemption for Pam's father, because he was not a citizen or resident of the U.S. or other qualifying country. Their son qualifies as a dependent, because he is under the age of 19.

Exemptions

80. a

A person who may be claimed by another as a dependent cannot claim a personal exemption.

TAX DETERMINATION

Taxable Income

81. c

($30,000 − $6,000 itemized deductions − $3,300 personal exemption) = $20,700. All Roth IRA contributions are nondeductible. William should itemize because it will result in a higher deduction than the standard deduction.

Taxable Income

82. a

Gross income	$46,000
Capital loss	(3,000)
	$43,000
Standard deduction	(5,150)
	$37,850
Additional standard deduction	(1,250)
	$36,600
Personal exemption	(3,300)
	$33,300

Note: $5,150 standard deduction + $1,250 additional standard deduction exceed the itemized deduction of $4,950.

Adjusted Gross Income

83. a

Adjusted Gross Income	$42,000
Less: Standard deduction (head of household)	(7,550)
Less: Exemptions (self, mother) $3,300 × 2	(6,600)
Taxable income	$27,850

Peter's standard deduction is higher than his itemized deductions since he can file as head of household.

Kiddie Tax

84. c

This question is related to the Kiddie tax, which applies to unearned income in excess of $1,700 (for 2006), by a child under the age of 14. Brittany, while under the age of 14, has only earned income. Amanda, age 14, is not subject to kiddie tax because of her age. Tony, age 3, had unearned income less than $1,700. Therefore, the correct answer is C. Kate, age 7, had unearned income of $1,800.

Kiddie Tax

85. b

$3,000 Unearned income

(1,700) Unearned income taxed at child's rate

$1,300 Taxed at parent's rate

Kiddie Tax

86. a

Statement 1 is incorrect; it applies to all unearned income of children under 14.

Statement 2 is incorrect; it should be under the age of 14.

Statement 3 is incorrect; it should be only unearned income.

Kiddie Tax

87. b

Unearned income	$1,800
Kiddie Tax Exclusion	(1,700)
Net unearned income taxed at parent's highest marginal rate	$100

Personal Service Corporations

88. d

Statement 1 is incorrect; personal service corporations, like other corporations, can have employee fringe benefits.

Statement 2 is correct.

Statement 3 is incorrect; personal service corporations, like other corporations, can take a dividend received deduction.

Statement 4 is correct.

STATUS FILING/FILING LEVELS

Filing Status

89. b

George correctly filed a joint return in the year of his wife's death. He will file as a qualifying widower (also known as "surviving spouse") for the two years following his wife's death if he continues to maintain a home for his dependent children.

Filing Status

90. c

Beth's 2009 filing status is Head of Household. Surviving Spouse filing status is available for only two years following death of spouse (2007 and 2008).

Filing Status

91. b

Married Filing Joint is allowed for a surviving spouse in the year of death. The "Married Filing Joint" filing status has the most favorable tax brackets and has the largest standard deduction.

DEDUCTIONS AND LOSSES

Unreasonable Compensation

92. d

The $60,000 of salary is reclassified as a dividend. Thus, River's taxable income increases by $60,000 because dividends are not deductible. John's gross income remains the same. His salary income decreases by $60,000, but his dividend income increases by $60,000.

Proprietor's Income

93. c

The illegal commissions and parking tickets are not deductible.

Income		$120,000
Expenses:		
Commissions to other brokers	$15,000	
Travel and transportation	16,000	
Supplies	4,200	
Office, phone and fax	3,500	(38,700)
Net Income		$81,300

Investigation of Business

94. b

If a taxpayer investigates a business that is <u>similar to the one he or she is already in</u>, the expenses are deductible whether or not he acquires the business.

If a taxpayer investigates a business that is a <u>new line of business</u> and acquires the business, the expenses should be capitalized and amortized. If he or she does not acquire the business, the expenses are non-deductible.

Since Randy is already in the business, he can fully deduct the expenses incurred in Florida and Alabama.

Commuting Expenses

95. d

Commuting expenses are personal, not business expenses, so Bill cannot deduct his commuting expenses.

Hobby Losses

96. c

Sara must include the $3,000 in income and deduct nothing. Hobby expenses can only be deducted if she itemizes. If she was able to itemize, her deduction would be limited to the income from the hobby and would be included as a miscellaneous itemized deduction subject to the 2% of AGI floor.

Vacation Home

97. c

A vacation home can be classified as a personal residence, a rental property, or a mixed-use property. A personal residence is a property that is rented out for less than 15 days per year.

Since the beach house was rented for eight weeks, it will be classified as either a rental property or a mixed-use property. The determination is based upon the number of days the taxpayer used the residence for personal use.

To qualify as rental property, the personal use cannot exceed the greater of 14 days per year or 10% of rental days. Since the property was used for personal use for 16 days, the beach house will be considered a mixed-use property.

Expenses incurred on a mixed-use property must be allocated between rental use and personal use. The rental expenses on a mixed-use property are only deductible to the extent of rental income received (the taxpayer cannot claim a loss).

Vacation Home

98. b

Since he will rent the home for 190 days, he can use the home as a personal residence for up to 19 days (the greater of 14 days or 10% of rental use) without jeopardizing the property status as a rental property.

Payment of Other's Obligations

99. a

Medical expenses for spouse and dependents are deductible. The other items are not incurred for the taxpayer's benefit or as a result of the taxpayer's obligation and are nondeductible. Property taxes are only deductible by the person who owns the property.

Related Party Transactions

100. a

Todd's sale to Trey, his son, is a related-party transaction, and therefore, Todd will not recognize a loss ($4,000 (FMV) − $6,000 (basis)). Trey's basis in the stock is $4,000. When he sells it for $5,000, he has a realized gain of $1,000. However, Trey will not recognize this gain since he can utilize $1,000 of his father's unrecognized loss. The remaining $1,000 of Todd's loss is gone forever.

Bad Debt Expense

101. a

Only the specific charge-off method can be used. Allowances for estimated expenses are not allowed for tax purposes.

Personal Bad Debt

102. c

No deduction is allowed for partial worthlessness in the year of bankruptcy for a personal bad debt. Personal bad debts are always classified as short-term capital losses. The $4,700 short-term capital loss may be used to the extent of gains or to a limit of $3,000 short-term capital loss against ordinary income with a carryover of $1,700 short-term capital loss to the future.

Personal Bad Debt

103. d

Non-business bad debts are deductible as short-term capital losses when the debt becomes worthless. The short-term capital loss of $3,500 is used entirely against $5,000 capital gains. Kevin would have a net $1,500 capital gain for the year.

Worthless Securities

104. c

Worthless securities are treated as becoming worthless at year-end. Therefore, the loss is a long-term capital loss even though the stock became worthless after 8 months.

Capital Assets Gains & Losses

105. e

The gain of $60,000 is classified as a short-term capital gain. Section 1244 small business stock rules apply only to losses. Since Pat held the stock for less than five years, he would not qualify for the favorable tax treatment provided under Section 1202 for gains on small business stock.

Worthless Securities

106. d

If a security becomes worthless during the tax year, the loss shall be treated as if it occurred on the last day of the tax year. The holding period will be long term.

Bad Debt Losses

107. a

No loss is allowed because the charge for services was never included in income since the taxpayer was a cash-basis taxpayer.

Personal Bad Debts

108. c

This is a nonbusiness bad debt (personal bad debt). Regardless of the holding period, it is treated as a short-term capital loss and the $3,000 limit applies. Kurt has a carryover short-term capital loss of $4,000 − $3,000 = $1,000.

If the loan had been a condition of Kurt's employment, it would have been classified as a business bad debt and would have been an ordinary loss in the year the debt went bad.

DEPRECIATION, COST RECOVERY, AMORTIZATION, AND DEPLETION

Election to Expense
109. c

His Section 179 deduction is limited to $15,000 (due to net income limitation). A Section 179 deduction cannot create a loss. He would still have $3,000 Section 179 carryover from the previous year.

Depreciation Convention
110. b

For personal property, the mid-quarter convention must be used if more than 40% of the property was placed in service during the last quarter of the year. SAW Furniture placed in service 67% ($100,000 ÷ $150,000) of the property in the last quarter. Therefore, the mid-quarter convention must be used for all personal property placed in service during the year.

The mid-month convention only applies to real property. The mid-week convention does not exist.

Depreciation/Amortization
111. b

A copyright is an intangible asset, and is eligible for an amortization deduction.

A is incorrect. Land is never eligible for a depreciation deduction.

C is incorrect. A personal residence is not allowed a depreciation deduction, because only property used in a trade or business or for the production of income is allowed a depreciation deduction.

D is incorrect. Inventory is not depreciable.

Depreciation/Amortization
112. d

Land can never be depreciated for income tax purposes.

A computer used in a business is eligible for a depreciation deduction.

Rental real estate is used for the production of income, and is therefore eligible for a depreciation deduction.

A sports utility vehicle, used in a trade or business, is eligible for a depreciation deduction.

PASSIVE ACTIVITY LOSSES

At Risk/Passive Losses

113. d

Options (a), (b), and (c) are all true. The correct analysis of the tax treatment of Bob's income is that he is limited to a $50,000 deduction against his other income since that is his at-risk amount. The remaining $25,000 would be a loss carryforward. Bob's at-risk investment would now be zero. He will have to increase his at-risk investment to use the $25,000 loss carryforward. Partnership income in the following year could increase his at-risk amount enough to utilize the loss carryforward. Since he is a material participant, the passive activity loss rules do not come into play.

At Risk/Passive Losses

114. a

The at-risk rules must be applied before the passive loss rules. Under the at-risk rules, a taxpayer can only deduct losses to the extent of his or her amount at risk. Passive losses can only be deducted against passive income.

Joseph invested $30,000 in the passive activity. Therefore, his at-risk amount is $30,000. Since his share of the loss from the activity is $45,000, he will only be allowed to deduct $30,000, his amount at-risk. $15,000 of the loss ($45,000 total less $30,000 deductible under the at-risk rules) has been suspended (disallowed) because of the at-risk rules and must be carried forward.

Even though Joseph has a $30,000 loss after applying the at-risk rules, he will not be allowed a deduction for the $30,000 loss, because he has no passive income. Therefore, $30,000 ($30,000 loss deductible under the at-risk rules less $0 loss deductible under the passive loss rules) of the loss has been suspended (disallowed) under the passive loss rules and must be carried forward.

At Risk/Passive Losses

115. b

George's losses are deductible in both years because he is a material participant in the activity. However, the at-risk rules limit his total losses to $100,000. He can carry the remaining $20,000 forward until he has increased his basis in the partnership.

At Risk/Passive Losses

116. b

The maximum deductible real estate loss is $25,000 per year. This maximum loss is phased out at AGI of $100,000 – 150,000. Since Fred's AGI was $125,000, the maximum loss he can deduct is $12,500, calculated as follows:

Reduction Amount = 125,000 – 100,000 = 25,000 × 0.5 = 12,500

Allowable Loss = 25,000 – 12,500 = 12,500

At Risk/Passive Losses

117. d

Philip's AGI, after considering the passive investment, is $175,000 ($140,000 active income + $35,000 portfolio income). He cannot offset the passive loss against active or portfolio income.

At Risk/Passive Losses

118. b

Option (a) is incorrect: Arthur would have to participate for more than 500 hours for Option (a) to be correct. Option (b) is correct: an individual who participates for more than 500 hours is a material participant regardless of how much others participate. Option (c) is incorrect: Arthur participates for more than 100 hours, and this is not more than the participation of any other individual. Option (d) is incorrect: Arthur's participation constitutes substantially all of the participation, even though Arthur's participation is less than 100 hours.

Passive Losses

119. a

An exception to passive loss limits regarding real estate allows individuals to deduct up to $25,000 of losses on real estate activities against active and portfolio income. The annual $25,000 deduction is reduced by 50% of the taxpayer's AGI in excess of $100,000. The deduction is entirely phased out at an AGI of $150,000.

Passive Activities

120. b

Only Statement 2 is treated as a rental activity according to IRS regulations. If a rental is 30 days or less <u>and</u> significant personal services are provided, the activity is a service rather than rental activity.

Passive Activities

121. a

The answer is zero. Losses from publicly traded partnerships cannot be offset against income from nonpublicly traded partnerships.

Passive Income

122. a

Rental income is passive; all of the others are portfolio income. Passive income is defined as income or loss from:

- Any trade, business, or income-producing activity in which the taxpayer does not materially participate, or;

- Any rental activity, whether the taxpayer materially participates or not.

Note: Remember there are exceptions to the rental activity classification.

EMPLOYEE EXPENSES

Employee Expense
123. b

The deduction is based on the distance between jobs. There is no deduction for commuting expenses (mileage) to or from a taxpayer's primary place of employment.

Travel
124. c

Less than 7 days of travel requires no allocation for foreign travel. Additional exceptions regarding allocation are:

1. If less than 25% of the time is used for personal purposes, or

2. If the taxpayer does not have substantial control over the trip arrangement.

Domestic travel transportation expense is either entirely deductible if predominantly business related, or not deductible at all.

Travel
125. a

[$1,200 + (8 × 150) + 1/2 (8 × 90)] = $2,760. Since Ashley used less than 25% of the time (10 days × 25% > 2 days) on personal business her airfare does not have to be allocated. Lodging and meals are allocated based on the number of business days on the trip.

Education Expense
126. c

[$2,000 + 0.5(1,000) + 700 + 200 + 700] = $4,100. Taxpayers may deduct expenses of additional education if additional education is required by the employer or imposed by law. The education cannot be for the purpose of meeting the minimum requirements for the job. Meals need to be reduced by 50%.

Employee Expenses
127. a

$25	Cover charge
$128	Dinner
$25	Tips
$178	Total
x 50%	
$89	
$30	Transportation
$119	

Transportation is not subject to a 50% reduction. The door cover charge, dinner, and tip are all considered part of the meal and are reduced by 50%.

Entertainment

128. b

50% [(15 × $25) + $455] = $415. The cost of the skybox is not deductible. The deduction is limited to the cost of the face value of nonluxury box seats, and all seats are counted, whether occupied or not. Meals (refreshments) and the seats are both subject to a 50% reduction.

Business Gifts

129. b

$29 (25 + 4) + 24 = $53. The cost of gift wrapping is allowed. No deduction is available for a gift to a superior. The limit on gifts is $25 per person.

Business Gifts

130. b

The limit is $25 per individual.

(3 × $12 = $36) + (12 × $25 = $300) = $336.

Employee Expenses

131. a

The listed deductions are all itemized deductions taken from AGI. If Foster takes the standard deduction, he will not be able to deduct any of the listed expenses.

ITEMIZED DEDUCTIONS

Itemized Deductions

132. c

Adjusted gross income is $55,000 ($60,000 − $5,000). Medical expenses must be reduced by 7.5% of AGI.

($60,000 − $5,000) × 0.075 = $4,125 is the floor for medical expenses.

$7,500 − $4,125 = $3,375 deduction.

Miscellaneous Itemized Deductions

133. e

Generally, full-time active duty military personnel cannot deduct the cost of uniforms (Option (a)). Job-hunting expenses for the first job (Option (b)) are not allowed, nor are job-hunting expenses allowed when the taxpayer is changing professions (Option (c)). The basic cost of one telephone in a home is not deductible, even if used for business (Option (d)).

Itemized Deductions

134. a

Gambling losses are miscellaneous itemized deductions that are not subject to 2% of AGI floor. All of the other miscellaneous itemized deductions listed are subject to the 2% of AGI floor.

Itemized Deductions

135. d

As a general rule, penalty taxes are nondeductible.

Itemized Deductions

136. c

Foreign taxes can be taken as either an itemized deduction or as a credit (foreign tax credit). Qualified moving expenses and health insurance premiums for self-employed individuals are both deductions for AGI. Professional dues for an employee are miscellaneous itemized deductions (subject to the 2% of AGI floor).

Medical Expenses

137. e

All are excluded. Deductible medical expenses are defined as expenses incurred for the diagnosis, cure, mitigation, treatment, or prevention of disease, or for the purpose of affecting any structure or function of the body. Nonprescription drugs (except insulin) and cosmetic surgery (except to correct congenital defect or defect due to disfiguring disease or accident) are not deductible.

Medical Expenses

138. c

The charge for tuition, room, and board to The Dalton School does not qualify, since the school does not provide qualified medical treatment.

Medical Expenses

139. c

Only $8,000 of the system qualifies since $2,000 of the $10,000 increased the value of Sidney's residence. The utilities also qualify – $1,000. Total = $9,000. The appraisal fee qualifies as an itemized deduction (subject to the 2% AGI floor) but not a medical expense.

Itemized Deductions – Taxes

140. b

Option (a) is incorrect because a state tax refund is not offset against the state income tax itemized deduction. Option (c) is incorrect since Donna claimed the standard deduction for the previous year, and she received no tax benefit from a state income tax deduction.

Itemized Deductions – Taxes

141. b

[(180 days ÷ 243 days × $2,000) + $120] = $1,601. Real estate taxes for the entire year are apportioned between the buyer and seller on the basis of the number of days the property was held by each during the real estate tax year. The day of the sale goes to the buyer. The correct answer can be selected using an estimate of 6 out of 8 months: 2,000 × 6/8 = 1,500 + 120 = $1,620.

Itemized Deductions – Taxes

142. c

($7,200 + 3,000) = $10,200. The interest on the deficiency is personal interest and is not deductible. The refund will be reported as income in the current year, if the payment was deducted in the prior year (tax benefit rule). It does not affect the deductible amount.

Interest

143. c

The interest on the loan to purchase household furniture is nondeductible personal interest. The interest on the loan to purchase Louisiana state bonds is not deductible because interest expense on debt used to purchase tax-exempt bonds is nondeductible (). The interest on the home mortgage is qualified residence interest and is deductible.

Home Mortgage

144. b

Home equity loans are limited to the lesser of:

1. The fair market value of the residence, reduced by acquisition indebtedness, or

2. $100,000.

Thus, $400,000 (fair market value) − $320,000 (first mortgage) provides a limit of $80,000. Interest on the remaining $50,000 of the loan will be treated under the consumer interest rules (i.e., not deductible).

Charitable Deductions

145. b

80% of a contribution which provides the right to purchase athletic tickets to a college or university is deductible. Therefore, $1,600 (80% × $2,000) is deductible. The $500 expenditure for the tickets cannot be claimed since it provided George with a benefit.

Charitable Contributions

146. b

If ordinary income property is donated to charity, the donor's charitable income tax deduction is the lesser of the adjusted tax basis or the fair market value of the property. Inventory is considered ordinary income property, and therefore Jeff's deduction is $6,000, the lesser of the adjusted tax basis or the fair market value.

If intangible property has been held for the long-term holding period (more than one year), the taxpayer can deduct the full fair market value of the property as a charitable income tax deduction. Stock is considered intangible property, and therefore Jeff's deduction is $40,000, the fair market value.

If tangible personal property is donated to charity, the donor's charitable income tax deduction is based upon whether the property is use-related (art donated to an art museum) or use-unrelated (art donated to boy scouts). If the property is use-related, the taxpayer can claim a deduction equal to the fair market value of the property. If the property is use-unrelated, the taxpayer can claim a deduction equal to the adjusted tax basis of the property. A coin collection is considered tangible personal property. Since it was donated to a church, the donation will be considered use-unrelated, and Jeff's deduction will be $1,000, the adjusted basis of the property.

Jeff's total deduction is $47,000 ($6,000 + $40,000 + $1,000).

Charitable Contributions

147. d

The cash contribution to the church is limited to 50% of adjusted gross income. Since 50% of the AGI is $60,000, the full $5,000 deduction for the cash contribution will be allowed.

With respect to the land, since it was held long-term, the taxpayer can choose either to deduct the fair market value of the land or the adjusted tax basis of the land.

If the taxpayer chooses to deduct the fair market value of the land, the deduction will be limited to 30% of AGI. Therefore, the deduction would be limited to $36,000 ($120,000 × 30%) this year, with a $34,000 ($70,000 fair market value less $36,000 current deduction) carryforward to next year.

If the taxpayer chooses to deduct the adjusted tax basis of the land, the deduction will be limited to 50% of AGI. Therefore, the deduction would be limited to $60,000 ($120,000 × 50%) this year, but the taxpayer would only receive a deduction of $40,000, which is the basis. The taxpayer would not have a carryforward to next year.

The allowable charitable deduction would be $41,000 ($5,000 cash plus $36,000 land) this year if the taxpayer chooses to deduct the fair market value of the land. There would be a $34,000 carryforward to next year.

The allowable charitable deduction would be $45,000 ($5,000 cash plus $40,000 land) this year if the taxpayer chooses to deduct the adjusted tax basis of the land. There would be no carryforward to next year.

Moving Expenses

148. c

Only the direct cost of the move is deductible. The lease penalty is not deductible. Additionally, the taxpayer must be employed on a full-time basis at the new location for 39 weeks in the 12-month period following the move.

Charitable Gift

149. c

He will receive a deduction of $100 because the property is use-unrelated. If tangible personal property is use-unrelated, the donor's deduction is based on the adjusted tax basis of the property.

Itemized Deductions – Medical

150. d

A taxpayer can pay medical expenses for those who could qualify as dependents (for this purpose, the joint return test and the gross income test are both waived in determining dependence status). Both transactions are deemed to have taken place in the current year. The IRS considers the credit card charge as a payment to the service provider (e.g., the doctor) and a loan back to the credit card holder.

Casualty Losses

151. b

The key is "sudden and nonrecurring." Negligence is not an issue unless it is willful negligence. To be a casualty loss, the event causing the loss must be identifiable, damaging to property, sudden and unexpected, and unusual in nature.

Casualty Losses

152. a

Casualty loss (lesser of FMV or Basis)	$10,000
Less: $100 floor	(100)
Less: 10% AGI (10% × $30,000)	(3,000)
Itemized deduction	$ 6,900

Casualty Losses

153. a

To qualify as a casualty, an event must be sudden, unusual, and unexpected. Termite damage does not qualify as a casualty; therefore, her deduction is zero.

Casualty Losses

154. a

Services donated to charity are not deductible. Therefore, the CPA can deduct $0.

Charitable Deduction (CFP® Certification Examination, released 8/2004)

155. a

When an individual donates long-term stock to charity, the individual is entitled to claim a charitable contribution based on the full fair market value of the stock. However, this deduction is limited to 30% of the taxpayer's adjusted gross income. The fair market value of Jorge's stock is $30,000, but his current deduction will be limited to $12,000 ($40,000 AGI × 30%). He will have a carry forward of $18,000. Note: An election is available to deduct only the basis of the stock, thus allowing an AGI limit of 50%. However, since the basis of the stock is only $7,000, this election would not be appropriate.

ALTERNATIVE MINIMUM TAX

Alternative Minimum Tax

156. d

The alternative minimum tax applies to individuals, corporations, estates, and trusts.

The alternative minimum tax does not apply to partnerships, because partnerships never pay federal income tax. Instead, alternative minimum tax adjustments and preferences incurred by a partnership would be reported on the individual partners' income tax returns..

Alternative Minimum Tax

157. d

Casualty losses are not an adjustment for AMT. All of the other choices are adjustments in calculating the alternative minimum tax.

Alternative Minimum Tax

158. d

Tax-exempt income from a general obligation municipal bond is not a preference item for AMT. All of the other items are preferences for AMT purposes.

Alternative Minimum Tax

159. b

When an ISO is exercised, the bargain element (the difference between the FMV and the option price) on the date of exercise is a positive AMT adjustment. The exercise of an ISO has no effect on regular taxable income.

Upon exercise, the bargain element is $7,500 [($125 − $50) × 100 shares]. This is an adjustment for AMT purposes. The sale information is irrelevant.

Alternative Minimum Tax

160. a

Statement 1 is correct because the AMT credit can be carried forward indefinitely to future years.

Statement 2 is incorrect because the AMT credit can only be used to offset regular tax liability.

Statement 3 is correct because the AMT credit can be used to offset regular tax liability.

Statement 4 is incorrect because the AMT credit cannot be carried back to prior years.

Statement 5 is incorrect. The AMT credit for noncorporate taxpayers is available based on the AMT liability attributable to DEFERRAL items, not EXCLUSION items. Note: Exclusion items include itemized deductions, standard deduction, personal exemptions, percentage depletion treated as a preference, and tax-exempt interest treated as a preference.

Alternative Minimum Tax

161. b

Statement 1 is incorrect because casualty losses are deductible for both regular tax and AMT. Therefore, no adjustment is necessary.

Statement 2 is correct because state taxes are not deductible for AMT purposes.

Statement 3 is correct because miscellaneous itemized deductions that exceed the 2% of AGI floor are only deductible for regular tax purposes, not for AMT purposes.

Statement 4 is incorrect because charitable contributions are deductible for both regular tax and AMT. Therefore, no adjustment is necessary.

Alternative Minimum Tax

162. a

Statements 2, 3, and 4 are not preference items. Preference items also include the part of the deduction for certain depletion that is more than the adjusted basis of the property and 28% of the excluded gain on the sale of certain small business stock (Section 1202).

Alternative Minimum Tax (CFP® Certification Examination, released 8/2004)

163. d

1 is correct. Certain deductions that are allowable for regular tax purposes (e.g., real estate taxes) are not allowed for alternative minimum tax purposes.

2 is incorrect. The Alternative Depreciation System (ADS) is allowed for alternative minimum tax purposes. If a client ELECTS to use ADS for regular tax purposes, the depreciation deduction for both regular tax purposes and AMT purposes will be the same.

3 and 4 are correct. If AMT is due, it may be a good idea to accelerate ordinary income for regular tax purposes, and defer real estate taxes (which are disallowed for AMT) to future years.

TAX CREDITS

Earned Income Credit

164. d

The Earned Income Credit (EIC) may be received from an employer by filing Form W-5 with the employer. To qualify for the EIC, the taxpayer's AGI must be below a specific amount. A taxpayer does not have to have a qualifying child.

Earned Income Credit

165. d

All tests must be met. In addition to the tests, the taxpayer applying for the credit must provide the name, age, and taxpayer identification number of the qualifying child on the return.

Child and Dependent Care Credit

166. a

Total qualifying child-care expenses are $8,000 ($3,000 + $1,000 + $4,000). A provider of child care can also perform housekeeping chores. The amounts paid to Mrs. Skeckel qualify since she was not a dependent. 20% × $6,000 (maximum allowed) = $1,200 child-care credit for 2006.

Child and Dependent Care Credit

167. b

$600 = 20% × $3,000. The maximum unreimbursed expenses that are eligible for the credit is $3,000 (2006) for one qualifying individual and $6,000 (2006) for two or more qualifying individuals. Since Guidry has AGI above $43,000, the credit percentage is 20%.

Child and Dependent Care Credit

168. d

$4,000 (child-care expenses) × 20% = $800 credit for 2006. For AGI over $43,000, the applicable rate of credit is 20% for 2006.

HOPE Credit

169. c

The $1,650 limit is per student, per year, so Statement 2 is incorrect.

Books are not an eligible expense, so Statement 4 is incorrect.

Lifetime Learning Credit

170. d

Neither the HOPE credit nor the Lifetime Learning credit is allowed unless elected by the taxpayers. There is no limit on the number of years the lifetime learning credit can be taken. It is a per taxpayer credit and so it does not vary with the number of students in the family and cannot be taken in conjunction with the HOPE credit for the same student.

Lifetime Learning Credit

171. c

Qualifying expenses	$10,300
Maximum allowed expenses	$10,000
Credit %	× 20%
Maximum credit available	$ 2,000

Non-Refundable Credit

172. a

The client will receive a refund of $2,000 this year, because he is eligible for a nonrefundable credit. Non-refundable credits are limited to the taxpayer's liability.

Tax before credits and payments	$20,000
Less: Estimated payments	(6,000)
Less: Amounts withheld	(13,000)
Equals: Tax before credits	$ 1,000
Less: Allowed credit (limited to tax liability)	(3,000)
Equals: Tax refund	$ 2,000

PROPERTY TRANSACTIONS – CAPITAL GAINS AND LOSSES

Capital Gains

173. d

Amount realized	$5,500
Basis (FIFO)	(5,000)
Capital gain (long term)	$ 500

Because John did not specifically identify the shares of stock sold, a FIFO presumption is made. The first shares he purchased will be the first shares sold.

Capital Gains and Losses

174. c

The business computer is Section 1231 property, not a capital asset.

A capital asset is any asset that is NOT:

1. Copyrights or creative works.
2. Accounts or notes receivable.
3. Depreciable property used in a trade or business or for production of income (such as a computer).
4. Inventory.

Capital Gains and Losses

175. d

The net long-term capital gain is $5,000 ($20,000 LTCG – $15,000 LTCL) and the net short-term capital gain is $12,500 ($20,000 STCG – $7,500 STCL).

Capital Gains and Losses

176. b

STCG	$11,000	LTCG	$0
STCL	(6,000)	LTCL	(6,000)
STCG	$5,000	LTCL	($6,000)

Net Long-Term Capital Loss = $1,000 (by netting $6,000 – $5,000)

Capital Gains

177. b

The amount realized is the sales price less the commissions paid on the sale ($5,200 – $80 = $5,120). Her basis in the stock is the purchase price of the stock plus commissions paid at purchase ($4,000 + $50 = $4,050).

The amount realized is reduced by her basis in arriving at the taxable gain of $1,070 ($5,120 – $4,050).

Capital Gains

178. d

Baseball cards are considered a collectible. The maximum long-term capital gain rate for collectibles is 28%. He purchased the cards three years ago, so the cards have been held long term.

Capital Gains

179. c

If property is received as a dividend, the taxpayer's basis in the property received is the fair market value of the property on the date of transfer.

Capital Gains

180. d

To meet the long-term holding period, property must be held for greater than one year. The date the asset is acquired is not counted when determining the holding period.

Therefore, the asset must be held until March 16, 2006, to be considered long term.

Capital Gains

181. c

When a gift of appreciated property is given, the holding period of the donor carries over to the recipient of the gift. Therefore, Larry would have long-term capital gain even though he sold the stock after owning it for only two days.

Since Larry is in the 15% bracket, he is allowed to use the lower 5% capital-gain tax rate.

Capital Gains

182. c

Equipment – the equipment is fully depreciated, so the entire gain of $2,100 will be taxed as ordinary income due to depreciation recapture.

Truck – the truck was held short-term (not more than one year), and as a result, the entire $1,200 loss is treated as an ordinary, not capital, loss.

Common stock – the sale of the common stock is treated as a long-term capital gain.

Summary of gains/losses:

Capital Gains/Losses		Ordinary Gains/Losses	
Gain (Stock)	$2,000	Gain (Equipment)	$2,100
Loss	$0	Loss (Truck)	$1,200
Net Capital Gain	$2,000	Net Ordinary Gain	$900

Capital-Loss Carryover

183. d

The capital-loss deduction is limited to $3,000. In computing the $3,000 deduction, short-term capital losses must be used first. Therefore, $3,000 of the short-term capital loss is used, and none of the long-term loss is used. Therefore, $5,000 of the long-term loss is carried over. Her total capital losses carried forward are $7,000 ($5,000 long term + $2,000 short term).

Basis

184. b

Assuming no gift tax paid by the donor, the donee's gain basis for the property received is the same as that of the donor. The donee's loss basis is the lesser of:

1. The donor's adjusted basis, or

2. The fair market value on the date of the gift.

Basis

185. a

The son's gain basis is $80,000. His loss basis is $70,000. Since his selling price of $78,000 is between the gain basis and the loss basis, he has no recognized gain or loss.

Wash Sale Rule

186. c

Amount realized	$8,000
Adjusted basis (30 × $280)	(8,400)
Realized loss	($400)
Recognized loss	$0

Since the transaction qualifies as a wash sale, the realized loss of $400 cannot be deducted. This postponed loss is added to the adjusted basis of the shares purchased 29 days earlier to determine the basis of the new shares. Therefore, the adjusted basis for these shares is $7,900 ($7,500 + $400).

The wash sale rules apply to a loss sustained upon a sale or other disposition of a stock or security. The loss is not allowed if, within a period beginning 30 days before the date of the sale and ending 30 days after that date the taxpayer has acquired or has entered into a contract or option to acquire substantially identical stock or securities.

Basis

187. c

Simon's initial basis will be $50,000 ($60,000 basis less $10,000 depreciation), the donor's carryover basis. Carryover basis on a gift for which no gift tax was paid is the donor's adjusted tax basis, unless the FMV on the date of the gift is lower than the donor's basis. Basis must be reduced by any depreciation taken. If the FMV on the date of the gift is lower than the donor's basis, the donee will have a double basis. Then, the FMV of the property on the date of the gift will be the basis for losses, and the donor's basis will be the basis for gains.

Basis

188. b

When Tommy's uncle died, the stock received a step-up in basis to the fair market value as of the date of death. Therefore, Tommy's basis in the stock is $6,000. Since Tommy sold the stock for $6,500, his taxable gain is $500 ($6,500 sales price less $6,000 basis).

All inherited property is considered long-term.

Basis

189. b

The basis to Scott is carryover basis of $50,000. No taxable income would result from the gift.

Gain on Sale of Inherited Property (CFP® Certification Examination, released 8/2004)

190. a

The XYZ stock received a step-up in basis upon the relative's death. All inherited property is long-term.

Value on date of sale	$6,250
Less: selling expenses	- 250
Amount realized	$6,000
Less: basis	- 5,750
Capital gain	$250

PROPERTY TRANSACTIONS: NONTAXABLE EXCHANGES

Like-Kind Exchange

191. d

Business equipment is considered like-kind property.

None of the other types of property listed are eligible for like-kind exchange treatment.

Realized vs. Recognized

192. a

The realized gain is the economic gain received by the taxpayer.

Option (b) is incorrect because the recognized gain is the gain reported on the tax return. The gain reported may be different than the realized gain.

Option (c) is incorrect because, if a loss is recognized, it is reported on the tax return currently.

Option (d) is incorrect because a recognized (reported) gain can never exceed the realized (economic) gain.

Like-Kind Exchange

193. b

Statement 1 is correct because like-kind exchange treatment is automatic, not elective.

Statement 2 is incorrect because a loss can never be recognized from a like-kind exchange, even if boot is received. Only gains are recognized when boot is received.

Statement 3 is correct.

Statement 4 is incorrect because prior depreciation deductions must only be recaptured (under Section 1245 or 1250) when a gain is recognized. If no boot is received in a like-kind exchange, no gain is recognized, and therefore, no depreciation recapture.

Exchanges

194. d

	Machine (A)	Building
Amount realized	$30,000	$35,000
Adjusted basis	(40,000)	(20,000)
Realized gain (loss)	($10,000)	$15,000
Recognized gain (loss)	$0	$15,000

The realized loss on the like-kind exchange part of the transaction (i.e., the machines) is not recognized. The realized gain on the boot (i.e., building) is recognized.

Exchanges

195. a

	FMV New Building	$ 800,000
−	Mortgage of Transferor	(275,000)
=	New Building (A)	$ 525,000

	Basis of Old Building	$ 600,000
−	Mortgage of Transferee	(275,000)
=	Old Building (B)	$ 325,000

	New Building (A)	$ 525,000
−	Old Building (B)	(325,000)
=	Realized Gain	$ 200,000
	Recognized Gain (net boot received equals net boot given)	$ 0

This is a like-kind nontaxable exchange wherein realized gains or losses are not currently recognized.

Involuntary Conversion

196. b

Gain realized equals $80,000; gain recognized equals $10,000 (i.e., $200,000 amount realized minus $190,000 amount reinvested); and basis equals $120,000 (i.e., $190,000 cost minus $70,000 postponed gain).

Involuntary Conversion

197. c

Gain realized equals $5,000 ($15,000 insurance proceeds less $10,000 basis); gain recognized equals $3,000 (i.e., $15,000 amount realized minus $12,000 amount reinvested).

Exchanges

198. d

Related parties can enter into a nontaxable exchange although disposition before a two-year holding period will trigger recognition.

Involuntary Conversion

199. d

The form of the involuntary conversion is the condemnation of real property used in a trade or business. Therefore, the taxpayer has three years, rather than the normal two years, from the close of the taxable year in which gain is first realized to replace the property. The gain is considered "realized" when the insurance proceeds are received.

Like-Kind Exchanges (§1031)

200. a

	FMV New machine	$10,000
-	Boot Given	0
+	Boot Received	0
=	FMV Old machine	$10,000
-	Adjusted Basis (old)	(5,000)
=	Potential Gain (PG)	$5,000
-	Boot Received (recognized gain ≤PG)	0
=	Remaining Gain	$5,000
	FMV New machine	$10,000
-	Unrecognized Gain	(5,000)
=	New Basis	$5,000

Like-Kind Exchanges (§1031)

201. b

	FMV New machine	$10,000
-	Boot Given	(4,000)
+	Boot Received	0
=	FMV Old machine	$6,000
-	Adjusted Basis (old)	(5,000)
=	Potential Gain (PG)	$1,000
-	Boot Received (recognized gain ≤PG)	0
=	Remaining Gain	$1,000
	FMV New machine	$10,000
-	Unrecognized Gain	(1,000)
=	New Basis	$9,000

Like-Kind Exchanges (§1031)

202. c

	FMV New machine	$10,000
-	Boot Given	(6,000)
+	Boot Received	0
=	FMV Old machine	$4,000
-	Adjusted Basis (old)	(5,000)
=	Potential Gain (PG)	($1,000)
-	Boot Received (recognized gain ≤PG)	0
=	Remaining Gain	($1,000)
	FMV New machine	$10,000
+	Unrecognized Loss	1,000
=	New Basis	$11,000

Like-Kind Exchanges (§1031)

203. b

	FMV New machine	$10,000
−	Boot Given	0
+	Boot Received	4,000
=	FMV Old machine	$14,000
−	Adjusted Basis (old)	(5,000)
=	Potential Gain (PG)	$9,000
−	Boot Received (recognized gain ≤ PG)	(4,000)
=	Remaining Gain	$5,000
	FMV New machine	$10,000
−	Unrecognized Gain	(5,000)
=	New Basis	$5,000

Like-Kind Exchanges (§1031)

204. b

	FMV New machine	$10,000
−	Boot Given	(400)
+	Boot Received	0
=	FMV Old machine	$9,600
−	Adjusted Basis (old)	(5,000)
=	Potential Gain (PG)	$4,600
−	Boot Received (recognized gain ≤ PG)	0
=	Remaining Gain	$4,600
	FMV New machine	$10,000
−	Unrecognized Gain	(4,600)
=	New Basis	$5,400

Like-Kind Exchange

205. c

In order to qualify for favorable tax treatment under Section 1031, property exchanged must be considered "like-kind."

The following property is not considered like-kind property:

-Personal use assets (personal residence, etc.)

-Ordinary assets (inventory, etc.)

-Securities (stocks, bonds, etc.)

-Personal property exchanged for real property

-Domestic property exchanged for foreign property

-Different sex livestock

A is incorrect. Securities are not considered like-kind property.

B is incorrect. Inventory is an ordinary asset, and is not considered like-kind property.

C is correct.

D is incorrect. Domestic property exchanged for foreign property is not considered a like-kind exchange.

Like-Kind Exchange

206. c

Option (c) is correct. Assumption of John's liability by Mary would result in boot being received by John, potentially causing John to recognize gain if there is a realized gain.

Option (a) is incorrect because the payment of boot will not cause a taxpayer to recognize gain on a like-kind exchange.

Option (b) is incorrect because the assumption of Mary's liability by John is considered a payment of boot by John to Mary.

Option (d) is incorrect because the transaction would result in a realized loss.

Sale of Personal Residence

207. a

Capital gains realized on the sale of a personal residence can be excluded from gross income (if elected) for gains up to $250,000 for single taxpayers ($500,000 for married taxpayers filing jointly).

The purchase of the condo is irrelevant when calculating the recognized gain.

Sale of Personal Residence

208. b

Any realized gain on the sale of the residence that exceeds the exclusion amount must be recognized as a capital gain on the taxpayer's income tax return.

Option (a) is incorrect. There is no age requirement

Option (c) is incorrect because the home need only be used as a principal residence for two years, not four.

Option (d) is incorrect. There is no limit on the number of times the exclusion may be elected.

Sale of Personal Residence

209. b

Both spouses must use the home as a principal residence for at least 2 of the 5 years before the sale to qualify for the full exclusion of gain.

Sale of Personal Residence

210. a

Capital gains realized on the sale of a personal residence can be excluded from gross income (if elected) for gains up to $250,000 for single taxpayers ($500,000 for married taxpayers filing jointly) if they have lived in their personal residence for 2 of the 5 preceding years.

Sale of Personal Residence

211. a

Section 1041 provides for nontaxable exchange treatment for the transfer of property between spouses or between former spouses as a result of divorce. The transferee's (Marge) basis is equal to transferor's (Ron) basis immediately before the transfer. Marge's carryover basis is $160,000.

Sale of Personal Residence

212. c

Single taxpayers can exclude up to $250,000 of gain on the sale of a personal residence.

($75,000 = $445,000 amount realized – $120,000 basis – $250,000 exclusion).

Sale of Personal Residence

213. b

Age is not a factor. The exemption can be used every 2 years (more frequently if certain conditions are met).

Sale of Personal Residence

214. a

Capital gains realized on the sale of a personal residence may be excluded (if elected) up to $250,000 for single taxpayers ($500,000 for married taxpayers filing jointly).

Sale of Personal Residence

215. c

Doug meets both the ownership and use test so he can exclude $250,000. Cary does not meet the ownership test, but doesn't have to because Doug does. However, she must meet the use test. Since she doesn't and the move isn't due to a change in job, health or other unforeseen circumstances, she gets no gain exclusion.

Sale of Personal Residence

216. c

She has no taxable gain because she can exclude one-half of the $250,000 gain because she has owned and used the condo for one year and she moved for a job change.

Sale of Personal Residence

217. d

The loss is disallowed because the residence is a personal-use asset, and a loss on the sale of a personal-use asset is nondeductible.

SECTION 1231 AND RECAPTURE PROVISIONS

Section 1231 Gains and Losses
218. c

When the taxpayer has a net Section 1231 gain for the year, the lookback rules may recapture some or all of the net gain as ordinary income. To the extent the lookback rules do not apply, the net gain is treated as a long-term capital gain. The lookback goes back 5 taxable years, not including the current taxable year.

1245 Recapture/1231 Gains
219. e

Ann's total gain is $240,000 − $60,000 (basis) = $180,000. The gain attributable to depreciation must be recaptured as Section 1245 gain ($140,000) and the excess is Section 1231 capital gain ($40,000).

1245 Property
220. a

Section 1245 property includes all depreciable personal property, patents, copyrights, and leaseholds. Section 1245 requires any recognized gain to be treated as ordinary income to the extent of depreciation taken on the property. This "depreciation recapture" occurs when there has been a taxable event with respect to the property.

A is correct. An installment sale is a taxable sale that will result in depreciation recapture if a Section 1245 asset is sold.

B is incorrect. A distribution by a partnership to a partner is a return of basis, not a taxable distribution. Therefore, no depreciation recapture will result.

C is incorrect. A disposition in a tax-free transaction, such as a like-kind exchange, will not result in depreciation recapture. Depreciation recapture only applies to taxable transactions.

D is incorrect. A gift is not a taxable transaction, so no depreciation recapture would result.

1231 Property
221. a

The file cabinet is Section 1231 property, and will be subject to depreciation recapture upon sale. The depreciation recapture will cause some (in this case, all) of the gain to be taxable as ordinary income.

Sales Price		$250
Original Cost	$400	
Less: Depreciation Taken	(220)	
Equals: Adjusted Basis	$180	(180)
Recognized Gain		$70
Ordinary income (Lesser of Recognized Gain or Depreciation Taken)		$70

1231 Property

222. d

The overall gain to be recognized is $34,000. Section 1231 gain is typically taxed as a capital gain. However, depreciation recapture will convert some or all of the capital gain to ordinary income in the year of sale.

In addition, the lookback rule requires a taxpayer to "look back" for any unrecaptured Section 1231 losses. These unrecaptured losses will also cause some or all of the current year Section 1231 gain to be treated as ordinary income.

The capital gain in the current year is determined as follows:

Total Gain – Current Year	$34,000
Less: Current Year Depreciation Recapture	(15,000)
Less: Unrecaptured Losses in Past Five Years	(9,000)
Equals: Capital Gain	**$10,000**

The remaining gain of $24,000 ($34,000 less $10,000 capital gain) will be taxed as ordinary income.

TAXATION OF INVESTMENT TRANSACTIONS

Small Business Stock (1202)

223. d

The capital gains rate on Section 1202 stock is 28%. The effective rate, after the 50% gain exclusion, is 14%.

Double Basis Rule

224. a

Mary Francis gifted loss property to her son. Therefore, the double basis rule applies when her son sells the stock.

Since her son sold the stock at a gain, he would use Mary Francis' original cost basis (gain basis), resulting in a gain of $50,000 ($550,000 sales price less $500,000 basis).

The gift tax is ignored, because gift tax is not allocated to basis when loss property is gifted.

Specified Identification

225. b

Using the specific identification method, she would choose to sell the shares with the highest cost basis. She should sell:

100 shares at $21=	$2,100
200 shares at $19=	$3,800
200 shares at $13=	$2,600
Basis for 500 shares sold	$8,500

Therefore, the lowest amount of gain she could report is $1,500 ($10,000 proceeds less $8,500 basis).

Taxation of Investments (CFP® Certification Examination, released 8/2004)

226. b

The CD, blue chip stock, and savings bonds (in that order) would result in the lowest tax liability upon liquidation.

CD – since the interest on the CD was taxable each year, the basis in the CD would be equal to the value. Therefore, no federal or state income taxes would result upon liquidation.

Blue chip stock – the appreciation of the blue chip stock would be taxed, but at favorable capital gains rates.

U.S. Savings Bonds – the appreciation would be taxed at ordinary income tax rates for Federal income tax purposes. However, savings bonds are not subject to state income taxes.

Traditional IRA – The appreciation only (client has basis for the contributions because they were non-deductible) would be taxed at both federal and state ordinary income tax rates.

401(k) Plan – The entire amount would be taxed at both federal and state ordinary income tax rates.

BUSINESS ORGANIZATIONS

Forms of Business Organizations
227. d

A sole proprietorship is owned by one individual who is personally liable for the business. Therefore, the business depends solely on the owner.

Forms of Business Organizations
228. d

Interest in the business being personal property is characteristic of a general partnership. More than one owner being personally liable indicates a general partnership business form. Common shareholders, preferred shareholders and limited partners do not have personal property at risk, only the investment in the company is at risk.

Forms of Business Organizations
229. c

The ease of raising financial capital is a main strength of the corporate form of business entity.

Forms of Business Organizations
230. e

Limited liability, proxy, and a board of directors are all characteristics of the corporate form of entity. Therefore, Statements 1, 3, and 4 are correct. Limited life is incorrect because the death of a shareholder does not dissolve or otherwise automatically adversely affect the corporation (as with a partnership).

Forms of Business Organizations
231. d

All are strengths of the partnership form of business entity.

Forms of Business Organizations
232. d

The question specifies that the taxpayer is concerned about liability issues that would mean that forming a corporation is desirable in order to protect personal assets. A sole proprietorship and a partnership would expose the personal assets of the taxpayer to creditors. Since losses are expected in the first year, it would be desirable to take advantage of these losses on a personal level. An S corporation allows the benefit of pass through of corporate items to the individual, therefore, this is the more appropriate form to elect. A Personal Holding Company is a status, not a form of business organization, which is determined by an IRS test.

Forms of Business Organizations
233. d

Form 2553 – Election by a Small Business Corporation has to be filed by the 15th day of the third month of the tax year. Statement 1 is incorrect because the shareholders secure the consent to be taxed as an S corporation. Statement 3 is not correct because in general only one class of stock is allowed.

Forms of Business Organizations
234. b

All of the statements except Statement 3 are disadvantages of electing S corporation status. Section 179 expenses are allowed at the individual level by virtue of the pass through of selected items to the individual shareholders.

Forms of Business Organizations
235. d

All other statements are true. (a) is correct. Keogh plans are only available to self-employed business. A sole proprietor, partnership, and an LLC could establish a Keogh plan. C corporations and S corporations cannot have a Keogh plan. (b) is correct. The self employment tax is applied at a rate of 15.3% of net self employment earnings. (c) is correct. Guaranteed payments made to a partner are typically reported on form 1040 and are taxable to the partners. (d) is incorrect. Flow-through income from an S corporation is not subject to self-employment tax. (e) is correct. Salary is subject to FICA.

Forms of Business Organizations
236. b

A limited partner's interest in the partnership is personal property that may be freely assigned unless agreed to the contrary. Therefore, Statement 2 is correct.

Forms of Business Organizations
237. a

One similarity of both a partnership and a corporation is that they may both hold and convey property. (1) is correct. Partnerships and corporations can both hold property. (2) is incorrect. Only a corporation is regarded as a distinct entity for tax purposes. Partnerships are flow through entities. (3) is incorrect. Corporations may retain profits. Partnerships are not required to distribute profits equally among the owners. (4) is incorrect. Corporations pay tax on income.

Forms of Business Organizations
238. a

The taxable income/losses of an S corporation flow through to the shareholders. Option (a) is correct because losses can be utilized by the shareholders on their individual tax returns in order to reduce their own liability. Option (d) is incorrect because although a corporation may borrow money from shareholders, this is not exclusive to S corporations and is, therefore, not a valid reason to select such a corporate status. Options (b) and (c) are incorrect.

Forms of Business Organizations (CFP® Certification Examination, released 11/94)
239. e

The question asks about legal forms. Partnerships (Options (a) and (b)) are excluded due to disruption if a partner left. Corporation (Option (c)) is excluded due to implicit double taxation and no need for capital accumulation. Professional Corporation (Option (d)) is not available for a franchise operation. Therefore, the S corporation is the best choice – a flow-through entity, offering limited liability and ease of continuation and exchange of ownership. A limited liability corporation may well have accomplished the same goals had it been a choice.

Forms of Business Organizations (CFP® Certification Examination, released 11/94)

240. e

Statements 1, 2, 3, and 4 describe an S corporation nonemployee shareholder; therefore, Option (e) is the correct answer. Compensation is not used in item one as it is ordinarily used in taxation. Compensation usually means earned income from employment when used in taxation. Dividends declared from an S corporation are nontaxable distributions to the extent of the accumulated adjustments account.

Forms of Business Organizations

241. b

An S corporation will allow losses to flow through to the brothers, continue in the event that one brother should die, and will have the protection of a C corporation.

S Corporations

242. e

Fringe benefits for greater than 2% shareholders are not deductible. Therefore, the premiums are taxable to Bill and Diane.

Family Limited Partnerships

243. e

The general partner of a family limited partnership can be an individual or one of the entities listed.

Family Limited Partnerships

244. d

A limited partner may not receive a distribution to the extent that the distribution will cause partnership liabilities to exceed the fair value of partnership assets. FLPs often restrict a limited partner's ability to transfer an interest. A limited partner may withdraw from the partnership upon the occurrence of events specified in the partnership agreement.

Family Limited Partnerships

245. b

Appraisal fees may be required to support underlying asset valuation and discounts taken.

C Corporation

246. d

Statement 3 is incorrect. LIFO Recapture Tax only applies to S corporations. All other selections are taxes that could apply to C corporations.

S Corporation
247. c

Statement 1 is incorrect because the S corporation does not pay alternative minimum tax. The AMT adjustments and preferences are passed through to the shareholders, who are responsible for paying any AMT. Statements 2 and 3 are correct. The LIFO Recapture Tax and the Built-in Gains Tax may be applicable to S corporations that were formerly C corporations. Statement 4 is incorrect because the Personal Holding Company Tax is applicable only to C corporations.

S Corporation Taxes
248. c

Statement 1 is incorrect because the Built-in Gains Tax only applies to S corporations that were formerly C corporations. Statements 2 and 3 are correct. Statement 4 is incorrect because the Built-in Gains Tax is paid by the S corporation, not the shareholders.

S Corporation Taxes
249. e

Statement 1 is incorrect because the LIFO Recapture Tax only applies to S corporations that were formerly C corporations. Statements 2, 3, and 4 are correct.

S Corporation
250. c

Statement 1 is correct. Statement 2 is incorrect because the income from an S corporation is not considered self-employment income. Therefore, the shareholders cannot establish a Keogh plan, which is a qualified plan for self-employed individuals. Note: If the shareholder has self-employment income from another source, he or she can establish a Keogh plan. Statement 3 is incorrect, because dividends from a C (not S) corporation are subject to double taxation. Statement 4 is correct.

C Corporation (CFP® Certification Examination, released 8/2004)
251. c

1 is correct. The first $50,000 of corporate taxable income is only taxed at 15%, and the next $25,000 of corporate taxable income is only taxed at 25%. These rates are much lower than the maximum individual tax rate of 35%.

2 is incorrect. When accumulated profits are distributed to shareholders as a dividend, they are double taxed. The dividend is first taxed at the corporate level, then to the individual. Note: recent legislation reduced the dividend rate to equal the capital gain rate, however, dividends are not actually considered capital gains. This favorable tax treatment of dividends is scheduled to expire.

3 is correct. Corporations can provide many tax-favored fringe benefits to shareholders, such as group term life insurance. Several of these fringe benefits are not available to other types of entities, such as partnerships.

4 is incorrect. Once a corporation has been established, it is not easy to change the form of business. When a corporation is liquidated, both the corporation and the shareholder must pay tax, resulting in double tax treatment.

Personal Service Corporations

252. c

Under the personal service corporation rules, the corporation is taxed at a flat 35% rate if at least 95% of the stock is held by active or retired employees. Otherwise, graduated rates apply.

A is incorrect. The rules apply to companies involved in fields of health, law, engineering, architecture, accounting, actuarial science, performing arts, or consulting, in which at least 95% of the stock is held by active or retired employees.

B is incorrect. The losses incurred by the corporation remain inside the corporation, and can only offset income earned by the corporation.

D is incorrect. Personal service corporations may earn passive income.

Personal Holding Tax

253. b

In determining the undistributed personal holding company income subject to the personal holding company tax, the corporation is permitted to deduct the dividends paid to shareholders.

A is incorrect. The tax rate is 15%.

C is incorrect. The objective of the personal holding company tax is to discourage individual taxpayers from using the corporate entity solely for tax avoidance. The alternative minimum tax reduces the tax benefits from certain types of deductions and tax preferences allowable for regular tax purposes.

D is incorrect. The personal holding company tax does not apply to S corporations, life insurance companies, banks, and certain other financial institutions.

Personal Holding Tax

254. d

The personal holding company tax will apply because greater than 50% of the value of the outstanding stock of the corporation is owned by five or fewer individuals and at least 60% of the corporation's adjusted ordinary gross income consists of personal holding company income.

A is incorrect. The flat 35% tax applies to personal service corporations, not to personal holding companies. Robbins Company is a personal holding company.

B is incorrect. Corporations are only entitled to a dividends received deduction when they receive a dividend (not interest income) from another corporation.

C is incorrect. A personal holding company is not a flow-through entity.

TAXATION OF TRUSTS AND ESTATES

Fiduciary Deductions
255. c

A fiduciary is prohibited from deducting any losses that have previously been claimed as a deduction on an estate tax return.

All of the other items may be deducted by the fiduciary.

Taxation of Trust Distributions
256. d

The taxable portion of the distribution is based on the taxable portion of the distributable net income (DNI).

Therefore, $750 [$1,000 distribution × ($15,000 taxable DNI ÷ $20,000 total DNI)] of the distribution will be taxable to the beneficiary.

Taxation of Trust Distribution
257. c

The taxable portion of the distribution is based on the taxable portion of the distributable net income (DNI).

Therefore, $12,000 [$15,000 distribution × ($40,000 taxable DNI ÷ $50,000 total DNI)] of the distribution will be taxable to Kerri, and $16,000 [$20,000 distribution × ($40,000 taxable DNI ÷ $50,000 total DNI)] of the distribution will be taxable to Melody.

Taxation of Estates & Trusts
258. a

This is a grantor trust, and the grantor (Billy) will be responsible for the tax on all of the income.

The power to borrow trust assets without security will cause the trust to be a grantor trust for income tax purposes.

Taxation of Trusts (CFP® Certification Examination, released 8/2004)
259. a

Since the trust is revocable, the trust is considered a grantor trust for income tax purposes. The grantor, Ronald, will pay taxes on all income earned by the trust.

AUDIT, PENALTIES, AND TAXPAYER'S RIGHTS

Statute of Limitations
260. e

25% of ($320,000 gross receipts + $20,000 capital gains) = $85,000. Section 6501(e) states that if the taxpayer omits from gross income (total receipts, without reduction for cost) an amount in excess of 25% of gross income as stated in the return, a six-year limitation period on the assessment applies.

Tax Audits
261. d

Chances of an audit do not increase for those previously audited where the result was no change in tax liability.

Preparer Ethics
262. b

Preparer must withdraw if error is material and affects current return and should consider withdrawing if the error is material but does not affect the current year. (#2 and #4)

Innocent Spouse
263. c

Option (a) is wrong since liability arises from a joint return. Option (b) is incorrect since the 1998 Act relaxed the standard to simply "erroneous." Option (d) is incorrect because the election is made by the spouse seeking relief.

Penalties
264. c

The penalty is determined as follows:

Failure-to-pay penalty		
[1/2% × $5,000 × 2 (2 months violation)]		$ 50
Plus: Failure-to-file penalty		
[5% × $5,000 × 2 (2 months violation)]	$500	
Less: Failure-to-pay penalty	(50)	450
Total penalties		**$500**

Negligence Penalty
265. c

A 20% penalty applies to the negligence component.

Failure-to-File and Failure-to-Pay

266. b

The failure-to-file penalty is netted against the failure-to-pay penalty [$60 + (600 − 60)] = $600.

Penalties (CFP® Certification Examination, released 11/94)

267. e

Sara owes a penalty and interest on the $400 that she owed on April 15th.

Sources of Authority (CFP® Certification Examination, released 8/2004)

268. d

Treasury regulations have the highest precedential value of all the options listed. Only the Internal Revenue Code has a higher precedential value.